March 13, 1963

COPPER TOWN:

Changing Africa

COPPER TOWN:

Changing Africa

THE HUMAN SITUATION
ON THE RHODESIAN COPPERBELT

Hortense Powdermaker

PROFESSOR OF ANTHROPOLOGY,
QUEENS COLLEGE, THE CITY
UNIVERSITY OF NEW YORK

HARPER & ROW, PUBLISHERS
NEW YORK AND EVANSTON

To Gotthard Booth, M.D.

Contents

Tables

Acknowledgments

I am deeply indebted to the Guggenheim Foundation for making the field work possible. To the Wenner-Gren Foundation for Anthropological Research, I am grateful for financial aid for research and secretarial assistance after I returned.

Many people have aided in different ways in the development and completion of this research. The field work could not have been done without the cooperation and helpfulness of innumerable people in Luanshya (the site of field study): African research assistants, particularly one who worked full time during the entire study, the general manager, the African Personnel Department, Welfare Department, and the Hollerith Machines Department of the Roan Antelope Copper Mine, the district commissioner, the teachers in African schools, and innumerable others of both races who gave me friendship and pleasant hospitality as well as data. In Lusaka, the helpfulness of the acting director of the information department and the heads and members of its sections—broadcasting, publications, and movies—was invaluable.

The book could not have been written without the previous publications of the Rhodes-Livingstone Institute concerning the Copperbelt—particularly those of J. Clyde Mitchell, A. L. Epstein, and the late Godrey Wilson—and the writings of Audrey Richards, Elizabeth Colson, Max Gluckman, J. A. Barnes, and many others on Africans of

Northern Rhodesia and related areas. The integration of an anthropological theory of cultural change with a psychological one of individual change was largely possible through the writings of Erik H. Erikson. I tend to be influenced by the humanistic anthropologists, in general anthropology by the late Alfred Kroeber, and on Africa by Melville J. Herskovits.

The whole manuscript was read by Carl Withers, LeRoy Leatherman, and Elizabeth Colson; two-thirds of it by Arthur Tuden; half, by Lloyd A. Fallers; all chapters in which psychoanalytic psychological thinking is involved, by Alan Drummond, M.D.; the chapters on leisure, radio, and movies, by Kurt Lang; the theoretical chapter on social and individual change, by Sidney Axelrad and David M. Schneider. It is difficult to express the depth of my appreciation to all these readers, not only for their suggestions and criticisms, but also for their encouragement.

I am greatly indebted to the MacDowell Colony, where I wrote under perfect conditions for two summers. I appreciated residence at Montalvo for six months.

Ostrander F. Taylor was helpful on some of the detailed economic factual data; William O. Brown provided library facilities at Boston University; and George M. Foster, at the University of California, when I was in their respective neighborhoods; Pat Fenn took the photographs. To all of them, my thanks. I am likewise grateful to Sidney Axelrad, chairman of my department, and all its members for their understanding release of me from committees and other departmental duties when I was working intensively on the book.

For reasons best known to themselves and to me, I should like to express my gratitude to Saxton Pope, M.D., to Mayflower Brandt, to Margery Day, to the late Joan Sanger, to my sister Florence Powdermaker, to my foster son Won Mo Kim, and to Hope and Joseph Klapper.

Despite the help of many friends and colleagues, I must accept the responsibility for the data, presentation, and interpretations.

HORTENSE POWDERMAKER

Queens College, The City University of New York
February 27, 1962

Introduction

Like many anthropologists and a multitude of other people, I am interested in the social changes which are taking place in Africa. In the past I have tried to understand the inner coherence and logic of a tribal society. Today, I am concerned with attempting to discover the inner coherence and logic of complicated social and individual changes in a contemporary African society—specifically, a modern heterogenous community on the Copperbelt of Northern Rhodesia, composed of a majority of Africans, most of whom had come from small homogeneous, tribal villages and a minority of Europeans who, if not indigenous, had come usually from South Africa, Southern Rhodesia, or the United Kingdom. I arrived in September 1953, shortly after the Federation of Northern and Southern Rhodesia and Nyasaland had come into being, and left in June 1954. With the exception of a month spent partly in Lusaka, the capital of Northern Rhodesia, and partly in a tour of a rural area, all my time was spent in Luanshya, the site of the Roan Antelope Copper Mine.

The Problem

The problems in the field and even in the writing of the book changed in the course of their doing. The original problem was concerned with the communication of modern Western culture through the mass media—radio, movies, and newspapers—and was part of a larger study of leisure activities as an index of social change in this mine community. Both traditional and modern leisure activities existed here; some helped the participants to relate to the modern world, and others appeared to be a way of returning to the past. Since the choice of leisure activities is largely voluntary, it can be used as a significant index of social and individual change.

A study of the communication of Western culture has to include those who represent and communicate it, directly and personally, as well as the impersonal mass media. These were usually white people, or Europeans, as they are called colloquially, and they, too, were living in a society of rapid social change. (The occasional American was grouped with Europeans.) Although there was little social relationship between individuals of the two races, yet the societies of each were closely intertwined. Any changes in one had repercussions in the other, and both were linked with the ever-quickening changes on the continent of Africa and in the world beyond.

Many years of working as a cultural anthropologist, doing holistic studies of tribal and modern communities, inevitably conditioned me to seeing leisure activities and the process of cultural change in their social setting, which included such obvious aspects as economic organization, the power structure, family life, concepts of the supernatural, and the values which underlay them all. Likewise, no study of social change can be made without a historical base to answer the question of "change from what" and without a knowledge of continuities as well as changes. As Herskovits has emphasized in many of his publications on Africa, culture changes, and culture is stubborn.[1] It was not possible for any one individual to carry through such an ambitious, holistic frame of reference with any completeness, particularly when time was limited. But the availability of many monographs on traditional societies and the excellent surveys and special studies on the Copperbelt, done usually under the auspices of the Rhodes-Livingstone Institute, made it possible to attempt such an inclusive frame, even though the data in it are uneven. Interest in the general process of social change became stronger, and eventually the study of leisure activities became only one aspect of it, described and analyzed in about a third of this book. But it provided an excellent way of both initiating the field work and of opening up general problems of change, cultural and individual.

Methods of Work

More than twenty years ago, Audrey Richards wrote that "the whole picture of African society has altered more rapidly than the anthropologist's technique."[2] This is infinitely truer for the study of a rapidly evolving African society since then. My study was exploratory, and therefore methodology had to be flexible. As the problem expanded or deepened, so did the methods. I used any method which had potentialities for securing relevant data, which I was capable of handling, which fitted into the time and financial limits of my study, and which was feasible within the power structure, European and African. Some methods were based on current anthropological practices and my previous field experiences; others were devised on the spot to meet the particular situation. There were problems which lent themselves to quantification, while others excluded it. The ideal of narrow exactitude may lead to good surveys and statistical data but sometimes excludes the formulation of other significant problems. Mannheim writes, "Instead of attempting to discover what is most significant with the highest degree of precision possible under the circumstances, one tends to be content to attribute importance to what is measurable."[3]

As in all field work, whether in a tribal or a modern society, it was necessary to have at least the consent and, if possible, the cooperation of those in authority. No one could work on the mine township without the permission of management, and I got their approval before I began. It was, likewise, essential to have the cooperation and good will of the Africans. I made contact with them initially through the African Education Department, and on my first Saturday afternoon in Luanshya, the African Education Officer called a meeting of about fifteen members of the African intelligentsia. These were teachers, clerks, social workers, and trade union officials. I talked about my forthcoming study, answered questions, a number of which were concerned with the auspices under which the study was being made, and asked for their help, which, at the end of the meeting, they promised.

I soon saw that in spite of the social segregation between the two races, the situation was "open"; namely, that it was possible for me to mingle socially, admittedly with discretion, with members of both races. A previous field study in Mississippi, where social relations or the absence of them between Negroes and whites was not too different from that in Luanshya, was valuable training. The systematic field work was done primarily among the Africans. With the exception of some work among white school children, the data on Europeans was gained mostly through constant observation of them in public and private situations and through conversations, both planned and unplanned, all that was possible within the limits of my time. I had good friends among Africans and Europeans.

English was spoken by those who had gone to school for five or six years, but Bemba was the lingua franca for the majority of Africans. I was told by anthropologists who spoke the language that a modest fluency could not be gained in less than a year's concentrated work in a Bemba village where it would be the only language. My sabbatical year and Guggenheim Fellowship were limited to a year, and it did not seem wise to return to New York at the end of it with accomplishments limited to a knowledge of a vernacular language. If I had known in advance that I was going to the Copperbelt of Northern Rhodesia, I could have acquired a rudimentary knowledge of Bemba through a published grammar and texts. But my original plan was to work in Uganda, for which I had studied Swahili; for a number of reasons, a month before sailing, the locale was shifted to Northern Rhodesia; and after I arrived there, the Copperbelt was selected. I began working with an interpreter, but this turned out to be an uncomfortable situation for me, since I am accustomed to making very direct contacts. If I had persisted, perhaps this method might have been useful. However, I quickly decided that it was better for me to use educated African assistants, who knew English and Bemba and whom I could train. They worked in the vernacular, while I worked with the English-speaking Africans. Most of the anthropologists who worked in this urban area and who spoke a vernacular language still relied heavily on African assistants for collecting much of their data.[4]

Finding good assistants was not easy. After a period of trial and error, I found seven students in their late teens who were home on vacation from the Munali Secondary School in Lusaka. I employed them for five weeks for a survey of the use of the mass media. They worked with a schedule I had constructed and pretested, which brought in data on preferences in radio programs, movies, and newspapers; reactions to what was heard, seen, and read; reasons for non-participation in any of the mass media; attitudes towards illiteracy and other related points. The sample of 551 adults was randomly selected and was representative of different groups based on age, sex, tribe, occupation, education, rural or urban birth, pagan and Christian belief; correlations were later made with these categories. The young male assistants were bright and receptive. I gave them some initial training, and then they met with me every morning when I reviewed and discussed the interviews they had handed in the previous day. They quickly caught on to the goals of the study and to the method of asking open-ended questions to elicit attitudes, as well as specific questions for factual information. Among the most revealing questions were those which asked the respondent how he *felt* about what he had heard, seen, or read in one of the mass media and those which asked the reasons for his preferences. The survey provided pertinent patterns on the use of the mass media and of attitudes toward it, revealed many other themes and problems of life on the Copperbelt, and provided a base for much of the work which followed.

At the end of the month, the student assistants had to return to their school, and, in any case, I could not have afforded the employment of all seven for a much longer period. As it turned out, the best assistant out of the seven did not have the money to return to school because of his father's recent death, and he remained with me on a full-time basis for the duration of my study. During its course I also employed two African teachers and one woman part-time as assistants. Part of my assistants' work and of mine consisted of interviewing on selected problems. These interviews had depth, but did not represent as large or as well-selected a sample as those of the survey. However, they opened up problems, gave rich details, and deepened my insight. In addition to interviewing, I and some of my assistants attended the tribal dances on Sunday afternoons, ballroom dances on Saturday nights at the welfare halls, the movies at the African cinema, athletic events, and many other social affairs.

I knew some Africans and Europeans well enough to visit them casually and to discuss data and the local events and news.

One way of studying social change is through different age groups, and I did a limited amount of work with a selected group of boys and girls in their teens, as well as the more extended work with adults. In the study of the young group, I was particularly interested in their values, their self-imagery and imagery of Europeans, their concrete ambitions and their fantasies of what they would like to be. This data was obtained from essays written by boys and girls, ranging in age from twelve to seventeen, in Standards V and VI (corresponding approximately to our seventh and eighth grades) in two government schools. This was the highest level of education offered in the community, and since there were no girls in these standards there, I turned to a nearby girls' boarding school. The essays were assigned by African teachers to the students as part of their regular classroom work; essay writing was customary, and none of the students knew the essays were being done for me. The total sample for each of four essays ranged from 102 to 109 and represented all the young people in these standards in the schools of this community at the time of my study. The essay topics in the order in which they were written were:

1. If you went to London and met an English person who had never before seen an African and he asked you about them, how would you describe them? Include how they look, how they live, and how they behave.

2. If you went back to your village or your mother's village and you met a friend who had never seen a European, how would you describe them? Include how they look, how they live, and how they behave.

3. What would you like to do when you finish school? Include the kind of job, where you want to live, the kind of person you want to marry, when you want to marry, the number of children desired.

4. If it pleases God to make you anyone or anything you please, who or what would you like to be? Give your reasons.

The essays yielded rich data in traditional and modern elements, values, goals, imagery, and showed a marked difference between males and females.[5] I used the same technique of essay writing in the government-run evening classes for studying English, attended by African men. Although the adults' essays provided some data, they were not as full or as interesting as those of the young people, probably because the older group were just beginning to learn how to express themselves in writing while the young people had been doing it for several years.

While all these methods—survey, essay writing, interviewing, casual visiting, attending social affairs—brought in good data, I was not satisfied. I lived in the European part of the municipality, and it would have been impossible from either the European or African point of view for me to have lived on the segregated African township. Although I drove to it almost daily, I was missing the intimate knowledge and feeling-tone of daily life which comes from actually living in a community, seeing and hearing much that goes on, and participating in daily life, all of which is so essential to an understanding of any society. It occurred to me that I might get a vicarious sense of personal daily life if an assistant recorded everything that people said and did in his home and its immediate neighborhood, from the time they got up in the morning until they went to bed; so I asked one to stay home for a week and do just this. His family and neighbors were more or less typical. His brother-in-law, in whose house he lived, was a miner, as was the next-door neighbor. Neither they nor their wives had any European education, and the assistant was the only one who knew how to write; his written record of conversation did not have the same connotation for his family and neighbors as they would in a contemporary, Western, literate home, and his "work" was simply accepted as part of his white-collar job. At the end of the week, when he brought me the recorded conversations, I realized that these were really the stuff of life and that they provided what I had been missing. They gave much more than that: attitudes, opinions, and behavior, some of which I had not known existed. Its richness naturally prompted a continuation of the method, not only in this household and neighborhood, but in others and at the beer hall, the public washing stands, the welfare hall, the union meetings, on the road, and wherever Africans met. Africans love to talk, and they express themselves well. The conversations were about many things: news from the village, suspicions of a husband's adultery, incest in a neighbor's household, sickness and death, witchcraft, a fight between two women, argument and discussion of the pros and cons of a miners' strike, a trade union meeting, incidents at work, European supervisors, an intra-African court case, where the best beer was being brewed, a new suit of clothes, the price of food, and so on and on. Knowledge was shared, gossip exchanged, and traditional and modern points of view argued. These conversations about the trivial and the significant, which make up the fabric of personal and social life, had a quality of intimacy which was invaluable to me. In the book, they give a personal dimension to an objective study. The reader hears individual Africans talk, as well as listening to the author's description and interpretation.

A few themes were constant. Whether discussing witchcraft or a strike, the modern European-educated young men were more detached and critical than the tradition-oriented individuals. The latter also had a narrow range of identifications, not going much beyond relatives, while the range of the modernists was expanding not only beyond the kindred, but also beyond tribe and, more gradually, into the world. These and other significant differences between the two groups which emerged in the conversations were then studied in different contexts. The conversations also revealed that small groups of relatives, neighbors, workmates, and friends acted as a form of social control. The assumption of many sociologists that this type of control completely disappears when people move from a small village to a large industrial community was not borne out.[6] The tendency toward the rather quick formation of small groups exercising a measure of control has also been noted in studies of the social organization of hospitals, mental institutions, public housing projects, and other such institutions; and it is obvious in a college faculty.

The conversations were recorded verbatim, without any selectivity, at intervals for a period of six months. There was much repetition, and my editing has been restricted to deleting unnecessary reiteration, so that themes emerge more clearly, and to occasional explanations for clarification. The translations were by an African, and I have not changed his English.

Before I hit upon the recording of personal conversations, I used a similar technique in getting spontaneous reactions to the movies. There was so much conversation in the audience about the movie being seen that the sound track was unheard. My assistants moved about in the audience and recorded what people were saying, which provided a different kind of data from that obtained in interviews.

(This method could not be used for reactions to radio programs, since the listeners did not talk during them.) I was present while the movie was being shown, observing the overt emotional reactions of the audience as well as looking at the movie.

There was not sufficient time to do systematic work on the functioning of the churches on the township or any detailed studies of the schools. My knowledge of the former is impressionistic; and of the latter, mainly through documentary sources. Obviously, it would have been better if I had known the Bemba language and if I had had two or more years rather than one for the field project; some of the methods were designed to reduce the effect of these limitations. There is also the unavoidable delay between the time of the field study and the completion of the book. Most of the sustained work on the organization of field notes, library research, and the integration of the two in the writing of the manuscript was primarily restricted to summers and one semester on leave without pay. I had approached a number of foundations for a grant which would have enabled me to take off a year from my professional duties to write the book. Several foundations kindly indicated that they would be glad to entertain an application for another field study, but that they did not give money to "write-up." I mention this point, because it is a problem for many American anthropologists, particularly those who are teaching at a college rather than at a university with its provisions for research. Since I left Northern Rhodesia, I have kept up with the continuing situation through publications, journals, newspapers and magazines from the area, letters from Africans and Europeans there, and contacts with those who have come here. In the book I indicate some recent trends, about which I have information. But I do not aim to be a journalist, and even under the best possible circumstances there would be a considerable lag between the completion of any field study and its publication. My goal is to describe and interpret a fundamental process of social and individual change, the basic elements of which continue to be much the same, even though the rate of change has quickened. The accelerated changes of today are closely related to those of yesterday.

Plan of Book

The book endeavors to bring into an ordered frame of reference
seemingly unrelated facts from many different sources and those
which are quite obviously related. Professor Ithiel de Sola Pool, of
the Massachusetts Institute of Technology, writes, ". . . science includes both the radical free play of imagination in ordering miscellaneous facts regardless of how these facts were collected and also
the systematic controlled observation which tells whether new facts
fit the theory."[7] Data is both quantitative and qualitative, factual and
interpretive, and extends from generalizations about social change to
personal conversations between individuals. I have not tried to force
them all into one form for the sake of an artificial consistency, but
have let the different kinds of materials dictate the form in which
each is given. Some chapters are primarily descriptive, others more
interpretive, and still others recount an event completely through
the conversations of Africans. Statistical tables are at the back. When
possible, generalizations are illustrated with specific examples of
individual cases. Traditional tribal life is described and interpreted
and the history of the coming of the Europeans related, because
otherwise it is not possible to understand contemporary African life.
Then, too, the theme of changing relations between the two racial
groups runs throughout the book. An attempt is also made to understand Europeans and Africans who do not want to change, as well
as those who desire to change. Finally, I have tried to relate the
complex process of social change to that of the equally complex
process of individual change.

Societies change because some individuals in them want to change,
and this happens through the introduction of more advanced technology and of new values and ideas into the society. This is a circular
process. Most anthropologists have given up looking for original
causes or separating cause from effect in their studies of both physical
evolution and of social behavior, and speak rather of their inter-
relationship. To understand the relationship between individual and
social change, I have integrated concepts from cultural anthropology
and other social sciences and from psychoanalytical psychology.
Anthropologists have been studying social change, beginning with
prehistoric periods; and historians, sociologists, and economists have

described and interpreted historical and contemporary social changes, some revolutionary and others gradual. Psychoanalysis deals with continuities and changes, on a conscious and unconscious level, within the individual.

I have not hesitated to use insights from all these disciplines to illuminate the knowledge gained from my field work and the work of others, but have avoided as far as possible their technical language. Though I am only too well aware of the limitations in both my knowledge and insight, my goal has been to understand some of the universal characteristics of social change, some of its distinctive qualities on the Copperbelt of Northern Rhodesia and its meaning for the Africans and Europeans who live there. I have focused on the human situation, as well as on the abstractions of social change.

PART I

THE PAST
IN THE PRESENT

township. Here, too, were the orderly rows of rectangular white houses of from one to three rooms, provided by management for its African employees and their families, totaling about thirty thousand people. Only the inevitable ant hills broke the uniformity of the evenly set white houses. At the time of my study the average house, made of sun-dried brick, plastered and lime washed outside and inside, with concrete floor and corrugated iron roof, had two rooms. Each room usually had one window, and there was a bed, a table, a few chairs, an oil lamp, perhaps a battery radio, a few dishes and cooking utensils, and a wire bin to protect food from insects. A picture of Queen Elizabeth was likely to be on the wall. The house had a lean-to kitchen, although some of the preparation of food, such as the pounding of mealie-meal, was done outside. There was a small, but increasing number of European-like bungalows, with a veranda, three rooms and a kitchen, electricity and inside sanitation, occupied by senior employees. Unmarried men lived in dormitory blocks with a central communal kitchen. The orderly rows of white houses and the lack of trees and flowers seemed to me to lack a pleasing esthetic quality. But the Africans thought the houses a great improvement over their traditional village homes.

The township has now expanded to four and one-half square miles, and the standard of housing is constantly improving. In 1954 there were 146 houses with electricity, while in January 1961, there were approximately 4,920 out of a total of 7,708. Some of the better houses had flower gardens.[5] The substandard houses without electricity are now scheduled to be demolished within the next few years and replaced by electrified ones.[6] Houses were the property of the mine and were allotted to employees for the duration of their employment at a subeconomic rent. In the past, it was always assumed that all Africans would return to their rural villages. With more Africans being born on the township and with town life becoming increasingly a permanent way of life, return to a village can no longer be taken for granted. An African home-ownership scheme has been recently introduced by the copper-mining companies, whereby an employee may purchase or build his home outside the mine townships, with the assistance of the company and through a housing plan controlled by the government, a municipal council, or a management board.[7]

The township had nine sections, each with its public latrine and bath house, and a stone washing stand with running water where the women gathered to do the family washing. (At this writing there are eleven sections.) There were many amenities: a large sports stadium, a swimming pool used almost entirely by youngsters, a main welfare center with library, tea shop, and radio loudspeaker. The center provided a meeting place for various clubs and Saturday night dances. Attached to the center was a large open-air movie theatre with a biweekly program of Westerns, serials, and current-events films. The theatre was likewise used as a meeting place for the African Mine Workers' Union. Welfare subcenters were in different parts of the township. Scattered across it were also an open-air market, an African Co-operative Society store and a number of other stores, a photographer's studio, a carpentry workshop, a beer hall, and a hospital; and there were churches of many denominations, including Christian and Moslem, schools for children and for evening adult English classes, and centers for induction classes for miners. All this was on the surface.

Twenty-five hundred feet underground, reached by the "cage" (elevator), is the buried copper for which all the above existed. Here miners worked with axe, shovel, and drill, and drove the underground trains on rails through wet, slippery mud. These men and the others working on the surface in smelter, powerhouse, and concentrator were organized in gangs of from ten to fifteen men, each under the direction of an African boss-boy, who was responsible to a European "ganger," a foreman. Other Africans, skilled and unskilled, were employed in many supplementary jobs, such as compound sweepers, cleaners of latrines and bath houses, watchmen, policemen, building laborers, clerks, storekeepers, social workers, and hospital aides.

Unlike many early mining communities, this township was not predominantly male. In 1951 the population was 55.5 per cent adult male and 44.5 per cent adult female.[8] The differential percentage between the sexes has diminished since then. Most of the men had a wife, and a few had two; and in the household were their children, and often nephews and nieces. Adolescent boys and girls often slept in the home of a relative, the boys sometimes in the "single quarters," to avoid being too close to their parents' private life.

Driving in the township one evening about six o'clock I saw the mine shafts and derricks starkly silhouetted against the sky with its beautiful, continuously changing cloud formations, which seemed both close and vast. The smelter belched forth its smoke. I passed a meeting of the African Mine Workers' Union in the movie amphitheatre of the Welfare Hall, and a rehearsal, with the drums beating, of a tribal dance to be held the forthcoming Sunday afternoon, within earshot of the showing of slides of Noah's life by a missionary to a small congregation. Africans alone or in groups of two or three passed on bicycles, others on foot. At this time of the evening relatively few women were about. Earlier, I saw them walking, carrying their babies, and stopping to nurse the infants when they cried.

In this setting there were powerful forces of social change, some visible and some buried like the copper. The Africans in this changing society belonged to about seventy different Bantu tribes, in thirteen linguistic groups, with the Bemba language as the lingua franca. The people came from small villages, mostly in Northern Rhodesia and Nyasaland. Although the customs of one tribe differed from another, they all belonged to the same order of civilization. Now traditional and modern orders exist side by side. Men who participated in a tribal dance on Sunday afternoon might be dancing on Saturday night to jazz music at the Welfare Hall. Witchcraft-thinking did not prevent people from using the services of the clinic and hospital. They listened to modern songs and to current news and stories over the radio, and used their traditional proverbs and folk tales to make a point in colloquial conversation. The Mine Workers' Union was a unifying force for non-members as well as members, and at the same time tribal membership was a significant criteria for identity and a close bond between people. The goal of individual careers was new, but it had not eliminated traditional duties to kindred. Many people went to church, but they also followed some traditional customs at birth, puberty, marriage, and death. These were some of the dichotomies on the Copperbelt. Some people tended to be more traditional and others more modern in their general orientation, with many gradations between the extremes. The traditional and modern were found not only in disparate groups, but within the same individual.

Europeans as well as Africans were part of these forces of rapid social change. Like the Africans, many Europeans mingled traditional beliefs with new forms of behavior. Their values, behavior, and attitudes to Africans were conditioned, in part, by their national and class backgrounds. Some made use of the most recent scientific and technological developments and at the same time had strongly entrenched and disproved beliefs about race differences, stemming from another century. Europeans varied as much among each other as did Africans and could be classified on a similar scale, ranging from traditional to modern.

An official in the European-personnel mine office estimated that about 25 per cent of the Europeans employed by the mine came from the United Kingdom, about 20 per cent from South Africa, and 55 per cent from the local community. Of the latter group, most of them or their parents had come originally from either South Africa or the United Kingdom. In class backgrounds they ranged from the upper-class with the traditional sense of *noblesse oblige,* to the working class who feared Africans as potential economic, social, and political rivals. The changing types of Europeans in Northern Rhodesia—missionaries, colonial officials, industrialists, artisans, farmers, business men, and other settlers—and in 1953 a shift in the locus of power from the Colonial Office to the settlers through the Federation of Northern Rhodesia with Southern Rhodesia and Nyasaland, were significant factors in the contemporary scene. The Europeans represented another dichotomy for the Africans, for whom they were both models to be liked and imitated, and powerful people to be feared and sometimes hated.

The fifteen hundred or so European employees of the mine had their own residential area outside the compound. Its tree-shaded streets were lined with one-story bungalows set in gardens. When the rains came, this part of the community was vivid with color from poinsettias and roses and from the blossoming Rhodesian flame trees and the purple bougainvillea, the hibiscus, jacarandas, and frangipani. The large ant hills, some with small trees growing out of them, were part of the landscape in summer or winter, rainy or dry season. In this area were the red-brick administration building of the mining company, the European hospital, the offices of the European Mine Workers' Union, and the European Club, open to all white employees, with its swimming pool, tennis courts, golf course, library, bar, and dining room. The European miners and most of the other employees lived better and had more social amenities than people in their occupations in other parts of the world. An enjoyable feeling of alleged superiority because of their race was an additional bonus for many of the Europeans. In their small community was a sense of intimacy and of security, created by the dominance of one benevolent employer and by the social isolation from Africans and from the rest of the world.

The African mine township also seemed to have more unity, more security, more parochialism than did the municipal location. My initial survey of the use of the mass media on both and my systematic work on the mine township and casual visiting on the location suggested a hypothesis that the more heterogeneous life on the municipal location accompanied a greater sense of participation in the modern world and that, in general, these people were a bit more cosmopolitan in their orientation than were those who lived on the mine township. There the benevolently inclined management, with its hierarchy of jobs, its pension system, its extensive welfare activities, sports, personnel work, educational classes, provided a way of living as well as jobs. The union likewise provided an opportunity for group solidarity, not replacing the tribe, but giving a broader focus. The people on the municipal location, however, worked for many employers. The municipality rather than the employers provided the limited welfare activities. The domination of one large employer and one union on the mine township seemed, to some degree, to enclose and restrict it, though standards of living were higher, amenities more profuse, and economic opportunities greater there than on the non-mining township. However, the problems of change in the mining and non-mining townships of this area did not seem basically different, even though a minor difference in emphasis might be assumed. Since my study concentrated on the mine township, my data, with some exceptions, is from it.

The thirty thousand Africans on the mine township did not live isolated or anonymously. Friends, relatives, neighbors, and workmates moved in small groups with close ties, and these mingled with larger ones. The speed with which a rumor spread throughout the entire township was evidence of a broad web of social relations. Life was personal, with a quality of enormous vitality. Emotions were strong. Men and women loved, were jealous, quarreled, fought, and

sometimes made up. They drank, they danced, they shouted their
approval at the Western movies, they played football, they enjoyed
listening to the radio, they went to a union meeting, they visited
relatives at home, and relatives came to see them. They talked endlessly about all things that interested them: a strike, an unfaithful
husband, the price of food, a debt to be paid, an overcoat they
wanted, political news, illness and death, the visits of relatives, where
native beer was being brewed, a football game, an approaching marriage, a court case, going home on leave, witchcraft, the birth of a
baby, a stolen bicycle, and on and on about the little and the big
things that were important to them. They worked the eight-hour
shift, some in the dark corridors of the mine and others on the
surface. They were happy sometimes, and sad sometimes. They knew
life was changing about them. Some knew it more than others. Some
fantasied a return, even an exaggerated return, to a part of their
tribal past. Others looked toward a new future. For the anthropologist,
it was a moment in history to be understood.

Now we leave the physical and social setting and proceed to a
theoretical frame, necessary to an understanding of social and individual change in this part of Africa. The problems of change there
are part of the universal phenomenon of human change, and the
frame, therefore, cannot be limited to one place or to one period of
time. After the theoretical contours have been given, we return to
the people, Africans and Europeans.

2. Social and Individual Change

CHANGE is as old as the human species. Probably some alteration occurred in the way of life in the different ice ages because of changes in the physical environment. Since then, most of the changes in culture have been due to technological innovations in the man-made environment and to accompanying new values. The "Neolithic Revolution" was marked by the domestication of animals, the beginnings of agriculture, and the invention of tools. Then came the "Urban Revolution," with its use of metals, improved agriculture, irrigation, wheeled transport, and many other inventions which resulted in the growth of cities, empires, and dynasties. The Industrial Revolution was a third one, and we are probably in the beginning of a fourth, the Atomic Revolution. Each historical period becomes shorter than the previous one, and the slow processes by which past civilizations came into being are not recapitulated today. As Henry Adams observed, the march of mankind constantly accelerates.

Change is possible because it is an inherent part of the human organism. It occurs from the moment of conception. Change for the individual is involved in growing, learning, and maturing, all necessary for his adaptation to the environment.[1] Obviously, no individual comes newly to terms with it. Besides his biological heredity, he has a social heritage—the traditions, customs and all the ways his an-

[11

cestors have discovered for meeting their problems. The anthropologists call this culture, and it is never static, although the rate of change varies widely. Social change in Africa, as elsewhere, is the result of historical events, economic processes, and communication between peoples. The subsequent set of institutional arrangements, a social system, is related to dominant values and is "ultimately mediated through individual human action."[2] This is a circular process. The influence of institutional arrangements on human personalities in turn generates movements of change in the original social system.[3]

The same themes seem to underlie biological, psychological, and social change. Pierre Teilhard de Chardin relates all three to increasing selective differentiation, followed by convergence and incorporation of differentiation into an organized and unified pattern.[4] As Julian Huxley notes in his introduction to Teilhard, after *homo sapiens* began to differentiate into different races, migration and intermarriage led to increased interbreeding between all human variants. Huxley writes: "Man is the only successful type which has remained as a single interbreeding group or species, and has not radiated out into a number of biologically separated assemblages (like the birds, with about 8,500 species, or the insects with over half a million)."[5]

The psychological development of the individual, or as it is often called, the development of the ego, involves increasing differentiation within the individual's inner world and includes the separation of thinking from feeling, of perception from imagery, of means from ends, and of a growing separation of the individual from his early bonds of dependency on parents.[6] Again, differentiation is followed by integration of the elements within the self and of the individual with the world of men.

Changes in a culture may be initiated from within the society or come from without it, but the latter has been by far the most frequent during the course of history.[7] Cultural diffusion, occurring through migration and ever-improving systems of communication results in cultural differentiation, and this is then followed by cultural convergence. Cultures formerly distinct become increasingly similar.

The same process happens within a social system. For instance, the web of kinship underlies all social institutions in tribal societies, and the basis of marriage is usually a preferred mate in an extended kinship group. When the choice of mate depends on personal attraction and friendship outside a group of kindred, courtship is differentiated from kinship. To take another example, in modern society, political institutions are freer from kinship loyalties and religious beliefs and practices than they were in tribal ones.[8] Yet it is well known that the economic, political and social elements of a modern social system become increasingly interdependent.

Social change is not limited to conscious planning, but takes place also through the adjustments of people who are dissatisfied with traditional goals and who wish to further new ones. The Industrial Revolution, the development of science, the Protestant Reformation, and the beginnings of capitalism were all interrelated, in that they helped to free man to make his own place in the world, a place formerly set by accident of birth, and at the same time made him more responsible for the place he made. Geographical and social mobility gave him new goals. The destruction of the medieval feudal order, the rise of the bourgeois class and the beginnings of modern capitalism took approximately from the middle of the twelfth to the middle of the seventeenth century. Changes now occurring in Central Africa have some similarities to, and, of course, many differences from, that period in Europe; and the timetable today is different: a few generations instead of five centuries. Nor can we anticipate that the results will be the same, or exactly what an African society will be like in a hundred years. We cannot prophesy even for our own culture in this revolutionary age. We can, however, analyze the process of social and individual change now occurring and point to directions in which it may move.

Changes occur through the introduction of new tools, improved technology, and new ideas. These result in modifications in the social system and in the personalities of the people living in it, who, in turn, modify the social system. It is relatively easy to learn new techniques, such as riding a bicycle, driving a car, reading and writing, and the various manual skills required in mining and other occupations. All over the world most people accept with great eagerness an iron spade and later a plough and do not revert to a primitive hoe. A bicycle, and then an automobile, become much-desired means of transportation, and then most people do not want to walk. Once a sewing machine is introduced, nothing can keep an Alaskan, a Melanesian, or an African from wanting it. These technological changes are on a conscious level and for easily understood goals. The more advanced technology enables people to live better and with less effort; voluntary technological regression is rare.

But we assume with Redfield "that the moral order which refers to the nature of the bonds between men and to their values—their conviction of what is right and wrong—will change more slowly than the technical order in which men are bound by things rather than by sentiments."[9] Traditional values and the concepts associated with them are learned early in life and, to a large degree, unconsciously; and they become part of a complex ideational matrix. For instance, magical thinking is part of tribal man's relationship to the supernatural, to his fellow men, and to the natural world. The theories of causation which underlie magic are based on preliterate man's concept of the universe. It is not surprising, therefore, that difficulties are encountered in attempting to substitute scientific thinking, based on a different view of the universe, for magical thinking. Often when a new concept is introduced it will run parallel to an old one. Thus Africans may believe in witchcraft as a cause of illness and also use modern medicine to cure it. The simultaneous existence of outmoded and of modern theories of causation are not confined to Africans. In modern political life, attempts to find a scapegoat as the cause of all our problems—Hitlerism, McCarthyism, and other such isms—exist side by side with modern and rational techniques for understanding social problems. In the United States, the struggle over integration in southern schools reveals new values in conflict with outmoded ones, which still function with considerable vitality.

But all men, African, European, or other, have potentialities for learning; and many new values and concepts take their place beside the old, are substituted for them, or integrated with them. The process is obviously easier for the second and third generation after a concept has been introduced. However, cultural and individual growth and change are not necessarily either harmonious or contentious. We take for granted that men will vary in their attitude to change. Lawrence K. Frank has discussed potential reactions in our society to the implications of rockets, sputniks, and other characteristics of men in space. Some men fail to perceive or deliberately ignore new events and new ideas; some try to apply new concepts in a limited way; some attempt to apply them to an ever-broadening range of situations; still others try to communicate their new perceptions to people.[10] Reactions to cultural changes are the same phenomenon, whether they are the responses of tribal Africans to a modern industrial society, of Europeans in Africa faced with a dissolving colonialism, or of all of us in this new Atomic Age.

Among significant changes now occurring in this part of Africa are:

1. The concept of space is drastically broadened, as the result of direct contacts with other cultures and, indirectly, through new forms of communication: the printed word, radio, and motion pictures. The quality of life in a relatively small, isolated, preliterate society, dependent on the spoken word for communication, is radically changed when the scale of society broadens, and mobility and personal freedom increase.[11] The small, relatively closed world becomes ever wider, more open, and more heterogenous, with increasing differentiation and consequent choice. Man no longer almost automatically becomes a herder or farmer. He can choose to follow a traditional path, or he can try one of the new ones opening up in industry, in education, and all the other expanding areas of the changing society.

2. The imagery of time changes from one in which activities follow the cycle of nature to one of clocks, of work and vacations, and other such differentiated regularities.[12] Time not only becomes more precise, but also acquires great depth. The conscious traditions of preliterate peoples usually go back no more than ten or twelve generations. A man in tribal society might know his genealogy for three or four generations and be able to talk about past wars and migrations, but he would be ignorant of the every-day doings of two generations back.[13] Today, the African is becoming "heir to the ages."

3. The introduction of a money economy and radical changes in the economic system transforms traditional communal goals of the extended kinship group to those of personal achievement and individual careers. This results in changing the structure of the family and the position of men and women in it and in the community. The family on the Copperbelt tends to become the modern nuclear one, and new roles are slowly opening to men and to women. But ties to the extended family and to the lineage remain.

4. The traditional concept of respect of young for their elders, of women for men, and of commoner for chief accompanied by elaborate etiquette and ritual now vies with a new social system in which European education, ways of living, and amount of money rather than age and rank determine status.

5. The newly achieved status affects the form and nature of leadership. In the past, chiefs, who had their position because of royal birth, controlled goods, services, and people. In a sense, they were maintenance men with the duties of maintaining, through their secular and ritual behavior, the health, fertility, justice, and defense of the group and peaceful cooperation within it. If they did not serve well, they lost their following. Although the clearly defined roles for superior and subordinate were not egalitarian, everyone lived on much the same subsistence standard. Today, the situation is somewhat in reverse. The new leaders achieve their position by democratic means through trade union and political organizations. They are usually young men as compared to the ruling elders of the past, and control neither goods or services, nor do they have despotic power over people. Their functions are defined in terms of changing conditions and of ability in obtaining for their followers new benefits which do not yet exist, such as political independence and higher living standards. These new leaders are given respect and honor, but maintain their position only as long as the people think they are being well served. On the other hand, the egalitarian standards of living are disappearing.

6. European standards, not equally accessible to all, have become important and mark the beginning of self-conscious status groups: the intelligentsia, the new middle class, and the masses of still illiterate people who are unskilled workers or subsistence farmers.[14] On the Copperbelt, the intelligentsia were usually considered by Africans to be those with eight or more years of schooling, who were teachers, political and trade union leaders, social workers, business men, clerks, and other white-collar workers, and those in any other positions requiring at least the elementary education of eight years. (The educational system is described in Chapter 17.) The new middle class included those with less education and were semi-skilled workers, building laborers, policemen, taxi drivers, servants in European houses, and business men and others who did not meet the edu-

cational requirements of the intelligentsia. The lower class were the unskilled mine workers, often illiterate and with no education or one or two years of schooling.

7. Modern education introduces a fundamental shift in emphasis in theories of causation. We have long known that preliterate man was both reality-oriented and magical-oriented. Through his observation and thinking he knew empirically the relations between certain means and ends in farming, hunting, fishing, and many other pursuits. But his cosmos was also a highly personalized one, in which good and bad fortune were attributed to magicians and witches and to the observation of rituals and taboos, by the individual, by the chief, and by the group. However, for the Africans, and all other men in our contemporary world, the cosmos becomes increasingly impersonal. Thinking is more and more based on experimentation or the testing of reality and the delegation of responsibility for well being to the self and to non-magical specialists and experts, even though our capabilities in this direction are still quite limited.

8. The African is affected by a world-wide change in knowledge about race, in attitudes to peoples of different races, and in ideas about colonialism. We have progressed from the early days of empire-building in the seventeenth century, when colonizers thought they had the right to take land wherever they settled and to enslave indigenous people, force them onto reservations, exploit them for labor, or kill them. The *ad hoc* ideology of that period about the alleged superiority of the white race gave way in the late nineteenth century to the more respectable and "scientific" theories of social Darwinism, based on the oversimplified concept of the survival of the fittest.[15] Then came colonial policies of trusteeship, or "the white man's burden," in which a guardian looked after his ward. This involved the idea that the European was responsible for turning the "primitive" man into a "civilized" man like himself. In the meantime, scientific research established that the range of potential abilities is the same for people of all races; and practical experience has validated the theory. As Herskovits writes, history rather than biology today explains the differences between peoples. Historical factors have a stubborn continuity, but they are of quite a different nature than biological factors. Many educated Africans know this. Europeans got power because

history favored their capabilities at a certain time.[16] But times change, as do the capabilities of men.

9. The Africans not only have more knowledge, but also more self-awareness. According to Teilhard, an increase of consciousness is part of man's development and has been happening since the end of the Tertiary era. Modern man reflects, looks at himself as an object with its own consistency and values, and knows himself more than did his ancestors.[17] The African becomes increasingly aware of his own personality, of his existence apart from the tribe, of his place in changing history.

10. All of the above developments contribute to the change from tribalism to nationalism, from a homogeneous to a heterogenous culture, from a society set within narrow geographical limits to one which is part of a continent and looks out on the world.

There are, of course, other innovations, but these are among the most significant in the changes taking place in the African's image of himself and his relationship to other men and to his environment and in his goals. The changes are in the direction of greater differentiation, followed later by convergence, that is, integration of the differentiated. This brings the possibility of a tremendous creative surge within the African cultures.

Neither all Africans nor all Europeans change at the same pace, and there are those who resist change as well as those who desire it. Why do some individuals (in all races) pursue, in the main, a form of adaptation to their environment which envisages a future radically different from the past while the adaptation of others is based on a desire to return symbolically to a past?[18] As is well known, all men find security in an established order, because their position in it and their internalized values are not threatened. At a time of rapid and intensive social change, they are apt to lose their point of reference and so be faced with insecurity and anxiety. It is generally assumed that some individuals have more strength—ego strength, as it is often called—to withstand the ambiguities and anxieties of change than do others. Individual genetic factors may be relevant, although we know very little about them, i.e., we know more about the cultural factors, which may influence both the amount of anxiety and its nature. In this context, the following questions are relevant: Does the individual think the changes are advantageous or disadvantageous to him? Does he have the opportunity of achieving new goals, if he desires them? Does he have some understanding of the rational underlying the changes? Do the changes threaten his traditional internalized values? Have these changed, too? Such questions are not bound by race, but apply to Africans, Europeans, or anyone else living in a society of rapid change.

In tribal Africa young people were in a disadvantageous position in regard to their elders, women in their relationship with men, and commoners with royalty; and this is true for many other societies. Choosing a modern goal and achieving it reduces some of the disadvantages of being young, a woman, and a commoner. In one sense, there is built into every differentiated social system a source of strain from the feeling of being in an unsatisfactory or an oppressive position; the need to eliminate it eventually acts as a mechanism of change.[19] Then, too, the availability of the means for achieving new goals is not the same for all. Young Africans, and males more than females, have had more opportunity for attaining the necessary European education than their elders. The education gives not only training, but also introduces new values, sets new goals, and may give some understanding of the changes involved. Likewise, many more men than women have direct contacts with Europeans, which is an exposure to new values.

But young and old, men and women, royalty and commoner are affected by the new money economy. Everyone needs and wants money to pay taxes, to raise his economic standard of living, and to buy the new, attractive goods. However, it is possible for an individual to achieve monetary goals with little change occurring in his internalized and traditional values. Money and the things it buys fit well into the traditional prestige system, and "showing off" is not a new trait. More significant and more complex are those new goals and ways of thinking which demand new emotional commitments. The choice of an individual career is one of these. It conflicts with the mores of tribal family and communal social life and requires considerable planning and the giving up of some present satisfactions for the sake of future gains. The acceptance of scientific thinking and its substitution for the traditional concept of magical causation is likewise not just an intellectual process, but a major psychological change for the individual and is still part of human development.

Some of the factors involved in this process can be understood by theories of identification and identity. The term "identification" is derived from psychoanalysis and, as Axelrad and Maury write, was first used to explain certain processes in the parent-child relationship. The initial helplesses of the infant establishes a need for a dependable model, usually the mother. The child can explore an unknown world only through the medium of those who have knowledge of it and who represent security. The favorable emotional relationship of the child to another person provides the necessary anchor for further explorations and for further identifications. As the child grows up, the distance increases between him and the original objects of his identification. But through the unconscious process of internalization, he has made some of their characteristics his own. In this type of identification an individual desires to be like another, either in a single characteristic or in many traits. He becomes like the other by assimilating one or more of the latter's characteristics. This is part of all normal growth. Another form of identification has as its function a defense against danger, described by Anna Freud as "identification with the aggressor." The anti-semitic Jew is an example of this type. A third type of identification is based on the perception of a common quality, and examples are found among those who have a common leader, goals, ideology, or scapegoat, or similarity in work.[20]

From infancy on, every culture provides opportunities for many identifications, beginning usually with the mother. Erikson notes that the most important element in this initial relationship is trust. If there is basic trust rather than mistrust, the ground is laid for healthy development, for trust in one's self, and in others. Other identifications follow the initial one with the mother, and by adolescence the values of the ego gained from successful identifications culminate in a sense of "ego identity." This is "the accrued confidence that one's ability to maintain inner sameness and continuity (one's ego in the psychological sense) is matched by the sameness and continuity of one's meaning for others."[21] A problem for the adolescent in many societies is the gap between his image of himself—the continuity between what he was as a child and what he is now becoming—and the community's image of him, particularly as represented by his parents, teachers, and others in authority. The process of identity formation is, of course, not restricted to any one period of life, but is continuous throughout the life history of an individual. Always he must try to make sense to himself and to his community.[22] Many Africans face not only the discontinuities in intra-African life, but they also have to suffer the wide discrepancy between their image of themselves and the Europeans' image of them. An African clerk comes into contact with some Europeans who think, "all Africans are monkeys, just down from the trees."

It was indeed easier to make sense to one's self and to the community in tribal society than in this rapidly changing life. The traditional homogeneous culture offered for identification a small number of stable stereotypes differentiated primarily by sex and age. The values and expectations of parents and of other significant elders for their children were those which young people had internalized by the time they reached adolescence. In tribal life, the group identity, called by Erikson the "life plan" of a society—its basic way of organizing experience—included an intimate relationship to an extended group of kindred, to tribe, to ancestral spirits, and to the land. Since the arrival of Europeans there have been new models for identification, and parental values internalized in childhood may clash with new values. The recent models included Europeans and Africans: European missionaries, traders, colonial officials, employers; European and African teachers; African political and trade union leaders and successful business men. Nor are prototypes limited to experience with real people, but include characters portrayed in myths and folklore, in movies, radio, songs, stories, history, and literature. In a period of rapid change, such as is now occurring in Africa, adult socialization is important; and those who lead the way in the modern world are involved in its process.[23] Their new experiences, new values, new group identity, and the resulting changes in the social system, all become significant in the socialization of their children. The process is endless.

The homogeneity of tribal society, with its well-defined social roles for each sex and age group and its slow rate of change, is in sharp contrast to the discontinuities in contemporary Africa. The broadening of space and time imagery and the increased knowledge of other peoples, of other mores and institutions, extend the possible areas of perception, of action, of self-awareness, and the range of identities. The personality of modern Africans is not only different from that of their tribal ancestors, but there is probably a sharper differentiation between individual Africans today than in the past. The principle of differentiation operates also within the social system, creating more and different kinds of divisions between people; but, at the same time, there is another kind of convergence in the new nationalism.

The world of the Europeans in Northern Rhodesia is also rapidly changing, and they are threatened in varying degrees by the changes. The European's status in society and his motivations for coming to Northern Rhodesia are among the determining factors for his attitude to social change. Those immigrants who were in a low economic and social class at home, who migrated to raise their standard of living, who looked to Africa as the promised land of opportunity for themselves and their descendants, are threatened by a competition from Africans who learn modern skills. The children of these immigrants often have the same fears. Those with an upper-middle or upper class background, who are in professional occupations, who still have roots in England, are much less threatened, as are their children, too. But some of this group who strongly desire to maintain a standard of life, which includes servants, no longer possible for them in England, feel imperiled by the changes. Those who come to this part of the world out of a desire to help the Africans, and often the descendants of such people, may not feel endangered at all. And there are always some individuals whose reactions cut across their backgrounds.

Threats may be to the Europeans' values as well as to economic standards. These values range through the "brotherhood of man," "Africans are essential as workers to develop the country," to Africans are "monkeys just down from the trees." European goals range from a truly integrated society, to one of partial integration, to one in which Africans are permanently in a lower social, economic, and political position.

Europeans in Northern Rhodesia (like colonials elsewhere) have lived in a relatively closed world, much more closed than in England; and their image of themselves as an allegedly superior race occupying their rightful place at the top of a power structure is being rapidly shattered by changing events. Their society has been fixated on race differentiation. Can the Europeans take the next step of convergence with another culture? Do the Europeans have a capacity for more trust and creative growth, or is their mistrust, with its accompanying rigidity, greater?

In the United States, there has been a more gradual change in the nature of the American identity in relation to the world. The traditional identity based on "an image of insulated spaciousness" has come into conflict with "the new image of explosive global closeness."[24] As a result, our anxieties are greater than those of some of our European allies, who have been living for centuries in explosive continental closeness. The problem for all of us is one of expanding identities in an ever larger and closer world. This is the third type of identity described by Freud, based on the perception of common qualities in an enlarging group. While the earliest infantile identification has its origin in an emotional relationship, usually with the mother, this third type results in another and broader type of emotional relationship.[25] This is similar to the convergence or integration of Teilhard's theory.

The counterpart of acceptance and relatedness is *"distantiation,* i.e., the readiness to repudiate, to ignore, or to destroy those forces and people whose essence seems dangerous to one's own."[26] A crisis may compel one group to fight to maintain its new identity and another group to hold on to an outworn one. Some African leaders talk about a new "African personality" emerging in the new social structure. Can a new European personality with expanding identities develop? Can a new life plan, a new group identity, which includes both races, be forged? Or is it too late?

In the next chapter, some of the theoretical generalizations discussed in this one are focused on the tribal cultures of the area. Obviously, any study of social change must proceed from a historical basis. The tribal African had the same potentialities for the development of his personality as do members of the human species in general; but the actual personality was related to the customary and specific modes of interaction with his environment and with the human beings significant in his life history. Every African differed in some ways from every other African in his tribe, but common culture patterns produced similarities in their personalities and in their behavior as they do everywhere.

3. The Tribal Past[1]

$\mathbb{A}$LTHOUGH THERE ARE a hundred or so different tribes on the Copperbelt, their histories have many elements in common: peaceful migrations or military invasions, intertribal warfare, early contacts with Arabs and participation in the slave trade, and finally submission to the British. It is predominantly a saga of power, of dominance and subjection. In condensing the tribal past of this area in one chapter, it has been necessary to concentrate on major common themes, omitting many variations and differences between tribes. The more detailed data is on the Bemba tribe, since they are the most numerous people on the Copperbelt.

Dominant Tribes

About a century ago there were four powerful kingdoms indigenous to what is now Northern Rhodesia; these were the Bemba, Lozi, Ngoni, and Lunda. In nearby Nyasaland were the war-like Yao. Most of the people on the mine township belong to the Bemba tribe or to related groups, such as the Bisa, Lala, Lima, and Lamba, all from the Northern Province of Northern Rhodesia. The lingua franca on the Copperbelt is the Bemba language. The matrilineal Bemba people came from the Congo basin, probably before the eighteenth century,

24]

and set up a strong military state under their paramount chief, Chitimukulu. They occupied a high plateau of poor soil and practiced a shifting slash-and-burn type of agriculture. Their legends say the country was empty on their arrival and so they did not have to conquer or drive out another people. Toward the end of the last century, however, they enlarged their territory by pushing back other tribes. Their political organization was centralized with a well-developed hierarchy ranging from a hereditary paramount chief to lesser chiefs.

The Ngoni, a dominant tribe in the Eastern Province, were numerous on the Copperbelt. These patrilineal, cattle-keeping people came originally from Natal and had been driven northward by the Zulu despot, Shaka, about 1812. When they reached Lake Tanganyika, their chief died and the people split into a number of groups led by his sons. They settled in different places in the Fort Jameson district of Northern Rhodesia, in Nyasaland, in Tanganyika, and in Portuguese East Africa. They were a war-like people with well-developed tactics for fighting which made conquests of neighbors easy. There are about a dozen groups who call themselves Ngoni, and there are others not using that name, but who are classified as Ngoni because of common origin.

In the northwestern part of the Territory, the Lozi tribe, a numerical minority on the Copperbelt, was the dominant group in the Barotse state, the most highly developed of the indigenous kingdoms. They reckoned kinship through both sides of the family, but with an emphasis on the father's side. The fertile river plains where they lived provided rich land for gardening, grazing for cattle, and excellent fishing sites. A powerful king organized the internal economy upon an exchange of goods through tribute and gifts. The Lozi subjugated many tribes, from whom they extorted tribute in kind, and the conquered received in exchange protection from their enemies, as well as gifts and loans of cattle.

The fourth powerful tribe of Northern Rhodesia was the Lunda, who now with the Bemba are among the majority on the Copperbelt. They came from the west, probably after the Bemba, in the beginning of the eighteenth century and established a powerful kingdom under the strong Chief Kazembe, but were conquered later by other tribes.

Africans from Nyasaland were also on the Copperbelt, and among these were the Yao, who are supposed to have migrated peacefully to Nyasaland in family groups from what is now Portuguese East Africa in the late eighteenth and early nineteenth century. They were matrilineal, agricultural and war-like people, who "set themselves up as ruling classes over the indigenous Nyanja."² But the Yao never developed the strong state structure found among the Bemba and Lozi; there was, instead, a constant division of power by independent chieftains.

Hundreds of tribes with weak political organization were raided and conquered by the stronger. Among the important weaker tribes were the Chewa, Bisa, Ila, and Plateau and Valley Tonga.

The Slave Trade

The dominant and the weak tribes were all profoundly influenced by the slave trade and by intra-African slavery. The slave traders on the east coast were Arabs and Portuguese half-castes who constantly pushed inland as elephants became scarce along the coast. The demand for ivory increased with the development in Europe of luxury industries which manufactured billiard balls, piano keys, fans, and objects of art in the nineteenth century. Slaves carried the ivory from the mainland to the coast and were both a cheap means of transportation for it and valuable merchandise in themselves; they were sold to work on the great clove plantations on Zanzibar and the Pemba islands, and they were also exported to the markets of Persia, Turkey, and Arabia as domestic retainers and concubines.

Status in Muslim slavery was not fixed, but had many gradations from misery to wealth. Arab and half-caste Portuguese slave traders differed greatly from the Europeans who came later. For the Arab practiced polygamy like the Africans, took Negro wives, and believed in assimilating the Africans. A typical incident in the Arab conquest is the story of an Arab trader who came from Zanzibar with a large caravan and settled on the western shore of Lake Nyasa, where he lived on friendly terms with the local Nyanja chief. Later, when friction arose between them, the Arab defeated his former host and reduced him to the status of a headman. Other African chiefs came afterward with their people to settle under the new ruler, who gave offices impartially to Bemba and Yao retainers and to those who had come with him from Zanzibar. He protected all the people against other raiders. Like African chiefs, he collected grain from local head-men, levied tribute from caravans, and received a share of all ivory shot in his domain.

The Arab traders not only fitted into the Bantu power structure, but also profoundly influenced it. They gave guns to the African chiefs in return for men and ivory and thus increased the ferocity and extent of tribal warfare and strengthened the power of chiefs, who had a monopoly of ivory and control of war captives. Bemba chiefs engaged directly in the slave trade with Arabs from 1865 to 1893. The Yao, Bisa, and various other tribes participated in the network of slave trading even prior to 1865. Among the Bemba, the slaves were either captives from other tribes, or Bemba who had been deprived of their liberty as a legal punishment or as a com-pensation for irreparable injury, such as murder or destruction of gardens. Not all slaves were sold to Arabs; some became part of the owner's household. A chief or other notable fed and protected them, provided for their marriage and the upbringing of their children. In return he had rights over their labor, movements, residence, and their life and death. The slaves lived as members of the owner's large household, sleeping in their own huts but not possessing granaries of their own. The only observable difference among the Bemba be-tween a slave and a poor relative was that a slave worked harder and ate only left-overs.

The Yao, who had contact with the Arabs for about two hundred years before the coming of the Europeans, were also active slave traders. Yao chiefs, competing with each other for power, engaged in slave hunts to get followers. The captives were incorporated in the chief or headman's retinue; the men engaged in farming and building, and the women became junior wives. The Ngoni, too, raided for slaves to increase the manpower of the tribe. Captives were as-similated and could rise to important posts. By contrast, the Lozi king, who had a monopoly of ivory and rubber, traded these for guns, but hardly ever dealt in slaves.

The pattern of the slave trade therefore varied, depending on the complexity of a tribe's economy, on ecology, and on the strength of its political organization. But whether slaves were sold to Arabs or incorporated into the tribe, intertribal warfare became increasingly destructive, and the power of the chiefs was augmented. Burton, a British explorer, estimated that in order to capture fifty-five women, whom he observed in one caravan, at least ten villages had been destroyed, each having a population of between one and two hundred. Some were killed; others died of starvation or lost their lives on the way to the coast.[3]

Through the slave trade, strong tribes became stronger, and the traditional dominance-subjection theme which underlaid the whole social system was reinforced. The image of the powerful and the powerless governed the relations of young and old, men and women, as well as chief and commoner. But conquerer and conquered, the strong and the weak, all belonged to the same order of civilization.

Village Life

An African was born and grew up in his village, where his life was interwoven with the lives of relatives, friends, and neighbors, and in it he achieved his closest associations with nature as well as with people. In Central Africa, the villages were small, usually consisting of from thirty to fifty round thatched-roof huts, although the village of a king or paramount chief was much larger. Among the Bemba, the one-room huts were built in an oval or circular space, surrounded by food gardens. The huts were windowless, but each had its veranda and door, and inside there were a fireplace and a bed, a reed mat stretched over a small platform. The house was used primarily as a bedroom and kitchen, although much of the food was prepared outside. Granaries were near the owner's huts. A men's club house—an open shelter, consisting of a roof supported on poles—was at one end of the village. Life was lived mostly in the open. People sat and talked on their verandas or on the ground in front of them, and there was much visiting back and forth. There were no strangers; there was no anonymity.

Much of the time was taken up with food-producing activities. Relatives and fellow villagers cooperated in clearing the fields, in planting, in hunting, and in the preparation of ritual feasts; among cattle-keeping people, herding was likewise important. There was a sharp division of labor between men and women. Among the Bemba and other agricultural peoples, the husband cleared the field and the wife planted and weeded. The husband built the house, kitchen and granary, and kept them in repair. The wife cleaned and tidied the hut, looked after young children, cooked the daily meals, collected wood for the fire, fetched water from the stream for bathing and drinking, and looked for "relish"—wild spinach, mushrooms, gourds, and pumpkins. She was responsible, also, for the threshing, winnowing, and grinding of grain, and for the making of porridge and the brewing of beer, both staples of the diet. The husband, usually an enthusiastic hunter, provided the meat. He was also responsible for providing mats and clothes, and he made all the household utensils except the pots. Although the wife cooked the daily meals, the family did not eat together; the groupings at the main meal clearly reflected status positions based on age and sex: the woman and her young children ate separately from the man. When boys were seven or eight years old, they ate with other boys in their age group. The mother and her daughters continued to eat together and apart from the males. The status of women was lower than that of men, but there were "big women": the wives of chiefs for whom other women worked and, among a few tribes, women chiefs. Grandmothers always had high status, as did successful gardeners, whose advice on soil and on seeds was sought. But men were the masters and were respected as such.

There was leisure time for beer-drinks, for gossip, for courting, for sexual affairs, for storytelling, and for the important rites of birth, death, initiation, marriage, the installation of a new chief. Wars and slave raids broke into the round of work and leisure. There were also times of famine or near-famine, when everyone suffered.

Man's Relationship with Nature

The cosmos of these tribal Africans was relatively undifferentiated. Human beings, animals, land, and ancestral spirits were supernaturally related and interrelated. Animals figured prominently in myths and folklore, in which the transformation of people into animals and vice versa was a prominent motif, still persisting in fantasy. In essays written by boys and girls of two Copperbelt schools in Standards V and VI (corresponding to our seventh and eighth grades) on the topic, "If it pleases God to make you anyone or any-

thing you please, who or what would you like to be?," a majority
of the boys (64 per cent) and almost half of the girls (48 per cent)
expressed a fantasy desire to be non-human. Of these, three-fourths
of the boys and half the girls wanted to be birds. Other animal
fantasies for each sex included cats, elephants, lions, and insects.
Almost a quarter of the non-human-wishing girls fantasied being
inanimate: a flower, a tree, a river; only one boy was in this category.[4]

The sense of oneness of animals and humans occurs in all peasant
folklore. It is still prominent in many fantasies of our own times, as,
for example, in the sophisticated cartoons of the *New Yorker*
magazine and in the popular Walt Disney and other movie cartoons.
The close relation between human beings and animals is therefore
not an entirely "primitive" or archaic phenomenon, but in tribal
society it was more consciously meaningful.

So also was the relation of Africans to land. In all of Africa
people were mystically related to the land on which they lived. In
West Africa men worshipped the earth. In Central and South Africa,
kings and paramount chiefs were identified with the earth; the Barotse
word for king means "earth." The Lozi believed there was a divine
and mystical relationship between the land, the dead ancestors buried
on it, the kingship, and the nation. Among the Bemba, the power of
the chiefs was similarly related to the good will of supernatural
beings, the guardian spirits of dead chiefs; this inherited mystical
power enabled the chief to influence the prosperity of the land. It
was believed that the chief's private life—his good or ill health,
his sexual life, his observance of taboos and the following of rituals
—affected the fertility of the land and the welfare of his people. A
chief's sexual power was supposed to give vigor and "warmth" to
the land, but it was also a source of danger, for harm could come
to a community if the chief did not perform a ceremony of purifica-
tion after sexual relations. This mystical relationship of man to land
and to the spirits of his ancestors is found in most tribal civilizations,
but it is in Africa that the connection with power has been so
emphasized. In New Ireland (Southwest Pacific), for example, the
Melanesian people were also mystically related to the land and to their
dead ancestors, but the emphasis on power was relatively slight,
as compared to Africa. Among the Melanesians power was com-

paratively unimportant, and there were only the rudiments of political organization.[5]

Man's Relationship to His Kindred

Men were not only related to nature and to the land, but also to each other through extended ties of kinship. As in most preliterate societies, every African was a functioning member of his immediate family and of an extended and, usually, unilineal kinship group, such as a lineage or clan.[6] In a matrilineal society, a person was closely related to his mother's brother, his mother's sisters and their children, and others in his lineage. In a patrilineal society, the system functioned through the father, his sisters and brothers, the brothers' children, the paternal grandfather, etc. Intertribal wars of the past sometimes brought matrilineal and patrilineal peoples together. The patrilineal war-like Ngoni, for example, incorporated into their tribe men and women captives, who "came from matrilineal, matrilocal tribes, and the values associated with these systems of organization were not entirely forgotten."[7] In the area of my study, matrilineal descent was typical, although not universal. Among the Bemba, and many other matrilineal tribes, children belonged to the mother's family, and her brother assumed responsibility for them and had authority over them.

Whatever the way of tracing descent, each individual in tribal society was intimately affiliated with the members of his lineage group from birth to death, and, supposedly, even after death, when he joined his ancestors. Members of this lineal group were in dominant-subordinate roles and were linked together in a complex of reciprocal ritual, social, and economic obligations. An individual could rely on members of his lineage or clan for assistance on all ritual occasions, such as occurred at birth, initiation, marriage, death, and for help in the affairs of daily life; and he, in turn, was obligated to help them. Ties, involving sentiment and affection, and sometimes obligations, existed also with many kindred of the opposite side, i.e., the one in which descent was not counted. The pattern of living was woven by the kinship system. From birth to death, no one stood alone.

Marriage

Kinship determined which marriages were permitted and which were preferred. Since the range of possible incestuous relationships was large, often including all members of a lineage, clan, or even still more extended groups, the choice of spouse was limited. The Western concept—individual choice of mate coupled with romantic love attached to one spouse for life—did not exist. Kindred frequently selected mates for members of their lineage, and their approval was always necessary; betrothal of girls in childhood was fairly common. But there was considerable diversity. In some tribes girls could be forced to marry men whom they feared or disliked, but in others, girls could refuse to enter the marriages arranged for them. In matrilineal societies, the authority of a woman's brother over her children was exercised over their marriages. But she and her husband were frequently consulted, and rarely was the latter completely ignored.

Among the Bemba the young man made his choice, then talked it over with his relatives. If they approved, one of them took the betrothal gift of a traditional copper wire bracelet to the girl's relatives. The matter was discussed in the girl's presence, and she had apparently the right to refuse. The acceptance of the bracelet meant that she said, "Yes." The girl, with a number of friends of her own age, periodically visited her future husband's village, and they talked and played with him and his friends, the girls retiring at night to a hut which had been prepared for them. Later, the future husband moved to the girl's village, built himself a hut, joined his prospective father-in-law's working team and made small payments to him between betrothal and consummation of marriage.

Marriage was always a contractual agreement between two groups of kindred and involved the giving by one to the other of a woman and her potential children. In return, some form of "marriage payment" or "bride price" was given to the bride's family: services of the son-in-law, goods, cattle, or combination of them. For some years the Bemba bridegroom was in a position of economic dependence on his wife's family to prove his worth as a husband and father. His wife could be taken away if he failed to carry out his obligations. He had to cut gardens for his father-in-law, and do any other work his wife's family required of him. At harvest time he had to carry the grain from his garden to the granary of his wife's family, and he was not allowed to build one of his own for some years. During this time his wife was also dependent on her mother's household, and she was part of her working team. The Bemba man thus had sexual rights over his wife long before he became the economic head of the household. The power to allot food and beer to his friends was won gradually, as was also the assumption of responsibility by husband and wife for their own household; this could take from five to fifteen years. Only gradually did the husband have the right to choose his place of residence and move his wife and children to it. He did not become really important until he had a married daughter.

Among the Plateau Tonga, bride wealth consisted of cattle, goats, hoes, and spears; and the completion of the payments took from two to four years, and sometimes as much as ten years. Until the final payment was made, the husband and his wife "may not have a cooking fire at their house; the wife may not brew beer there; they may not entertain their friends; she may not cook separately to provide for his need; he may not dedicate the house to his ancestors, who in any event have not yet been appraised of the fact that the marriage has taken place."[8]

Marriage frequently involved the separation of one spouse from his kindred, since one of them went to live in the other's village.[9] Patrilocal residence, in which the wife left home and joined her husband, was the most common in Africa, and the marriage rituals symbolically emphasized that a woman was leaving her kindred. For many of the matrilineal peoples there was a compromise, such as was noted among the Bemba, where although the wife remained with her kinsmen and was joined there by her husband, he eventually moved his household to his own people.

Polygamy was the desired form of marriage in almost all of Africa, and a man's high status was correlated with the number of his wives. But only a minority of men could afford more than one wife; and, futhermore, the normal distribution of sexes would have made it impossible for all men to have been polygamous. In polygamous establishments each wife and her children had their own hut; but the first wife had a senior status.

Adultery appears to have been common, and the mores sanctioned it for men, except on certain occasions. Among the Tonga, if a man died without ever having been charged with adultery, his mortuary rites included a mock claim for damages and their payment. But women were not supposed to have the same privileges. However, data from many monographs indicate that they had adulterous relations, no matter how exclusive the sexual rights of husbands were supposed to be. Moreover, there were probably not sufficient widows and divorcees to have made the practice of adultery so widespread. With a few permitted exceptions, as in the case of a sterile husband, an adulterous woman and her lover were punished if caught. There was also a general fear of supernatural consequences; and among the Chewa, it was believed that the salt which an adulterous woman put on her husband's food would poison him, or that harm might come to him in a dangerous occupation, or that the woman would have difficulties in childbirth. While extramarital relations were the norm, although not socially sanctioned for women, there was a sense of reasonable limits as well as some prohibited occasions, and excessive promiscuity was not regarded favorably. Within the social limits, sex relations in and out of marriage appear to have been a source of lusty satisfaction.

The right to divorce was held to be an essential liberty, although there was criticism of those who repeatedly changed partners. Divorces were common and procedures not too complicated. Among the Tonga, a woman could seek a divorce if her husband "discriminates against her in favor of another wife, fails to provide clothing, beats or curses her unreasonably, is impotent, or is generally unpleasant around the household, encroaching upon the woman's prerogative of managing the household, food, stock, or refusing to allow her to offer hospitality to her relatives or generally showing himself hostile to her kin."[10] The Bemba added another reason: if the husband was a bad worker. A Ngoni husband did not need specific grounds for divorcing a wife; but, in practice, among them as in many other tribes, wives were usually divorced if they quarreled persistently, were lazy about preparing food, disrespectful of their husbands, or, in the case of patrilocal residences, always running back to their own village.

The instability of marriages in this area and in other parts of Africa has been generally noted, and there has been interesting theoretical speculation about it. An obvious conflict existed between the interests of the nuclear family and those of the extended kinship groups, for each one may demand allegiance at the expense of the other. In the matrilineal society the bond between a man and his sister was often stronger than with his spouse. Outside of the Plateau Tonga, men did not usually talk over their affairs with their wives. The Ngoni had a maxim: "Never confide in your wife, for tomorrow you may divorce her."[11] Among the patrilineal Soga in neighboring Uganda, there was a belief that "traditional marriage consisted in a kind of 'theft' (*obukka*) of the bride by the bridegroom."[12] This belief is found underlying marriage in tribal societies in many parts of the world. The mock fighting in marriage rites between members of opposite moieties among the matrilineal Melanesians in New Ireland indicates a similar belief.[13]

Max Gluckman suggests that a fundamental conflict centers on the position of women in Africa. Natal kin and husband held two different kinds of rights over a woman: the first had rights over her as a child-bearer; and the second, as a wife. In a matrilineal society these two rights were held by different sets of men. In patrilineal societies, the woman's kin transferred both rights to the husband, and it is Gluckman's hypothesis that the latter situation made for greater stability of marriage. But as Fallers rephrases Gluckman's thesis, patriliny tended to stabilize marriage only when the woman was socially absorbed into her husband's lineage and when her childbearing properties were completely transferred to it. I question whether the previous conditioning in one corporate group would permit complete *emotional* absorption into another, and I think that loyalties might still remain divided, consciously or unconsciously. This may partly account for the lack of stability which has been so characteristic of African marriage in general. Among the matrilineal and matrilocal people of Central Africa, this tendency was strengthened or weakened, depending on the distance between the villages of husband and wife. On the mine township new factors both strengthened and weakened marriage bonds.

Since fertility was among the greatly prized values, a barren wife or sterile husband was reason enough for taking another mate; and a marriage often was not regarded as consummated until a child was born. Children were a form of insurance and security for the future, as they are among other peoples. Children were also a form of power, for through marriage they extended family connections and brought new members into it. In a society which honors ancestors, children likewise ensured that traditions would be maintained and that the living would be honored after death.

Political Power

In all the kingdoms the hierarchy of political power had a religious basis and was rooted in the mystical relationship of the king or chief to the land and to ancestral spirits. Chieftainship and kingship were based on descent. Although kings and chiefs had a considerable degree of absolute power, the structure of the state implied that they ruled by consent. Public opinion could make itself felt through a council of elders. There are some examples of a ruler, like Shaka of the Zulu tribe, becoming a tyrant and incurring popular disapproval; in such a case, a revolt was led by members of the royal family or subordinate chiefs, who were often kinsmen of the king. But the occasional rebellions against particular kings or chiefs were not against the institution of kingship or of chieftainship, since this was the only system the people knew.

The Bemba paramount chief acted as an overlord to a number of territorial chiefs, drawn from his immediate family. Beneath them were subchiefs, also drawn from the royal clan but more distantly related. A council of thirty to forty hereditary officials, many of royal descent, functioned in tribal ceremonies and in other matters of importance. Each chief also had his own councillors appointed by him from old men of the village. Further down the hierarchy there was a headman of each village, who might have his position by inheritance, through individual initiative and by the chief's permission, or through nomination by a chief to whom he was related. Every headman had his councillors, chosen from the elders of the village, and on the "grass roots" level there was an informal democracy, with all adult men in the village participating.

In this area of Africa there was a customary judicial procedure functioning through a hierarchy of courts. Among the Bemba, cases could go on appeal from the subchief to chief, and from him to paramount chiefs. As Epstein has described in detail, each chief chose his advisors from the elders. Witnesses were brought by each contender in the case; the chief summed up and gave the judgment. The function of tribal law appeared to be the elimination or lessening of social frictions by achieving a balance between the contending parties. Compensation for the injured person rather than punishment for the guilty was the guiding principle. Again, following Epstein's analysis, in a society of face-to-face personal relationships, the need to settle disputes was urgent. Informal courts often brought the disputants together and sometimes achieved a settlement. The standards in both the informal and formal courts were based on the concept of what was reasonable and customary in a particular situation. Gluckman makes the same point for the Barotse, namely, that ". . . a Barotse *kuta* [councillor] cross-examines and assesses evidence by the standard of how a reasonable man or woman would have behaved, meticulously according to custom. . . ."[14] In general, there was, thus, a certain degree of flexibility in legal interpretation, and emphasis was on the spirit rather than the letter of the law. The concept of reasonableness is basic to the African's thinking, whether about politics, family affairs, or union activities, and came up over and over again on the Copperbelt in casual conversations as well as in court cases.

Although there was great emphasis on differences in status, in the past everyone lived on much the same standard of living, subsistence by our contemporary values. There were rich, and there were poor, but the rich controlled goods and services rather than owning them; their main interest was to gain followers by giving them land for which they had no other use and surplus stocks of cattle and grain. Shaka amassed large herds of cattle through his successful raids on other tribes, but he did not use them to raise his own standards of living: "he ate the same boiled beef as his followers, and having many cattle he gave most to his subjects for them to eat as boiled beef. He, too, like his subjects, lived in a pole and grass hut. . . . Not even the first introduction of firearms and European trade-goods broke up this egalitarianism."[15]

Food and Authority

The close connection between the distribution of food and authority in all status relationships has been stressed by Richards. Food is obviously of deep biological and symbolic significance to all peoples, but for those on a subsistence standard who know recurring famines, it is even more important. The Bemba had learned in infancy that he could always rely on his mother and a group of close kinsfolk for food. As he grew older, he was never refused food if there was any in the house, and he had the same expectations in the households of his mother's sisters and of his grandmother. He expected food from all those in authority, as later he expected food and cattle from a headman or chief to whom he was attached. The association between authority and the power to give was made early. At the same time, the association with power and the right to take was made. Older siblings and cross-cousins could take food from younger children. When the children were grown, their elders expected presents from them as payment for the food and clothes which had been given them. On the Copperbelt, at the time of my study, adolescent girls at a boarding school were expected to work before marriage to reimburse their parents for the expense of their education.

The reciprocity of obligations existing in all relationships was emphasized not only in Africa but in many preliterate societies and, as anthropologists have noted, helped to maintain a social equilibrium. The dominant-subordinate relationships in these African tribes were not one-way streets. Authority and power were always tied to generosity, as well as to the right to tribute. In her study of the Ngoni, Read reports that she heard people praising a former chief or a chief's wife by recounting their lavishness in giving gifts and by comparing the chief's generosity to that of a father or mother giving freely to their children. The Bemba brought tribute of food to the chief, and he was obligated to distribute to his followers. If a chief attempted to dry meat and keep it for future gifts, the Bemba said, "We will shake the tree until it gives up its fruit," meaning they would nag the chief until he divided his supplies; and he was usually forced to do so.[16] Among the Lozi, too, Gluckman notes that the generosity of the king was constantly emphasized, and tales of the past describe his distribution of goods and foods to the people. Even when European trade-goods entered the country, the king shared the cloth with his followers. Cattle taken in war were similarly distributed and sometimes returned. In return, the Lozi had to work for the king, fight for him, and render tribute. But they had the king's protection against enemies, his help in time of trouble, and the right to use the products of his land. In a cross-cultural study Yehudi Cohen indicates a correlation between early repetitive food gratification and a predisposition for adults to share food with each other, and hypothesizes that these predispositions are maximized or minimized by different social structures. The maximization is emphasized in those structures which represent a maximum of solidarity, based on common descent, ownership of land, physical proximity between households, and face-to-face personal relationships.[17] These conditions were present among many of the tribes in this area.

Status and Etiquette

Although chief and commoner lived on the same egalitarian standards, their difference in status was constantly affirmed. In any society high status involves power over people and access to desirable goods. The formal etiquette and ritual behavior which accompany status emphasize the social distance between those with power and those without it. By social distance is meant the boundaries beyond which persons in the particular status relationship cannot go. The elaboration of status positions with the accompanying etiquette and ritual was naturally greatest in the highly developed kingdoms, such as are found among the Lozi, the Ngoni, and the Bemba. But in the tribes with less highly centralized political systems, the status hierarchy was also important and was based on the same factors of age, sex, rank, and kinship.

The Lozi were continuously concerned with the proper behavior between persons of different rank, which was implicit and explicit in every relationship—parent and child, husband and wife, king (or royalty) and commoner. Arguments and disputes occurred over the relative ranking of royalty in their elaborate hierarchy. The Lozi term *likute* covered politeness, respect, good taste, appropriate behavior; and it was high praise to say a man had *likute;* to say he lacked it was to damn him.

Of the Bemba she studied more than a quarter of a century ago, Richards writes, "They are obsessed with problems of status and constantly on the lookout for their personal dignity, as is perhaps natural in a society in which so much depends on rank. All their human relationships are dominated by the rules of respect to age and position, and I should hazard a guess that more quarrels were caused by imagined slights than by material damage of any kind."[18] A Bemba greets his chief most obsequiously by lying prostrate on his back on the ground, with his head toward the chief, and clapping his hands; no commoner may stand in the presence of a chief, nor may a young man stand in the presence of an elder. A woman kneels when she presents something to her husband. The customary grouping by age and sex at meals has already been noted. In the subsistence tribal economy Bemba people were often hungry, and a high status position carried an advantage with regard to food: elders and men ate more relish (vegetables, meat, fish) with their porridge than did women and children. Chiefs drank more beer than commoners, elders more than young men, and usually males more than females. It is probable that appropriate etiquette always validates significant status roles.[19]

Rank and the appropriate etiquette were all-pervading motifs in the African social system. According to a thesis expounded by Yehudi Cohen, ritual or formal behavior in status positions is a symbolic denial of aggression in situations where some people are excluded from attaining high prestige and where the power inevitably imposes limitations on those who do not have it; the result for them is often the creation of conscious or unconscious feelings of frustration which could lead to aggression.[20] The automatic etiquette and ritual behavior required of lower-status persons toward those of higher status symbolically and unconsciously deny the aggression and are necessary to the comfort of both groups and to maintain and preserve the power structure. Cohen gives an example of military etiquette and writes that the hand salute symbolizes the social distance between enlisted men and commissioned officers, and is a ceremonial expression of the trustworthiness of the former. The salute indicates that the enlisted man has no dangerous weapon in his right hand and that the right arm itself is not going to be used aggressively. I suggest that the prostrate position of commoners before chiefs, the kneeling of women before men, and of young people before elders are similar unconscious denials of feelings of aggression. The same etiquette of respect was accorded the first Europeans and, I assume, had the same unconscious function.

The political hierarchy from commoner, headman, chief, to paramount chief or king seemed more stable than family life. On the broader level, the reciprocal responsibilities and sanctions underlying the power of some to command and of others to obey and the formal etiquette apparently channeled potential conflicts. But Gluckman reports that there were expressions of ambivalence: the Lozi said they loved the prince until he was elected king; then they hated him and also loved him. This is apparently the familiar human ambivalence toward authority, but in Africa this hate was rarely expressed overtly, and then only in an occasional rebellion against a king, when he was deposed and a brother put in his place.

Channeling of Anxieties

Although the political hierarchy was stable, with unconscious hostilities apparently well channeled into ritual and etiquette, unresolved conflicts in family life were more open. The clash between lineage and family ties (with the lineage being the stronger), the extramarital relations, the frequent divorces, the emphasis on differences of status between men and women, young and old, were sources of hostility and of anxieties, conscious and unconscious, much of which appeared to be channeled through witchcraft.

Good and bad magic and witchcraft exist among all tribal societies. They are based on a theory of personal causation and a belief in a supernatural power in the universe which men can control through their knowledge of magic and the following of taboos. There is almost no activity in life which cannot be assisted or hurt by magic. Benevolent white magic involves the use of spells, or "medicines," or rites, or a combination of them, and is used to cure illness, to cause the crops to grow well, to have a good catch of fish, to win a woman's or a man's love, to make the rain fall or the sun shine, and in many other situations in which there is uncertainty. Black magic is evil and has its medicines; and its spells and rites bring misfortunes, such as sickness, death, barrenness, sterility, loss of love, failure of crops, and death of cattle. Witchcraft, sometimes synonymous with black magic, involves a witch who knows and uses black magic. The identity of the witch in some societies is not known; anyone—a friend or neighbor—may be a witch. In other places, people who are not witches but who want to use black magic may pay a witch for the medicines or the making of spells.

In Africa, the emphasis appears to have been more on black magic and witchcraft than on white magic. As Gluckman notes, any unusual success was considered to be at the expense of one's fellows. Although emphasis was on the welfare of the kinship and local group, at the same time kinsmen competed for the headmanship of a village, co-wives competed for the sexual and other favors of their husband, and men for the sexual favors of women. The successful person was then suspicious of the witchcraft of his envious rivals. Illness, death, or other individual disaster was always thought to be caused by witchcraft. Why is one man rather than another killed by a lion, or bitten by a poisonous snake, or why does he suffer the loss of his wife to another man? Why does misfortune happen at this time and not at another time? The African answer is witchcraft. The system is closed, since there is always "proof" of its effectiveness. If a sick man became well, it is believed the witch withdrew the magical poison from the patient, or that another witch made counteractive and stronger magic for the patient to regain his health. If the patient dies, the witch did not withdraw the poison or the counteractive magic was not sufficiently strong. The thinking is logical, but circular and closed, since the initial premises are not questioned or tested.

Projection of one's own hostility, a very common human mechanism, underlies witchcraft. This came out very clearly in the practice of divination, through which the victim tried to find out who used witchcraft against him. He gave the names of people whom he feared or hated to a diviner, who then with the aid of a magical rite selected the one who had made the witchcraft. The similarity of witchcraft-thinking to paranoia is quite obvious. The question of whether the two are the same phenomenon is not easy to answer. M. J. Field, a clinical psychiatrist, working in West Africa, studied rural people in Ashanti, who came to shrines to be cured of illnesses they believed were caused by witchcraft or to be protected from being turned into a witch. In Africa, as elsewhere, people suffer pains and aches due to anxieties which come from having done something considered wrong, such as adultery, cheating a kinsman, or committing some other unsocial act; and revenge is feared. Field found that some of the people coming to the shrines were clearly mentally ill from "fantastic delusions of sin and guilt," and she classified them as depression cases.[21] On the other hand, she writes, "mentally ill people comprise only a very small proportion of the pilgrims who flock to these shrines not only from within Ashanti but from distant parts of Akan Chana. The great majority are healthy people supplicating for 'protection.' Financially successful men are full of fear lest envious kinsmen should, by means of bad magic or witchcraft, bring about their ruin. Unsuccessful men are convinced that envious malice is the cause of their failure. Thus, a strikingly 'paranoid' attitude is normal. Healthy intelligent Africans have some insight into the prevalent distrust and envy, and often refer to it spontaneously as one of the weaknesses of 'us black men.' "[22]

Revenge through witchcraft is a cultural belief, and it is a cultural fact that witchcraft is practiced to harm people. If these premises are accepted, is witchcraft-thinking an evidence of paranoia? The answer does not seem to lie in a straight "yes" or "no." Field found people who were disturbed, with a vague sense of malice all around them, although they did not admit of any misdemeanors and had no evidence of ill will directed toward them. These people, she notes, were more disturbed than mentally healthy people who said they were ill because they found a talisman of bad magic under their pillow. She writes, too, that there were "a few well-balanced successful people who are able to accept calmly the indubitable fact that less successful people do bear them ill will."[23] From Field's work in West Africa and my more casual impressions of witchcraft on the Copperbelt and reports of it in the nearby rural areas, there seemed to be many degrees of intensity to the paranoia-like theme underlying it. There were those who feared and saw malice in every situation, and who might well be described as pathological. There were others whose fears and the resulting anxieties were limited to specific situations defined by the culture as connected with witchcraft. These could hardly be called mentally ill or paranoid. There were still others who could interpret failure or success on a reality level. My hunch is that there might have been similar variations in the Middle Ages in the breadth and intensity of the Christian belief about burning in hell for one's sins.

Witchcraft is one answer, culturally sanctioned in tribal Africa (and in many other societies), to aggressive impulses, stemming in part from social conflicts, in part from individual personality problems, or some combination of them. Africans, as well as the rest of us, differ from each other in degree of tension and how much they can "carry," without becoming mentally ill. Witchcraft provides a relief from tensions, without touching their source.

Some anthropologists have tended to stress the social function of witchcraft. Hostilities are directed against a few scapegoats rather than many. Open social conflicts are avoided and the equilibrium of society is maintained. However, I tend to agree with Nadel that "every witchcraft accusation . . . adds to the stresses of the society, through causing a serious disturbance of social life, entailing blood revenge and the like."[24] In our society religious or political witch hunts undoubtedly relieved the tensions of some fearful people, but they added to the strains of others and were socially disturbing. An occasional lynching in the Deep South of the past by the Ku Klux Klan and their more recent riots against segregation probably channeled the aggression of the Klan members and other participants and helped maintain the status quo, one form of equilibrium. But most people do not consider these functions a social justification.

Witchcraft was not the only socially approved mechanism for relieving anxieties. Another very common relief the world over is found in alcohol, and it may also serve to release aggression. Beer-drinking was an integral part of African life. Among the Bemba and most other African tribes beer was food, a payment for labor, a necessary element on ritual occasions, an important part of hospitality and entertainment. A beer party was the reward for the communal work required in cutting and clearing bush ground and the hoeing of the cleared land, and most householders brewed at least once a season for this purpose. A meeting of a tribal council, a wedding rite, or an initiation ceremony could not take place without beer. Less important occasions were also accompanied by beer-drinking. For instance, among the Ndembu, a ritual to cure an ill person was accompanied by dancing, and the dancers were given beer and food by the patient's kin and the headman of his village.[25] Almost any time those who brewed beer were expected to share it with relatives and friends. Beer-drinking thus provided an important break in the monotony of tribal life.

Bantu people make beer from maize, millet, kafir, cassava, bananas, and honey. The Bemba and a number of other tribes in this area preferred millet beer. When drinking, Africans did not usually eat other foods, for beer was considered a food. It was a source of vitamin B, lacking in much of their other diet. Its alcoholic content was estimated as about 4 per cent, and Richards wrote that among the Bemba the average consumption on any one night was about one and one-half pints for an older man or woman, one pint for younger ones, and a one-half pint for a young girl. Chiefs, to whom beer was given as tribute, drank more than commoners and some-times subsisted on it from day to day. The amount of beer drunk was correlated with status, based on age and rank.

In spite of the low alcoholic content and the relatively small amount drunk in an evening, some drinkers became excited, garrulous, apt to quarrel or to indulge in illicit love-making. Richards describes this as "slightly intoxicated" and attributes it to the fact that the beer was drunk hot, often in a small very hot hut crowded to capacity, and was accompanied by singing and dancing.

In the past, according to the same author, it was impossible for anyone except a chief to get enough beer to become a regular drunk-ard. But chiefs who drank regularly apparently "carried their liquor" better than the commoners, who drank less frequently. In most vil-lages beer was brewed about once a week in the harvest months, from May to July or August. In the subsequent months, brewing was less frequent, and at the end of the rains during the scarce season could be found regularly only at a chief's court. Drunkenness or a milder form of intoxication was regarded with tolerance or envy, but those who were known to become quarrelsome at beer-drinking parties were often avoided by their friends.

There were, and are, other outlets for anxiety and aggression, common the world over: nagging, petty quarreling, gossiping, making fun of people. Major forms of aggression such as homicide and suicide were relatively rare. A recent study by Bohannan and his colleagues of five African tribes in Uganda, Kenya, and Central Nigeria indicate that strife was well controlled and that the communities were relatively stable.[26] The rates for homicide and suicide, as far as they could be determined and compared to Western rates, were relatively low, but both occurred most frequently within the domestic situation. The tribes studied by Bohannan and his colleagues were not in the area of my study, but were sufficiently similar to those in Northern Rhodesia to give additional weight to the point that there was more strain in the tribal family and in the domestic situation than in other institutions. The second situation in which suicide and culpable homicide were committed were those in which status and rank were considered very important.

Common Patterns in Life Histories

The life histories of these tribal Africans followed certain patterns which were consistent with the structure of society. It is more or less generally accepted that there is a relationship between socially approved patterns of behavior in infancy, childhood, and youth and the type of adult personality valued in the society. Psychoanalysts, such as Erikson, assume that there is a "ground plan" for physiological and psychological growth according to inner laws of human development, which create a "succession of potentialities for significant interacting" with human beings in the immediate environment, and that this mode of interaction varies from culture to culture.[27] Or, put another way, certain personality trends fit into the general cultural patterns, and vice versa.

Psychoanalysts and psychoanalytically oriented anthropologists have tended to stress infantile and childhood social conditioning. This is obviously important, particularly in a stable society. In a period of rapid change, adult socialization is also highly significant. Changes in the social system permit sufficiently flexible adults to internalize new values; the children of these people are then conditioned differently from their forebears; society is then further changed. The process is circular. In the following description of a possible modal life history in tribal society, the emphasis is on infantile and childhood conditioning and its "fit" with adult social patterns. In a later discussion of contemporary social change, the stress is on adult socialization. Obviously, within any individual life history, all socialization from birth to old age is related.

Infant care was similar among all the Bantu peoples of this area, and from a Western point of view, was characterized by much indulgence. The Bemba infant was suckled for two, and sometimes three, years, and was given his mother's breast whenever and as often as he wanted it. Mother and infant were hardly ever apart during this period. "Sleeping or waking the baby is pressed close to her back, or sitting astride her hip in a sling of goat or antelope skin, where it dozes as she tills the fields, with only a head visible above the fold of the skin. . . . At night it sleeps on its mat by her side."[28] (Sexual relations between husband and wife were taboo during the nursing period, accounting for men's adultery during it.) This period of complete indulgence to the infant came to an end abruptly with weaning. Disciplinary measures, such as a custom of putting pepper on the breast, were then used to prevent the baby from suckling. At this time the sexual taboo between parents was ended, and the child's place on the mat was taken by his father. The baby, however, continued to sleep in the same room; perhaps a grass mat hung between him and his parents. But among some tribes it was not uncommon for the child to be taken to the house of his grandparents immediately after the weaning rites and to be temporarily adopted by them.

Colson writes that among the Plateau Tonga, small children after weaning wail to be carried on the mother's back or try to sit on her lap. The mother may permit this for a few months when she is not busy, but then she threatens, "I will beat you if you try to sit on my lap again! You are no longer a baby. You must stop it!" The toddler goes through a period of temper tantrums, especially if there is a new baby enjoying its old privileges.[29]

Among the aristocratic patrilineal and patrilocal Ngoni in Nyasaland, the pattern of infant care described by Read was somewhat different. The new infant was cared for by a nurse girl who brought it to the mother at more or less regular intervals for suckling. The time for weaning was decided by the mother-in-law and other senior women of the father's family who would come suddenly one morning and put a hot paste of pounded chilies on the mother's breasts and hold the child near enough to smell it. Then, "they said to the child, 'Leave it alone. The breast is now bad'—and they spat downwards as they did when something was really bad. While the child was howling with fright and frustration, the mother's breasts were covered with a cloth." These Ngoni asserted "that weaning was a shock to the child, even if it happened at two years old."[30]

With occasional exceptions, such as among the Ngoni described above, the infant was continuously with his mother, and there was complete indulgence in suckling for the first two or three years. Among all the tribes on which there is adequate information weaning seems to have been sudden. This might well have been traumatic for the infant. On the other hand, there were compensations of attention and love from grandparents, elder siblings, and other relatives. It is important to note, also, that the mothers conveyed no uncertainty in their behavior, since there was only one pattern of child training. However, the abrupt weaning after the long indulgence might have left anxieties from a feeling of "being empty" and "being left," similar to those of patients in our society with this kind of unresolved infantile conflict. In the African society with its recurring periods of famine, there was a real danger of "being empty."

After the sharp break of weaning, the years of childhood and youth were a gradual induction into well-defined social roles. Children learned these easily, mainly through observation and gradual participation in adult activities. Among the Bemba, typical in this respect, little boys were with older boys and the latter with their fathers and other men; little girls were with their older sisters, their mothers, and other women. Children were continuously present at adult activities, watching and, by degrees, playing a role in them.

Like little girls everywhere, African girls of five or six practiced housekeeping. They dug holes in the ground and pretended to pound grain with imitation pestles. When somewhat older they begged for scraps of food which they cooked in old pots on the edge of the village where they made small huts of grass and "played at houses." Small boys paired off with little girls in a game of being married. By the time a girl was ten or eleven, she cooked more seriously on her mother's veranda, serving meals to friends or elders. Instruction, whether in cooking or learning about different kinds of edible mushrooms or wild spinaches, was given by older girls, rather than by mothers. By the time of the initiation rites which preceded marriage, the girls of fourteen or fifteen knew well all their household duties. The rites further impressed on them the traditional attitudes to their responsibilities. Young people learned their roles well through imitation of adults.

This kind of almost complete role identification is not conducive to spontaneous growth or self-awareness.[31] The gradual and extended induction into adult life happened apparently without any significant or successful revolt from authority. There may have been temper tantrums in childhood, but they passed, and obedience was substituted. Nor was there any sharp break at adolescence. Initiation rites were the formal social recognition that the individual was able to assume more responsibilities. However, neither this recognition nor the assumption of more responsibilities appeared to have led to any rejection of the elders' authority. The probationary period before a husband could make the last payment of the bride-wealth or perform the last service for his in-laws and, consequently, become the real head of his household often took many years. It has already been noted that marriage was unstable, extramarital relations were the norm, and divorce was frequent.

From a psychological point of view, it is possible to see positive and negative aspects in the modal tribal life history and its relationship to the social system. This is different from naively making a one-to-one correlation of any particular aspect of infantile training with adult personality.[32] The close relationship of the infant to the mother was probably a source of basic trust, and the mother's generous breast a symbolic model for many adult relationships, particularly those involving authority. A chief or king *must* be generous. The Bemba chief was not permitted to keep tribute for future use, but had to distribute it immediately, and praise of former chiefs or kings was frequently about their generosity. The same trait was likewise valued in relationships between kindred and friends. Generosity was a major tribal value and is still basic, although in conflict with other values today.

It is possible that much insecurity was caused by the unsatisfactory resolution of the weaning crisis, by the economic factors of a subsistence economy and recurring periods of famine, and by the social structure in which one mate at the time of marriage left his lineage group, to which he had deep ties. All these factors were probably unconsciously interwoven and can account, at least partially, for the wide-ranging sexual life of the adult, for instability of marriage, and for the preoccupation through witchcraft with unseen hostile forces. The mother's breast may be simultaneously both a symbol for generous giving and for disaster through its loss. Field writes: "In African societies, if a child resents the mother's relationship with the father, it is less likely to be because she sleeps with him than because she pampers him with food."[33]

The crucial crises of growing up, so common in modern society, in which young people break from authority figures, seem to have been bypassed in childhood, adolescence, and youth. The African achieved his adult status and identity by going through the prescribed practices and rituals which accompanied his physiological growth. He does not appear to have experienced a quest for a more developed personal identity, in which the struggle against traditional authorities is usually highly important. If there was an inner struggle, there is no evidence that it was won. Rebels were most exceptional, if present at all. There was apparently no break in the circular relationship of the individual with kinsmen, land, tribe, ancestral spirits, and powerful chiefs, all mystically interrelated.

Tribal Africans knew the uncertainties of war and the slave trade; they had an unstable family life; and they had anxieties, conscious and unconscious, channeled largely through witchcraft. Yet their world also offered deep psychological satisfactions. An individual was not just a tiller of the soil, a herdsman, a chief or a commoner, a man or a woman; he was also an integral member of an extended kinship group and of a tribe, sharing its fortunes, good and bad. Although status and rank were much emphasized, the wide gulf which separated the serfs from nobility in the Middle Ages or the working class from the aristocracy at the beginning of the Industrial Revolution did not exist. All the Africans lived more or less on the same subsistence standards, thought they had the same destiny, felt the same intimate relationship to nature, to animals, to ancestral spirits, and believed in the same external verities. The satisfactions from this relative lack of differentiation—the merging of the individual with family, kindred, land, nature—are deep and conducive to basic trust and to stability. At the same time, there seems to have been a fixation on the oral level, which discouraged the development of self-confidence and the autonomy necessary for the further development of ego identity. Nor did the social system encourage autonomy. Even the occasion of marriage among the Bemba and related tribes did not make a man the head of his household.

The African was part of the whole and his integration with it prevented the development of more self-awareness and the search for personal autonomy. This could not happen as long as the prototypes for identification were limited to parents, older siblings, other close relatives, neighbors, chiefs, and characters in myths and folk tales— all cast in a traditional mold.

The break in the circle, the social differentiation which shattered the cohesion of tribal man's identity with nature and with kinsmen could come only after new prototypes and new values appeared. This began to happen with the coming of Europeans.

4. The Coming of the First Europeans[1]

THE OCCASIONAL early explorers, Portuguese and others, and the Arab slave traders did not disturb the fundamental aspects of African society in this area. It was the British who, without intention, revolutionized tribal life by introducing new prototypes, new values, and a new form of civilization. The first of these who came to Northern Rhodesia were a varied group, including missionaries, officials of a chartered trading company, administrators of mining companies, and miners, railway workers, farmers, traders, shopkeepers, and colonial officials.

Missionaries were the first to arrive and "they came not only as the apostles of a new faith, but also as the representatives of a new way of life; they believed in individual salvation instead of tribal collectivism, hallowed by beliefs in ancestral spirits and the magic of a chief; they stood for a creed of individual economic effort and advanced productive techniques, instead of a system of tribal cooperation based on a low level of technical efficiency; they represented the values of the Christian and monogamous family, instead of those of extended kinship groups practicing polygamy."[2] Individualism was one of the basic new themes introduced by Christianity and by the new economic organization.

David Livingstone, medical missionary, explorer, and natural scientist, traveled through this area between 1851 and 1872. Although he did not found any mission stations, his work in Central Africa was an essential part of the subsequent European penetration. Livingstone formulated the policy that Europeans should bring not only the Gospel to Africans, but that they should also replace the slave trade with "legitimate" trade. His work and ideas made a deep impression among both missionary societies and businessmen in Britain. In 1877 the established Scottish Church and the dissident Free Church decided to send missionaries to Nyasaland. Glasgow businessmen backed them by founding, in 1878, the African Lakes Company to supply the missions and to engage in trade with Africans. During the last two decades of the nineteenth century and the first decade of the twentieth, many other churches were involved in evangelical work in Central Africa: the London Missionary Society (founded by the Congregationalists), the Universities' Mission for Central Africa (Anglican Church), the Plymouth Brethren (a lay body that had seceded from the Anglican Church), the White Fathers (Roman Catholic), the Paris Mission (French Protestants), Primitive Methodists, American Seventh Day Adventists, and others. All these different societies, with their varying beliefs and types of organization, competed with each other for converts. This was quite different from the monopoly which the Jesuits enjoyed in their work among some of the American Indians.

But in spite of differences in creed, there were sociological similarities in the work of different missions in Central Africa. The first missionaries were like chiefs, ruling their mission stations, making use of native labor, and attempting to enforce their standards of sexual morality. Some, such as Bishop P. Dupont among the Bemba, had considerable political power and influence. All of them were responsible for establishing the first schools, in which the elements of European education were given, and for giving training in industrial skills such as bricklaying, carpentry, and printing. "Mission boys" were employed by trading and mining companies and became part of the intelligentsia and the new middle class. Many of the contemporary political and trade union leaders received their elementary education in mission schools. Since missions were started earlier in Nyasaland than in Northern Rhodesia, "Nyasaland boys" were in demand for white-collar jobs on the mines and in government; they were the most literate African group on the Copperbelt.

Although it is difficult to assess the results of the missionaries' work, I agree with Gann that in spite of their fervor and many converts, relatively few of the converted radically changed their thinking or their way of life. But the missionaries' crusade against slavery, their establishment of schools, their medical and welfare work, and the vistas they opened to the elite were all profoundly significant.[3] The Africans accepted many of the secular values of the missionaries, and these provided the base and the shape for a benevolent image with which these Africans could identify.

The African's Christianity contrasted sharply to the deeply religious conversions of American Negroes in the Deep South. They had been quick to make Christianity their own and to internalize such major Christian concepts as "All men are God's children," "The meek shall inherit the earth," and "Love thine enemy." Christianity was a deep and pervading force in the life of the American Negroes; it gave them a sense of human dignity in a situation which generally disregarded it and a feeling of the righteousness of their cause and of eventual victory. Negro ministers were and still are leaders of social protest movements, and today many of them are in the forefront of the struggle in the South over integration in schools.

The historical situation of the American Negroes, separated from their ancestral lands and fellow tribesmen differed markedly, of course, from that of the Africans, still related to their tribal land and mores. The vacuum caused by the forced migration was filled for the American Negroes by Christianity; they made the church their own. Their ministers, especially in the rural South, were usually uneducated and had little or no formal training; they had a vision and were called by God; they preached with evangelical zeal. In Northern Rhodesia there was no equivalent of these revivals and of the "getting religion" experiences of the American "Bible Belt." Instead, there were the typical restrained British church services, dominated by missionaries who often complained about the lack of African leadership, but who, at the same time, said that it took three generations to train a responsible African priest or minister. To anyone who knew the feelings of American Negroes toward Christianity, the responses of Africans seemed weak and membership in the church rather nominal. (The evangelical Watch Tower sect which came from the United States was an exception.)

The secular work of the missionaries, their devotion to African welfare, their sincere belief in the brotherhood of man, and their promise that those who accepted their training "would enjoy the fruits of civilization which were displayed in every-day European life,"[4] these were the values which sparked the revolutionary changes in Africa. The mission-trained African elite, with the Bible as a source book and the benevolent image of the missionary as a guide, were able to contrast the gospel of the brotherhood of man and the missionary's attitudes with the missionary's behavior and with the attitudes and behavior of other Europeans. The 1915 revolt in Nyasaland, for example, originated not in resistance to European rule, but in resentment over the alleged betrayal of promises made by missionaries.[5]

Nevertheless, the missionaries became the protagonists in the struggle for African rights and were the first representatives of African interests in the Northern Rhodesia legislature. On the Copperbelt they were still sharply differentiated from other Europeans in the African's mind. During my study, two girls about twelve years old were discussing a woman missionary and one of them referred to her as a European. The other said, "She is not a European: she is a missionary"; her friend accepted this as true. After I talked to a group of African men, one of them said that I must be a missionary. It was difficult for him to believe otherwise, even though my talk had been concerned with the study I was making. When he came up after my talk and I explained again that I had no connection with a mission, he still looked unconvinced. Probably I was the only "European" he had met or heard of, other than missionaries, who treated him as a fellow human being.

If David Livingstone was a prototype for missionaries, Cecil Rhodes had the same function for empire builders. Rhodes' whole life was given to the struggle for power. Diamonds were discovered in South Africa in 1867; by 1888 Rhodes controlled the diamond industry, and in 1890 he was prime minister of the Cape Colony. He had a vision of British expansion northward for the reported minerals there, for native labor, and for extending the British Empire. It was his plan that development of the country north of the Cape Colony would come through chartered commercial companies, which would supply the capital, open up new areas, and make them safe for commercial development. The British Parliament, after the experience with the North American colonies and the failure of the colony in Senegal, did not think political control was necessary for trade and was willing to charter private commercial companies to occupy and develop Africa. The abolitionists and the empire builders concurred: the former saw legitimate trade as the answer to the slave trade and as a means of raising the African standard of living, and the latter envisaged great wealth through the development of natural resources and the extension of the Empire.[6]

The most successful and long lived of the companies was the British South Africa Trading Company. It engaged in banking, mining, the making of land grants, and other economic activities. It even set up its own police force. The company was obligated by its charter to respect native civil law, eliminate slavery, and prevent Africans from securing liquor. The distant British Secretary of State had supervisory powers over it, such as vetoing ordinances and arbitrating disputes between a tribe and the company.

Although the transoceanic slave trade had been officially abolished in 1873 by an alliance of Great Britain and the Sultan of Zanzibar, the Crown was powerless to stop the trade in the interior. The company's initial problems were, therefore, the elimination of the slave trade and the establishment of peace between warring tribes, so that European settlement would be possible. Some tribes, like the Matabele in Southern Rhodesia and the Yao in Nyasaland fought skillfully, but were eventually conquered. On the other hand the Barotse, who wanted protection against the Matabele and were influenced by the missionary Coillard, did not oppose the British and made a treaty quickly. By the end of the nineteenth century, the Bemba had surrendered, the Ngoni had been defeated, and the weaker tribes offered no problem after the defeat of the big chiefdoms.

These white victors differed from the early missionaries, hunters, and concession seekers, who more or less treated Africans as equals. However, the company's rule was "semi-paternal in nature, limited in its activities, relied upon prestige as much as on compulsion."[7] Its officials acted not only as administrators, but also as policemen, tax collectors, and judges. Rhodes held out a promise to Africans of becoming Europeanized; and his slogan, "Equal rights for all civilized men," assumed that Africans would become civilized. In many areas the Africans accepted the company's officials as patrons and protectors, stronger than their tribal chiefs.

Through treaties with chiefs, the British South Africa Trading Company had early established its claim to the mineral resources of Northern Rhodesia, then "The Far North." The extent of the resources was unknown, but included vast copper deposits. The British Government recognized this claim as a reward to the company for undertaking the administration of the country; the company then gave concessions to other companies in return for shares in them. As the development of the European luxury industries had earlier precipitated the need for ivory, so the need for copper was greatly increased with the expansion of the electrical industries at the end of the nineteenth century. Telegraph wires, submarine cables, electric lighting installations, machinery, and streetcars all made use of copper as raw material. The subsequent trek of the miners was part of the northward movement of the "miner's frontier" from the diamonds in South Africa and the gold in Southern Rhodesia to the copper of Northern Rhodesia.

The miners' need for adequate transport brought about the construction of a railway in Northern Rhodesia, causing social as well as economic changes. Heavy mining equipment and coal was moved in, and bulky ores were moved out. Africans could travel more easily from village to mines and other centers for employment. Village life was affected by its closeness to the railway, and even today the quality of life "on the line" is different from that in the distant and more traditional villages. The "line" was also a stimulus to European farmers, because for the first time they had a market in the mining townships.

The building of the railway brought in a new social group: the railway employees of many nationalities, including Italians, Central Europeans, and Afrikaans from South Africa. Working conditions were oppressive; a railway union was first organized in Bulawayo in 1911, and an effective one in Northern Rhodesia in 1919; the unions followed the South African pattern of segregation, preventing Africans from competing for skilled jobs. However, there was always a potential rivalry, for Africans learned the skills as they worked with Europeans. But the Railway Workers' Union and, later, the European Mine Workers' Union did their best to maintain their monopoly over skilled work and prevent competition from lower-paid Africans. For instance, when more skilled workers were needed, the railway men demanded that they be recruited from European immigrants. These Europeans were in sharp contrast to the missionaries, who were intent on the teaching of skills to Africans, and this is but one example of many in the conflicting imagery of the white man first presented to Africans.

The extension of the railway line into Northern Rhodesia made further immigration of settlers possible, and the company encouraged them with cheap land (from three to eight pence an acre in 1910) to farm and to provide food for the mining communities. The immigrants were attracted not only by the cheap land and cheap cattle, but also by the opportunity to be their own masters. Many of them had the habit of commanding, through their experience in the military police and in administration in South Africa. Although inexperienced as farmers and with little capital, they were "the first Europeans to enter into competition with the African for the latter's source of livelihood—the land."[8] But outside of a few small areas, the pressure on land in Northern Rhodesia was small. Only a few Africans lived along the new railroad line, and they received compensation to move away. One of the exceptions was the fertile districts in the Fort Jameson area, densely populated with as many as 140 Africans per square mile. When the first Europeans came there, most of the Africans stayed on as tenants for them; later the settlers demanded that the company set up native reserves, which were started in 1913. The land outside the reserves was retained for the Europeans, although this was contrary to the policy of the British Government. However, as compared to Southern Rhodesia and even more to South Africa, the relatively few white immigrants in Northern Rhodesia did not create any serious land problem in those early days.

The European traders differed from the farmers, miners, and other employers in that their relationship with Africans was not one of command and obedience. As Gann writes, the trader could not order Africans to buy goods any more than a missionary could order them to be converts. Westbeech, an important English trader in the seventies, worked within the frame of tribal structure, "Sat as an adviser on the Barotse tribal council and played an important part in native politics, which allowed him to give most valuable support to the missionaries."[9] In the northwestern part of the Territory many of the traders were poor East European Jews who had pushed northward from South Africa. As some traders became wealthy, they opened stores, and afterward they resented the competing Indian hawkers. In contrast to Uganda and other areas, Indians remained small in number. Whether as shopkeepers or as hawkers, the traders both created and fulfilled new needs of the Africans for blankets, clothes, cooking utensils, oil lamps, and nother material things of Western society. Debts for these often piled up and were then an incentive for Africans to seek employment. Most of the Europeans— officials of the chartered company, railway men, miners, and farmers —thought the proper place of the native was that of cheap laborer. They assumed he would never live permanently in towns, but would always return to his village when his job was over. In spite of considerable evidence to the contrary, many Europeans still have this assumption.

The rule of the chartered trading company began to give way early in the nineteenth century; Nyasaland became a protectorate in 1907; Southern Rhodesia became a self-governing colony in 1923, with the settlers retaining power; Northern Rhodesia became a protectorate in 1924. The two protectorates were administered by a Colonial Office benevolently inclined towards Africans, while the government of Southern Rhodesia was controlled by settlers interested in making their country a white man's land.

The British administration of its African protectorates was known popularly as indirect rule, or, more precisely, as the Native Authority system.[10] Chiefs and other traditional leaders were recognized as local agents of government and given the title of "Native Authority." This Native Authority could be a single individual, a group of chiefs, or a council of elders; recognition of its power could always be withdrawn by the British. The Native Authority had judicial, legislative, and financial powers, subject to British supervision. Like the Arab slave traders, the British tilted the balance of power in favor of the chiefs. The Colonial Office thought it could remove the abuses from the chieftainship and then use it constructively; its goal was "to democratize the government of chiefs without destroying it."[11]

As Mair points out, the assumption that "a political system can be modified by external action in just the direction which is desired . . . is false."[12] I would label it naïve, but it was in keeping with the prevailing ideology of that period, which did not recognize the intricate and dynamic nature of social change.

The British civil servants now replaced the personnel of the Trading Company. These colonial officials were often remarkable men: strong, carrying the tradition of stern British justice, but at the same time benevolent and paternalistic toward the Africans. District and provincial officers were usually university men with high ideals. Their goal was to help the Africans, to prohibit abuses in their working conditions, to protect their land rights, and, like the missionaries, to bring European civilization to them. The stated policy was one of trusteeship. In 1923, a Conservative secretary of state enunciated the principle that African interests were paramount.[13] A Labor secretary of state repeated the same principle in 1930. The British Parliament made clear in 1931 that "the term meant that the interests of the African majority should not be subordinated to those of any minority, however important."[14]

The district officers were often dedicated men; they enjoyed their work in the bush and had chosen their career as a way of life. They knew the Africans personally in their districts and often stayed in their villages, sometimes hunted with them, and when the day's hunt was over joined them at the campfires. Although they were different from the missionaries, the district officers were likewise benevolent father figures to the Africans. As late as 1947, members of the African Representative Council (an elected group) referred to the British government as "our father." A representative ended his speech on a motion to increase the number of European representatives of African interests in Legislative Council, ". . . and they [the Africans whom he represented] want the government to listen to their cries. The government is our father."[15] Another representative, in a different context, said, "Our missionaries lost their lives in nights of darkness and in days of darkness. Our commissioners and our district officers have borne the burden of civilizing the Africans in this country. . . ."[16] This benevolent image of the missionaries and district officers runs all through the proceedings of the African Representative Council.

These African tribal societies, with their strong emphasis on rank, were able, with relative ease, to incorporate the early Europeans into their status hierarchy and to regard them as the new chiefs. Like the traditional chiefs, they made demands in the form of taxes, but they also gave many advantages and opened new vistas. Richards notes that the proud Bemba were submissive and servile to them. In a brief tour of rural villages I saw a Bemba man greet a district officer in the same way he greeted his chief, by lying prostrate on his back on the ground and clapping his hands. The warlike Ngoni who looked down with contempt upon other tribes identified with the Europeans. They assured early European travelers that they themselves were white and related to them. One such traveler was described by them: "He is a Ngoni and a white man."[17] The strong Yao looked upon their submission to the whites in much the same way as they regarded the former submission of other tribes to them.[18] A member of the Lunda tribe, in talking about the history of his people in the Luapula valley, said, "First of all we lived without chiefs and we had no wars and we were happy. But then the chiefs came, and the Bemba came and conquered us, and then Kazemba [a chief] came and conquered us, and then the Europeans came and conquered us."[19]

Contrasted to this benevolent image of authority was an earlier and different one of Europeans. In the nineteenth century Arab slave traders spread the rumor that the Europeans who were coming to East and Central Africa had no intention of freeing slaves, but wanted to ship them abroad and eat them. In East Africa, Shepperson and Price report that many Africans had an image of Europeans as cannibals, as hungry for Africans' flesh as for their land. The cannibal stewpot used by Victorian mamas in England to scare their children appears to have existed in reverse form in East and Central Africa.[20] Today, it is common both on the Copperbelt and in villages for African mothers to frighten children who are misbehaving by telling them that Europeans will "get them."

The two images were formed early and continue to exist, each ready to be precipitated by particular events and by specific people. For example, two children of an African woman with whom I had a pleasant relationship boasted to neighboring children that they had a "European friend." An African clerk lost his suspicion of Europeans through a long, meaningful relationship with one European civil servant who was genuinely interested in him. But for most Africans, the ambivalence continues. In their imagery is the picture of the "good" or "proper" Europeans—the missionaries, the district officers, and an occasional employer or supervisor—all interested in helping them enter the modern world; on the other side are the bad Europeans, the settlers, with their alleged cannibalistic desires in the background and in the foreground their overt manipulations to keep Africans on the lowest economic and social level. One group is temporarily in Africa to help the Africans. The other hopes to be there permanently and to hold on to its political and economic power.

The European power structure changed radically in 1953, when the protectorates of Northern Rhodesia and Nyasaland were linked with the self-governing colony, Southern Rhodesia, in a Federation, in which the European settlers gained power at the expense of the Colonial Office. The Federation came into being against the strong opposition of all Africans. They did not desire independence; they wanted to remain under the benevolent Colonial Office until they were ready to assume independence. In the discussion of the proposed federation in the African Representative Council, the following statement was typical: "Our present Government is trying to bring us along like children who are learning to walk, and we are just beginning to see the light and to have a little wisdom, but those who are looking to this country say, 'When those young children grow up, we shall not be able to do the things we want to do in that country.' For these reasons my people have asked me to come here and say that they do not want this new constitution. They do not want it at all. We want our Government to go along with us. When the day comes when we realize that we are fully developed, we shall be able to go forward and say, 'Father, we are now grown up, cannot we do this?' . . . There is good fertile land here, we have wells underneath the ground, and the time will come when we will be able to develop our land and use what we have in the ground. We should not let other people have these things. These people say that if they do not get these things now, then they will never be able to get them in the future."[21]

These men were fearful of the proposed alliance with Southern Rhodesia, because that colony was well known for its many restrictions on Africans, such as those relating to land and the formation of trade unions, and for its generally repressive policies. The speeches of members of the African Representative Council of Northern Rhodesia when the proposed federation was being discussed reflect the fears. A member of the council said: "... The truth is that the Colonial Office policy that the interest of Africans should be paramount frightens our European settlers. They are trying to drag us to the South where our interests would remain inferior forever. ... I cannot go into details about the hardships which the Africans are experiencing as far as land questions are concerned both in Southern Rhodesia and the Union of South Africa. ... Since the motive behind the demand for self-government is to amalgamate or federate with Southern Rhodesia, a country whose policy is one of economic and political discrimination and racial segregation, and since Southern Rhodesia is a white man's country, the whole issue, however well intended is absolutely unacceptable. Northern Rhodesia should remain under Colonial Office rule until such time as the Africans themselves begin to demand self-government."[22]

But in spite of speeches, motions and protests, the Federation of Northern Rhodesia, Southern Rhodesia and Nyasaland came into being in October 1953. When I began my field work, the meaning of the new political union became quickly apparent to me because the fear of federation and the loss of land was dragged into almost every interview and conversation, regardless of context or relevancy. I never interviewed specifically on the subject of federation, but most Africans, with or without European education, young and old, appeared to have a compulsive need to talk about it and the related fear of losing their land.

No land has been taken from Africans under the new Federation, and the native-land policies for Northern Rhodesia are still under the jurisdiction of the British Crown and not under the Federation. But Africans were and are fearful of the possible dominance of Southern Rhodesia with its restrictive African policies and of the increased power of the Northern Rhodesian settlers. The "father," the benevolent colonial official, who was leading them into European civilization with the promise of eventual independence, seems to many Africans to have sold them down the river. Statements of responsible Federation officials did not reduce this fear. When I began my field work I was puzzled by questions from African school boys in their teens, as well as from adults, about past and present population figures of North American Indians, until the connection was made with a previous speech of the Prime Minister, in which he had threatened that the Africans would disappear like the "vanishing Indians" of North America, if they did not cooperate in the Federation. The African school boys and others knew the Indians had lost most of their land and the analogy aroused great anxiety.

The mystical relationship among land, fertility, and power has already been discussed. Land was life, and it is therefore easy to understand that loss of land is a symbol for annihilation. Nor is it surprising that the resulting anxieties have become tied in with the witchcraft-thinking. This is illustrated by an incident which occurred while the Africans were protesting the coming of federation. A couple of African government clerks secretly printed and distributed circulars which stated that Europeans had poisoned the sugar to make African men impotent and African women sterile. Although Africans love sugar and usually consume a great deal, they ate none for a considerable time afterward. This incident is revealing. Witchcraft is customarily used by those who envy another's possessions. Europeans are supposed to envy the Africans for their land and to want it. A basic element of witchcraft is the making of poison to kill the victim. Europeans have remarkable powers and knowledge of many medicines, and in this case their "poison" was allegedly aimed at African survival. Thus, the rational fear of the Federation moved into the realm of the supernatural and of direct personal annihilation.[23]

Interestingly enough, some of the Europeans' fears appear to be of the same order. Some of them think the Colonial Office, with its policy of liquidating the Empire and granting independence to Africans, has sold the Europeans down the river; and they fear annihilation at the hands of the Africans. Thus, black and white "partners" in the Federation each fear they will be destroyed by the other.

The first Europeans in this area were the last conquerors in a history of tribal conquests, and they fitted easily into the prevailing African dominant-subordinate social structure. These new authority figures broke the cohesion of tribal life by introducing new values and new goals. Africans could no longer envisage the present and future in the image of the past. The European "fathers" were leading them into a new civilization, and in the process Africans had to break from their traditional authorities. Although indirect rule had in some ways increased the power of chiefs, Christianity, European education, and the top position of the Europeans in the hierarchy undermined the supernatural sanctions for the chiefs' power. The formation of a mission-educated elite shattered the tribal homogeneity. The small group in direct personal contact with the benevolent European "fathers" identified with them and accepted new secular values. Like the tribal elders, the new "fathers" were completely sure of their values, among which were education, health, saving for the future, monogamy, and freedom—with its goal of independence. The colonial officials had announced a policy of eventual independence for Africans. When it was effected, they would go home.

But there were other Europeans with different intensions. For the settlers—farmers, miners, railway workers, shopkeepers and others—Northern Rhodesia was and is home. They had come there to better their own economic and social position and not to help the Africans achieve independence. As Prime Minister Harold MacMillan of Britain noted in an interview in Capetown, after visiting Central and South Africa, the people there are now concerned with guaranteeing the rights of the whites rather than those of the Africans, and this is one measure of change since the coming of the first Europeans, when the primacy of African rights was proclaimed.[24]

PART II

THE NEW
ECONOMIC ORDER

5. The Europeans[1]

Ɪɴ ᴛʜᴇ ᴛᴡᴇɴᴛɪᴇꜱ the mining community of this study resembled a pioneer camp and was almost exclusively male. Today, however, the European men live with their families in modern bungalows, and many participate in a round of polite social life: dinner parties, "sundowners" (cocktail parties), afternoon teas, amateur dramatics, and social affairs at the Club.

Although the Europeans mingled socially at the Club, in the churches and on many public and semi-public occasions, the guest list at parties frequently recognized status distinctions. The managerial group—a few in the highest executive positions and a larger number on the second executive level—were at the top of the mine hierarchy. Many of these men were upper-, or more frequently, upper-middle-class English. Like the civil servants, they went home to England on their leaves, and most of them retired there. Their children, with career plans not confined to Africa, usually went to Great Britain for school and university training. On the second executive level, in addition to the English, there were others born in South Africa, Southern Rhodesia, or Northern Rhodesia. Africa was home for them. This was even more true for those below the managerial level: the mine captains, the shift bosses, the engineers, the electricians and other, organized in a Salaried Staff Association.

Beneath them were members of the European Mine Workers' Union: artisans, who broke the rock; timbermen, who erected posts to hold the wall after the rock was removed; and gangers, who directly supervised a group of five or six African miners, headed by their African boss boy.

Attitudes of Europeans toward Africans were conditioned by nationality, class, occupation and, of course, idiosyncratic personality factors. Unfortunately, there is no exact data on the country of origin for the European employees of the mine, but in the Federation as a whole, the Union of South Africa was the most important birthplace for Europeans, with 314 per thousand people, followed by the Federation, with 305 per thousand, and the United Kingdom, 274 per thousand.[2] In Northern Rhodesia the proportion was somewhat different. By nationality and citizenship the numbers were:[3]

United Kingdom and colonies	31,797
Union of South Africa	24,595
Southern Rhodesia	4,573

In the federal elections of November 1958, it was estimated by an official that 60 per cent of the members of the European Mine Workers' Union could not vote because they were not citizens of the Federation. About 50 per cent were said to be South Africans.

The idea held by many Africans and by English, too, that all South Africans, particularly Boers, were hostile to Africans and that those who came from England were favorably disposed toward them was a conventional stereotype.[4] Two African miners discussing their respective bosses, expressed a commonly held opinion:

FIRST MINER: That Boer was very angry, even throwing gloves around on the floor [gloves worn by those who work in the smelter]. Even though I had done nothing wrong, he said, "I can beat you Kaffir," and then he clapped [hit] me. I am going to report him to the foreman.

SECOND MINER: Yes, we cannot be cursed at, and even when we have done nothing wrong. Now my *bwana* [master] is good. He does not do such bad things. One day I was late because I overslept, and he excused me and told me to do my best to be on time.

FIRST MINER: Some Europeans are very kind to Africans.

SECOND MINER: Especially Englishmen, but not Boers.

FIRST MINER: It is because we and the Boers are both inferior to the Englishman, that the Boers try to make themselves better than us.

A survey of European attitudes to Africans was made in 1957 by Professor Thomas M. Franck in Salisbury in Southern Rhodesia and in Lusaka in Northern Rhodesia; the results, based on 1,142 responses in the former and 205 in the latter, indicate that the country of origin and length of residence in the Federation provided a high correlation with attitudes. A question in the survey was: "The Federal Government has recently decided that Africans travelling first or second class on the Railways should have the same dining-car privileges as Europeans. Do you agree?" Negative responses to this question, expressed as a percentage of the total affirmative and negative responses, were:

Emigrated to Central Africa from	"No" Responses (per cent)
South Africa	93.9
United Kingdom	50.5
Elsewhere	53.9

The negative responses of the South Africans who had emigrated to the Rhodesias twenty or more years ago was the same as those who had come during the last four years. Nor was there any appreciable difference between the Afrikaaner and non-Afrikaaner immigrants from South Africa. According to Franck, the British South Africans emigrate because they see no future for themselves in the Boer-dominated country. The author notes that the largest number of South African emigrants, whether of British or Dutch descent, are in the lower and lower-middle classes.[5] Class, therefore, as well as nationality could be a factor in the answers to this question on the survey.

Franck's survey also included a random sample of sixty-three young European males, between the ages of seventeen and twenty-two, and they were more conservative in their attitudes to Africans than were the adults of his survey.[6] My impressions of the children growing up in Luanshya was that they took their alleged racial superiority for granted. How could their attitude be otherwise, since this was the only one the majority of them knew? Children saw adult Africans only as servants, the "boys" who were to wait on them. One white youngster who came to school without his homework gave as his excuse that the "boy" had forgotten to put it in his schoolbag. Unlike the earlier situation in the American South, European children did not have African nurses, nor did they ever play with African children.

Although Franck's sample is heavily weighted for Salisbury adults whose "conservatism percentile" was 67.7 per cent, as compared to 57.9 per cent for the Lusaka adults,[7] it is probable that the general trends would have been the same if more Northern Rhodesians had been included and if a similar survey had been made on the Copperbelt.

It was the considered opinion of some Europeans, who had been in supervisory positions over other Europeans for a long time, that although the exceptionally hostile men were usually Boers or other South Africans, some workers from the United Kingdom were equally hostile. South Africans have usually been conditioned to believe in the alleged innate inferiority of Africans, but many of the English miners had belonged to socialistically oriented unions at home, had seen well-dressed Africans and other Negroes in London or Birmingham, and had believed that Africans were basically no different from other people. When they arrived on the Copperbelt, these English workers were completely unprepared for the Africans they found there—men with different customs and manners who did not know English and with whom they could not communicate. Some of these Englishmen, perhaps because of disappointment, then went to the other extreme in attitude and behavior. One such Englishman, contrary to Copperbelt custom, offered a cigarette to an African miner the second day he was on the mine township. Two weeks later he was calling Africans "dumb monkeys," and was disciplined for striking one of them, which was against the rules of the mine.

There were many reasons why English workers became intolerant. Some new arrivals, eager to fit into a new situation only half understood, leaned over backward in pushing the African around. Similarly, some Northerners in the United States who move to the South become more "southern" than their neighbors. Then, too, intense

resentment was often expressed by many Europeans, who said that
the Africans were "savages" until twenty-five years ago with no culture of any kind and that now they cashed in on inventions and
accomplishments of Europeans which had taken centuries. These
Europeans seemed to believe that they or their fathers and grandfathers were personally responsible for the richness of Western
civilization and that if the African absorbed it, the Europeans would
somehow be poorer. For some, the belief was a convenient rationaliza-
tion for the differential in wages betwen members of the two races.
An engineer told of a conversation he had had with a couple of
African miners on the subject of equal pay. He made the point to
them that his father and his grandfather had known about motorboats,
electricity, and all kinds of other wonderful things, and he then asked
the Africans, "Did your fathers know about these things?" Their
answer was "No." Then he asked, "Do you understand what makes
electricity or how the radio works?" and again the answer was, "No."
"Ah," the European said, "that is our secret, a secret we have had
a long time, and our fathers and our grandfathers before us. Since
we have this secret, we are entitled to more pay, and we will not
give you the secret." A very different attitude, indeed, from that of
the missionaries and early civil servants, who came to give their
"secrets" to Africans.

Others thought that the African could acquire European culture
only superficially, and one of them said,

> The African may talk English, but he thinks African, and if he goes
> back to his village he will revert. He inherits his African way of thinking
> and his character and he cannot change them. It took us thousands of
> years to develop our civilization, and it would take Africans equally long
> to learn it, if that is possible.

These men seemed to be unaware of how quickly people can take
on a new culture and of the possibility of a culture in which African
and European elements would be mingled. Nor did they know that
the mingling of cultures enriches them.

Class and occupation were important conditioning factors for
attitudes, and in general, the higher the status in each, the more
favorable were attitudes to Africans. Franck's survey also found
this close correlation consistently between social-economic class and

attitudes to race.[8] Most of the top managerial group on the Roan
Antelope Mine believed in advancing their African employees because they thought this policy was to their enlightened self-interest,
as well as to the interests of Africans. Sir Ronald Prain, chairman of
the board of directors of the Roan Antelope Copper Mines,
initiated and led the mining companies in this area in a
progressive policy of African advancement. There were also at the
top a few men with the traditional upper-class attitude of *noblesse
oblige* toward employees. One of them said, "We must advance Africans and do things for them because it is right, whether or not they
appreciate it." This was his answer to the often-heard statement,
"The Africans don't appreciate anything we do for them." There
were other executives, who while genuinely concerned about African
advancement, feared that the pace might be too fast. As former
African colonies gained independence, these fears deepened. Some
of these men distrusted many of the civil servants and missionaries,
whom they considered too sympathetic to independence for Africans.

On both the top and second managerial levels, there were bold
men who wanted to try innovations, timid men who could not give
a clear "Yes" or "No" to any policy, and others who dismissed a
problem by saying, "The Africans are not civilized and never will be."
Their beliefs about Africans had a similarly wide range. A few accepted the generally held scientific view that there are no innate
intellectual or psychological differences between races; and one of
these men said, "If the Africans had our educational and other
advantages, they could think as well as we do." Others thought that
Africans should be trained to accept more responsible jobs and
advance economically, yet doubted that they could ever become the
equal of Europeans. Many of these people believed that there is
something mysterious and unknowable about the African's mentality,
which radically differentiates him from other members of the human
species. They did not consider their belief subject to proof or disproof;
and it was held by some who worked with fervor for African progress,
as well as by others who wished to return to the "good old days."

In a social-psychological study of the European employees on the
Copperbelt made in 1959 by the National Institute for Personnel
Research in Johannesburg for the Northern Rhodesia Chamber of
Mines, attitudes to African advancement (industrial, political, and

social) were studied. The report is confidential, but the press release and a letter from the director of the Institute indicate that advancement in occupational opportunities evoked the least resistance, and the granting of full social and political rights the most. The majority were in favor of African industrial advancement, but only 13.5 per cent of all the employees accepted all the implications of political and social advancement, which included social mixing in schools, residential areas, or homes. However, 53 per cent of the salaried staff and 35 per cent of the daily-paid workers (members of the European Mine Workers' Union) were prepared to tolerate mixing in public places such as hotels, restaurants, and motion-picture theaters, which involve only impersonal and public social contact. The press release states that "the report finds it historically inevitable that the essentially conservative white attitude pattern of the rest of Southern Africa should have been transplanted to the Copperbelt. It could but be expected that the very prosperity and isolation of Copperbelt society would enhance rather than change the values of the European way of life."[9]

Those results of the survey which have been made public and my own field work indicate that the greatest intolerance toward Africans was among the lower-class European miners. These were the men who had the most direct contact with Africans, and their attitudes were therefore significant in shaping responses of Africans to Europeans in general. The European miners were constantly irritated by African manners and customs. Among those particularly provoking were:

When given an order which he does not understand, an African may say "Yes" and then do nothing. He considers it ill-mannered to suggest that the European has not expressed himself well.

An African whose command of English is poor does not know how to introduce a topic or make easy transitions, and the unintentioned effect is abrupt and rude.

When something goes wrong, an African often smiles and laughs out of sheer nervousness.

An African follows his traditional custom of a junior walking in front of a senior and entering a room first.

An African is not effusive in his thanks for a gift, because effusiveness about gifts is not customary.

An African may sit down before a European tells him to.

An African may not be as clean as European standards of hygiene demand.

An African is sometimes apparently unconcerned about breaking a piece of machinery, because he may think the accident is not his fault, but was caused by malignant witchcraft.

The very language most European supervisors and African miners used in communicating with each other was not conducive to understanding. It is called Fanagalo, or more colloquially, "kitchen-kaffir"; a hybrid of Zulu, English, and Afrikaans, it probably originated in Natal during the second half of the nineteenth century and then spread through South Africa and the Rhodesias. It has none of the basic phonetic or morphological characteristics of the Bantu languages and both the Bantu peoples and the Europeans must learn it.[10] Its vocabulary is limited and is confined to expressing a master-servant relationship in terms of command and obedience. For Africans it is an insulting language.

Some European supervisors were fond of their African "boys"—in their own way. One man said:

I've worked with them fifteen years underground and I'm fond of some of my boys, like I'm fond of a dog. Some of them like me, but we have our ups and downs. Sometimes they do things wrong, and I curse and punish them. The ups and downs make it interesting.

On some occasions there was a kind of camaraderie between Europeans and the Africans they supervised. The birth of a baby in the family of either might be enthusiastically announced, and congratulations did not follow the color bar. Neither did condolences, if a death in the family occurred. Occasionally, there was good-humored chatting. Sometimes a European sold old clothes or used furniture to his African workers, who were glad to buy them.

Fortunately, some Europeans in supervisory positions were polite and known for their sense of fairness. One miner talked admiringly about his supervisor:

He knows how to try African cases. I remember one man who was caught committing adultery and Mr. S—— said to him, "So you left your job and coaxed the wives of your friends while they were away at work.

So now you have lost your job." He settles cases like an African, and if you take your case to the Compound Office to be settled by him, you just know it will be settled properly.

Few in number were the Europeans who learned the Bemba language, who thought Africans were an interesting part of the new environment, who tried to understand their customs and who had African friends. It was exceedingly difficult to be friendly with Africans. At the time of my study, European mine personnel were not supposed to entertain Africans in their homes, but now and then a few did. Sinister rumors circulated about one such European. Casual familiarity was not liked either. One young European was seen during the lunch hour by his immediate supervisor, sitting on a fence and smoking a cigarette with an African clerk. He was later called down for it and told that he looked like an anthropologist! Several European women appeared genuinely interested and curious to find out more about the Africans in their community, but did not know how to proceed without embarrassing themselves or their husbands who were employed by the mine. These women asked if they could accompany me on my visits to Africans and to the African cinema. I regretfully had to say "No," since I was unsure of what their reactions would be and, in any case, their presence would have hampered my field work. These are small incidents, but they are significant in showing how the social climate made it almost impossible for well-meaning Europeans to get acquainted with any Africans on a simple, human, friendly level.

At the opposite end were the Europeans, also a minority, who were violent and cruel by temperament and for whom the situation of being in the dominant white group offered many temptations. Mr. T was of this type and although he does not represent a large number, an attempt to understand his extreme violence may offer some insight not only into him, but also into those whose fury was not so intense or open. An Englishman of working-class background, he went into the army from secondary school. During the last world war he was sent to Africa, and when it was over he stayed there, joined the Southern Rhodesia police force, and married a South African girl who was also of a working-class background. He was restless in the police force and left it after several years to look for adventure. With his wife he spent months in the bush searching for crocodiles, valuable for their skins, but had no success. Then he began prospecting for minerals and, again, had only misfortunes. His second-hand truck broke down, and he used up all his small capital. He would have liked to farm, but he did not have the capital required as a down payment for land; he was forced to look for a job and found one connected with the maintenance of houses and sanitary facilities on the African Mine Compound. He earned about a £100 a month and he remarked that he did little to deserve it.

His bitterness, his sense of frustration, his unconcealed feelings of violence were extreme. He talked compulsively and unceasingly about the "Kaffirs"; a deep and desperate hatred of them seemed to pervade his whole being. He brought out all the cliches:

The Africans have no brains. They can never be civilized, not even in a thousand years. They walk into my office without knocking. An African clerk had the cheek to tell me I made a mistake. The educated Africans are the worse—they do nothing but imitate the Europeans; did the Kaffirs ever invent anything? They can learn nothing; if you gave them a palace they would use it as a lavatory: The only good Kaffirs are the old men in the bush and the dead ones; when the educated native goes back to the bush, he reverts to type and goes wild and is just like a baboon.

As he spewed out his distilled hatred he did not notice his inconsistencies, such as that the bush Africans in the villages are the only good ones and that when the educated African goes back to his village he reverts and becomes a wild baboon.

He said rather hopefully that he expects the Mau Mau will come to Northern Rhodesia, and in fact, spread all over Africa. He wishes that he could have gone to Kenya when the Mau Mau were active and shot them down. He refers approvingly to the reported case of European officers there who kept a record on a scoreboard of the number of Africans they killed. If the Mau Mau would come to Northern Rhodesia, he would have his chance to kill. But now he is fined by the Mine Company when he is caught just cursing an African.

His hatred was directed toward other Europeans as well:

All the laws are to protect the Kaffirs. The D.C.'s and the D.O.'s are all pro-African. And the mine management wants to advance the Africans and oust the Europeans. African clerks now are taking the place of

European ones. Management is afraid of the African Union and gives them anything. And the British at home—they are even worse; even my father used to speak of the "poor Africans." And those M.P.'s who come here for a couple weeks and are given a free show and meet only educated Africans.

His frenzy reached a high point—unprintable—when he referred to the marriage of a prominent English girl to an African.

His wife added to his spleen by telling how she curses her house boy. She described a recent incident when she bought a large quantity of vegetables in the market and the cook prepared too many at one time. She was livid with anger and raised her hand as if to strike him. The threatening motion and her anger sent him hurrying out of the room, as she yelled that he had no brains and that his head was only to keep his ears apart. She told me that she is sure the cook makes mistakes on purpose to irritate her and remarked that she, as a South African, had always known what the "Kaffirs" were like and then, in an amused tone, mentioned that when she first met her husband, he talked civilly to them but now she said, smiling, he has learned—his civil talk is over and he curses and kicks them if he thinks he can get away with it. (Since he had been recently fined for these misdemeanors, he was now more careful.) She went to England for the first time a year ago, but did not like it, saying,

The people there are so poor. The women did their own cooking and housework. They thought I was very extravagant because I smoked a lot and threw out stockings instead of mending them.

Hatred poured out of Mr. T and his wife like the violent torrential downpours of the rainy season. They would be violent people anywhere, and they think of Africa as a place for violence. They did not want to return to "quiet England." Yet Africa had thwarted them; they were hemmed in on all sides by the "Kaffirs," by the liberal mine management, by the government with its "pro-African" laws. Mr. T's hunting and other adventures had failed and, ironically, he had a job concerned with maintenance of houses for Africans. He hated his job; he hated the "Kaffirs"; he hated the community in which he lived and its rules and laws which prevented him from expressing his violence. Perhaps his image of the "Kaffir" as a wild baboon was a projection of his own deepest nature.[11] The African setting lends itself to the extremes of Mr. T's personality.

The majority of miners were not so extreme. They resembled in some ways immigrant settlers all over the world. They came to improve their standards of living and to provide a good future for their children and grandchildren. But unlike immigrants to the North American continent, Australia, and other pioneer countries, who suffered hardships and worked hard, these European miners lived comfortably. To attract European technicians and artisans to Northern Rhodesia, the mining companies offered high wages and the many amenities already described. The European Mine Workers' Union, organized since 1936, had obtained a closed shop contract and, during World War II, many other advantages, since management did not then want to risk any interruption in the production of copper. By English standards the pay of the European miners was high and their income taxes low, as was also the rent of the company-owned houses. Many owned cars. Women who formerly did all their own work had at least one African servant, and some had two. The plateau, four thousand feet above sea level, provided a healthy climate; and in case of illness, there was an excellent hospital. Then, too, every European could enjoy the feeling of being a member of an allegedly superior race, regardless of ability and accomplishments. But fears and anxieties prevented these Europeans from enjoying their many advantages. They feared the Africans, who outnumbered them eight to one in Northern Rhodesia. They feared curtailment of their advantages and progress by African advancement, when skilled jobs would no longer be reserved for them purely because of their white skins. They feared the European management, which pressed for African advancement. When Sir Ronald Prain made a public announcement in 1954 about the desirability for the further advancement of Africans to more responsible jobs, many of the European miners expressed consternation and asked apprehensively how far Sir Ronald planned to go.

Relations between Europeans and Africans were not confined to the mine. The two groups also met in the municipality—in shops, public buildings, on the streets, and in the servant-mistress relationship in homes. Some of the European shops employed Africans to wait on customers; all used Africans to deliver orders. Treatment of these

African employees, few in number, varied; one employer treated them with courtesy; another often kicked his African assistant to get his attention. The kick, given as a matter of course, was not an unusual form of communication between Europeans and Africans. I saw a European man kick a middle-aged African sitting in his customary place on the pavement in front of the largest shop, with his wood animals which he sold to passers-by. There was plenty of room for the white man to have walked by the African without disturbing him. Instead, he gave him a kick and told him to move. The African moved aside; his face was without expression.

The relationships of European women with their African servants, or "boys," varied enormously. Many of the upper-middle- and middle-class women said "please" and "thank you" to their servants and taught their children to do the same. Other women, wives of artisans, who never had a servant before, continuously shouted "boy!" at their servants and never used any terms of normal politeness. They were furious over the smallest misdemeanor, such as breaking a glass. The standards for honesty were incredibly high: houses left unlocked; purses plainly visible; cars with packages in them open on the main streets. An occasional theft aroused a great fuss and was taken for a sign of the African's deterioration. No figures on theft were available, but it was my impression that theft from Europeans was rare and that intra-African thefts were more numerous. Europeans seemed to be unaware of the situations in other parts of the world, as for example, in New York or Mexico City, where no one would ever think of leaving packages in an unlocked car or of leaving an apartment or house unlocked.

There were a few oases in the town. The district commissioner at the time of my study was respected and liked by the Africans; he was known for his sense of justice; a few of the intelligentsia were his friends. A newly arrived Protestant minister and his wife established friendly and cordial relations with Africans. They entertained a group of schoolboys, for whom this was the first social occasion in a European's home. The boys were tremendously excited by this novel experience, and one of them, telling about the party, said, "Reverend R and his wife, and their children and their home, the way they talk and the way they act—are all wonderful. I would like to be just like Reverend R and live as he does." His identification with Reverend R was obviously immediate.

No matter how well meaning some Europeans and Africans were in their effort to have a more or less normal relationship, something often happened to disturb it. A European pastor insisted, over the protests of a few members of his church board (composed mostly of Europeans employed by the mine) that two ordained African ministers be invited to a ceremony for the laying of the foundation stone of his new church. He had to compromise with a couple of recalcitrant board members by promising that the African ministers would not be mentioned in the greetings given by the master-of-ceremonies. They were thus not officially recognized, but there was an unofficial recognition. A white woman standing next to the two dignified middle-aged African ministers leaned over to them during the ceremonies and asked, "Would you *boys* like to have a program?" as she handed them her copy of the mimeographed program with its hymns and responsive readings. The Africans said, "Thank you," as they took the program; their faces were as expressionless as that of the man on the pavement who had been kicked. But while the white man appeared to kick purposively to hurt the African, my impression of the white woman was that she thought she was being kind in offering the program and was completely unaware that she had insulted the two Africans. All Africans, whether cooks or ordained ministers, were "boys" to her.

Mine management had an educational program for their European workers to improve their relations with African workers. Supervisors were encouraged to learn the Bemba language and were given a bonus if they passed an examination in it. A course for supervisors, covering technical and management problems, included a few lectures on race relations and was designed to give a sympathetic view of Africans and to promote proper working relations, necessary for increased efficiency and for an expanded production of copper. I attended several of these lectures. In one of them the lecturer and one or two other representatives of management who were present made the general points:

What happens in race relations on the Copperbelt sets the tone for the rest of Northern Rhodesia.

Americans will not invest their capital in the mine unless race relations are harmonious.

The African Mine Workers' Union behaved with a sense of responsibility and filled a vacuum, which might have been filled with something worse.

Then the lecturer stressed the following positive injunctions for supervisors:

1. They should have a sense of dignity, which they can achieve by not reprimanding a boss boy in front of his gang, not losing their temper, not indulging in horseplay or manhandling labor in either fun or anger, and not calling Africans "monkeys."
2. They should have a sense of justice, hear all sides of the case, and know the facts before jumping to conclusions. The European should not necessarily be supported *right or wrong* against the African.
3. They should have a sense of responsibility for the safety and welfare of African labor under their supervision, making sure that work is allocated fairly, showing appreciation of a well-done job, and seeing that men leave their job with as little delay as possible when the day's work is done.
4. They should understand the way an African lives, feels, and thinks; never discuss political matters with him, but inquire about health and family and win his confidence by being firm, fair, and consistent.

It apparently did not occur to the well-meaning lecturer that he was talking primarily about personality qualities (dignity, sense of justice and responsibility, understanding, consistency) not attained through listening to lectures. The supervisors' questions, which followed the lecture, their facial expressions, and the tone of their voices indicated insecurities and fears. Among the questions and their answers were:

Does the African think as we do? ANSWER: Schools are building the character of the African and training him for responsibility.

Is the African getting the same kind of talk in race relations as we are? ANSWER: The European is the leader, and he should behave as a leader.

What should one do when an African says he can do what the European is doing? ANSWER: Encourage that.

Is the African payroll higher than that of the European one? ANSWER: Yes, but there are fifteen thousand Africans and fifteen hundred Europeans.

It African labor really cheap, since it is not as efficient as European labor? ANSWER: We can help Africans improve.

Do Africans really want to accept responsibilities? ANSWER: They accepted them in tribal life. When they come to the mine they do not know what their responsibilities are and must learn them.

Shouldn't the African be civilized first before there is all this talk of Africans advancing on the job? Civilizing a primitive mind takes thousands of years. ANSWER: Some are ready now for more advanced jobs.

What will happen if we are swamped by the blacks? Won't there be intermarriage and the end of the white race? ANSWER: The scientist says we'll all be a bit darker.

Deep anxieties, ranging from fear of losing their jobs to fear of losing their women, were expressed in the questions. The lectures probably did little to reduce the fears. It was fairly obvious that the European employees resented management's telling them how they should *feel* toward Africans and how they should treat them. It was all very well for the lecturer to say, "It is absolutely essential to keep a clear and unprejudiced mind. . . ."; but prejudice is a stubborn emotion which does not disappear after listening to a lecture. Both the lecturer and management were well meaning in their attempt to lay down "a line" for good race relations among their workers. But the educational approach was so oversimplified that I doubt if attitudes were modified by it. A more careful selection, based on personality factors of the European personnel who were in direct contact with African employees, might be more practical.

The effect of the anticolonial attitudes expressed in newspapers and by people in Great Britain was pronounced, but in a different direction from that intended. Great Britain has been long in the process of dissolving its empire and giving independence to formerly subject native peoples. But many parochial British settlers held on fiercely to the beliefs and code of empire-building days, when the white man's power over allegedly inferior native peoples was regarded as innately right. They fiercely resented the editorials and news stories about Africa in the *London Times, The Observer,* and similar papers, all of which they regarded as pro-African or Fabian. One settler, a professional man, explained that the British were ashamed of having built an empire and that now they beat their breasts in guilt and talked only about how the Europeans in Northern Rhodesia are exploiting the poor Africans. He had just returned from a visit to London and said that his friends shocked him so much that he doubted he would see them again. None of them, he said, had any understanding of the "primitive" Africans and of the settlers' problems. Although the Conservative party was in power, he and others thought the Colonial Office was following Fabian policies. Feeling misunderstood by friends at home and by an unsympathetic Colonial Office, the attitudes of some of these settlers hardened and grew more intense.

In 1960, a law passed by the Northern Rhodesian Legislature, forbidding racial discrimination in hotel dining rooms, restaurants, cafes, and movie houses, precipitated as many reactions as the diverse types of Europeans on the Copperbelt. According to reports from Northern Rhodesian papers, as well as from foreign correspondents stationed there, some groups of angry white men attacked the Africans who took advantage of this law on the first week end it was in effect. In one town on the Copperbelt white men ran through the streets, shrieking curses and obscenities. I assume that men like the violent Mr. T were in this mob. But all white men did not behave in this way. White policemen arrested white men in the mob and protected Africans from them. The disorderly whites were later fined by the courts. Another group of Europeans went out of their way to go to desegregated movie houses. Although the low incomes of most Africans prevent them from going to expensive restaurants, the law marked real progress in breaking down the social color bar. Reactions varied from violent opposition to acceptance, willingly or not, of a changing world.

Another recent event also produced a variety of responses. At the time of the Congo disaster in the summer of 1960, four thousand fleeing Belgian mothers with their children and some men flew to the safety offered by the Copperbelt. There were two reactions from the Europeans there and elsewhere in Northern Rhodesia: "I told you so. You can't advance these people"; and the opposite, "The trouble is that the Belgians didn't advance their workers fast enough and far enough, particularly in the governmental sense and in the sense of bureaucracy and management." It appears that on the Copperbelt the latter reaction won out, as evidenced by an agreement in November of the same year between management and the European Mine Workers' Union, which opened up new job categories to Africans and made a plan for a unified wage structure for both races.[12]

This tends to confirm the data from the National Institute for Personnel Research, cited earlier in the chapter, that the European workers on the Copperbelt had accepted the opening of occupational opportunities to Africans as more or less inevitable. The problems inherent in political and social advancement for Africans are still to be met.

6. The Africans

THE WINDS OF CHANGE blow even more strongly for the Africans than for Europeans, and the mine township was indeed a new world for them.[1] In it time is lineal instead of circular. Labor is sold for money instead of performed in a round of reciprocal obligations. Manual work is disparaged instead of respected. Differentiation in standards of living replace the tribal egalitarianism. Young leaders tend to supplant elderly chiefs, as the authority symbols based on age and rank are weakened. Yet history has its persistence, too, and the traditional mingles with the new.

In the past there was a time to do this and a time to do that, but it followed the cycles of nature. Work was largely seasonal, and sunrise and sunset determined the daily round of activities. Today there is the rigidity of clock time. The mine whistles blow in the early morning, and one group begins work as another shift ends. Periods of work alternate with "leaves," usually spent with relatives in the village. Many children are being conditioned to the regularities of school time, in which classes begin at one hour and are over at another hour. Among the intelligentsia some mothers had adopted a regular feeding schedule for their babies, instead of nursing them whenever they cried. Whether conditioned early or late, this new symmetry of time is experienced by all Africans on the mine township. Time also stretches ahead to a future of individual careers, independence, and a place in the modern world still only dimly perceived, instead of rotating between a past, a present, and a future, all quite similar.

Today a young man does not go through a life cycle which, formerly, was much the same for all men. He makes a choice. If he is born in a village and decides not to remain to farm, or fish, or tend his cattle, he can come to a town. A large number of Africans in this area came to a mining community. Formerly the young men traveled on foot, later by bicycle, and now usually by bus or train. If the men are married, there was an increasing tendency for wives to come with them or to follow shortly afterward. According to Mitchell's survey of 1951, 66.9 per cent of the men were married and had their wives with them.[2] As of 1961, 80 per cent of the Africans had wives and children with them (the proportion for Europeans was about the same).[3] "Wives" in this context included those who had come from the villages, others who had married on the township and, probably, some who did not have the benefit of a marriage ritual.

When unskilled Africans first come to the mine, it appeared to be quite easy for them to learn how to handle the tools and the new techniques. An induction class for new miners, in which an experienced African taught them the names and functions of the new tools, provided a good beginning; and it took relatively little time to gain the necessary familiarity with the implements. It took longer to get used to working underground. A miner described his reactions:

> I do not like working underground. Always your life is in danger down there, and I do not like work which does not vary. When I went underground the first time, it looked like a rat's hole, and when you get down there, you are like a rat. The hole goes downward and is very deep. You cannot see the blue sky, but only rocks. I am going on leave soon, and I hope when I come back to get a job on the surface.

Other miners appeared to get used to working underground and did not complain. In 1954 (at the time of my study) on the Copperbelt as a whole, 15,682 Africans were working underground as compared to 19,671 on the surface. In 1960, the numbers and proportion had changed to 20,079 underground and 14,810 on the surface.[4]

The economic revolution produced by copper mining and other industrial developments in Africa differed from the beginning of the Industrial Revolution in Europe, when everyone had long been accustomed to differences in occupation, income, and standards of living. Peasants and serfs had always worked hard with their hands and lived on a lower economic standard than the lords of manors. The low status of manual work is an old concept in Western society, but the African came to it late, with a tradition in which physical strength was valued and manual work, whether hoeing or tending cattle, pounding the maize or cooking, was highly respected. But at the top of the mine hierarchy are the Europeans, who do no manual work. Even those on the lowest rungs have at least one African servant. Many Africans doing hard manual work, which often involves underground dangers, were really perplexed by a system which pays more to men, European and Africans, who sit in offices on a job which requires no physical strength and has no unusual hazards.

The hierarchy of labor is differentiated according to the skill, responsibility, and education required for the job. At the bottom are the unskilled laborers, those in groups 1 to 3: the lashers, the underground men who shovel and load the rock after blasting, "handle boys," "spanner boys," and surface workers such as compound sweepers and night-soil collectors. From 1948 to 1959, the unskilled African employees of Roan Antelope declined from approximately 74 per cent to 65 per cent. In the semiskilled groups (groups 4 to 7), among whom were boiler attendants and stokers in the power plant, mine police, watchmen, painters, plumbers, tinsmiths, the percentage in the same decade rose from 25 to 31 per cent. In the highest groups (8 to 13), the skilled and supervisory employees (boss boys, skilled mine workers, supervisors, clerks, social workers, record keepers, storekeepers) the percentage grew from about 1 to 4 per cent in this period.[5] At this writing, nearly 40 per cent of the African employment on the Copperbelt is in the lowest three categories, and there are a thousand advanced jobs for the thirty-eight thousand employees.[6]

The economic position of the African mine employee can be understood only in the context of the biracial situation and, more specifically, in the attitudes of the members of the European Mine Workers' Union. During the last world war, when it was important to avoid any interruption in the production of copper, a strategic material, the European Mine Workers' Union insisted on a color bar in its closed shop agreement with the mine companies, and it took ten years before management succeeded through negotiations with the union in removing the color bar. In 1955 the thousand jobs previously mentioned were opened up in twenty-one new categories; and in November 1960, sixty more job categories were added, again at the initiative of management and through negotiations with the European union.[7] It voted favorably on a plan drawn up by the Mining Joint Industrial Council to abolish separate categories of jobs for Europeans and Africans, and to have "one ladder of promotion depending only on competence and character," with the same rate of pay for all.[8] Eighty per cent of 4,700 members of the European Mine Workers' Union voted, and the majority in favor of the proposal was 580.[9] Although the majority is not large, it represents a substantial change in attitude, due, perhaps, to the realization of the European mine workers that they now have little actual choice in this matter.

As new categories in skilled and responsible jobs have opened to Africans, training for them has also become available. There were underground training schools to prepare candidates for blasting, as hoist and loco drivers, pipe-layers, and other such jobs. Today there are boss boy trainee courses and training for administrative and senior supervisory posts and for skilled technical work.[10] In 1961, two African personnel assistants from the mine township, as well as one European who was an African-personnel officer, were about to leave together for Britain to take a special course in personnel work.[11] But as of this writing, no Africans have reached positions of relatively high responsibility.

The Africans thought they were poorly and inadequately paid. The average earning of all African employees on all the mines on the Copperbelt (including the value of food provided) in 1954 was £123 and in 1960 £258, an increase of 209.7 per cent.[12] The average earnings of the European employees in 1954 were £1,734 and in 1960, £2,150, an increase of 118.2 per cent.[13] Another recent and slightly differently estimated account of the wages of African employees of the mines owned by the Rhodesian Selected Trust Company, which includes the Roan Antelope Mine, is "from about £22 to about £72 per month, and taking into account housing, welfare and money wages—that is, fringe benefits, the average African is estimated to be about three times better off in 1960 than in 1950 in terms of real income."[14] It is extremely difficult, if not impossible, for anyone unfamiliar with the technicalities of mining jobs to know the exact degree to which jobs done by Europeans and Africans are comparable. However, the general impression is that the pay for jobs done by Africans is only a fraction of that for comparable ones performed by Europeans. It is well known that this is a major point of tension.

Although the Africans knew their standard of living was improving and was decidedly higher than in rural and in other industrial areas, a deep bitterness underlay their complaints about wages. For the economic order of the Africans was not an entity of itself, but part of a biracial community in which the Africans were well aware of the big disparity between their earnings and those of the European workers. Evidence of the Europeans' much higher standard of living surrounded the Africans and typical comments were:

We like money as much as the Europeans. We and the Europeans come to the mine to seek our fortunes. We all need money. But we are paid very little and the Europeans get very much. Also, they discharge us from time to time. For example: Birds eat the fruit from a fig tree because they are hungry. Now it would not be right for one hungry bird to chase another hungry bird from the tree, so that he can eat all the fruit alone. This is not fair at all. Hunger is the same for all, and so those birds should be patient and eat the fruit together.

There are strikes sometimes against the injustices of the Europeans to Africans. We cannot be treated like dogs as they did in the past. They introduced trade unions and that makes us powerful. We are now fed up with the ill treatment. God gave us this land to live in. Europeans, too, were given their own country. They are very unfair, indeed.

It is not fair at all. We do a lot of work and yet we receive very little money and we are also poorly fed. Some Africans have been working for more than ten years, but cannot see what they have been working for because they have been given so little money. A European comes and works for only two years, and he grows rich and buys a car. An African can't buy a car even if he works for fifteen years. We want more money so that we can also buy cars and have money in the bank to start a business.

First, I was just a spanner boy giving spanners to the mechanic. I watched him when he was doing his work and I saw how he was using his tools and what kind of spanner he was using for every particular part, until I knew the work of every part of the engine and the use of all spanners. So one day I asked my boss to let me try and fix an engine. He unscrewed all the parts and let me put them together. I put them together all right and he recommended me as a mechanic. Now there is no part that I cannot fix. . . . But I get very little money. If I was a European, I would be getting very much money and be able to buy many things. You see our fathers who were first employed by Europeans were wrong in accepting anything they were given, and that is why we receive so little now. We must make demands from time to time to be given more.

The complaints of Africans about wages were intensified by anger at those European supervisors who constantly belittled and sometimes insulted them. As noted earlier, many Europeans regarded Africans as inferior beings, sometimes hardly human, "like monkeys down from the tree." The term "boy," in universal use toward African adults, was regarded by them as an insult. In a conversation between two Africans about the promised advancement, the idea that the invidious distinction between the terms *bwana* (master) and "boy" would be abolished was almost as important as the hoped for increase in wages.

FIRST MINER: The union officers said that all mine employees, both European and African, should have equal pay for the same kind of job. It is just a suggestion now, but later it will be taken to the Supreme Council for further discussion. There would be no boys or *bwanas* at work. Even a boss boy would not be called a boss boy.

SECOND MINER: This will happen to those not yet born.

Africans give the title *bwana* (formerly reserved only for white men) to their political leader, Mr. Kaunda.

One day, an African assistant, who was working in my house, answered the door when someone knocked and told me "two gentlemen" wanted to see me. I went to the door and found two African boys about ten years old who inquired if they could cut the grass.

My modern assistant had been so bedeviled by the term "boy" that he could not use the term, even when he knew it was appropriate.

In the past there were people of high and of low status, and the former commanded the services of others. But this was done in the structure of reciprocal obligations and with dignity. The African's strong sense of courtesy and his punctilious etiquette were observed by many early writers on this area, two of whom described him as a "polished gentlemen,"[15] and the relationship between this etiquette and the rather rigidly defined roles was noted earlier. The highly personalized insults of some European supervisors to Africans is in sharp contrast to the traditional impersonal formal etiquette which still persists in much of intra-African daily life. Even in the modern bureaucracies of the West, those in positions of command have learned that it is easier for employees to take impersonal orders than personal ones.

The hierarchy of labor in the mine township introduced radical changes from the homogeneity of tribal life, with its divisions based primarily on sex and age. Instead of an egalitarian standard of living, the kind of house and the amount of pay determined the worker's place in the hierarchy. But educated, skilled workers were separated from the uneducated and unskilled men not only by the nature of their work and the amount of money they earned, but also by the way they spent their money, by their values and goals, and by the image of their destiny. The new middle class and intelligentsia had expectations of a more cosmopolitan way of life dependent on an increasing participation in modern society. They often planned further education for themselves and a higher education for their children. Some of them were committed to saving money, to taking correspondence courses and to using leaves for returning to school. Although a boss boy earned as much as or more money than a member of the intelligentsia, he lived differently and did not have their social prestige. At the time of my study it was not necessary for him to know English or have any European education, although he had more responsibility and more pay than the other miners. (At the time of this writing Standard III is required.) The values and ways of life of the boss boy were the same as those of the other miners, except that he had more money to spend on beer, clothes, and luxuries.

Whether skilled or unskilled, everyone wanted money, as much as he could get, for clothes, food, beer, a bicycle, furniture, a watch, a radio, presents for kindred at home and payment of kinship obligations; some wanted it also for the education of their own children and for further training to advance their own careers. The new European goods displayed in the windows of the European and Indian shops were endlessly enticing, as were the popular mail-order catalogues from South Africa and England. Africans have always loved to show off, and in the past killing a lion or an enemy was the one way of doing it. Clothes are another way.

But the craving for clothes is not new. Richards, in her study of the rural Bemba about a quarter of a century ago, noted the constant talking about clothes, the intense interest in them, and the swaggering of booted and trousered young men in front of the young girls of the village. Cloth was valued in this area ever since it was introduced by Arab traders in the middle of the nineteenth century. Then, the exchange of slaves for bales of cloth was the chief's monopoly, and to wear cotton cloth instead of the indigenous bark cloth was a sign of royal favor. In the early thirties, clothes were also a "sign of distinction between the civilized men and the bush native."[16] Only a few tribes, such as the Ila, do not have this long history of intense interest in clothes. But for almost everyone on the mine township, male and female, clothes were of great importance, and new ones were a source of pleasure and prestige. They were a perennial subject for conversation and for boasting.

The following conversation between two miners was typical:

FIRST MINER: Mr. Banda ordered an overcoat from Oxindales [a mail-order house] at seven pounds, fifteen shillings. It is very wonderful, indeed.

HIS FRIEND: Ah!

FIRST MINER: Yes, there are three other kinds of overcoats in the Oxindale catalogue, but they are not good. The one which this man ordered is wonderful. In June [African winter] he will be wearing it to the beer hall, since he is a strong drinker, and people will all be looking at him. The coat is brown in color and has very long hair. If he wears it in town, policemen can be asking from where he got it. [Theft suspected.] The other day when he put it on, three Europeans asked him where he got it. Ah, it is wonderful.

HIS FRIEND: You will order one, I guess.

FIRST MINER: Yes, I must make sure that I get one. I shall order it
before I go home next time. People at home will just fall
off the chair when they see that coat. It is very wonderful!

Good clothes were an important distinction between village and
town people. A man who saw some poorly dressed boys passing by
said:

Do those boys have no fathers? Why are they in such ragged clothes,
just as if they were in the rural? Men get a lot of money here and should
buy proper clothes for their children.

If an unemployed man did not dress well, he was suspected either
of being a witch or of having no common sense. Only a witch or a fool
would dare to flout the strongly entrenched mores surrounding the
prestige of clothes. The conversation below occurred between a white-
collar worker, a miner's wife, and a boss boy:

MINER'S WIFE: That man, Ba Chivwa, does not wear good clothes.

WHITE-COLLAR   That is why he is suspected by some people of working
   WORKER: for magic.

MINER'S WIFE: But his wife has a lot of dresses.

BOSS BOY: That man is senseless. When he buys a shirt and a pair
of long trousers, he does not like to buy any more until
those he has bought are completely finished.

WHITE-COLLAR   He is no better than anyone in the village. That friend
   WORKER: of his, whom you call a Julias, looks the same, too.

BOSS BOY: Yes, he has a lot of patches on his clothes, too.

MINER'S WIFE: But a Julias has got a lot of monkey nuts [peanuts]
from his gardens in his house.

BOSS BOY: And he kills a lot of animals from the bush.

WHITE-COLLAR
   WORKER: On what do they spend their money?

BOSS BOY: They drink a lot of beer. Ba Chivwa drinks beer nearly
every day.

MINER'S WIFE: He only allows his wife to buy clothes and not himself.

BOSS BOY (*jokingly*):
Perhaps he fears to see Indians at the shops.

WHITE-COLLAR   They think that Indians will chase them away since they
WORKER: are very dirty. But Indians like anyone who has money.

BOSS BOY: Why don't they buy from these small shops here at the
                 mines or from the cooperative store. His wife is not
                 very reasonable.

WHITE-COLLAR
WORKER: Yes, that is true. The wife is not good.

MINER'S WIFE: If he were my husband and we went to a place where
                 there were many people, and if some of them asked me,
                 "Is that your husband with you?", I would answer that
                 my husband had remained behind and the man I am
                 with is not my husband. If I would say that he is my
                 husband, my friends would be laughing at me because
                 of his poor clothes and say that I had married a poor
                 husband.

The *nouveau riche* of any Western culture have more diversity in
showing off. In the United States, the latest model of a prestige car,
a professionally-decorated apartment at the "right address," as well
as expensive clothes are all significant. Because of the low standards
of living in Central Africa, clothes were generally the most important
means of display.

However, money was spent on many other things. Most kinship
obligations, from the still important bride-wealth to small services,
were commuted in terms of money. When relatives visited a miner,
he was usually "cleaned out" of any cash he had. The rationale was
that if he had not been working in the mine township, he would have
been in the village helping his kindred. The men on the township and
their wives grumbled to their friends, neighbors, and to me about
having to give money to visiting kin, but they did not even consider
withholding it. No African could imagine standing alone, separated
from the members of his extended family and his lineage.

Money for beer was also a drain on the wages of some Africans.
Almost everyone drank beer, some in moderation and others to get
drunk. The beer hall, under the jurisdiction of mine management and
selling only the commercially bottled beer, was a social center for the
community. But the heavy drinkers preferred the native beer, now
illegal, but brewed, as in the past, by women and sold and drunk in
their homes. Occasionally, there were raids by the mine police on

these homes; but neither the brewing nor the drinking stopped. Food was also an expense, but lessened by growing some of it in the gardens on the edge of the township. Taxes, oil for a lamp, and soap were among the smaller items; and blankets, a bed, a table and chairs, and other furniture, among the larger ones. If any money was left over, a bicycle, radio, and other luxuries were bought. Today, an occasional African owns a car.

When Africans stopped working for the mine, they lost the right of residence on the township; they could go to other mines, to non-mining towns, or return to their villages. In the decade between 1950 and 1960, the average length of employment for the African workers on the Copperbelt lengthened from two and three-quarter years to seven years. (For Europeans it is around eight years.) The African turnover rate is about 20 per cent per year, and the largest turnover is among the first- and second-year men, some of whom come and do not like working on the mine or are not good workers. The European annual turnover rate usually varies between 20 and 25 per cent.[17]

Mitchell, in his 1951 survey, attempted to get attitudes toward remaining in town or leaving it. He classified as labor migrants those who said they would go home "soon," "as soon as possible," or "as soon as wealthy"; and 58.5 per cent of the men on the township were in this category. He regarded as temporarily stabilized those who said they "will return home at some future date," "will stay, but will keep contact with the village," "will return home on retirement"; and this represented 35.2 per cent of the group. The category of permanent stabilization was given to those who said they "will always be on the Copperbelt" and those who were born and bred in town: "It is as if it is my village"; and this represented 6.3 per cent of the sample.[18]

There appeared to be a correlation between age and increasing stabilization. With the exception of men under thirty, born and brought up on the Copperbelt, it was the older men, who had spent ten to twenty or more years there, who tended to say that they would remain until they retired.[19] Mitchell's data represent what men thought they would do in the future and not what they actually did. Unfortunately, this has not been studied. In the decade since Mitchell's survey more African adults are in the group who have been born in town. It is probable, too, that the new opportunities for advancement into skilled and responsible jobs lengthens the time spent on the Copperbelt, and a new scheme for home ownership sponsored by mine and government creates the possibility of remaining there indefinitely.

The mine provides pensions of from £4 to £6 a month to which Africans are not required to contribute, for those who have reached the age of fifty and completed twenty years of employment. Long-service and retirement bonus are also paid. A voluntary savings scheme, in which more than 60 per cent participated, enables employees to save through payroll deductions.[20]

Thus when a man worked until he retired, he had his pension; and many who stopped earlier usually had some savings. The former worker frequently had relatives in his village, and many Africans still on the township mentioned that it would be good to die among them. But before that happened, he might return to the village and use his pension or savings to farm, sell fish, drive a bus, open a tea shop, or work as a tailor or carpenter if he knew one of these skills. If he decided to live in a town, he could engage in any of these occupations except farming, and he also had the possibility of owning and driving a taxi. The tendency was to want a work situation in which there would be no direct dependence on Europeans. To work for one's self and not to have a European boss was a new goal.

About 60 per cent of those we interviewed on this subject said they planned to go home upon retirement or when they thought they had accumulated enough money. Typical statements from this group were:

> When I am old I must do the work which will suit my age, like being a tailor. I shall stop work when I am growing weak and buy a sewing machine and go home to the rural and start business there. I will not wait until I am too old, as do some of the men I see here. I do not know what they work for. I want to go back home, because it is good to die there, where there are many relatives and they can bury me properly.

> When I leave the mine I shall go home and build a big house there, and live in a modern European way of life, and be an example to my people. I will buy a good number of cattle for use in ploughing my farm, and I shall be selling milk and skins from my cattle; also, the farming business will add to the example I shall try to set for my people at home.

> I shall not stay here for good, as I do not always want to be cursed by the white while at work. I want to go and make my own work, where I

can be an employer, too. I will use my savings for running a store which will go to my children and make good wealth for them.

After I have worked enough on the mine, I shall go back home to the rural and start ploughing. And I shall start making nets to kill fish. And I shall be looking after my mothers [real and classificatory]. Those who do not want to go back to the village came here with magic and so they fear to go back to their homes, where they have killed relatives.

The accusation of witchcraft was leveled at many who departed from the accepted norm, whether it was by refusing to spend their money for new clothes or by not returning to their villages.

Others did not plan to return to a village, and the following statements were typical of them:

I shall stay on the mines because this is my home, where I have lived for a long time. When I stop working, I will use my money for buying fish from the rivers, and then bring them to the mine to sell. After I will be rich enough from selling fish, I will set up a tea room here.

If I leave the work I shall not go anywhere else, because all the people of my family are town dwellers. So I will only stay on the mine, and buy a taxi-car, which will give me a little business while I am in this hard life.

The ambitions of teen-age boys (twelve to seventeen years) now in Standards V and VI (comparable to our seventh and eighth grades) in school on the mine township were relatively modest. To be a skilled worker (carpenter, mechanic, other building laborers, chauffeur) was the goal of 42 per cent of the boys. Thirty-five per cent of them wanted to be white-collar workers (teachers, clerks, medical orderlies, social workers, and religious functionaries). I was told that clerical jobs had been more popular in the past. Eleven per cent desired to be shop-keepers; another 11 per cent, farmers. No one wished to be a mine laborer or a domestic servant, and apparently none thought of becoming political leaders. Seventy-one per cent of the boys wanted to live only in urban communities.[21] As more people are born on mine townships or in other urban communities, a higher proportion of them will obviously become permanently urban.

A group of young men born on the Copperbelt, who had finished Standard VI and who were in their late teens or early twenties, had not yet settled down. They were in and out of employment, as drivers, attendants at gas stations, delivery boys for European shops, and in other miscellaneous jobs. Girls, radio, music, dancing, and sports filled their spare time. The Copperbelt was home to them, and they did not consider living in any other place. It is not possible to know what they will be like in another decade or two, but some of them will probably be interested in careers involving more skill and higher status.

In the past, ambitious men with some education tended to become teachers, clerks, civil servants, social workers, or to go into business. Many of the intelligentsia, particularly those over thirty, began their education in a rural mission school, continued it at a teacher-training school, and became teachers. I found many dedicated to their work. It was a pioneer job, with inadequate personnel, funds, and buildings. There was opportunity for advancement to principal or headmaster and, for a few, to supervisory work in the government education department. Many teachers, not so dedicated or more ambitious, left the school system and worked as clerks, welfare workers and in minor administrative posts, in all of which salaries were higher than those of teachers. Some government departments in Lusaka, particularly the Broadcasting and Publishing Division of the Information Department, employed Africans in creative posts, such as broadcasting to Africans and writing for them. (With the removal of the color bar from mine employment more young men with education and ambition will probably enter it.)

African organizations such as trade unions and cooperative societies offered opportunities for a few of the ambitious. The leaders in each were generally educated, and a few of the trade union leaders had spent a year in England learning about the labor movement. The African Cooperative Society, started in 1949 and sponsored by the government, gave training to its workers in the principles of cooperative societies, in bookkeeping, and in other aspects of commerce. Political participation, whether in African organizations or in the Northern Rhodesian and Federal Legislature, today was of interest to many of the intelligentsia, but could provide jobs for only a few leaders.

The following are a few examples of careerists on the mine township. Mr. Banda had a white-collar job in the African Personnel Department. Like that of most of the intelligentsia, his background included education in a mission school and teaching. After that he was active in two social movements, first as charter member and then as a organizer of the local African Cooperative Society, and later as an organizer of the African Mine Workers' Union and as an officer of its local branch. He was a representative to the African Representative Council and its delegate to London several times. He spoke excellent English and appeared to think in it: his speeches in the African Representative Council were noted for their logic and clarity. He spoke eloquently against federation, making the point that it would take away much of the status of Africans as "protected" people (i.e., protected by the Colonial Office) and, at the same time, would not give them parity with the feared European settlers.

I was told that in the past he had been very suspicious of and hostile to Europeans. A long and pleasant friendship with a district commissioner apparently reduced the suspicion and hostility, and he seemed even less suspicious than the average African. He was present when I spoke to a group of the intelligentsia, called together by an African Education Officer at the beginning of my field study. I was attempting to enlist their cooperation. One man talked at great length and asked me many questions, indicating much suspicion and implying that I might be an agent of the Federation. Mr. Banda, whom I had not met before, interrupted him, saying he was tired of listening to this man's long harangue and that one should not be suspicious of *all* Europeans.

Mr. Banda lived with his wife and two young children in one of the "special-group" houses and his wife graciously served tea to me when I visited them. The house was superior to most of those on the township, but inferior to that of a European of Mr. Banda's status. It appeared to be difficult for most Europeans on the mine or elsewhere in the protectorate to give adequate recognition to the new intelligentsia or fully to accept the fact that there is such a class. For instance, when Mr. Banda and eight other members of the African Representative Council flew to Lusaka for a conference with the Colonial Secretary, an open vanette was sent by the government to bring them in the pouring rain to the Secretariat. They were drenched. Mr. Banda described the incident with more irony than bitterness. He had an apparent knack of being able to cope emotionally with the lack of etiquette and of ordinary politeness from Europeans.

Other ambitious young men on the mine and in the municipal loca-

tion had goals directed to business. At the time of my study, eighteen
Africans from the municipal location, each with the necessary capital
of £500, had applied for permission to the Luanshya Municipal
Board for sites on which to open shops: grocery store, butcher shop,
bakery, tea room, and laundry. The leader of this group of would-be
business men, Mr. Soko, in his early thirties, had an intelligent face
and was always well dressed, his tweed jacket, trousers, shirt, and tie
being in excellent taste.

Mr. Soko attended a mission school and was trained for hospital
work, after which he was a medical orderly in a hospital. Then he
moved to Luanshya, became a building worker and at one time
worked for the Building Workers' Union. At the time of my study he
was employed by a European contractor to teach bricklaying to
Africans and to be a foreman over them. He participated in civic and
political affairs, served on the African Affairs Committee of the
Luanshya Municipal Board (composed of Africans and Europeans
under the chairmanship of the district commissioner), was a member
of the Urban Advisory Council and its representative on the Provincial
Council.

He was married, had two children, and was assisting two brothers
and two sisters, one of whom was living with him. He also helped his
parents, who lived in a Nyasaland village. When he gets the site for
his shop, he did not plan to give up his present job; his wife and
brother would run the shop, and in the beginning an uncle, who has
a shop in nearby Mufilira, would come over and help. Mr. Soko will
take care of the accounts in his spare time.

He had friendly relations with the district commissioner, a missionary, some Europeans in the Master Builders' Association, and particularly with his employer who, he said, had been very helpful to him.
He thought it very important for Africans to become educated and
enter professions, such as law or medicine; he would have liked to
have become a physician. He believed that when Africans advance,
they should live peacefullly side by side with the Europeans and said,
"It would not be right to make the Europeans leave after you have
learned so much from them." But he was very resentful of his low
salary and remarked that he saw Europeans, who knew no more than
he, earning £100; fingering the skin on his hand, he said, "It is just

because of the color of my skin, that I get only twenty-five or thirty pounds."

There were other Africans ambitious to move upward economically, but with lesser goals. Many of these were taking correspondence courses, which they hoped would eventually lead to matriculation. One young man with a Standard VIII education, working in the Sanitation Department, was studying to be an accountant. He had three more years of the correspondence course ahead of him, at the end of which he thought there was more chance of employment by an Indian merchant than by a European. He was not politically active but read the *Northern News,* a daily published for Europeans.

All the Africans in this community, educated and uneducated, skilled and unskilled, manual laborers and the intelligentsia, lived in an almost completely intra-African society, mingling with peoples of many different tribes. It was my strong impression that many had relatives on the mine, but unfortunately there is no quantitative data on this point. But it was clear that many small groups of face-to-face relationships existed and that the social controls exercised by them were not missing. Workmates, neighbors, friends, and relatives were in close and frequent contact. They discussed the latest news and gossip, boasted about new clothes or other possessions, borrowed money from each other, advised one another on personal problems, and drank and played together.

Ties with relatives in the village also persisted. Miners and their wives spent leaves in the village, and relatives came to see them. Letters also went back and forth between township and village; the literate wrote and read for the illiterate. One of the most popular parts of the radio program was a request program, *(Zimene Mwatifunsa),* in which listeners sent messages to distant relatives, accompanied by their favorite musical record.

African life on the mine was not confined completely to its township. The municipality, with its shops, the Boma, the Urban Court, and other places of interest, was within walking or cycling distance. Relations between Europeans and Africans there ran the same gamut as on the mine township. Africans could go into the Post Office and banks, but had to use separate entrances and windows in each. But they could not even enter most of the shops. The local Chamber of

Commerce had declared that Africans could go into shops, but they were unable to control the actions of individual shopkeepers. At the time of my study Africans had to do their shopping in most European stores through a "hatch," a small square window at the back of the store. Here they lined up, pushing and struggling with each other to get to the hole in the wall; many were not shopping for themselves, but were servants of Europeans with their daily orders. The chemist's shop (drug store) had no hatch and Africans had to line up outside the entrance and hand their prescriptions or give their other requests to a clerk who came outside. Africans were exceedingly bitter about the segregation in shops: "Is this what they mean by partnership?" asked many of them. One member of the intelligentsia commented bitterly about having to stand an hour and a half in the line at the drug store to get medicine for his sick wife. Of course, all white customers, regardless of their time of arrival, were served before any African. In 1960, the hatch and other forms of segregation in shops and all public places, including restaurants and movie houses, were legally forbidden in Northern Rhodesia. But the legacy of frustration and hostility from the recent former practices remain.

A new world for the Africans, indeed! The new economic order, essentially urban with its wage labor and increasing differentiation of work, dominated the social scene. Europeans were part of the same economic order, but there was an absence of social relations with them. Many of the Europeans with whom African miners had contact on the job appeared to be ignorant of all the niceties of etiquette, so important to Africans, and gave them little respect, regardless of their age, sex, or social position. But there were compensations in this new world: there was money and the things it would buy; management was advancing Africans into more responsible and highly paid jobs, and there were opportunities for individual careers; there was a pension and a savings system; a union looked after the interests of Africans; a welfare department provided new leisure activities such as sports, radio, movies, clubs, classes for adults; management also gave medical services in a hospital and clinics. The African Mine Workers' Union and the Mine Welfare Department, each in its own way, were sources for some of the compensations and both played important roles on the township. They are described in the next chapter.

After working hours: a convivial scene near the beer hall.

of the large ant hills
h dominate the land-
:, and on which children
o play.

Two miners returning home after the day's shift of work is finished.

This brightly dressed woman is carrying her baby and her bundles in traditional and typical manner.

The open-air market is a sociable place, primarily for selling and buying food. It also has a small book stall.

Neighbors and friends often cook the evening meal together outdoors.

7. Two Faces of Security and Authority: Welfare Work and the Union

THE COMPOSITE NATURE of the symbolism of the African Mine Workers' Union and management, as represented by its Welfare Department, is illustrated by an incident which occurred at the beginning of my field work. With the help of African assistants, I made a survey of the use of the mass media and of attitudes toward it. Several of the assistants had an initial difficulty in getting some people to consent to be interviewed, even though they carefully explained the innocuous nature of what they were doing. A number of the prospective interviewees remarked that they would cooperate if they heard the study announced over the loudspeaker of the main Welfare Hall by either a union official or an African welfare worker, who was, of course, an employee of management. The sponsorship of either one was apparently equally good. It was quicker and simpler to arrange to have the announcement made by the African welfare worker, and he did it several times in succession when the amphitheatre was filled to capacity with a movie audience. Interviewing proceeded without opposition afterward. Incidentally, the same amphitheatre was used for union meetings.

The social cohesion or "unitary" structure of the mine township has been noted by Epstein.[1] He stresses the self-contained aspects—industrial, residential, and administrative—of the community and the way the mine impinged on the Africans' life at every point. He points out further that the union, developing within this structure, had also taken on some unitary characteristics and was asked by members to take up problems outside the usual scope of a trade union. Epstein contends that "within the 'unitary' structure of the mine, Union and Management, represented by the African Personnel Department, occupy positions which are, in a sense, structurally equivalent though opposed."[2] But while the two organizations might be structurally opposed, particularly from a Western point of view of labor-management relations, they were not necessarily psychologically opposed in the Africans' imagery. At the time of a strike, management is the enemy and the union is the protector, but much of the time the Africans' imagery of mine management had many benevolent characteristics. The incident quoted at the beginning of the chapter illustrates the composite nature and, to some degree, the interchangeability of the union and management as a benevolent authority symbols.[3]

The benevolent aspects of management in the Africans' image were due, of course, to the management's paternalistic policies. Although Africans complained bitterly about the large discrepancy between their wages and those of the Europeans mine employees, yet most of them knew that Roan Antelope Mines had taken the initiative in advancing Africans to more highly paid and more responsible jobs and that their wages were better than comparable wages in other Rhodesian manufacturing employment. The Africans on the mine townships were well aware, too, of their higher economic standards of living as compared to that of the rural villages. But the Africans' image of management was not limited to its economic policy. Management provided a way of life and many social amenities through its Welfare Department, under the leadership of its able welfare officer, Mr. Robert Howie, who had several African assistants and two European "lady welfare officers." By 1958, he had a European male assistant and thirteen African male asssitants at the main center, and at the sub-centers there were five full-time and twelve part-time African employees.[4] The main center housed an office for the staff, a tea room, recently grown to a restaurant, a movie amphitheatre, a radio with loudspeaker, a reading room, which served also as a writing room, where an African assistant helped the illiterate write letters and address parcels. Nearby was a hobbies building, where carpentry work was done. Smaller buildings in different sections of the township were centers for many other activities: literacy classes, day nurseries for preschool children; classes for women in cooking, sewing, knitting, nutrition, and infant care; girl's clubs; and other social and educational pursuits. Dances were held on Saturday nights at the large and small centers. Perhaps the most popular activity of all was sports, particularly football, track, and high jumping.

The football eleven played teams from the Copperbelt and other parts of Central Africa at the mine stadium and also traveled to other towns for games. These always drew large and interested audiences of men, women, and children. For the players the games were an exciting and important part of their life and provided satisfactions other than the fun of the sport. It was an occasion for showing off; often a player pirouetted with the ball, with an obvious eye to the impression he was making on the audience, particularly the females in it. As one young man said, "If you happen to play well, you may have sex relations with six girls on the same day, because girls like one who plays well." The intertown games provided also an occasion for making new friends, on whom the player could rely for hospitality if later he went to their town. A member of the team said, "I like football because through it you can easily be known and make friends in a short time. Then you will have a place to stay, if you go to Ndola or some other town where you have no relatives."

Football games and athletic meets were among the few occasions for cordial relations between the two races. Young European men in administrative positions on the mine volunteered to coach the African teams, and playing the game well was more important than racial differences. In the office of the Welfare Center were several large posters of "Commonwealth Sportsmen," each portraying two fine-looking athletes, one European and one African. At any major athletic event for Africans, management was always well represented. The seating arrangement was segregated, but Europeans and Africans were at least enjoying the same event, which was unusual. When the Central African Olympics were held sometime ago at the mine stadium, there was an unsegregated tea party for the athletes and top European personnel. In reminiscing about it, one of the Europeans mentioned how much he had enjoyed this novel occasion—

the first time he had ever sat down with an African and had a cup of tea. Everywhere, common participation in sports, whether as participants or in an audience, tends to weaken tensions between peoples of different races and nations.

Some European men in administrative posts below the top level were volunteer teachers of English to Africans in evening courses. The role of these Europeans was similar to that of the early missionaries, giving the "secrets" of modern civilization to Africans. The course was a valuable learning process for teachers as well as for Africans, and provided one of the few opportunities for Africans and Europeans to meet outside of the relationship of worker and boss. From this point of view it was, therefore, superior to the government-run classes with African teachers. One hundred and fifty adults regularly attended night classes run by mine and government in 1954. Four years later the attendance was 709.[5]

Many educational, social, and athletic activities are increasingly being carried on through clubs, under the direction of African welfare assistants. The African movie amphitheatre was another popular feature of the welfare department, which also provided loudspeakers in its centers for listening to the radio. (The impact of radio and movies is discussed in a later section on leisure.) A newspaper, *The African Roan Antelope,* was published by management (but not under the auspices of the Welfare Department) for its African employees; and it, too, is discussed in a later chapter.

I did no special study of the African clinics and hospital provided by management. But it was apparent that the Africans went to both readily, even though they used their own medicines and magic to cure illness. If one failed, the other might work. The prenatal clinics were popular with young mothers, and the medical facilities in general were much appreciated. From 1938 to 1958 hospital attendance for African employees of Roan Antelope increased from about three thousand to fifteen thousand and the mortality rate during the same period decreased from 5 per one hundred to 1.5 per hundred.[6] Medical services were run by the companies and were free to employees. A contribution toward the maintenance of the clinics was made by the government. On the hospital staff were European doctors, nursing sisters, male nurses, and trained African orderlies and nursing assistants as well as trainees. Clinics were situated in different parts of the township and were visited regularly by doctors and staffed with European sisters and trained Africans, including midwives.[7]

Welfare activities for women at the time of my study were not as successful as for men for a number of reasons: activities for women were started later; African women on the Copperbelt were more conservative than men; it was difficult to find able African female assistants; the European "lady welfare officers" were not as knowledgeable, understanding, and sympathetic to Africans as was the male European welfare officer. The womens' classes had periodic demonstrations of their work in cooking, sewing, knitting, and other homecraft, when prizes or certificates were given for the best work. Wives of top-level mine officials were invited to judge the work. At one such exhibition of handiwork from a sewing and knitting class, there were about seventy-five Africans present—the pupils, their children, their friends, and a few husbands—and about fifteen European women. The Europeans were asked by the "lady welfare officer" to look at the work laid out on tables inside the Welfare Center, and then they were served tea and cake as they sat on comfortable chairs in the exhibition room. Outside were the Africans, some sitting on an inadequate number of benches provided for them, others sitting on the grass, or just standing around. They had nothing at all to do while the Europeans were seeing the show and having their tea. Later, the Africans were invited into the Center to see the handicraft and were then served bottled soft drinks. Certificates of merit were awarded by the wife of a senior mine official.

The comments of the Africans were resentful and mocking. Three women sitting on the benches outside talked:

FIRST WOMAN: Look! These Europeans are foolish. They have invited us for the show, but are sitting away from us and drinking tea themselves without giving us some. Why have they invited us?

SECOND WOMAN: Hah! What would happen if we used the same cups that these Europeans are using? Would we leave our black skins in their cups?

THIRD WOMAN: I imagine they think that we don't drink tea in our homes. We sometimes drink more tea in our homes and have better cups than these. Don't they see Africans buying tea cups and tea sets in their stores?

The value of the certificates awarded was not plain. A friend of one of the competitors in the exhibition laughed cynically when the certificates were given and said to the woman next to her:

Look at our friends. They were telling us that at the show there would be given money prizes. Alas, they have not been given even a farthing. The winners are given only pieces of paper which have no use at all and will only be torn by the children. If they were not given money, it would have been nicer if they would have been given needles and cotton. These women are no better than we, who do not go to classes.

The men, whose wives were exhibiting work, talked to each other:

FIRST MAN (*as he sees the Europeans entering the show room*):
    Why is it that they put the things inside where we cannot see them? We husbands would like to look at the things and see what the women do, because they spend a lot of time here and neglect some duties at home.

SECOND MAN: If I do not have the chance of seeing what my wife does, I won't allow her to come to welfare classes.

FIRST MAN: We won't be given a chance at seeing. Why have they not invited us inside? We are here as intruders. These people have no regard for us. They invite a number of their fellow Europeans and no black people. Is it because they think we have no interest in what our wives do?

SECOND MAN: It is difficult to understand why these Europeans should think so. After all, these things have been done by Africans and not by Europeans.

The "lady welfare officer," rather new on the job, seemed more interested in impressing the wives of the mine officials than in making any friendly communication with the Africans. The European women visitors appeared to be similar to the "Lady Bountiful" type. They lacked the spontaneous, friendly interest of the European men who coached the football players or taught English to the miners. A missionary who conducted classes in homecraft for African women said she was embarrassed by the patronizing attitude of some European women who wanted to help her. One, who visited her class, exclaimed in a surprised tone and in a voice loud enough to be heard by all the members, "Oh, they are clean!" Since contacts between black and white women were extremely limited, those that did occur took on an out-of-proportion significance. (The position of African women is discussed in detail in a later chapter).

Welfare work with children was more successful and recently has been carried on through day nurseries, which cared for children who were awaiting admission to the overcrowded local government schools. (Educational facilities on the Copperbelt and in the Territory of Northern Rhodesia are discussed in a later chapter). The official age range of the boys and girls was from five to twelve, but some older girls who brought their little sisters and who did not like being illiterate joined the group. The subjects taught were the three R's, scripture, and hygiene. In 1958 the enrollment varied between 360 and 720, and when they were tested, over 200 were accepted for the second year in the township schools. Recently the Welfare Department has organized clubs for girls who have left school between Standards IV and VI (corresponding to our seventh and eighth grades) and who have nothing to do with their time. The main activities of the clubs were handicraft and recreation; netball and swimming were particularly popular.[8] In tribal society these girls would have been busy helping their mothers in the fields, in the preparation of food, in taking care of younger siblings, and in participating in the dances and all the other village activities. In the township there was the customary urban separation between activities of adolescents and adults.

All reports note the continued growth of the welfare work. Athletics remain important. The adult education center and the number of clubs as well as their activities expands. The work with women may have matured and improved, but this can not be determined from reports. The director of welfare work is also chairman of the Northern Rhodesian Youth Council and works in many ways to encourage youth leadership. Two trainees in this work, one African and the other European, were sent abroad to take part in a Commonwealth Youth Council meeting.

Much of the welfare work was taken for granted by the Africans, and they did not talk about it nearly as much as they talked about their grievances over pay or indignities suffered from supervisors. Most people talked more about their troubles in life than their satisfactions, but many of the Africans would have felt lost without the activities offered by the Welfare Department. Although teen-age school boys did not want to be miners, they wanted town jobs (skilled and white-collar work) where they could enjoy the modern recreational and other social amenities of the mine township.[9]

Management, through the activities of its Welfare Department, was obviously playing an important role in the induction of Africans into Western culture. Although differently motivated, the functions of some of the activities of Management were similar to the earlier work of missionaries and civil servants. The Africans' image of these Europeans of a half century or so ago had been two-sided: benevolent fathers leading them into a new and better world, and cannibals eager to devour them. Management likewise has two faces: one advances Africans into better-paid and more responsible jobs over the opposition of European employees, provides excellent medical facilities and adult education classes, and offers many enjoyable recreational opportunities; the other devours their work without giving them adequate pay, and employs some supervisors who are insulting and who treat Africans as if they were "monkeys down from the tree." Even with the two faces, the image of management was much more favorable than that of government, as represented by the Federation political officials, who were considered responsible for bringing the Federation into being and maintaining it. This group, headed by the Prime Minister, had only one aspect for the Africans: that of the enemy. But the advantages of the new economic order represented by the mine were apparent to all Africans.

Some of these advantages have been obtained through the African Mine Workers' Union, in existence since 1949 and a symbol for security and authority, not only for its members, but also for most Africans on the Copperbelt. Preceding the union, the African's first role in the administration of the mine township was created by the Europeans in 1931, when the compound manager (now known as African personnel manager) introduced a system in which tribal elders, elected by members of their respective tribes on the mine, represented the interests of the workers and handled their complaints.[10] The choice of tribal elders was in accord with traditional practice, in which leadership was the prerogative of the old, and was also in keeping with the British colonial policy of indirect rule. The prevailing European view at that time was to regard the African worker on the mine as a tribesman living temporarily on the mine township.

But the traditional wisdom of the elders, based on their knowledge of the soil, of magic, of tribal customs, and of rituals, was of little use and offered no precedents for the new problems which arose in the mine community. In the disturbances and a strike on the Copperbelt in 1935, the elders lost control and were regarded by some Africans as agents of the Europeans. But after the disturbances the elders partially regained their former status, and no other group of leaders arose to challenge them then. However, in 1942, a Boss Boys' Committee was formed to discuss grievances with the compound manager. About the same time welfare societies, an early feature of African urban life, began to function more actively. Although their membership included some tribal elders, the more active members were younger men with European education, many of them school teachers, some of whom later became leading political figures in the Territory. The Welfare Society was neither official or political but exercised influence on local problems such as the quality of maize sold in the stores and the making of a road between the municipal location and the mine.

In this period the urban advisory councils were created by the government to work on social problems with district commissioners. African representatives from the mine compound and the municipal location were on the council. In the beginning most of the members were tribal elders, but by 1944 there was a high proportion of young English-speaking members: clerks, teachers, and medical orderlies.

In the meantime the tribal elders had been reorganized as tribal representatives and the Government Labor Officer had instructed them in the presentation of workers' cases to management or government. But their power was short-lived. In 1947 the British Labour Party, then in power, sent a representative to Northern Rhodesia to help Africans organize in trade unions. Two years later there were branches of mine workers' unions on the Copperbelt, which amalgamated to form the present African Mine Workers' Union. However, the tribal representatives (or elders) were still part of the administrative machinery, and there was much rivalry between them and the union executives over the division of their respective spheres of authority. At the union's request a vote was taken under government supervision to determine the wishes of the mine employees on who should represent them. Approximately 85 per cent of the workers voted, and of these almost 97 per cent voted against the retention of tribal representatives. The Africans clearly thought that their interests as industrial workers cut across tribal affiliations. This was a revolutionary change in the power structure. But tribe is still important as a point of reference in placing an individual. "What is his tribe?" is often the first question asked about a stranger. Tribal affiliation and tribal rivalries play a role in union leadership, in intra-African politics and in many other aspects of life. But on the mine township, leadership shifted to the trade union officials, usually young men with European education and with some knowledge of modern industrial problems.

However, as late as 1958, some representatives of management were still treating visiting chiefs and other tribal dignitaries not only with respect, but with courtesies not given to African trade union or political leaders. Mr. Wina, a former *Ngambela,* or prime minister, of Barotseland visited his nephew, who was a male-nurse instructor. Although the visit was a private one, Mr. Wina was asked to stay at the mine guest house, usually reserved for European guests, and was shown many other courtesies.

Mr. Wina's letter of thanks to the mine's paper for African employees follows:

It is with great pleasure that I am given the opportunity of saying something in your paper before I leave.

I have been exceptionally impressed by the welcome I have received from Mr. Cook and his friends. It is something I did not expect, being on a private visit to my nephew who is employed by the Mine. Indeed, I owe Mr. Cook a great debt and also Mr. Manson who introduced me to him. You have given me a wonderful time which I will not forget.

I have enjoyed my visit here and been impressed with what I have seen. The Africans are given good houses with lights and they get their water nearby. Their latrines are kept very clean indeed, and I am sure they are a happy lot. All these things made me come to the conclusion that Roan Antelope Company has got the welfare of its African employees at heart.

I have visited several places here, and at each place I have been impressed with what I have seen, and the facilities given to the Africans at work and at home are very encouraging. They have got a wonderful hospital, very clean and patients seem to be very well looked after.

I am grateful for what I have seen and really impressed by the kindness of the people of Roan Antelope Mine, first of its kind I think since my arrival on the Copperbelt, of which I will tell people at home when I arrive in Barotseland in two weeks time.

Lastly, my advice to you all is this: Respect your employers, you have left your homes and these people are now your fathers, cooperate with them and always receive their advices with both hands.

I wish you all everlasting happiness in your every undertaking.

Good-bye,

NAMAKANDO WINA[11]

The incident indicates that this African chief and the European mine administrator who issued the invitation probably wished for the "good old days." But there were others, African and European, who were trying to usher in new days. In the same newspaper two years later there was a sympathetic profile story and picture of the chairman of the local African Mine Workers' Union.[12] He was described as believing passionately in the trade union movement, but having a full sense of responsibility. In the interview he criticized management for the communal lavatory system (which had been praised by the chief) and for the smallness of the houses; he gave praise for the welfare services, mentioning particularly the medical facilities and the Adult Education Center. The publication of a profile of a trade union leader marked a long step from an earlier period when the union was not mentioned in this paper, except possibly at the time of a strike and then unfavorably, and when management never publicly acknowledged the responsible behavior of a trade union official to Africans.

Membership in the union was voluntary, since the mining companies have not conceded the principle of a closed shop. When the union was first organized, the check-off of dues was done by management and handed over to the union. In 1953 management discontinued collecting them. But in 1958 the union again won the right to the check-off system by management. The membership varies: at the beginning of the union's existence, membership was estimated as between 70 and 80 per cent of the total labor force; in 1954, it had fallen to 22 per cent;[13] in 1961, the proportion in the union for the Copperbelt was approximately 50 per cent[14] and about 45 per cent for the Roan branch, that is, 3,150 out of 7,000.[15] According to Epstein's study, those members with higher wages and with longer periods of service on the mine apparently tended to seek protection of their interests through the union more than did those in the lower groups, in which the highest rate of labor turnover occurred.[16]

The union was originally an industrial one, taking in all workers—skilled, unskilled, clerks, hospital orderlies, and all other African employees. In 1953 the white-collar workers negotiated for separation from the parent group, because they regarded their status and their problems as quite different from those of the manual workers. The subsequent formation of the African Staff Workers' Association, in 1954, with a membership of approximately 100 was a blow to the egalitarianism of the industrial union and a recognition of the growing social and economic distinctions between Africans. As of 1961, the membership of the Staff Workers' Association was 284.[17] The mine policemen have their own association, with a membership, in 1961, of 119, almost 100 per cent.[18]

But in spite of the formation of the Staff Workers' Association, the African Mine Workers' Union remained a powerful organization. Its meetings were held about once a month, in an open amphitheatre used for movies and attached to the Welfare Center; the union office was in a small building also donated by management. The meetings were open to the public, to non-members as well as members; and some women occasionally went to them. In conversations and in interviews with women as well as with men, with members and with non-members, it was obvious that they all regarded the union as an institution intimately related to their general welfare, which included such matters as the brewing of illicit beer and the employment of "proper" women welfare workers by management. During a one-week strike which occurred during my study, everyone, members and non-members, white-collar and manual workers, stopped work. The union leaders counseled all to be peaceful and not to engage in fights or in any other violence. The orders were completely obeyed and the township was far more peaceful during the strike than ordinarily.

Some of the traditional respect and obedience accorded to chiefs and tribal elders is given to the young trade union leaders. They have responsibilities for the welfare of the miners, as the chiefs had for their subjects. But the miners have indicated on many occasions that they are not passive subjects, that they think for themselves and, occasionally, even differ from their leaders. Disapproval of officers' views may be expressed at meetings as well as privately, and it has been reported that speakers have occasionally been howled down at meetings.

Both the union and management represent authority. At the time of a dispute or a strike, the union is the protector and management is the enemy. But when miners complained about their low wages, particularly in comparison with the earnings of Europeans, the blame seemed to fall on a rather generalized picture of unfair Europeans. A distinction was also made between top-level management and Europeans on lower levels in the hierarchy; and these status-conscious Africans usually preferred the former. There were even some few occasions when it was believed that management was handling the interests of the Africans better than their union. This occurred when the union officials, angry and frustrated over an incident in their dealings with management, ordered their members to withdraw their savings from the Savings Fund, a voluntary savings plan instituted by management. Many miners individually refused because they had little confidence in their ability not to squander or lose the accumulated savings if withdrawn, and they trusted the company to hold them. The following conversation between two miners gave their point of view:

FIRST MINER: I heard that Mr. Katilungu wants the Mine Bank to give all the savings straight away back to the Africans.

SECOND MINER: That is not a good idea. How can people keep their money in the house?

FIRST MINER: It is not a wise plan at all, because most of us will lose it quickly. The mine is doing a good thing by keeping the money for us. I do not like this idea of getting the money from the Mine Bank and then keeping it ourselves or putting it in other banks. We Africans cannot keep money by ourselves. If we get the money in our hands, we will not think of taking it back to a bank. Many people drink a lot, and they would spend it all on beer.

SECOND MINER: Some people might get a hundred pounds, or even a thousand pounds, and when they get all that money they will think that it will never finish. A lot of people become bankrupt after they take their money to go on leave or if they are discharged. Then they have no place to go. Some of them are here at Kamalasha [the name of a nearby hamlet where charcoal is made]. Also there are a lot of thieves around who can steal your money. Yes, I have a concrete example: There was Jim who sold mealie-meal and had a lot of money. Someone stole nine pounds from him, and he never got it back.

FIRST MINER: If I had been at the meeting [of the Union] I would have opposed the taking of the money from the Mine Bank.

Obviously there were both similarities and differences in the labor problems on the Copperbelt compared with those in other industrial communities. There were conflicts between employer and employees and between whites and blacks on the mine; the two conflicts were often intertwined, producing a three-sided situation. When white workers resisted the policy of management for advancement of Africans, management was aligned with one group of workers against another group; and from another point of view, upper-class Europeans and African workers were joined together against lower-class Europeans.

The two symbols of authority and security—the union and the welfare work of management—are not static, but respond to the changing economic, social, and political situation. As noted in Chapter 6, new opportunities in the skilled job categories have been steadily increasing since 1955, and it is possible that the African Staff Workers' Association might therefore become more important. But it is probable that the African Mine Workers' Union will remain significant economically and politically in the foreseeable future. In 1953, approximately 74 per cent of African employment on the Copperbelt was in the lowest three categories, while in 1960 the percentage had been reduced to about 60.[19] It is generally recognized that the gang system used in these low categories is inefficient, and the tendency is to move away from it by granting higher wages. This could mean a reduction in the number of African employees and, as Africans move up into more skilled jobs, a similar reduction of Europeans in their lower groups. It might likewise be predicted, on the basis of similar situations in other countries, that the social as well as economic distance will diminish between members of the two races holding skilled and responsible jobs.

As an indication of such a trend, in 1960 a study course on industrial relations organized by the Labor Department for the Copperbelt was attended by twenty-five Africans and Europeans, representing the Africans Mine Workers' Trade Union, the African Staff Workers' Association, and the mine personnel departments. Representing this mine community was the branch secretary of the African Mine Workers' Trade Union, two European members of the African Personnel Department, and the labor officer.[20] This course provided a new kind of communication between Europeans and African leaders on the mine. Members of the two races were together learning some of the "secrets" of industrial relations.

There is still the problem of narrowing the gap between the attitudes of management toward Africans and the attitudes of many European supervisors, who are in direct contact with African employees. Some of these supervisors remain from an earlier period and resist any fundamental change. They are, in part, responsible for the continuation of the duality (benevolent father and cannibal) of the Africans' image of Europeans on the Copperbelt. It has already been noted that lectures on the Africans' background and on biracial problems do not *make* people just, dignified, and unbigoted. These character traits were lacking in many of the European personnel, some quite high and others low in status, at the time of my study.

The selection of the proper kind of European personnel becomes particularly important in view of the changing attitude of management. The new policy is away from the past benevolent paternalism and toward a gradual shifting of responsibility to Africans. This is happening in the work of the welfare department, in the management of the township, in the increasing emphasis on education, and, probably quite soon, in political activities.[21] The new policy fits into the general trend of Africans assuming more responsibility for their own welfare. However, it is highly probable that the union and management will both remain strong symbols for security and authority on the Copperbelt in the foreseeable future.

In the next chapter, some of the many complex attitudes toward union and management are revealed in the recorded conversations of Africans during a strike.

8. A Strike[1]

THE STRIKE lasted only five days; and as strikes go, it was unimportant. But the recorded conversations are given at considerable length because they illustrate a number of significant points discussed in the preceding chapters: the self-imagery of Africans and their imagery of Europeans; the diverse attitudes to union leaders, to supervisors, and to management; the importance of the hospital for Africans; the security of having villages to return to if fired. The conversations are also of interest because they reveal nuances of life on the Copperbelt at the time of this study, many of which remain or underlie attitudes of today and, probably, of tomorrow.

The strike was called by a newly elected chairman of the local branch of the African Workers' Union, who was very different from most of the union officers, usually young clerks with no experience underground or in any other manual work on the mine. At the time of his election, the new chairman was a boss boy and a representative of the underground workers on the union executive committee. He had no formal European education, and he had only a slight command of English. In his youth he had been a fine football player, and he was now chairman of the Football Club. His reputation for belligerence and for being unafraid of Europeans was reported to have been influential in his election. It was regarded as a triumph of manual workers over former officers, white-collar workers, who had sometimes been accused of being too conciliatory in negotiations with management. The pick-and-shovel workers seemed to have thought that the educated clerks identified more with the Europeans than was apparently the case.

The new chairman called the strike almost immediately after his election, and some of the intelligentsia said he was showing off, which could have had some relationship to the tribal tradition of a chief raiding another tribe on his ascension to power. However, the reason the chairman gave for the strike was the alleged dismissal of two African workers without cause, and he demanded the discharge of the European supervisor who had fired them. But the request for the summary discharge of a European supervisor did not come within the union's contract; moreover, the chairman did not use the regular channels for the handling of disputes. The president of the African Mine Workers' Union for the entire Copperbelt, young and European educated, was apparently not informed of the strike in advance; but he supported it after it was called. Probably, due to his influence, the official cause of the strike was changed after a few days to a grievance that the general manager had not seen the trade union committee promptly and within the contractual limit of days.

The recorded conversations occurred among miners, boss boys, clerks, and other white-collar workers and their wives. On the day before the strike was called, Mr. Mhango and his wife Mary were discussing the troubled situation with Mr. Sichinga, a neighbor and workmate. Mr. Mhango, a large, attractive-looking man in his thirties, born in the rural area, had never been to school and was illiterate. He came to the Copperbelt in 1942 and had progressed to being a boss boy. His thinking and attitudes were traditional-oriented. Mary, his wife, belonging to a different but related tribe, was a shapely, attractive-looking woman in her twenties and had been born in the rural area. Like her husband, she had no European education, was illiterate and was traditional-oriented. Mr. Sichinga, a workmate and friend, was in his thirties and had had a few years of elementary education.

PATSON SICHINGA: I have come to hear what you heard from the Compound Office yesterday.

JAMES MHANGO: Hm! There was trouble there. All the local trade
                 union leaders were there and the new chairman.
                 Some of the boss boys like myself were sent to listen.
                 One of the trade union leaders said: "We have
                 come here to inform you that we are going on strike,
                 if this European, Mr. Jones, isn't discharged from
                 work, because he is discharging a lot of Africans
                 for no special reasons. We want you to do one of
                 two things: Either you discharge him, or you send
                 him to work where there are no Africans."

PATSON SICHINGA: That means discharge, because there is no place
                 where Africans are not found working.

JAMES MHANGO: The manager, not really the manager, but head of
                 African Personnel Department, answered: "I have
                 no power to discharge any European. The general
                 manager is not here. He has gone to Kitwe for a
                 meeting and will return this evening." The trade
                 union leaders replied, "If this European is not dis-
                 charged tomorrow, we shall go on strike. He has
                 discharged a lot of Africans. He must either be
                 discharged, or work alone with his fellow Euro-
                 peans."

PATSON SICHINGA: Ah, that is impossible.

JAMES MHANGO: The manager grew very timid, because of the way
                 the trade union leaders spoke, and he said, "Please,
                 I beg of you, I have no power to discharge this man
                 from work. We cannot discuss it until the general
                 manager comes from Kitwe. I shall tell him about
                 this matter, and we shall meet again tomorrow. I
                 know something will be done. You come again
                 tomorrow."

PATSON SICHINGA: Was the European, Mr. Jones [the man they want
                 discharged], there?

JAMES MHANGO: He was there and he looked very sick.

PATSON SICHINGA: He will now learn a lesson. He will go back to Eng-
                 land when he is discharged.

JAMES MHANGO: Perhaps so. The trade union will not allow him to
                 work with Africans because he does not like them.

PATSON SICHINGA: The trade union is very strong.

The next day management issued the following notice:

NOTICE TO ALL AFRICAN EMPLOYEES

The Assistant Personnel Manager has held meetings with the local Branch of the Northern African Mine Workers' Trade Union during the past two weeks to discuss complaints regarding the supervision of the Maintenance Gang in the African Township.

The Company has investigated the complaints and are perfectly satisfied that they are completely unfounded.

At a meeting held on Thursday with the African Personnel Manager, the African Union has demanded the removal of the Supervisor in charge of the Maintenance Gang and have informed the African Personnel Manager that unless this is done a strike of African Employees will be called.

It has been pointed out to the union that their claim for the removal of an employee from his present occupation does not come within the scope of terms of the Agreement signed between the Union and the Company and, therefore, this matter is of no concern to the Union. It has also been pointed out to the African Union that a regular procedure exists for the handling of complaints and that this procedure has not been observed.

The Management wish to make it clear to all African Employees, whether members of the union or not, that they have no intention of acceding to the Union's request and that neither threats of strike nor strike action will make them alter their decision.

The Management also wish to state that if the Union calls a strike on this issue the Management will take whatever steps they may think necessary to terminate the strike and resume mining operations.

However, a decision to strike was taken at a union meeting shortly after this warning by management.

After attending this union meeting, some miners were walking to their homes, about six o'clock in the evening.

FIRST MAN: No work tomorrow. I shall keep in bed until nine o'clock. No work.

SECOND MAN: So they think we can worry if they don't accept what we want? We shall show them. They will just get tired of expecting us to work.

THIRD MAN: We cannot be worried at all. We have gardens and we shall eat our maize. [The reference is to gardens on the edge of mine property.]

SECOND MAN: I shall go for beer tomorrow. I am tired of working. There will be a lot of beer in the compound, and why worry about the strike?

FOURTH MAN: I shall have plenty of time to go to the gardens with my wife tomorrow.

FIFTH MAN: Keep your money properly, for tomorrow we shall strike. There will be no food for you, if you don't keep your money.

FOURTH MAN: I have enough money which can keep me for a couple of weeks, if I don't work. Let the Europeans be taught a lesson. I shall drink beer tomorrow.

FIFTH MAN: This time Africans have got plenty of food in their gardens. It is not wise for Europeans to allow them to strike when they have plenty of food.

Shortly afterward, Mr. Moula, a boss boy and a distant relative of Mary's, came from the meeting to Mr. Mhango's house. Mr. Mwenda, a younger brother of Mary Mwenda, who lived with her and her husband, was there, too. Stockily built and twenty years old, he was born on the Copperbelt, when his father was working there as an unskilled laborer. Mr. Mwenda had completed the second year at a government boarding school and had stopped only because his father had died and there was no money to continue his education. He was bright, quick in his thinking, spoke two African languages and English fluently, and held a job requiring a high level of intelligence and initiative. He belonged to the intelligentsia, and like many of them, he was ambitious to own a business of his own. His wife, Catherine, a rural girl from his tribe, had recently come from her village to join him, and they were staying in Mr. Mhango's house until they could have one of their own.

SAM MOULA: I have just come from the meeting at the Welfare Hall. There will be a strike tomorrow. No one will go to work, including those who work in the hospital and clinics, and also the scavengers who clean the latrines.

PETER MWENDA: But that is not wise. The people in the hospital are not
                  Europeans, but are fellow Africans, and the latrines
                  are also used by Africans.

SAM MOULA: But everyone will not go for work. The people have
                  declared so.

A man came down the road, shouting: "A strike tomorrow! A
strike tomorrow! No work! If you have a blanket, use it. No work
tomorrow!" (Presumably the reference to a blanket was a symbol
for sleeping.)

The next morning, the first one of the strike, Mr. Mwenda and his
wife, Catherine, discussed the strike as they sat in front of the house.
She had just recently arrived on the Copperbelt and had never experienced a strike.

PETER MWENDA: So these people have not gone for work. All those
                  who work in the mines are on strike.

CATHERINE ALEFA: Hm . . . When will the people go for work again?

PETER MWENDA: There is no definite time, because it depends on when
                  they come to an understanding with the mining com-
                  pany. If they come to agreement today, they will start
                  work today; if it will be after a week or so, they will
                  start work then.

CATHERINE ALEFA: Will people be still getting their money?

PETER MWENDA: They cannot get money for no work done. They will
                  start earning the time they start work. Now, they are
                  just as good as loafers.

CATHERINE ALEFA: Whey should they go on strike if they cannot get any
                  money?

PETER MWENDA: They want to work under good conditions. It is not
                  good for men to be discharged without any special
                  reasons.

CATHERINE ALEFA: People seem very happy today.

PETER MWENDA: The main reason why workers are always ready to
                  strike is that they want to rest and drink a lot of beer,
                  or go to the gardens. It is not only that one of them
                  has been discharged from work. People like to rest
                  and loaf, and that is why they cooperate so well.

Strikes are not called often. If they were called very often, the men would not cooperate.

Mr. Mhango and his wife, Mary, came out of the house as several neighbors and workmates arrived. One of them was Mr. Kabeyo who lived next door; he and his wife, Edna, were of a different tribe from either Mr. Mhango or Mary, but they were all good friends. Mr. Katongo and Mr. Mwape and more casual friends also arrived.

JAMES MHANGO: There will be no proper work done today, and tomorrow it will be worse.

GEORGE KABEYO: Hm . . . Africans do not play. When we want something, it must be done.

HENRY KATONGO: These people think we are not united.

RICHARD MWAPE: That was long ago in 1940 when an African could be used in any way they liked, but not nowadays.

GEORGE KABEYO: The man who introduced trade unions made a great change in the lives of the Africans. The trade union is the greatest weapon we can use. We are not people to play with.

RICHARD MWAPE: This strike is great. No African is working now. Even the boys, medical orderlies, and scavengers will not work.

HENRY KATONGO: Do these Europeans think that we shall give in?

GEORGE KABEYO: We cannot give in. They must do what we want. Mr. Jones must be discharged, or removed to where he will not work with Africans.

JAMES MHANGO: Yes, he should work where there are no Africans, since he does not like to work together with Africans. Now the Europeans are sweating alone.

GEORGE KABEYO: Hm . . . they are already tired. They are not as powerful as we are.

HENRY KATONGO: They always praise their machines, saying that they do the work. But when there is a strike, those machines do not do any work. The miller will soon stop making a noise.

JAMES MHANGO: We should see the Europeans and Mr. Jones do all that work.

PETER MWENDA: After seven o'clock the smelter and the miller will be very quiet.

GEORGE KABEYO: Yes, Europeans alone cannot do anything.

HENRY KATONGO: How do they work at their home in England?

PETER MWENDA: They work very hard there. You will find Europeans working with picks and shovels in railway lines or digging things just as Africans do here. What can they do since they have no Africans to use there?

GEORGE KABEYO: These people here are proud because of the cheap labor we offer them. Here they work in offices, because they know that there are Africans to work for them manually.

JAMES MHANGO: As we are not in the mine now, they are already black with soot. Their trousers are even torn by now.

RICHARD MWAPE: Now supposing they worked for a long time, they would be worn out.

HENRY KATONGO: These Europeans do not treat us well; they get a lot of money and we get little compared to theirs, and yet we work hard.

GEORGE KABEYO: The time will come when we will get equal wages for equal work. I am a locomotive driver and yet I only receive thirteen pounds, and the Europeans who does the same job gets four or five times that.

JAMES MHANGO: We are now coming into light, and they will not cheat us any more. You saw yesterday the European bosses were issuing the notices from the company forbidding us to strike.

GEORGE KABEYO: That is what they always do. Even in the last strike, in 1952, the same notices were given to workers.

HENRY KATONGO: These [notices] are rubbish. They only want to persuade us to work.

JAMES MHANGO: Africans mean this strike. Everywhere, no one is working. We shall teach them a lesson. I am now going to drink beer. If they say, "you have been discharged," I can readily go home to the country. It is only those who have no rural homes who must worry.

RICHARD MWAPE: I don't mind either. I can go home and start killing
                 fish and then bring it here to sell.

GEORGE KABEYO: If I am discharged, I have got people at home to stay
                 with, and I can start gardening.

RICHARD MWAPE: Let us go to the beer hall to drink beer.

HENRY KATONGO: I understand there will be no water for people in the
                 bathrooms.

GEORGE KABEYO: We do not worry much about that. There is plenty of
                 water in that river at section eight, which is very nice,
                 and also water from the Makoma Dam.

PETER MWENDA: That will be very far for those in section one, two,
                 three, and four, especially for those houses on the
                 lower part of the compound.

GEORGE KABEYO: It does not matter.

JAMES MHANGO: Today we should see the European come and clean our
                 lavatories here.

PETER MWENDA: He can't come.

JAMES MHANGO: He must come. Why does he discharge Africans if he
                 knows he can't do the work alone? He will learn a
                 lesson. I am going now to fix my bicycle.

GEORGE KABEYO: I am now going to get some maize from my garden.

HENRY KATONGO: Let us go and hunt for beer in the mine compound. Is
                 the beer hall closed today? (*As he sees a beer hall
                 policeman passing by.*)

POLICEMAN: No, we are not on strike. Just come and enjoy your-
                 selves, if you have money.

RICHARD MWAPE: The beer at the beer hall is usually not very good. I
                 will first go in the compound and drink. Then after
                 that I shall go to the beer hall to drink some bottles.
                 ["Bottles" refer to the commercially bottled beer,
                 weaker and not liked as much as the beer brewed il-
                 legally by African women.]

The next morning, Sunday, Mary, Catherine, and their husbands,
Mr. Mhango and Mr. Mwenda, were talking outside their house.

MARY MWENDA: Yesterday, it looked as if it were Sunday, too. A lot
                 of people were drinking beer.

CATHERINE ALEFA: The people were drunk yesterday. Is that what they do when there is a strike?

MARY MWENDA: Yes, the first day of the strike looks like that: many people drunk and a lot of shouting. But when the money starts finishing in their pockets, they begin selling their best clothes to get money for food, and then they are not very willing to strike. In the last strike of 1952, there was much hunger, and people started selling their things at cheap prices. If you have money, just keep it; and if the strike continues like this, you will buy a lot of things cheaply. I do not think the workers will convince the Europeans. Europeans are very clever.

CATHERINE ALEFA: Yes, these people are wonderful. The things they have made are very astonishing.

PETER MWENDA: I do not know what the result of the strike will be.

MARY MWENDA: Europeans can work by themselves. Are they not many?

JAMES MHANGO: They are many, but not very powerful. They are only supervisors and do none of the real labor.

PETER MWENDA: Comparatively speaking, there is a greater number of Africans in Northern Rhodesia and in each mine than there are Europeans. But though fewer, they are as powerful as Africans. The Europeans are just lazy here, since they have the cheap labor from the Africans. However, I sometimes fear that with the coming of more Europeans, the trade union will not be very effective. The Europeans are coming in great numbers, and one day they will be as many as the Africans. Then, if the Africans go on strike the Europeans can continue working, and the Africans would just lose their jobs.

Later in the day, Mr. Thomas Chana, a friend of Mr. Mwenda, came to see them. Mr. Chana, twenty-one years old, born on the Copperbelt, had completed Standard VI and was employed as a delivery boy in a European shop.

PETER MWENDA: Hello, Thomas, I have not seen you for a complete week.

THOMAS CHANA: I have been very busy. I work all day carrying orders to the Europeans' houses. I do not have sufficient time to rest. What do you think, is this strike a good one?

PETER MWENDA: I do not think so.

THOMAS CHANA: No, it is not rightly carried on. They should not prohibit hospital orderlies and nurses from working, and scavengers, too. This is wrong. This means killing more and more Africans. Yesterday, a lot of babies were discharged from the hospital because there were no workers to look after them.

PETER MWENDA: Some of them will definitely die in the compound.

THOMAS CHANA: Mr. Katanga, the father of Nita, died on Friday night and was supposed to be buried yesterday.

PETER MWENDA: What was he suffering from?

THOMAS CHANA: Coughing. He has been in the hospital for about a month.

PETER MWENDA: I did not see him. Was he very old?

THOMAS CHANA: He was old, yes. He used to work in the tailoring shop at the compound office.

PETER MWENDA: That is very bad. Has he been buried already?

THOMAS CHANA: He was supposed to be buried yesterday. But because of the strike, he was not discovered dead until about two P.M. yesterday, and his body was carried to the mortuary by the European doctors. When his family went to mourn for him, they found his body was in the mortuary, which was locked, since no one was working there.

PETER MWENDA: See now, what is the use of including medical orderlies in the strike? These trade union leaders have not been very reasonable.

THOMAS CHANA: No, they are not. A lot of people were discharged yesterday from the hospital, even though they were not well. The few who remained were put in one room. It is very bad indeed.

JAMES MHANGO: Yes, I also understand that those who were in the hospital were discharged, even the babies.

PETER MWENDA:	Do you think that was good?
JAMES MHANGO:	No, it was not good to take out patients. But Europeans should have done all the work. When we went on strike we said that Mr. Jones with his fellow Europeans should do all the work because they did not consider African labor important.
PETER MWENDA:	But things like the hospital and the latrines and the Welfare Center are for your own benefit.
JAMES MHANGO:	Europeans should work there alone, because they argue that our labor is not important.
PETER MWENDA:	But Europeans cannot work at those places which are for us.

Mr. Katongo, a friend of Mr. Mwenda, came by.

HENRY KATONGO:	Hallo.
PETER MWENDA:	Hallo. Where are you going?
HENRY KATONGO:	I am going to the mortuary. My sister's baby has died.
PETER MWENDA:	Was he ill?
HENRY KATONGO:	Yes, he was discharged yesterday when other babies were being discharged from the hospital.
PETER MWENDA:	See, now, what the trade union has caused.
HENRY KATONGO:	Yes, I must hurry on.

Later, on the same day, Mr. Mwenda met some of his friends at the Welfare Center. They were Mr. Malango and Mr. Kalikeka, both clerks, and Mr. Bwalya, a welfare worker, all in their early twenties, with secondary school education.

GEORGE MALANGO:	These people [trade unionists] have not been reasonable in stopping the scavengers and the medical orderlies from working. It is against the law to do that. Essential duties should not be included in the strike.
SIMON BWALYA:	That is the result of having untrained leaders. The chairman is not educated at all.
PETER MWENDA:	People only chose him because he has no fear of saying anything before Europeans, but he does not know much.

SIMON BWALYA: Next time, I shall force them to make me a leader.

PETER MWENDA: The chairman started making mistakes when he was
                   elected, only a few weeks ago. That is the time he
                   should have shown his intelligence. But why can't the
                   Europeans only remove Mr. Jones, so that people start
                   work?

BILL KALIKEKA: That is not the main cause for the strike. The trade
                   union wanted to see the general manager at once, so
                   that he could warn Mr. Jones but not remove him.
                   But the general manager was at Kitwe, where he had
                   gone for a meeting. The trade union wanted him to
                   leave the meeting at Kitwe and come and attend to
                   them at once. Failure in doing that meant a strike.
                   We saw the statements when they were being taken
                   to the personnel manager.

GEORGE MALANGO: Yes, we saw the statements. The general manager
                   was supposed to be here late on Thursday from Kitwe,
                   but he did not come then. Again on Friday he did not
                   come, and so the trade union declared a strike because
                   the general manager did not attend to them at once.[2]

PETER MWENDA: Already, some of the babies who were taken out of
                   the hospital yesterday have started dying. Do you
                   know Peter Chibesa?

BILL KALIKEKA: Yes, he is an old friend of ours.

PETER MWENDA: His sister's baby who was discharged yesterday has
                   died.

GEORGE MALANGO: So now what can the presence of mothers, which
                   they are demanding, do? They claim that mothers
                   should sleep with their sick babies at the hospital.
                   [Mothers on the mine township wanted to stay over-
                   night in the hospital if their sick babies were in it. The
                   hospital had refused permission.]

BILL KALIKEKA: They demand that because everywhere on the Copper-
                   belt it is done, and so why not here?

SIMON BWALYA: Though it is done other places, it is wrong from the
                   scientific point of view.

GEORGE MALANGO: Let us go and play gramophone records.

SIMON BWALYA: Yes, let us go.

BILL KALIKEKA: Oh, very good.

Later in the day Mr. Mwape, a neighbor, came with his wife to see Mr. Mhango, and the two men and Mr. Mwenda talked about the strike.

PETER MWENDA: Mr. Mhango, you said it was good that medical order-lies and nurses should not work. Have you heard that some of the babies have already started dying?

JAMES MHANGO: It does not matter.

PETER MWENDA: You mean you don't mind if more Africans die?

JAMES MHANGO: Even if they die, they are not my relatives.

PETER MWENDA: But the ones you are striking for are not your relatives.

JAMES MHANGO: We should strike because Europeans are not treating us well.

RICHARD MWAPE: It was not good that the medical orderlies and nurses were not allowed to work. All those in the African hospitals are our own people. It were best if those African orderlies working at the European hospital were brought to the African hospital instead of stopping everyone. Moreover, we are the people using the latrines and so scavengers should be allowed to work, too.

JAMES MHANGO: It does not matter even if they die. Are they my rela-tives?

RICHARD MWAPE: Don't talk like that. The men we are striking for are not our relatives. I do not even know one of them. They may be the Nyakyusa, or Swahilis from Tan-ganyika. If I happen to meet them at their home in Tanganyika after losing my job because of the strike, they will not recognize me at all. Those who are dis-charged might get employment again, but those who die will never live again.

JAMES MHANGO (*Interrupting*):
Where shall we drink beer today?

RICHARD MWAPE: I am going to the beer hall now.

JAMES MHANGO: You have even carried a tumbler. I am coming after you soon.

RICHARD MWAPE:	I am thirsty.
JAMES MHANGO:	So am I.
SARAH MWAPE:	These people waste a lot of money.
MARY MWENDA:	With this strike they will be starving soon.
JAMES MHANGO:	If I find that I am starving, I can indulge in beer-drinking. It is only the one who does not drink beer who can suffer.

Elizabeth Mhango, the wife of Mr. Mhango's brother, known as Mr. Mhango II, arrived.

JAMES MHANGO:	Hallo, sister-in-law.
ELIZABETH MHANGO:	Good afternoon, thank you. Have you not gone to drink beer?
JAMES MHANGO:	I have no money. I wish someone would give me some money for beer.
ELIZABETH MHANGO:	You have finished your money, before the strike is over.
JAMES MHANGO:	Anyway, I shall be eating my maize from my garden. Where has Mr. Mhango II gone?
ELIZABETH MHANGO:	He told me that he went to Section One. The latrines are already dirty.
MARY MWENDA:	Yes, they have not been cleaned.
ELIZABETH MHANGO:	These people [unionists] have not done a good thing; no medical orderlies at work and no scavengers.
PETER MWENDA:	And the Welfare Hall is not open, either.
ELIZABETH MHANGO:	Isn't it? But the Welfare Department is not so important.
PETER MWENDA:	It is important. No Europeans use the Welfare Center. It is only used by Africans, and I do not know why it should be included in the strike. People should have places where they can pass time during the strike, so they will be entertained by different games. If they don't have all such, they will indulge in beer drinking, and when they are intoxicated they can damage anything they come across and start fighting, which will

cause the strike to be unsuccessful. When we mean business, we do not want to play.

ELIZABETH MHANGO: It does not matter if they close the Welfare, but the important things are the hospital and the lavatories, which affect our health.

JAMES MHANGO: I would like to go and drink some *mbote* [native beer] at Section One now.

Mr. Moula arrived.

SAM MOULA: There was a meeting last night, and it was decided that medical orderlies, pump boys, and scavengers should start work. The chairman was very angry because some people, including babies, were discharged from the hospital.

PETER MWENDA: It was because there was nobody to look after them.

SAM MOULA: No. Europeans should have looked after them and failing to do that, they should have been given a case by the trade union.

PETER MWENDA: But the hospital is for Africans. How can you expect Europeans to help you, when you don't try to help yourselves?

SAM MOULA: Europeans argue that our labor is not so important; we have done this so that we see how much they can do without us. Europeans should work in the African hospital, because every miner pays for medical treatment. They cannot stop looking after our people when we give them money. As for the underground, we should see them handle the drilling machines or controlling water. They think we are not powerful, but Africans are very powerful. See already when there are no Africans working, all the machines are quiet. We are very powerful. When we handle a drilling machine we just consider it as a very tiny, light thing. Without the powerful Africans, Europeans would not have done much.

PETER MWENDA: Did the union chairman ask the scavengers and pump boys and medical orderlies to start work?

SAM MOULA: The important Europeans came to ask him to let the orderlies start work. So he ordered some medical orderlies and nurses to start work; also he chose mine scavengers to do work from Section One to Section Nine.

MARY MWENDA: When will the rest start work?

SAM MOULA: It will be the time they will come to an agreement with the company. Now I have to go and settle a family trouble at Section Two.

PETER MWENDA: Do you think the Europeans asked for medical orderlies, or that the trade union leaders thought it wise to put the orderlies back to work?

MARY MWENDA: Europeans just say, "Let Africans die."

ELIZABETH MHANGO: I think the unionists realized that they were wrong. Let us go to the beer hall.

PETER MWENDA: I am going to the football ground.

Very early the next day, a man passed by Mr. Mhango's house crying out his announcement:

TRADE UNION MEETING AT THE WELFARE CENTRE TODAY
AT 8 O'CLOCK A.M.
Meeting at the Welfare Centre! Everyone is Wanted There!
Katilungu Has Come Today! Meeting at 8 o'clock!
8 o'clock Meeting at the Union! ! !

PETER MWENDA: Are you going to the meeting?

JAMES MHANGO: No, those who have gone will come and tell us. I am busy.

PETER MWENDA: What business do you have?

JAMES MHANGO: I have washed, and now I must iron.

PETER MWENDA: I will go to the meeting and listen. I especially want to see Katilungu in person, because I have only seen him in pictures.

At the meeting, only part of the president's speech was recorded, as follows:

It will not be very good to see some of you people go for work after you have started the strike. If it happens that some of you go, you endanger others who do not report at work. Carry on with your strike until you have got your demands. It does not matter how long the strike will take, but still hold on. You have got fields where you can get your maize, monkey nuts, and potatoes to eat.

You are the backbone of Northern Rhodesia, and if you do not work, then Northern Rhodesia will become poor. The harder you work, the richer this country will become. Europeans are dependent on you. Since you have stopped working, the mine has become poor.

Last week, on Saturday, the senior labor officer of Kitwe came to see me and asked me whether I knew of the strike at Luanshya; and I answered, "I do not know; I have just heard it from you." He said, "All those working as pump boys, scavengers, and medical orderlies have stopped work, and that is against the law. Policemen will be sent to Luanshya by the Government." I answered, "Yes, I know the duty of the policeman. The government can send policemen to keep order. There will be work there for them if our people start damaging machinery or start fights. But I do not think they will do that."

I know that you did not allow scavengers, pump boys, and medical orderlies to work because you were angry. But we have put that right now. All those doing essential duties should continue their work, for the mine is yours, too. You are miners, and you should not worry even if other people call you miners. You are much better than these other people, the cooks, the clerks, and delivery boys, and the others who work in town. They always laugh at us, but we marry their wives, and we will keep on marrying them.[3] (*The audience cheers!*) Just keep on. I praise you for your unity. This is all we want. I have to go now to a meeting with the committee members.

Union members talked as they leave the meeting:

FIRST MAN: We cannot give up.

SECOND MAN: Now the strike will spread.

THIRD MAN: Ah, then it will be worse.

FOURTH MAN: It is good that we rest.

FIFTH MAN: Yes, it is another kind of leave. We are tired of hearing Europeans curse at us as if we are dogs.

FOURTH MAN: I shall be eating maize from my garden.

Early the next morning, Tuesday, Mr. Chilufya and Mr. Ngosa, uneducated miners, come by Mr. Mhango's house to ask the literate Mr. Mwenda to read a notice which had just been issued by management. Mr. Mwenda read aloud:

NOTICE TO ALL AFRICAN EMPLOYEES

If you do not return to your work at once you are liable to be discharged.

There is a law in Northern Rhodesia which says what employees should do when they have a dispute with their employers. In a matter which the contract between your Union and the Mining Company recognizes as a complaint which can be settled between the Company and the Union, the Union first should meet the African Personnel Manager and then the General Manager. If the Company and the Union still cannot agree, then the law says that the Union should tell the Government that it has a complaint against the Company. If the Government agrees that this is a proper complaint, the Government will tell someone to hold a meeting between the Company and the Union to see if he cannot get them to agree. If they do not agree and the Union decides that the Company is wrong, *then* it can call a strike.

The trouble about which you have gone on strike is not one which the contract gives the Union the right to discuss with the Company. When the General Manager invited the leaders of the Union to discuss your intention to strike they [Union leaders] refused to meet him. The Union did not tell the Government that it had a complaint against the Company and so, when it told you to strike, it disobeyed both its contract with the Company and the law of Northern Rhodesia.

Your strike therefore is against the law [Trades Dispute Ordinance] and the contract [agreement] made by the Union and the Company, and you have broken your own contract with the Company and have made yourselves liable to discharge from your employment.

BEN CHILUFYA: They are just frightening us so that we can go for work tomorow.

PETER MWENDA: If some of you go for work now, then it will mean that those who will not go will be discharged. If you do not want some people to be discharged, then you either all go, or you all remain away.

BEN CHILUFYA: They are cheating. We shall not go.

SPIDER NGOSA: That man who has written this unwise notice is not the general manager; he is the acting general manager. The general manager is not there. Does this acting general manager want us to be discharged even though we have done nothing serious? The man who wrote this does not want Mr. Jones to be removed. Mr. Jones is a very cruel and hard man. We used to work with him at Fourteen Shaft.

BEN CHILUFYA: Perhaps they have no office to transfer him to.

SPIDER NGOSA: Ah, that one is a Boer. Boers cannot be put in offices at all.

PETER MWENDA: He is English.

SPIDER NGOSA: No, he is a Boer, that one. He is not English.

PETER MWENDA: But his name is English, and also a Boer cannot be a supervisor here. Such positions are very few. Boers are mostly in the smelters and underground. I shall go to the meeting. First-hand information is usually better than second-hand.

BEN CHILUFYA: Let us go to the meeting, Mr. Ngosa.

SPIDER NGOSA: I will be told by those who have gone there. I am already tired of going to meetings. I want to do some small work here at home. You go and listen.

BEN CHILUFYA: Yes, I shall go.

At the meeting, men waited for it to begin. The committee members tried to get the people who were attending to sit down. The chairman of the local branch was on the platform, awaiting Mr. Katilungu.

FIRST COMMITTEE MEMBER: Sit down, please. Those who do not want to sit down can move to the back, so that they don't shade those who are seated.

FIRST MAN: How can we sit on this soil? It should have been better if there were some grass.

SECOND COMMITTEE MEMBER: Sit down, if you want respect. If you have really come for the meeting, sit down. Those who are standing have not really come for the meeting.

SECOND MAN: If you want to ask people to sit down, ask them in a good way. Not like that.

THIRD MAN: Moreover, you do not force others to respect you.

FOURTH MAN: Let them start speaking now.

FIRST MAN: Sit down, you men in front. We want to see.

SECOND
  COMMITTEE   Those are committee members. Don't worry. It is ears
  MEMBER: which hear and not eyes.

THIRD MAN: Ah, one always understands better when one can see the
               person who is speaking.

FIRST
  COMMITTEE
  MEMBER: We should do as the Europeans do.

Mr. Katilungu arrived, and all the members stood for a few minutes.

PRESIDENT   Silence! I am going to speak now. After I have said all I
  KATILUNGU: have to say, then I shall allow you to ask questions.
               I remember what happened here at Luanshya in 1935
               when so many people were fired. That was because there
               were no people to lead others. That time there were no
               trade unions, and so everyone was a leader by himself. I
               was not here then, for I was a teacher at home.
               You also remember what happened at Kitwe in 1940.
               So many peeople were killed and so many wounded. There
               were seventeen dead bodies in the mortuary, and there
               were sixty wounded people. You would be very sorry if
               you saw them. Some had lost their legs; and others, their
               hands. It was really a terrible time. I was there then, and I
               had taken an active part. I remember when I lost my
               best friend, Mulenga. I managed to escape from the same
               danger, because unknowingly, I went to the gardens with
               my wife. Perhaps it was God who made me survive, so
               that I could be a good example to the people and lead
               them.
               All these things happened because there were no leaders
               to guide others; but this time we have trade unions. I
               have been the leader of the trade union for six years.
               I admire you in this strike, because you have convinced
               the man who says Africans are primitive and not edu-
               cated, that he is wrong. You have indeed shamed him,
               because since you started your strike, and it is now four
               days, there have been no fights and no damage. This
               shows that an African can behave peacefully without
               need for the police, and that an African can obey his
               leader well. It is also very good that we have no reports

of any men who have grown tired of the strike and started to work. This shows that we are now united.

You have all seen the notices which have been given to the people in the compound, telling you to start work at once and that failure to do that will mean discharge from work.

The notices have also stated that you have broken the contract between the union and the company, which says that if the union has a complaint the matter should be taken to the personnel manager, then to the general manager; that there is a law of this country which says that if the union has a complaint, it can take it to the government, which then will send a man to settle the dispute between the union and the company. These two things the union did not do. They also say we refused to meet the management, and so our people are liable to discharge.

There is an agreement between the union and the company which says that if there is any question or complaint it must be attended to within seven days of the notice. We wrote a letter asking to meet the general manager on the Seventeenth of March, 1954. There was no answer until after seven days expired, and the five days had elapsed, which now total twelve days from the first day of notification. So the local chairman with his assistants decided to strike and to show their strength.

You must keep on. If the mines will not consider your case, then I will call Mufulira, Chibuluma, Chingola, Broken Hill, and Kitwe to help to strike. We cannot agree to be discharged from work any time they want without any special reasons.

(The audience cheers!)

Two men commented to each other:

FIRST MAN: Mr. Katilungu is very intelligent.

SECOND MAN: I had not seen him in person, and so today I am lucky.

PRESIDENT KATILUNGU: Yesterday I had a question to ask you. But since I have seen these notices, I command you not to go to work tomorrow. I shall ask you the question later on.

I am the general president of the African Mine Workers' Trade Union, and so I have the power to stop all other mines from work. The trade union is like your body. Once you hurt yourself on the tip of your finger you feel as if all your body had been hurt. That is the same thing with the trade union. This strike here has affected all other trade unions in other mines in Northern Rhodesia. If all the mines stop work and our demand is not fulfilled, I shall call on the other trade unions in railways, shops, and transport to strike. I am the general president.[4]

FOURTH MAN: Ha, this man is important.

THIRD MAN: I am sure he is clever.

PRESIDENT   You keep on your strike peacefully, because it shows that
KATILUNGU: you are educated. Education does not just mean to speak English or pass a high standard at all. It means knowledge of how to do something. Now I have finished, and if there are any questions, you can ask after we have all breathed hard.
                (The audience cheers!)

Late on the same day Mr. Lembani and Mr. Kabeyo, neighbors and workmates, who had been to an afternoon union meeting, came to Mr. Mhango's house to discuss the latest developments.

MOSES LEMBANI: We shall start work on Saturday.

JAMES MHANGO: No, Mr. Katilungu said we would start on Thursday.

PETER MWENDA: I cannot understand that. How did Mr. Katilungu so quickly change his opinion? When I was there, he said that if the general manager would not agree to the demand, then he would call all the other mines to strike.

GEORGE KABEYO: Yes, that is what he said. But later, at another meeting, he said that the question was whether we should return to work, so that we could hold meetings with management. He said also that he had planned to ask the question earlier, but that the last notice from the general manager had annoyed him. But he asked us now whether we should return, and said that when we met with management, if they did not consider our demands, he would call another strike and then it would be the whole Copperbelt. The people agreed to return to work, and one man suggested that we return on Saturday and a second man said, Thursday. Mr. Katilungu then said that if the management agrees to hold the meeting, we should start work on Thursday.

PETER MWENDA: Yes, now I understand.

The next morning, Wednesday, neighbors and workmates talked in front of Mr. Mhango's house.

GEORGE KABEYO: We shall go for work tomorrow.

JAMES MHANGO: Yes, we shall. The Boers will be very pleased to see us again.

RICHARD MWAPE: They have failed to work alone. See! Everything is quiet! The miller, the power station, and in the smelter, no smoke is coming out.

BEN CHILUFYA: They always say that we do not work hard; now see, there is no work going on. Everything is still.

RICHARD MWAPE: They cannot make any copper now.

GEORGE KABEYO: Hm . . . They can't shovel the stones underground. See? The conveyor belt stopped moving the day we started the strike. We are very powerful, I can tell you. The mine now has lost a lot of money.

PETER MWENDA: Yes. Yes. In the last strike, each mine lost sixty pounds per minute, which is very much.

RICHARD MWAPE: Why could they not just discharge this European, Mr. Jones?

JAMES MHANGO: Mr. Katilungu said that you should not expect to see Mr. Jones removed at once, because Europeans are not discharged from work as we Africans are. With Europeans they give them notice, so that they prepare. Even if the mine agrees to remove him, it will be after some weeks, and then you will see him disappear.

GEORGE KABEYO: These men are no good at all. The good Europeans are quickly removed; only bad ones like Mr. Jones cannot be removed or discharged. There was Kamwefu [the bearded man], who was very good to Africans. Nearly everyone liked him, but the Europeans discharged him because he liked Africans.

RICHARD MWAPE: They have liked Jones because he discharges Africans.

JAMES MHANGO: Another good *bwana* is Chinyanja [a nickname, be-
                   cause he speaks Chinyanja]. He discharges Europeans
                   who are not good. When he sees that a European has
                   beaten an African for no reason, he gives the European
                   a note to take to the general office and you do not see
                   that European again. He is very muscular, and other
                   Europeans fear him. He makes Boers work very hard.

PETER MWENDA: Yes, there are very few Boers with good jobs in the
                   mines.

RICHARD MWAPE: I do not know what the European Trade Union will
                   think about this strike. Will they understand?

PETER MWENDA: They cannot understand at all. Those people are highly
                   paid, so that they have less complaints. Moreover,
                   there cannot be any proper relations between the Euro-
                   peans and African trade unions, because those people
                   who ill-treat us are in the European Trade Union.
                   There can be no good relations when the Europeans
                   who are our bosses maltreat us at work. You hear so
                   many cases of Africans being beaten or discharged
                   from work by those who are in the European Trade
                   Union. They make us suffer. The general manager or
                   the personnel manager does not go about discharging
                   Africans or beating them. It is the European workers,
                   and these are in the European Trade Union.

RICHARD MWAPE: Yes, that is true.

GEORGE KABEYO: Yes, it is not possible that there can be a good under-
                   standing between the two unions.

MOSES LEMBANI: We shall go for work tomorrow. It is good, so that I
                   receive my pay on Thursday next week.

The strike was over, and the Africans returned to work without
having gained the discharge of the supervisor or anything else. A
week later, some of the men were discussing the strike:

JAMES MHANGO: It was not good that we returned to work. We should
                   show these Europeans that we are the people who do
                   much work and not them.

PETER MWENDA: But you would have suffered from hunger.

JAMES MHANGO:	No, we have money in the bank, and so we could strike longer. We want to see that European, Mr. Jones, discharged. Then we will be pleased. We should not be discharged without reason. If they do not discharge him, then we shall go on a longer strike.
TOM BANDA:	We cannot be treated like dogs as they did in the past. They introduced trade unions and that made us powerful. That is the only way we can fight, since we do not have weapons and guns to use. Had we those, we should just have declared war on them. We are fed up with their ill-treatment.
GEORGE KABEYO:	I do not think it was good that we returned to work because I feel the Europeans did not learn a big lesson. Europeans should realize that we are the big owners of the work, and if we stop, no work in the mine can go on. It is not reasonable for them to discharge us from work with silly reasons. They say we do not work hard, and yet when we stop, no work goes on. So, they are only being silly.
PETER MWENDA:	But what about the medical orderlies and the scavengers stopping work?
GEORGE KABEYO:	There the union leaders were wrong. These people in the African hospital were our own people, and if they die, it will be our own loss. The latrines, too, are used by us, and so stopping the scavengers was also a mistake.
JACOB MUTENGA:	It was done like that because people were angry, but it was not a right thing, since these people are our people.
SPIDER NGOSA:	I did not like the strike because I did not know the cause for it. Also, I did not like the idea of stopping the orderlies and latrine cleaners, because that work is for our own good. It would be all right, if the African orderlies at the European hospital were stopped, because the Europeans are not our relatives.
JACOB MUTENGA:	Even then, it would not be good because death is the same. We should not play with the souls of God.
TOM BANDA:	Even so, I think the strike was right to show the strength of the union.

The themes and images which emerge from these conversations were dominant in the strike situation, and many of them were continuously present in the mine township. The African miners' image of themselves was of strong, powerful men who did the hard manual work, without which copper could not be mined.

They pointed proudly to the fact that during the strike, everything —the miller, the power plant, the smelter, and all other parts of the mine—was quiet. The Europeans, who constantly belittled the Africans, must learn how important they are. "If they are not important, why does all mining stop when the Africans are not working?" they asked.

In the quite recent past the muscles of these Africans, and of others like them, was their main source of strength. Today, this kind of strength is still important for some of the manual, unskilled workers, but the prestige comes largely out of the past, and there is ambivalence concerning it. The same Africans who boasted about being so strong also delighted in a fantasy of the tables being turned and the Europeans doing the "dirty" work. The low esteem in which Europeans hold manual work, which usually happens to be dirty, complicated the Africans attitude to it. There were other complexities in today's image of strength. In the past, the strong fighter was much respected. During the strike the trade union president exhorted the strikers to show that they are educated, and not "primitive," by refraining from fighting and by conducting the strike peacefully. It is beneath the status of educated men to fight. The union president, himself an educated man, flattered the strikers by implying that they were sexually stronger than educated men.

Many distinctions between the educated and the uneducated were apparent throughout the strike. The illiterate chairman of the local called the strike. The educated president of the union, whose advice had not been asked in advance, then had to "carry the ball," maneuver the strike into the contractual framework and, eventually, call it off. Ironically, it was one of the uneducated miners with the most belligerent and anti-European attitude who was not sufficiently interested to go to union meetings during the strike, but relied on others to bring him the news of what transpired at them.

The most significant difference between the educated and some of the uneducated was in their range of identification. This was indicated in their attitudes to the chairman's calling out of sanitation workers and hospital orderlies and the resulting inconvenience for all Africans on the compound and the distress and, sometimes death, of those in the hospital. The reaction of some of the uneducated was, "but these are not our relatives." This is a completely traditional attitude based on the deep economic, social, and emotional significance of the lineage group. The educated Africans were shocked at this attitude and were against the chairman's calling out of sanitation workers and hospital orderlies. They did not think that any Africans, relatives or not, should suffer unnecessarily. A few included Europeans in their range of identification, and thought it was wrong for the chairman to have called out African orderlies from the European hospital. The difference in range of identification is one of the most significant criteria for social change among all peoples.

The strike for many was a welcome break in the rigid regularity of the normal work schedule, which is in contrast to the seasonal rhythm of traditional work. The free time was likened to a leave or vacation, and relatively little anxiety was expressed. The Africans did not feel greatly dependent on their mine jobs, for as they said, they could always return to their rural villages.

The stereotype of the unfair Boer was so strong that the supervisor on whom the strikers' complaints were focused was incorrectly made into a Boer, and the Africans would not listen to anyone who said otherwise. Likewise, the rank of all the European personnel involved in the strike was important. It was not the general manager, but the acting manager who signed one of the notices; and this was considered a reason for not taking it too seriously. That it is the European supervisors who unjustly fire Africans and never the general manager was another statement associating injustice with low rank.

The strike call was obeyed by all. No African in or out of the union, clerk or manul laborer, went to work; and during the strike the leaders were obeyed absolutely. But within the unity there was division, based primarily on the level of education and the consequent differences in social status and in the range of identifications.

PART III

FAMILY LIFE

9. The Changing Nature of Marriage

Sentiments and attitudes concerning family life and marriage are more private and usually slower to change than economic values, although, of course, the two are interrelated. The new economic order, with its structured hierarchy of jobs, its regulations, its union and staff associations, and the considerable control by mine management was quite clear cut. By contrast, the picture of family life and marriage on the mine township was ambiguous and complicated.[1] Some traditional attitudes towards marriage, sexual relations, and the family persisted, a few in exaggerated form; others were in conflict with new attitudes; and there were many patterns of compromise. It should be remembered, too, that traditional forms of marriage showed considerable variation and that the conjugal family was always more unstable than the lineage, the firm core of tribal society.

Many of the past stresses and strains in marriages continued to exist, weakened, strengthened, or changed in the new situation on the township. The position of the husband has become stronger since he is now a wage earner and it is his earnings rather than cooperation with kindred, often scattered, which determine much of the family's well-being.[2] As standards of living rose and became diversified, conflict between the interests of the family and those of the lineage group was increasingly focused on the distribution of wealth and property. Tensions inherent in the past situation, in which extramarital relations, sanctioned only for the men, were the norm, have been aggravated on the township, with its increased opportunities and with the presence of a group of young women openly taking the initiative. The new values, emphasizing a choice of mate that is based on love, congeniality, and sexual attraction, obviously weaken traditional arrangement of marriages by kindred. But marriage payments and continuing gifts (in lieu of traditional services) to in-laws remained even in the marriages based on choice. Polygamy persisted, probably to a lesser degree, but it presented additional difficulties in the one house allotted to each mine worker. Intertribal marriages, an innovation, brought new problems. The right to divorce has remained a fundamental liberty and appears to be exercised more casually than in the past. Distrust and jealousy, openly expressed, were major themes in marriage. But many of the men and women who were unfaithful yearned for a faithful mate and more permanent marriages. These seemed to be more numerous among the intelligentsia and middle class, in which there was also an increasing emphasis on the individual family, rather than the lineage, as the basic unit. As a result of these changes and complexities, new attitudes toward marriage and new forms of family organization developed, and, of course, new problems.

On the mine township the word *marry* did not always mean the same thing, and there were many different kinds of unions. Some marriages were based on traditional arrangements between groups of kindred. Church members added a Christian ceremony. Kindred played a smaller sponsoring role in those marriages in which the mates exercised choice before getting the consent of the bride's nearest relative on the township. My impression is that this was the most common type. Mitchell found that the bride's own brother was the commonest sponsor in town, though, in general, there were fewer sponsors from her generation than from her parents'. At the time of Mitchell's study, payments varied from less than five shillings to more than a hundred and sixty, with the median payment being thirty-three shillings and six pence,[3] not a very large sum by Copperbelt standards. The groom paid the bride-price out of savings and earnings. Of course, gifts of money were also expected at the time of visits from or to in-laws. The word *marry* was likewise used for concubinage, in which a common ménage was maintained without any sponsorship by kindred or payment of bride-price. There were also affairs, of long or short duration, in which the women received gifts and maintenance money without being part of a common household. One type of marriage union often passed into another. The one kind forbidden to Africans in Northern Rhodesia was the civil marriage contract based on European law. Native courts considered tribal law the only basis for a valid marriage.[4]

A majority of the men and women on the mine township were married, in the sense that the marriage had been registered at a Native Court. According to Mitchell's 1951 survey (the last to be made and which included both the mine township and the municipal location), 64 per cent of the men on both townships were married and had their wives with them and 95 per cent of the women were married and living with their husbands. Eighteen per cent of the men were not married, and the remaining 15 per cent had left their wives in the rural home.[5] Wilson's survey, approximately a decade earlier (1940), on Broken Hill showed a much higher proportion, 46 per cent, of unmarried men. Only 40 per cent of the men were married and had their wives with them, while 14 per cent had left their wives at home.[6] The percentage of married men who have their wives with them has constantly increased and, as reported earlier (Chapter 6), about 80 per cent of the men on the mine township were in this group. Wives increasingly follow their husbands to the Copperbelt; young unmarried women from villages come there to get a husband; and both sexes of the generation born in towns probably remain there with their spouses.

I found that girls under twelve on the mine township were often betrothed in a traditional manner and that their mothers were planning marriage for them as soon as they reached puberty. There was no way of knowing how many of these would be consummated. Sometimes relatives in the village made arrangements for the marriage of a young townsman to a village girl. The unsophisticated rural girl was usually considered more moral than the town girl. The marriage of Kandala, in his late teens, followed some tribal patterns. He was a member of the intelligentsia, born on the Copperbelt, and holding a skilled white-collar job. His parents were dead; and an older brother (a classificatory one), living in the village, made the arrangements for him to marry a girl who had never been away from the rural area and who had gone as far as Standard III at a local school. Kandala was informed of the arrangements in a letter from his brother, who asked him to come home and see the girl. Shortly afterward Kandala took a bus to his home village; upon his arrival, the girl was told by Kandala's brother that he had arrived. Then the two brothers went to see her. Kandala described the meeting:

> We sat down, and the girl sat opposite us. I was satisfied with her. Then my brother spoke to me: "This is the girl I was talking about. What do you think of her?" Then I answered, "She is all right." Then he said, "Be sure, for we would not like to see you change your mind in the future. This is the time for you to refuse, if you do not want to marry her." Then I answered, "No, what I have said is true." Then the brother asked the girl, and she replied. "My words are unchanged as they were before." She had agreed to the marriage before because she had been told that I looked almost exactly the same as my brother, and when she looked at me she was satisfied.
>
> The matter was now begun. Three days later, my brother and I went to her mother's home to inform them of the marriage and to get her. The matter was fixed, a payment was made, and the next day we went to register our marriage at the Native Court and then at the church of the Dutch Reformed Mission. Then we had a wedding, and a cow was slaughtered and also some fowls and a pig. We went to stay with my wife's mother and after about ten days, returned to my home. I stayed home for two months, and then I came back to the Copperbelt, leaving my wife at home. A few months after I started working and had saved some money, I sent for her, and I was happy when she arrived here.

The young wife was attractive looking, but shy and not at ease in the township. She missed her mother and other relatives in the village, although there were occasional visits with them. The young couple had two children within the first three and a half years of marriage. But almost from the beginning, the relationship was marred by the wife's intense jealousy of her husband whenever he was out of her sight. After a while, the jealousy had some basis. She became a nagging wife, eventually returned to the village with the children; and the couple were divorced. Sometime afterward Kandala married a young woman, a nurse's aid, better educated than his first wife and of a different tribe. This marriage was based on choice, but Kandala made the arrangements with the girl's family and paid a large bride-price of £90. The new marriage had a congeniality and mutuality of interests lacking in the first one and gave more signs of permanence.

Intertown marriages were also arranged. Much visiting occurred between Copperbelt towns, and arrangements were made by parents and other close relatives, or some other appropriate kinsman in the flexible classificatory kinship system. Often, these intertown marriages were more casual, and the parents or other relatives were not told until the principals had already decided on marriage; sometimes, a divorce from a previous mate was involved. The courtship and marriage of John was of this type. John described it:

You see, she was married to a gentleman at Mufulira [nearby mining township], and he was very rich. He owned a tearoom and had a motor-cycle. She came over here for a few days to see her mother. While here she moved in the company of three girls, and all four were beautiful.

One Saturday night they came to a concert at the Welfare Center. I was there, and I had on my wonderful new pair of crepe rubber shoes and my new Champion bicycle with me. These girls sat together in one corner, and boys tried to sit with them. But the girls cursed them and said they did not want dirty people to sit with them. It was difficult for me to think which one of them I would like for my lover, since all four of them were so beautiful. I decided to try my luck and sit by them. To my surprise they did not chase me, but one of them said, "This is the type of boy we want," and another one, "He has a new pair of shoes which are very expensive, and also a new bicycle." After some time, they said that they were sleepy, and they started to go home. When they left, I followed and coming up to them, said, "I want one of you to remain behind. I would like to talk to her." They asked me to choose the one I wanted to talk to, and after a few seconds, I pointed to one whose name was Mary. The rest went away, and Mary asked me what I wanted to tell her, and I replied that I wanted her to sleep with me at my house. She kept quiet for some time while looking at me, and then said, "O.K.," and we went home to sleep. I did not wake up until nine o'clock the next morning.

Then I told her that I wanted to marry her, and she told me about being married to a certain gentleman at Mufulira and that I would have to pay him. I told her I didn't mind. It was Sunday, and she took my bicycle and rode to her mother's house. Her mother asked her where she had slept and whose bicycle it was, and she replied that she had slept at one of her girl friend's house and that the bicycle belonged to her friend's brother. In the afternoon we went to the football field to watch a match, but I sat alone and she was with her friends.

Two weeks passed and Mary's parents knew she was playing [the term used for sexual relations] with a boy, and they asked her where she was sleeping. She told them, "There is a boy at Section Six who wants to marry me." The parents came to see me and said, "We have been told that you play with our daughter"; and I replied, "Yes, I do." They asked me if I did not know that she was married, and I told them that I knew and was prepared to pay whatever they asked. Then they said, "If you wanted to marry our daughter, why did you not come and see us?" and I replied that I was planning to come and see them. Soon, the whole family met to consider our marriage, and I went to see them. I paid the dowry and our marriage was confirmed.

After a few days my wife told me that she was going to Mufilira to collect her clothes. When she arrived there she told her husband she was married. He grew very angry and said, "We shall go to Luanshya together on my motorcycle, so that I see this man." They came here, and we started fighting seriously. I still have the scars which he made with his knife. But I was very strong and hurt him, too.

Although John's marriage was one of choice, based completely on sexual attraction and entered into casually, the girl's parents functioned eventually in a partially traditional manner.

Whether marriages were based on choice or completely arranged by kindred, the traditional services and gifts of the husband to his wife's family were commuted to money, which had to be given to the in-laws on their frequent visits to town. The modern men, and often their wives, too, interested in saving money for careers, in raising their standards of living, in educating their children, openly grumbled about this situation. Over and over again, members of the intelligentsia and other careerists complained about the visits of relatives and in-laws, to whom they had given cash on hand and savings. For instance, Mr. Bwalya, a white-collar worker, earning nine pounds and ten shillings a month, gave his mother-in-law seven pounds on her recent visit. Her demand was made indirectly, by mentioning that another son-in-law, whom she had just visited in nearby Ndole, had given her seven pounds. Mr. Bwalya felt he had to give an equal amount to maintain his status and to have a good record as a son-in-law, needed in case any future marital troubles became a court case. The frequency of divorce made this a possibility for almost everyone; the granting of divorce by the court depended, to some degree, on the records of the spouses. But seven pounds was a large amount for Mr. Bwalya, and he had to borrow most of it.

Women, too, complained about the demands of their husband's mothers. The wife of one of the leading members of the intelligentsia told how her mother-in-law left her family in the village with no one to look after them and had come to visit, "just to get money." She was given more than half of her son's monthly pay. In the past she would have been given food. Eating up food which was perishable was very different from today's demands, called "eating up earnings."

These men and women were aware of the conflict between the value of saving for the individual family and the frequent cash gifts to relatives, but they could not renounce completely the traditional ties formed early in childhood; and they were not sure enough of their position in the new economic order to risk foregoing their rights to help from kindred, if they were unemployed or in some other crises. The conflict was conscious and verbalized by the modern Africans, and the assumption is, therefore, that no high degree of unconscious anxiety was created. The traditionalists, more interested only in earning as much money as possible, but not in careers or in saving for the future, appeared to take the giving of money to visiting relatives more for granted and to enjoy the prestige which came from lavish gifts.[7]

Other rivalries and hostilities centering on money and property occurred between the conjugal family and the lineage group. In the past, members of the same household belonged to different lineages, but when everyone had the same subsistence standard of living, there was little economic rivalry. Today, with a diversity of standards and with some Africans enjoying a surplus, how a man spends his money becomes a cause of tension between his matrilineal group and his wife and children. When one man bought his wife a sewing machine, his sisters came on a visit and beat her up. When another marriage was dissolved, the husband's relatives came and took everything in the house, including even the wife's dresses. Colson found a like situation among the agricultural Plateau Tonga in Northern Rhodesia; and at the time of her study, the more successful farmers were demanding a change in customary laws and wanted to make a will and leave their wealth to their wife and children. As she noted, this could bring further problems, if the wife gave the inheritance to her matrilineal kindred.[8]

Polygamy also brought problems unknown in the past. There was no record of the number of polygamous marriages on the township, but my impression was that it was less frequent than in the villages of the past. In Broken Hill, at the time of Wilson's study, 5.7 per cent out of 3,500 women were polygamously married, and practically all of these were living on the five-acre plots outside of the compound.[9] In the past, each wife was an economic asset and a polygamous marriage carried more prestige for the husband than a monogamous one. On the mine township, an additional wife was an extra expense; and the prestige aspects, weakened by Christianity and European practices, seem to have disappeared with its economic advantages. The housing situation also made polygamy difficult. In the villages, each wife in a polygamous household had a house for herself and her children. But the mine provides only one house for its employee, regardless of the number of his wives, and two wives could rarely share the same house amiably. Quarrels between co-wives and charges of witchcraft were common. If they belonged to different tribes, there were added complications. Yet some men did take a second wife. If the first wife was barren, the husband might follow his customary prerogative of taking a second wife. But sometimes the polygamous household was merely one of convenience. For example, a man who had left his wife at home might marry again on the Copperbelt without bothering about a divorce. When the rural wife came to join him, a polygamous household was set up. Other times, it was a matter of desiring two women.

In one rather typical polygamous household, the first wife was of her husband's tribe and thirty-two years old, while the second wife was of a different tribe and twenty-four years old. The husband was about fifty and had been married and divorced several times. The second wife was pregnant when I knew them. The first wife told of her troubles:

We didn't sleep all night. My friend [the second wife] cried the whole night. She complained of the pain in her womb about seven P.M. and said that the baby was moving about and causing great pain. Nothing happened because it isn't time yet for the birth, but we decided this morning to take her to the clinic. I don't think she really had the pain, but that it was just a sign of longing for her husband. She is overproud of being a new wife and having a womb. If I had money, I would go home because I am not happy with this kind of life. My friend's relatives are here every month in search of help, and so when our husband receives his pay, he shares it with them. If I were the only wife, I could have enough money for food and clothing, but since we are two I cannot meet my needs. I am often tempted to play with other men because of my suffering.

Then besides, Mary [the co-wife] has no respect for me. When my husband first married her, I intended to treat her as my sister, playing and eating together. But she began to lie to her husband and tell him that I wanted to poison her food and water. One time she threw the meat from the pot at me because she thought I had poisoned it. Now she cooks at her friend's house because she is afraid of being bewitched.

I think the main trouble between us is also that we are from different tribes with different customs. I am from the same tribe as my husband, as was his first wife. Then he married a Biza woman, and that was followed by a Kaonde woman, then me, and now this Lamba woman. He is used to this kind of marriage and I think he will never go home, but will die here. But I hope to go home as soon as I can.

Occasionally I came across a relatively contented polygamous arrangement. In such a one, the second wife was employed as a nurse's aide in the African Hospital and was therefore entitled to her own house. Each wife lived separately, and the husband slept with each in turn, but "stayed to rest" more with the second one. The first wife belonged to her husband's tribe, and the second one was of another tribe. Discussing the marriage and her co-wife, the second one said:

We used to fight each other. She would start it, because she thought that the husband would then divorce me because of too much fighting. But it did not help her because he loved me as much as he did her. Now we are friendly and visit each other. Sometimes she cooks and brings food for me.

It is all right because I have my own house and am employed. It would be impossible if we lived in one house. Then we would be quarreling all the time. There are still some difficulties, particularly about money and how to share it between us. It is never enough even for our simple domestic requirements. Of course, I don't have to suffer much because I am working and earning money.

But there will be trouble when he decides to leave for his home. If it was not polygamy it would be simple. I would go with him, because he loves me and we understand each other. But because of this other wife, I cannot agree to go. She would go too, and I fear that she would poison me or that her relatives would bewitch me. I would be alone among people of a different tribe, and might die or become mad.

Even the one polygamous marriage which followed a traditional pattern did not work out. A barren wife helped her husband select his second wife, her niece, so that he could have children. But the first wife made the life of her niece, now co-wife, so miserable, that the latter was forced to leave and take the child with her. The wife admitted the right of her husband to take a second wife, since she had not given him a child and knew that her husband was thinking of marrying again anyway. But by one subterfuge and another, she was trying to prevent it.

It is difficult to see how polygamy could continue very long in the present situation, in which the co-wives have to share the same small house and the wages of one husband. Furthermore, the general trend towards Europeanization is contrary to its continuance.

Intertribal marriages bring a new problem to monogamous, as well as to the polygamous, households. In Mitchell's 1951 study, almost three-fifths of the marriages were outside of the tribe.[10] However, he computed that there were nearly six times more intratribal marriages than if there had been a purely random selection.[11] This was about twice the proportion in Broken Hill in 1940, where over 30 per cent of the marriages were intertribal.[12] Problems in intertribal marriages were apt to come to the fore when they ended in divorce and the question of custody of children involved a conflict of matrilineal and patrilineal principles. There was also the problem of going home, either for a visit or upon the husband's retirement. A wife felt strange and often feared to stay with her husband's relatives from another tribe, particularly if they were in a distant part of the territory. The fear of witchcraft in this situation was strong.

A woman who had been married some time ago to a man from another tribe from a rather distant part of the territory told of her experience. After she had had four children, her husband decided that they should all visit his home. Her father advised her, "My daughter, you are going very far, and it is better for you to take only one child with you and let the rest remain here with me." But the woman did not heed her father's advice and journeyed with her husband and all the children to his distant home. After staying there for some time, the husband told his wife that they would now return, but would leave the children behind. The wife answered, "Ah, but this place is very far from my home, and I cannot leave my children here alone." But the husband, supported by his relatives, made the children remain. When the woman returned, her father was much annoyed that she had refused to take his advice, but he reported the whole matter to the government, which sent a messenger to bring back the children. The husband's relatives could not refuse the government messenger, and so the mother and her children were united. She divorced her husband and shortly afterward married a man from her own tribe. At the end of her story she said, "I was very lucky."

Many of the mothers whom we interviewed were against inter-tribal marriage for their daughters, and there was much awareness of the problems resulting from it. But propinquity and attraction, as well as a possible difference in the sex ratios of any one tribe on the mine township, led to such marriages. Problems connected with them will probably diminish in the future, when the tribe becomes less significant as a point of reference.

Divorce and remarriage were common. In Mitchell's 1951 survey, which included both mine and town locations, 62 per cent of the men's marriages and 55 per cent of the women's marriages were re-marriages.[13] In general, those remarrying tended to pick mates who had also been married before. Although there was no exactly comparable data from rural areas, Mitchell thought that town marriages were probably no more unstable than those in villages today.[14] On the other hand, in Broken Hill, Wilson thought marriage was more unstable than in the country.[15] I assume that the percentage of divorces and remarriages in town might have been higher on the mine township than Mitchell's study indicated. His study was limited to people registering their marriages in the Urban Court of Luanshya. The marriage certificate issued by the court was introduced for administrative reasons, and a house for a couple was not allotted on either the mine or municipal township unless the certificate was shown. Couples who had been married for years, as well as those entering marriage, found it necessary to register their marriages and the "Africans themselves are beginning to recognize the certificate as a mark of stable marriage.[16] But there was great casualness in many of the remarriages, particularly when the men had been married a number of times; and they did not always apply for a new certificate. A new wife might simply take the place of the former in the household, and the administrative authorities were none the wiser. A husband could erase the name of a former wife from the certificate and write in the name of a new one.[17]

The reasons for divorce varied. The most common, for either spouse, were: attraction to someone else, continuous infidelity of mate, constant quarreling, and interference by in-laws. The husband's reason for divorce also included wife's lack of fertility and her extravagant demands for money and clothes; the wives' reasons also included husband's sterility, his failure to give enough money and clothes, refusal to accept a polygamous household, much fighting with husband and being beaten by him, and, in the case of intertribal marriages, not wishing to go to the husband's home. As in all societies, there was very often a combination of motives for divorce. I have no exact data on what happened to the children in the many cases of divorce on the Copperbelt, but my impression is that they tended to remain with the mother. This created a problem, since the men often resented giving up the children after they had paid a large sum of money as bride-price. As one man said, "Why is it that when men pay a lot of money to marry a girl, and yet when parting, the women take all the children? I do not see why we men should not take the children."

The talk of divorce was much in the air, often precipitated by a small dispute. For instance, a woman started quarreling with her husband over her petticoats. She complained that he did not buy her good ones and that when she bathed in the communal bathroom, her friends laughed at her coarse petticoats. Her friend, who witnessed the quarrel, sagely remarked, "Probably she has already seen another man whom she wants to marry." Sometimes a couple divorced for a trifling reason and later remarried. In such a case, a man came home very late after losing his money in a card game. His wife scolded him, and he beat her. They were divorced. Later, they remarried. Between the divorce and the remarriage, the woman lived with relatives on the township and the man lived with another woman, without benefit of any ritual.

A new phenomenon which contributed to the instability of marriage was a group of young women who were rather openly "on the town." These were called "champions," sometimes regarded as a synonym for prostitutes. But this is not accurate. These girls, ranging in age from the late teens to the midtwenties, were interested in freedom of choice, in taking the initiative if they so desired, and in the money and material things gained from their sexual relationships. But they would not have a relationship with a man which did not give them sexual satisfaction, and their liaisons often lasted for a number of months. They were well dressed and tidy and, reputedly, experts in sex. Some had been married and divorced; most of them planned to marry. They maintained relationships with their families, visiting their mothers whenever they could. Several of them were friends, going to beer halls and dances together. They loved European forms of dancing. One of them said:

I shall never stop dancing, even if I should have a child. While I am dancing, I will give the child to my husband to take care of. And the child I have by playing with ordinary darlings, I can give to anyone while I am dancing.

Grace was typical of this group. She was born on the Copperbelt about twenty-five years ago, although she looked younger according to African standards. She had a slender body, and was regarded as pretty or attractive, but not beautiful. She began playing with boys before puberty, customary in her tribe, and had been married three times. During the first marriage she had a baby, who died immediately after birth, and she has had no children since.

Recently, she ran away from her husband, a policeman in a nearby Copperbelt town, because he beat her too much. She said:

He was very jealous. He did not like me to greet any boy. If one just stopped to greet me at the beer hall, he would beat me when we got home. When he was told by his friends, "Your wife is adulterous," he would come right home and beat me. I told him that he should not listen to what other people said about me, but that he should prove it by finding me doing it. But he would not take my advice. The last time he beat me, I nearly died. I was in the hospital for two weeks, and look at the scars I still have.

He spoiled me very much. He would not allow me to go to the bush

to collect firewood or make charcoal as other women do. He was afraid
a snake would bite me, and so he bought the firewood and charcoal.
And he bought me expensive things, too. I have a coat which cost six
pounds, and once I had three pairs of sandals at the same time. Many
women were jealous of me because of my clothes and wanted my husband. I once found one who was taking food privately to him, and I
cursed her and then I cursed him, and we had a big fight. He has written
me that he would like me to be his wife again. But I have refused, and
my mother will not allow me to go back to him because he beat me so
much.

Grace was now sleeping rather regularly with an unmarried young
man, one of the intelligentsia, and was reputedly not faithful to him.
He was not planning to marry her, and she had her eye on someone
else, a clerk, whom she wanted to marry. According to gossip, he
would not marry her because he wanted someone who was not
"morally weak."

There was another group of young girls not yet married who
slept around with many boys, but who were not champions. They
appeared to be primarily interested in enjoying themselves through
frequent sexual relations with different partners, and they did not
expect clothes or money or permanence. There were also a few
prostitutes.

Men who were looking for sexual opportunities were not
restricted to the champions or other fast young women, but could also
satisfy themselves with married women. The opportunity for extramarital relations was greatly increased by the miners working on
shifts, as it was quite easy for a woman whose husband was on a
night shift to entertain a lover who was on the day shift. Mistrust
of each spouse's infidelity was common. If a woman stopped to talk
to a man for a few minutes on the road, it was assumed that they
were arranging an assignation. If she was late coming from the
market, or had a few shillings that she could not account for, she
was suspected of adultery. A man was suspected if he accepted food
from a woman, outside the bounds of ordinary hospitality, or if he
came home late. A church elder could not visit a parishioner's home
if the husband was not there, and my young male assistants could
not interview women. (It was not too long ago that sexual jokes about
the iceman and the milkman were common in the United States.) On

the Copperbelt, suspicions seemed to be endless, and recriminations between spouses were constant. The following conversation was typical of what went on ad infinitum in most households:

(The wife has returned home from market where she had gone to buy some fish.)

HUSBAND: You have taken so long! What were you doing?

WIFE: Where do you think I had gone? You know it takes time to buy something from the market, for one has to go from seller to seller to find out where there is good fish at a good price. Some of the fish costs two shillings, or two and six, and even three shillings. Could I buy that? Where else do you think I had gone?

HUSBAND (*looking convinced*):
   I thought you had gone to see a Megalita [sister-in-law].

WIFE (*angrily*):
   You are suspicious of me, because you do bad things with girls, and you think I do the same. Yesterday when you came home late and said you were lost, I did not believe it. I know you were with some girls.

HUSBAND: You think I went to do bad things with girls when I told you I was lost?

WIFE: Yes, I do! *(becoming more angry)*. And you are always coming home late from Monday to Sunday. You say you are drinking, but you are not the only one who drinks, and they do not all come home late. If you are going to continue doing the same, I shall leave you and go to my home.

HUSBAND (*trying to change the subject*):
   I am going to buy a valve tube for my bicycle.

WIFE: You are cheating; you are just going to the beer hall to drink beer with women.

HUSBAND: No, I shall come back quickly.

An interesting example of the mingling of old and new patterns is illustrated in the attitudes of a husband in a court adultery case, which concerned his young pregnant wife who said she was assaulted while her husband was away at work by a man who came to the house and asked for beer which she had brewed. The accused denied the assault, saying that the woman had willingly committed adultery. The court did not think the case clear-cut, since there was no evidence from nearby neighbors that the wife had called for help. The man was fined eight pounds as the principal wrongdoer, and the woman was fined two pounds ten shillings as having been a party to the "assault." The husband was a faithful member of the Church of England, whose missionary had requested that adultery cases be settled by the mission rather than by the Urban Court. Several missionaries took this stand because they suspected that some husbands encouraged their wives to commit adultery in order to get the court fines. However, the husband in this situation took the case to court despite the urging of the missionary, because he said that if his wife died in confinement or had unusually difficult labor pains, he or his wife (according to tribal custom) could be blamed for adulterous behavior. The court decision was necessary to establish his innocence. He was following a tribal pattern; but he was also a good Christian and refused to take the compensation of eight pounds which the court awarded him, saying that it was not Christian to make money out of sin. He thus satisfied his Christian conscience and followed pagan, tribal behavior.

Love and affection appeared to exist in both stable and unstable marriages. An adulterous husband might still love his wife and return to her, and an unfaithful wife might continue to love her husband. This situation is not peculiar to Africans. It is interesting that although extramarital relations were the norm, they were not emotionally accepted, as they are in some societies where they are customary. It was as if these Africans yearned unendingly for a faithful mate, but were compulsively unfaithful. There can be a number of explanations: historical, sociological, and psychological.

Neither monogamy nor a husband's faithfulness were traditional values. But although adultery and divorce were common in the past, there had been restraints: the smallness of the village created difficulties in keeping extramarital relationships secret; men had to pay compensation if caught, and there were other sanctions against women; canons of good taste and eligibility for future remarriage imposed limits; the presence and interests of in-laws and kindred acted as controls. The large township provided more opportunities for extramarital relations, and men and women were less segregated in daily social life. The concept of platonic relationships between the sexes is relatively new and was, and is, absent in Africa, as well as in many other places of the world. Then, too, men had more money to pay compensation and to secure a divorce. Standards of taste and eligibility for marriage were changing. Girls who in the past would have been married at puberty could postpone marriage if they wished. A group of young avant-garde women were available for sexual relations, and they exercised the very unorthodox right of choice. So did an increasing number of other adults. Men had the all-important money to buy clothes, and the intense desire for them created new temptations for women and were a cause of strife in marriage and in concubinage. The latter type of union, since it did not offer the security of marriage, tended to increase jealousy. The situation in regard to marriage and sexual relations was changing faster than mores of control could develop.[18]

On the unconscious level there can be another explanation for the frequent changing of mates and for the distrust in the past and today. The complete indulgence of African infants by their mothers for the first couple of years and then the sudden cessation, when the father literally took the place of the infant in the mother's bed, could be responsible for an unconscious quest for the utopia of infancy, combined always with the fear of disillusionment and the suspicion that the mate, like the mother, will be unfaithful. It should be remembered that the very close relationship with the mother was followed by a more diffused relationship with a number of "mothers" in the extended group of relatives. There was no pattern for a relatively exclusive and continuous relationship with one person throughout childhood. Wives in the polygamous households in the past seemed to get along well. It has already been noted that in one of the polygamous families on the township, the second wife took it as a matter of course that her husband loved both her and his first wife.

Meaningful new models of marriage and family organization were not present, as they were in the economic and political spheres. The African Mine Workers' Union was modeled directly on European unionism. British trade union leaders came to Northern Rhodesia to organize the miners; and later, African leaders went to Britain to study union organization. The functioning of the European Mine Workers' Union was also known, to some extent, to most of the Africans. From the early days of the Protectorate new political models, such as the African Representative Congress, were introduced. The increasing representation of Africans in the Federal and Northern Rhodesian Legislature, the knowledge of European parties and politicians in the Territory and Federation, the formation of predominantly African political parties, all provided the know-how of modern political life. There was nothing comparable for family life. The missionaries' teachings concerning monogamy, fidelity, and other Christian virtues did not appear to have taken deep root among most Africans in this area, even though many were members of a church and solemnized their marriages in them. The complete social segregation between the two races created ignorance and misunderstanding. The tales of cook boys and yard boys about their employers were in the nature of folklore. The position of the African "boy" in the kitchen, in the yard, or waiting on the table, overhearing scraps of conversation only half understood, was not conducive to understanding. For instance, all Africans, servants as well as others, firmly believed that Europeans were paid when they extended hospitality to friends and relatives. This is regarded as highly immoral by the Africans. The belief may have originated in the early days when there were no hotels and traveling district officers and district commissioners gave their per-diem expense allowances to whoever gave them a room and meals.

European life as depicted in movies also gave rise to the idea that Europeans were basically immoral. Africans regarded the kiss as a direct prelude to sex relations, and those who have grown up in town kiss in their love-making, but privately. The champions sometimes kissed in public when they were drunk. When an elderly man in a movie kissed a child, many in the audience gasped with horror, assuming it was the child's father and a prelude to incest. In another movie there was a scene of a man and a woman skiing. The Africans in the audience commented on the beautiful body of the woman and the exposure of her thighs in the tight ski pants. The following comment was typical of many:

> White people are not ashamed of anything. If an African girl was dressed like that, many men would be following behind her wherever she went. In fact, no girl would dare do it. If she was dressed like that she couldn't move even fifty yards. She would be lifted up at once. But European women do not care. They are very immoral.

Stable marriages did exist, even though they seemed to be a minority. My impression was that they were more frequent among the intelligentsia and middle class, and that a relatively high bride-price was paid by the men in this group, which would contribute to their stability. New values concerned with raising standards of living and having careers seemed also to increase marriage stability. Then, too, fathers in this class did not want to lose their children, who, in matrilineal tribes would go with their mother in case of divorce. The members of this small educated group also were aware of their status position, which would be hurt by open promiscuity and excessive divorces.[19]

There were other elements which contributed to family stability for Africans in general. There would presumably be more emotional involvement in marriages based on choice than in those based on contractual arrangements, and this could add to stability. The continued validity of marriage payments and sponsorship of marriage by some relative had, likewise, a stabilizing function. Epstein thought that the Urban Court was a "guardian of public morals." The court, composed of representatives of the major tribes on the Copperbelt, heard all divorce cases, held up standards for appropriate behavior, and admonished those who departed from them. For instance, it refused to give a divorce to an adulterous husband because he had been "running about loosely as though he were an animal in the bush."[20] However, we do not know whether the husband became less adulterous after this admonishment and the refusal of a divorce. Although the court members were appointed by native authorities in the tribal areas, Epstein wrote that their judgments were influenced by the social changes occurring on the Copperbelt and that their standards for reasonable behavior included some of the new practices on the Copperbelt.[21] However, the actual effect of the court decisions on marital behavior could only be learned in a more detailed study of the latter.

Although the township was large, it did not have the anonymity of a modern city. Relatives on the township, neighbors, and friends knew a great deal about the intimate life of each other; and this group sometimes acted to maintain norms of conduct they considered proper. "A Case of True Love," the next chapter, is an example.

10. A Case of True Love

THESE CONVERSATIONS record an important and frequent event of life on the Copperbelt: a member of a family leaves to visit his or her family in the rural village. Since women are usually unemployed, they make more of these visits than do the men. The collection of the necessary gifts, the journey, the temptations of the spouse who is left behind, and the consequent concern of town relatives, neighbors and friends, are familiar themes.

Mary Mwenda, the wife of James Mhango, whom we met in the conversation about the strike, was going home to visit her mother, who lived in a village in the eastern part of Northern Rhodesia. Mr. Mhango came from Nyasaland, and he and his wife belong to different but related tribes. He is in his thirties and she is in her late twenties. They are illiterate, without any European education, and this is the third marriage for each. Because they have no children, they have adopted Joseph, the three-year old son of Mary Mwenda's sister. Living in the household temporarily were Peter Mwenda, Mary's brother, in his early twenties, educated, and a member of the intelligentsia; and his wife, Catherine Alefa, who had gone to school for only a few years and had recently come from her village. Many of the friends and neighbors belonged to different tribes from those of either Mary Mwenda or her husband James Mhango.

It should be remembered that generally wives do not take their husbands' names although a few do; formal terms of address between close friends and kindred are common.

Part I

The Wife's Departure

JAMES MHANGO: Oh, by the way, do you know that I am sending Mary to her home for two months? I fear that her mother will blame her if she does not go soon. She will take Joseph with her.

PETER MWENDA: No, I didn't know.

JAMES MHANGO: They will be going next week, when I am in the afternoon shift.

PETER MWENDA: But, what about you?

JAMES MHANGO: My money is not sufficient to take me to Nyasaland. I wanted to take six months' leave, but I fear that when I reach my wife's home, I would have to share whatever I have. Then when I reach my home, I would find that people are poor, and I would have to give them some things. It is very expensive to go home on leave.

PETER MWENDA: Yes, that is true.

The next day the family discussed the journey and Mary Mwenda began with gossip which Mr. Sichinga, a workmate and friend of her husband, was spreading. Mr. Sichinga has had no education.

MARY MWENDA: Do you know, Mr. Sichinga has started spreading news that you are sending me to your home to see your mother, whose leg has been cut off?

JAMES MHANGO: He is foolish. Why does he talk of my wife's journey wherever he goes, as if when his wife was going home I went around and talked about that. I shall blame him when I go to work.

MARY MWENDA: Mr. Lyson, to whom he was talking, said, "How can a woman go alone to the home of her husband, to see people whom she has not seen before and who

have not seen her? It would not be wise for Mr.
Mhango to do that, since we do not know what
would happen to Mrs. Mwenda in Nyasaland."

JAMES MHANGO: Yes, that is true. If I wanted you to go to my home,
we would have gone together. You could not go
alone when you have never been there. Mr. Sichinga
is silly, and that is why he is ruled by his wife in his
house. Last night, I told the boys we work with that
Mr. Sichinga is not being given food by his wife
and is being treated very badly just because he lost
his bicycle. All the boys started laughing at him, and
he was very sad indeed.

PETER MWENDA (*to his sister Mary*):
Are you going by bus or train?

MARY MWENDA: We are going by train.

PETER MWENDA: But you should go by bus. The bus station is closer
than the railroad, and you have much to carry.

CATHERINE ALEFA [Mr. Mwenda's wife]:
You will have lots of trouble on the way because
you have to carry a very big bundle containing plates
and pots and other things, and a suitcase and blankets
tied together, and a big basket, and a bicycle.

PETER MWENDA: These are many things, indeed, and the little boy
Joseph will also be troubling you. You will have
much trouble when you get off the train at Lusaka
and go to the bus station there because they are far
apart. Why do you not go by bus from here?

MARY MWENDA: Someone yesterday discouraged me from taking the
bus, saying that I would have to pay for carrying the
goods on a bus from here to Lusaka. So I decided to
go by train.

PETER MWENDA: Nay, he was not telling you the truth. Here at the
bus station they do not charge for any luggage at
all. I am usually at the bus station on Sundays when
people go back home with heavy luggage. The only
thing charged for is a bicycle. People start paying
for luggage when they catch buses which take them
to the rural and not when they go to Lusaka.

However, Mary did not take her brother's advice and five days later she and the family got ready to go to the railroad station.

JAMES MHANGO *(to his wife Mary):*	We should go soon. You should cook something for us, so that we eat before starting. Do not touch this and that for nothing, when you know it is growing late. The train does not wait for any person.
MARY MWENDA:	Yes, let me cook food at Mrs. Kabeyo's house where there is a fire. [Mrs. Kabeyo is a friend and lives next door.]
CATHERINE ALEFA:	One who goes on a journey should not sleep too much. Mary should have got up earlier.
PETER MWENDA *(to Mary):*	Why did you not use a sack for wrapping on the outside of the dishes. This material which you have put outside will get torn. [The material is dress goods intended for a present at home.]
JAMES MHANGO:	I have already told her that, but she does not agree. She wants to show off how rich she is.
CATHERINE ALEFA:	All those goods which go on the van are covered with sacks because they are handled roughly by the railway men.
MARY MWENDA:	I do not have a light sack to put outside, and a heavy maize sack would only increase the weight.
PETER MWENDA:	But the material you have used is much more expensive than the extra pennies you would be charged for weight.
JAMES MHANGO:	She wants to show off. She will arrive at home as a wife of a chief, who does not use sacks to cover goods but uses good cloth.
PETER MWENDA:	But remember that some people at home are poor, and you should use this material properly before you give it away. Also, it is a new material.
MARY MWENDA:	I don't mind.
JAMES MHANGO:	You should think of the people you will find at home who would like this material.
MARY MWENDA:	But I have no good sack to use. Come, the food is cooked. Let us go inside and eat.

| JAMES MHANGO: | Let us eat quickly, so that we can start for the station soon. |
| | |

(After they have finished eating, they all come outside.)

JAMES MHANGO:	We should be starting now. We may be late.
MARY MWENDA:	Yes, let us be going now.
CATHERINE ALEFA:	I shall carry the basket.

They started off. Mr. Mhango took the little boy, Joseph, with him on his bicycle. Mr. Mwenda went on his bicycle with some of the packages. The women, laden with packages, walked. The railroad station was about three miles away.

CATHERINE ALEFA:	Some people at home have already started dreaming that something is going to happen soon.
MARY MWENDA:	Yes, everyone in the morning is trying to explain the strange dreams she had.
PETER MWENDA:	By the way, did you tell your niece, Mrs. Saulani, that you were going home?
MARY MWENDA:	Yes, I went to see her, so that I can tell her mother whether she is well or not, when she asks me.

(Mr. Mwenda and Mr. Mhango arrive at the station.)

JAMES MHANGO:	Where are the others? They are very slow.
PETER MWENDA:	I passed them on the way, but not very far off.
JAMES MHANGO:	I have already bought the ticket. It was ten shillings and nine pence.
PETER MWENDA:	Yes, I know that the charges for the train have been increased.
JAMES MHANGO:	And I have been charged eight shillings for the bicycle. Now I am waiting for that big dish, so that it can be weighed.
PETER MWENDA:	There they come.
JAMES MHANGO:	They are very slow indeed.

(The women arrive.)

| JAMES MHANGO: | Let us weigh the luggage. |

Mr. Mhango and his wife attended to the weighing of the luggage, while the others went to the rest rooms. Mr. Mwenda returned.

PETER MWENDA: Has the luggage been weighed?

JAMES MHANGO: Yes, it has. Here is the ticket.

PETER MWENDA: So you paid six shillings and eleven pence.

JAMES MHANGO: Yes. It is very expensive, and I know it will be worse when on the bus from Lusaka to home.

PETER MWENDA: Yes, there it is more expensive. Has Joseph been paid for, too?

JAMES MHANGO: They said that he is small and needs no ticket.

MARY MWENDA: Shall I have to pay again when I arrive at Lusaka?

PETER MWENDA: You have paid everything for the railway now. Your work is to keep these tickets you have been given very safely. If you lose them you will not get your luggage and bicycle at all.

JAMES MHANGO: When you arrive in Lusaka show these two white tickets to the man in charge of luggage.

MARY MWENDA: How shall I know the office?

PETER MWENDA: When you arrive you will see the men carrying luggage from the van to a big building.

MARY MWENDA: Oh, shall I give the tickets to one of them?

PETER MWENDA: No, just follow them and you will find a European there, and he is the one to whom you will give the tickets.

MARY MWENDA: Oh!

JAMES MHANGO: You will not be asked to pay again there. You will just be given your things when you give them these sheets of papers. The European will also have his papers with the same numbers.

MARY MWENDA: Oh, I see.

PETER MWENDA: But keep the things very safely and near you. Marriage receipt [certificate] and tickets, and leave-pass should all be in the handbag, which should be in your hand all the time, day and night. Do not leave it anywhere alone.

MARY MWENDA:	Yes.
JAMES MHANGO:	Women are usually not very careful. She will forget all we are telling her very soon.
PETER MWENDA:	Do not forget, because if you miss some of the things, you may be troubled very much by the policemen who inspect.
JAMES MHANGO:	If everything is not correct, the policemen will think you have just stolen the marriage receipt.
MARY MWENDA:	I shall not forget.
CATHERINE ALEFA:	Look at these two boys. They are looking at us very much. When they looked at the suitcase, one showed his friend the keys he has.
MARY MWENDA:	These are thieves who like stealing people's things at the stations. The time I was going to Chinsali some boys were chased by the policemen.
PETER MWENDA:	You should be very careful with them. See? They are looking at us and the suitcase.
CATHERINE ALEFA:	Look at his eyes; they are very swollen.
PETER MWENDA:	And he has not even combed his hair. I heard these two youths say that they are going to Ndola [a nearby town].
CATHERINE ALEFA:	Look at him. He does not want to take his eyes from us and the suitcase.
JAMES MHANGO:	Let me go and ask them where they are going. (*He goes over.*) Where are you going, Sir?
FIRST YOUTH:	We are going to Lusaka.
JAMES MHANGO:	I see. (*Mr. Mhango leaves them; he turns to his group.*) They say they are going to Lusaka.
PETER MWENDA:	These people are cheating. They have been saying that they are going to Ndola.
CATHERINE ALEFA:	You should keep an eye on them.
MARY MWENDA:	Hm . . . My suitcase will be very near me. Look at them. They are very dirty, and they have not even washed their faces, and yet they say they are going on a journey.
JAMES MHANGO:	The train has come now. I can hear it.
PETER MWENDA:	Yes, I have heard it, too.

When the train arrived, the two men helped Mary Mwenda and little Joseph aboard. They waved good-bye, and the train started.

JAMES MHANGO: I can only use a taxi-car when my wife will come from home. Now I shall go on my bicycle.

    (They all leave the station.)

Part II

The Erring Husband

Mr. Mwenda and his wife, Catherine, were at home; Mrs. Mary Mwenda had geen gone three days.

CATHERINE ALEFA: As I told you yesterday, Mr. Mhango followed a woman who pretended that she did not know him, and today he bought fish for six shillings and gave it to her. Then a little girl came, probably her daughter, and he gave her a piece of soap.

PETER MWENDA: That is very bad indeed. He has begun this even before his wife has arrived at home.

CATHERINE ALEFA: I told Mr. Mhango that what he was doing was not good at all. I asked him whether he had forgotten his wife, and he said, "No, I cannot forget my wife. I am just playing with this woman." Then I and Mrs. Banda told him that we would write a letter to Mary to tell her that he was marrying another woman. Then he answered, "I told Mary that I should have a lover and she agreed."

PETER MWENDA: Hm . . . A woman can never say that. Even if she is mad.

CATHERINE ALEFA: We told him that, too. But he just went away. The children of that woman came to Mrs. Chanda's house. You will see them. [Mrs. Chanda is a neighbor.]

The next day, Mr. Mwenda and his wife, Catherine Alefa, were outside their house and were joined by Mrs. Kabeyo, the next-door neighbor and a very good friend of Mary Mwenda, and by Mrs. Kunda, another neighbor and friend.

PETER MWENDA: Where has Mr. Mhango gone now?

CATHERINE ALEFA: His window is open, and so he must be in his room. (*She peeps in.*) Yes, he is there, and there is food tied in a handkerchief.

PETER MWENDA: Has it come from Mrs. Kwezekani [Mary's niece]?

CATHERINE ALEFA: Mrs. Kwezekani does not have that kind of material. It may have come from his lover. (*She turns to Mrs. Kabeyo.*) Has anyone come here while we were visiting in Section Two?

EDNA KABEYO: No, I did not see anyone.

CATHERINE ALEFA: (*She sees the children of the woman who is supposed to be Mr. Mhango's lover.*)
                    Ah, there are the children to whom Mr. Mhango gave soap, and it was their mother whom he bought the fish for.

EDNA KABEYO: These men are not to be trusted at all. Especially these men in towns are no good. Once you go away on leave they marry other women.

CATHERINE ALEFA: Mr. Mhango told me that he will marry this woman while his wife is away and then he will divorce her when his wife returns.

ALICE KUNDA: Hm . . . The woman might not so quickly agree to be divorced, and Mrs. Mwenda may find her in the house.

CATHERINE ALEFA: Mrs. Mwenda told me that if she finds her husband married, she will not come to this house. She will stay in Mrs. Kwezekani's house, and she will get married again, too.

                    (*Mr. Mhango wakes up and calls out from his room.*)

JAMES MHANGO: Has half-past two gone already?

EDNA KABEYO: No, only one o'clock has gone.

JAMES MHANGO: I should be leaving now. Has my friend Mr. Nkoma come by?

EDNA KABEYO: No, he may be at his brother's house.

JAMES MHANGO: He should not have gone. He told me that he would come and get me.

Mr. Mhango came outside and called to the little daughter of Mrs. Chanda to come and get his empty plates. The little girl came over and took away the plates. Mr. Mhango left.

CATHERINE ALEFA:	See, I knew that the food did not come from Mrs. Kwezekani.
EDNA KABEYO:	This is very bad indeed, and it is not right that Mrs. Chanda should let this woman come to her house because when Mrs. Mwenda hears of this they will not be on good terms. She will think that Mrs. Chanda was encouraging that woman to marry Mhango.
ALICE KUNDA:	These local tribes are no good at all. Even if a woman is your friend, when you go away she can sleep with your husband.
EDNA KABEYO:	Old people had a saying, "You chew some and leave some, because you do not know what will take place tomorrow." Mrs. Mwenda was right to take all the plates and pots home with her.
PETER MWENDA:	I shall ask Mrs. Chanda where the food has come from.
EDNA KABEYO:	You ask her. You can also ask Mr. Mhango. You should not fear.
	(Mr. Mwenda, Mrs. Kabeyo, and Mrs. Kunda all go over to Mrs. Chanda's house.)
PETER MWENDA (*to Lucy Chanda*):	Are you the one who has cooked food for Mr. Mhango?
LUCY CHANDA:	I am not the one who has cooked food. It has come from the woman he is marrying. Has he not told you that he is marrying another woman?
PETER MWENDA:	No, he hasn't.
EDNA KABEYO:	Ah, so he is marrying, and we do not know anything at all.
ALICE KUNDA:	Which woman does he want to marry?
LUCY CHANDA:	That woman who came here on Thursday evening. The one who was talking about her husband whom she has divorced.

PETER MWENDA:	So she is not married?
LUCY CHANDA:	No, she is not married; she is staying with her relatives in the special-grade section.
EDNA KABEYO:	That is very bad indeed. Some women are only after their friend's husbands.
CATHERINE ALEFA:	Whose children are these?
LUCY CHANDA:	They are from the same woman.
CATHERINE ALEFA:	And their father is the one who has been divorced?
LUCY CHANDA:	Yes.
CATHERINE ALEFA:	These women here are useless. Divorcing men who can give them children.
PETER MWENDA:	They do not seem to worry about that. They love money very much.
ALICE KUNDA:	But I know the woman is wasting her time. Mr. Mhango loves his wife very much. He is doing all this because these men do not want to be without lovers.
EDNA KABEYO:	I think Mr. Mhango knew this woman before his wife went away. For how could the woman start bringing food so soon?
PETER MWENDA:	I shall tell his brother about it.
EDNA KABEYO:	Yes, you should tell him.

Mr. Mwenda went to the mine bakery, where Mr. Mhango II worked.

EDWARD MHANGO:	Hallo, brother-in-law.
PETER MWENDA:	I have something to tell you. You see, when Mrs. Mwenda left on Wednesday, Mr. Mhango came home very late that night. Then on Thursday he bought fish for six shillings and gave it to a certain woman whom he says he wants to marry. Then on the same day he gave a piece of soap to the daughter of this woman, and today this woman has brought some food for him. When Mrs. Banda and Mrs. Alefa told him that he should not waste soap in that way and also money, he only laughed and said that he wanted to have the woman temporarily.

EDWARD MHANGO: I must see him tomorrow morning. He has started doing such silly things again. What tribe is that woman?

PETER MWENDA: She is one of these local women. She may be a Lamba or Swaka.

EDWARD MHANGO: They are useless indeed. I will blame him very much and he will hear me, since he fears me. When he married your sister, we thought he would settle down, and now again he has started doing useless things. I shall come and see you tomorrow. Is Mr. Mhango going for work in the afternoon?

PETER MWENDA: No. He will go in the morning.

EDWARD MHANGO: I shall come, so that you can show me that woman. I would like to curse her.

PETER MWENDA: Thank you. I must go now.

EDWARD MHANGO: Thank you.

The next day, shortly after Mr. Mhango came home from work, a young boy brought some food and Mrs. Chanda also arrived.

CATHERINE ALEFA: Where is that food coming from, Mr. Mhango?

LUCY CHANDA: So you did not tell your brother-in-law that you are marrying a new wife?

JAMES MHANGO: Hm . . . (*He goes into the house shamefacedly. They talk through the open door.*)

CATHERINE ALEFA: Do you think Mrs. Mwenda will be pleased to hear what you are doing?

JAMES MHANGO: So you people are much worried about it?

PETER MWENDA: The thing which worries us much is disease.

JAMES MHANGO: I am clever.

CATHERINE ALEFA: You have done a very bad thing because you started doing this the same day Mrs. Mwenda went home and it is giving her misfortunes. The bus in which she travels may overturn.

JAMES MHANGO: Ey. You people do not talk like that.

CATHERINE ALEFA: Yes. When Mrs. Mwenda comes home we shall tell her that you have married another woman, who has started bringing food.

JAMES MHANGO: I did not tell this woman that it was marriage; it is only friendship. I shall now tell her not to bring food here. If you continue talking, I shall let my wife stay at home for only one month instead of two. I love my wife very much, I cannot marry another woman.

CATHERINE ALEFA: Then if you love your wife, why do you sleep with another woman?

JAMES MHANGO: I cannot help it. I shall tell the woman that she should not be bringing food.

(Richard Mwape, a friend and neighbor, comes by.)

RICHARD MWAPE: Let us go and drink beer in Mr. Chipepo's house. He came in the morning to ask for you.

JAMES MHANGO: Yes, I shall go and drink some beer.

(Mr. Mhango and Mr. Mwape leave.)

CATHERINE ALEFA: Mr. Mhango will not come home until very late.

EDNA KABEYO: Yes, he will go to his woman.

CATHERINE ALEFA: He does not want to be advised by his friends at all.

EDNA KABEYO: Yes, yesterday Mr. Mwape and I tried to ask him where he was going and he said, "No one should be asking me where I am going. I do not have any one to look after me, and I have no child left behind who can be looking for me. If some people want to report to my wife they are just troubling themselves. She will not listen to them. She and I know our position better. I arranged with her about what I should do when she is gone."

PETER MWENDA: No woman can ever agree that her husband should marry another woman after she is gone.

CATHERINE ALEFA: And he said that he will have two wives and that the one who will not be satisfied will go away.

EDNA KABEYO: It is certain that Mrs. Mwenda will leave him, and she will marry another man here. She is quite fresh [young].

PETER MWENDA: Mrs. Mwenda will never agree to be a co-wife.

EDNA KABEYO:	He is quite senseless. He does not want to accept advice from his friends. He likes acting as a small boy.
PETER MWENDA:	I think better than he does.
CATHERINE ALEFA:	He will lose Mrs. Mwenda. The bad thing is for him to give disease, which he will contract from this woman, to Mrs. Mwenda.
EDNA KABEYO:	Yes, that is what we fear.
PETER MWENDA:	Before I went home Mr. Mhango infected her with a disease of bleeding, and she was very ill.
EDNA KABEYO:	And he has not yet learned a lesson.

Early the next morning, Mr. Mhango arrived home shouting.

JAMES MHANGO:	Good morning, sister.
CATHERINE ALEFA:	Good morning, brother.
JAMES MHANGO:	We have drunk a lot of beer. We have been drinking all the night at a house where I was taken by Mr. Nyawale. Yes. He took me to a certain Ngoni man's house in Section Five, where there has been free beer for a funeral.

Mrs. Kabeyo and Mr. Mwape arrived while Mr. Mhango was talking.

JAMES MHANGO:	I do not know the name of the wife and husband. We drank a lot of beer there. I do not have a wife here, and so I have to pass my time by drinking a lot of beer. I have nothing to do at home. This is not my house now, because my wife is not here. It belongs to Peter now. Anyway, I want my wife to come very soon. I am sending money so that she comes immediately. I cannot do without my beloved wife.
CATHERINE ALEFA:	What about your new wife?
JAMES MHANGO:	Ah, do you think I can forget my wife because of these women here? You will see my wife here soon. I had wanted her to remain at home for two months, but now she will not complete the two

	months. She will come when I shall be in the night shift.
CATHERINE ALEFA:	So soon?
JAMES MHANGO:	Yes, my wife cannot stay at home for a long time.
EDNA KABEYO:	You think much about your wife now.
JAMES MHANGO:	I always think much about her. When my wife comes I shall buy her some more new clothes, especially Fitenje because when she wears that she looks like a star. [Fitenje is the name of a figured material which comes from the Belgian Congo.] After some time has passed, I will go with her to my home.
CATHERINE ALEFA:	You will first go to her home, so that her relatives see you, and then you can take her to your home.
JAMES MHANGO:	Yes, I shall do that first.
RICHARD MWAPE:	Today you want to talk only about your wife.
JAMES MHANGO:	Yes. There is nobody else I can talk about. When your wife will go home you will not feel happy at all. That is why I spent my time drinking beer in houses so that I do not think much about my wife. Now I want to go and bathe; then I shall go to drink beer again. I cannot stay at home today, but starting from tomorrow I shall not be moving much. I will stay at home so that I am not late for work at night.
CATHERINE ALEFA:	That will be good.
JAMES MHANGO:	Now my wife is enjoying herself in the village.
CATHERINE ALEFA:	She has already gone to the garden.
JAMES MHANGO:	Ah, my wife cannot go in the bush. Before she left I told her that she should not go to the gardens because she might be hurt.
CATHERINE ALEFA:	But she cannot enjoy remaining alone in the village while other people have gone to the gardens. Moreover, this is harvest time, and there is much food in the gardens, and people will enjoy themselves with pumpkins and potatoes and sugar cane while they are gathering the maize.
JAMES MHANGO:	My wife will come with a lot of food when she returns. She will bring pork, too.

CATHERINE ALEFA:	You should send her enough money for her fares, and the two little ones [a young niece, as well as her nephew, Joseph] who will come with her and the things she will carry.
JAMES MHANGO:	Yes, I am sending her three pounds now, and she will borrow some money from her brother, and after she returns I shall send the money back.
CATHERINE ALEFA:	Yes, that is a good idea.
JAMES MHANGO:	I am going for beer now, but I shall come back soon, before twelve o'clock, so that I sleep.

He left and Mr. Phiri (a classificatory brother to Peter Mwenda and his sister) arrived.

DICK PHIRI:	I have come to tell you that I am leaving this afternoon by bus for Ndola, and as you know, from there I go home.
PETER MWENDA:	Ah, we have not written the letter yet. But you can greet the people at home. Mr. Mhango is sending money with you so that his wife uses it for returning here.
DICK PHIRI:	Yes, he gave me three pounds to carry to her. He said he would not keep it himself because he feared wasting it.
PETER MWENDA:	Yes, and we are writing letters tomorrow to go by the post.
DICK PHIRI:	Thank you. I must hurry now and pack.
PETER MWENDA:	Thank you.

At about half-past six Mr. Mhango returned.

CATHERINE ALEFA:	Is this your coming?
JAMES MHANGO:	Yes, I went to drink beer. Where is Mr. Mwenda?
CATHERINE ALEFA:	He is inside writing.
JAMES MHANGO:	Are you writing my letters now?
PETER MWENDA:	No.
JAMES MHANGO:	Now I want you to write a letter to my wife. Tell her that I have given Mr. Phiri three pounds to give

her so that she comes here soon. She should come
back with Joseph and her niece. I want her to come
soon. Tell her that she should borrow some money
from her brother for the fares of the little ones
and the luggage. I shall return the money when I
receive my pay next month. I gave her two months
leave, but I did not realize how hard it is to live
alone without a wife. I am bringing an envelope
for the letter. Will you send it very early tomorrow?

PETER MWENDA: Yes, at seven o'clock.

JAMES MHANGO: All right. I shall go now to work.

He put on his work clothes and left.

Mary Mwenda returned in about three weeks. She and James
Mhango happily resumed their marital relations.

A few themes emerge clearly from these conversations. A small
group, consisting of a few kindred and friends, who are neighbors,
were critical of the behavior of one of their members and regarded
themselves as custodians of his moral life. The fact that the friends
and neighbors were not related and belonged to different tribes
appeared to be unimportant. They, with the relatives, knew everything that was going on and acted as a social control, very similar
to those in the village. Proximity and friendships were strong bonds,
taking on some of the functions of village lineage groups. The expense of going home and, at the same time, the pleasure from the
prestige of bringing many gifts were obvious. The thinking of the educated Mr. Mwenda differed from that of the uneducated members, as
he belittled the desire to "show off" and counseled thrift and the best
means of transportation. But educated and uneducated men in the
group looked down upon a woman's capacity to remember and to
meet the hazards of a journey to the rural areas.

Mr. Mhango's dilemma illustrates well the pull between the desire
for immediate sexual gratification and love for his absent wife. This
problem is not unique on the Copperbelt, nor for other members of
the human species.

11. The Changing Position of Women

Personally, I should be very pleased if God had made me a man, for men have very little to worry them. Again a man can do whatever he wants to do. In addition to this men are stronger than women. If I had been a man, I should have been very troublesome to women, particularly to the educated girls who are very proud. Again as a man I should have gone for further education and probably the highest course in the world. I should have chosen a dignified job and a well-paid job.

In fact, being a man is a good thing. Men have more reasoning powers than women and are more courageous than women. Women get angry quickly while men keep their patience. Men get angry when there is really something bad. Of course, there are some men who only look for trouble in their women, but there are not many. Say, for instance, a man gave to a woman a penny, and if she annoys him you will hear him demanding more, say ten shillings, which in reality should be a penny. Such practices I dislike and I should be pleased to see that I do them to others and not to be done to me.

IN ESSAYS describing their fantasies, 73 per cent of the girls in Standards V and VI of the nearby government boarding school wished to be men. The essay above is typical of these. The girls were breaking from the past and seeking a new identity modeled on the privileges and power of men. In the essays, boys, as well as girls, expressed the desire to have less suffering, less work, and more independence. The boys envisaged this desired condition in the lives of Europeans; and the girls, in the lives of African men. The girls also envied the men for their greater strength, bravery, and power.[1]

Men and women started from different positions in tribal life. Women were an integral and respected part of the economic and social order, but men were definitely the masters. Among the agricultural tribes the hoe was a symbol for the women's work; and the axe, for the men's; and most work was done by groups of women and of men working separately. These groups were responsible for the training of the young. Socially and ritually men and women were also usually separate. But today men and women are no longer partners in communal economic tasks. The emphasis is on the individual household and on men and women living together as couples. Most women on the township had no communal or social role, and their work was restricted to the household.

Lag in Women's Entrance into the Modern World

The entrance of women into the modern world proceeds at a different pace from that of the men. It was primarily the males who had contact with Europeans and who were taking over many aspects of modern culture, while, in general, females were restricted to acquiring the new material things. Mining is, of course, exclusively a male occupation, but even in the non-mining urban communities of Northern Rhodesia there were relatively few positions open to women. On the mine township, at the time of my study, women were restricted mostly to jobs as nurse's aides, as social workers at welfare centers, and as teachers. Nurse's aides were the most numerous; only a few were assistant social workers; and there were only two women teachers in the elementary school. Women were not employed as domestic servants for Europeans; African men held these positions. I am told that today more women are working as teachers, and occasionally as telephone operators, but that they are still mostly nurse's aides. In any case, the number of women working outside the home was, and is, extremely small. The woman's work and life are confined to her immediate household. She may spend a small amount of time cultivating a garden at the edge of the township, but her days go to the care of her home and children.

The large majority of women did not participate in political, civic, trade union, and social organizations. Only a small number engaged in sports, although they were interested spectators at athletic events. A few women performed in the tribal dances held on Sunday afternoon, playing the role of "nursing sisters" and wiping perspiration from the dancers' faces. The social ballroom dancing on Saturday nights at the welfare centers, where men and women danced together, was an innovation. Some women drank beer with the men at the beer hall and in their homes, but there were fewer women drinkers. A significant minority of women, but a much smaller proportion than of men, listened to the radio and went to movies. Since the majority of the women were illiterate, reading could have no significance for them. Women went to church and, from my impression, more than men did, but with what seemed like little real emotional commitment. Welfare activities for women have been discussed, and while they are increasing, the participation of women in them was, and is, much less than it is for the men. The differential between male and female participation in community activities is not unique to the Copperbelt or contemporary Africa, and it has been historically true in most societies. But the African women start from the tradition of being part of a female communal group, which had economic, social, and ritual functions and was an integral part of society. The contemporary situation is, therefore, a drastic change for them.

Daily Life

On the mine township, the daily life of a woman followed a routine closely correlated with her husband's working hours. If he was on the day shift—from seven A.M. to three P.M.—she got up at about five o'clock, heated water, and carried it to the bathhouse for him. Then she made tea and prepared food for him to carry: corn, sweet potatoes, and peanuts. After her husband left, she cleaned and swept the house, washed the pots and plates left from the night before, bathed herself, and washed the children. If she had money, she then went to the market or butcher shop for vegetables, meat, or fish. If her husband was in one of the lower ranks and on rations, she might get up early to avoid standing in line at the company store. When she came home from marketing, she sometimes pounded the corn in a mortar to make "mealies" for porridge, and then she did her cooking. Some days she went to the public washing stand and did the family washing. After these household chores were finished, and if it was not yet time for her husband's return, she might visit with women neighbors and friends to gossip and talk. Or she occupied herself with bead work, or perhaps she went for a hairdressing. If she went out, she was careful to come home before her husband, and again she had his bath ready as soon as he returned. Then she finished the cooking and served her husband. She and the children followed the traditional custom of eating separately, he at a table and they on the floor.

All the women were in agreement that they did not have to work as hard on the township as in the village. One said:

I am sometimes afraid of going back to the hard work in the village. You do more work in the bush, and most of it is very hard. We have work here, too, but it is all done at home, and not in the bush, so that when you feel tired you can relax comfortably in a chair or lie down on a sack. Not so in the village. You work hard in the garden, you return home and still have to do domestic duties, such as drawing water from a far-distant well, cooking, and pounding.

This sentiment was echoed by many. The women thought they looked younger longer in the towns, partly because they did not work so hard and because they had better clothes and had more time to spend on hairdressing and on other such personal matters. One woman, whose husband was leaving his mine job and returning home, said:

I am unhappy to go home, for I fear that I will look old there very soon, after all the clothes I am taking with me are finished. At home I will no longer look young, and men will not look at me.

The fear of witchcraft was another deterrent to going home. Many Africans believed there was more witchcraft in the rural area than in towns, and the women feared for the lives of their children, who might be bewitched. One said:

We have lost many children there—they died from being bewitched—and if we go back, we may lose those we have now.

The women also thought that there was less jealousy of money, clothes, and other material things in town and, therefore, less witchcraft directed toward them.

Another woman said:

This place is better than home. One reason is that you can play about with money, and there is no hatred. You can be as well dressed as you like, and there is no one to worry or backbite you. Even if you have better food, you do not have to worry. Your friend would just find money and go out and buy food for herself, whereas at home, you would be hated for all this and suffer.

Life in the village would also seem narrow and uninteresting after town life. A typical comment by a woman was:

At home there are not many places to visit. I am accustomed to town life after twelve years on the Copperbelt. I was first at Chingola, then Nkana, and now here. I don't think I shall ever go home.

The majority (65 per cent) of the adolescent girls (from twelve to sixteen years) in Standards V and VI (corresponding to our seventh and eighth grades) of a government boarding school also wanted to live in town when they grew up, because they did not like the monotony of village life and because they enjoyed the diversity of people in town, the higher standards of living, and the opportunities for jobs and for recreation. A minority preferred rural life because they liked farming and the simpler, cheaper, and relatively more secure life.[2] There was also a minority of adult women who looked forward to returning home. One of them said:

I am very happy that we will go home in June when my husband retires. I will once more be among my own people, the Lala. I hope my daughter will be betrothed and that her future husband will start working for us, and I will work for him in return.

Disputes over Money

In spite of the general preference for town life, the women were not too comfortable in it. They had more money and food and better clothes, but they felt insecure. A wife was completely dependent on her husband's earnings, and what he gave her was entirely up to him. Many women complained that they did not know how much their husbands earned. "I never know the amount my husband receives or what's in his savings account, and I am suspicious of how he spends his money." I heard this over and over again. Many

women in the Western world also do not know exactly how much
their husbands earn. But it was new to the African women. In the
past, their husbands did not have wages but, specific duties, known
to all. On the township, the wages of one man differed from another;
and it was up to each husband whether or not he told his wife
how much he earned. There was neither custom nor relatives to
dictate how much he should give her.

Men differed about whether they should tell their wives how much
they earned. Borrowing between men was common. Debts were
expected to be paid on pay-day, and many husbands did not wish
their wives to know about them; or the men simply wanted to keep
some money for their own use and not tell their wives about it. One
man was seen sitting outside the compound office on a pay-day,
counting the money he had received. He separated the money into
two piles, and put one in his shoes. When he was asked why he
was doing this, he answered: "Ah, I cannot show my wife all the
money I have received. I must hide some for my own use." He was
rather typical, even though most men did not use their shoes as a
hiding place. But there were others who felt differently. One said:

If you cannot show your wife how much you have, who will you show?
If you die here, your relatives may be far away, and if you do not tell
your wife how much is in your savings or what you have, then all that
money is lost, and it would have been better to have spent it on beer
while you are alive. [Presumably he did not expect the mine to make
an accounting of his savings to his wife.]

There was also confusion about the pension. In the past, what
belonged to the women and to the men was clearly determined by
custom. The pension is new, and while it is usually considered to be
the husband's, disputes occurred over it. One wife fought with her
husband, claiming that the pension money should be shared between
them, since she had been doing the cooking and keeping the house
in order while her husband was working. The comment of one of
the men observing the fight was, "Some women are senseless. When
a husband leaves his job, it does not mean that they have to share
the money, as if they were going to divorce each other."

A difference of opinion also existed between men and their wives
on how her earnings should be spent. Although few women had

jobs, a considerable number earned money by brewing beer in their homes and selling it. This was illicit, but widespread and done more frequently and in larger quantities than in the village. Women have traditionally been the brewers, but in the past beer was used only for hospitality, for ritual occasions, and to reward workers. On the township it was sold, and there was no lack of thirsty customers. Also, since the town women were not so busy with other duties, they had more time for brewing. In the past there might have been a shortage of the necessary grain for brewing, but today it can always be purchased. However they might earn their money, most wives did not think they should have to spend it on food; they wanted to keep it for themselves. But the husbands wanted it spent on food so that they could save or spend more from their own earnings.

Although disputes and problems between husbands and wives concerning money are common the world over, it is a new kind of problem for these Africans. In tribal life men and women were economic partners, and while their jobs were different, their work was considered of equal importance. On the Copperbelt men have more economic freedom than they had in the villages, where they worked for a considerable number of years for their in-laws before setting up their own households and their obligations to a wife were carefully observed by her relatives. There is no precedent for the new situation in which a wife is completely dependent on her husband who controls all the economic resources, nor for the situation where a wife can earn money for herself.

Parents' Responsibility for Education of Children

Another area of conflict between the conjugal family and the traditional extended family was the responsibility of the men for his sister's children and his increasing desire to help his own children get an education and other modern advantages. Men in the white-collar and middle-class occupations, who had higher incomes than manual workers and accordingly had more demands made on them, often accepted considerable responsibility for their sisters' children, as well as for the education of their own. One man in his midthirties who held an important post in the African education department had seven children in his household, four of whom were his own. Fathers usually paid any school fees involved in the education of their children. Thirty-two of fifty girls in Standards V and VI at a nearby government girls' boarding school were being sent there by their fathers; twelve were sent by a matrilineal uncle, a grandfather, or an older brother; four were sent by a mother; and two, by an older sister.

Essays written by the girls on this subject were very similar. The following was typical:

It was my father who decided to send me to this school. My father wants me and my brothers to be educated before he dies, so that in the future when we are alone, we shall not have so much suffering in this changing world. My father says he does not want to leave us without education or proper places, because all our relatives stay far away and many have died.

Education was expected to provide the security formerly provided by the lineage group. The girls wrote that they planned to work when they left school, in order to repay their fathers or whoever was paying their school fees. Parents on the township who were paying school fees, or who planned to pay them when their children were older said they expected to be reimbursed by the children. Before schools existed, children were educated informally by parents, by older siblings, and by adults of their own sex. Schools and fees are new; and the modern conjugal family, rather than the traditional lineage, takes the responsibility. But the idea of reimbursement of parents by children retains the concept of reciprocity.

Desire for Children

Almost everyone, traditional or modern, intensely desired children. The universally normal desire to have children was further strengthened by the fact that the basic value of fertility was traditionally related to supernatural and religious beliefs. Supernatural sanctions and taboos still surrounded procreation and sexual relations during certain periods, even though these were shortened by many modern young couples. In tribal life children were an economic asset. Their services and those of their potential mates were a form of security for parents in their old age. In the new order, here as elsewhere, parents can no longer rely on support from children, who may be in distant communities or preoccupied with their immediate family and career. It has already been noted that education for children is a new expense, particularly if they go beyond Standard VI or are sent to boarding schools. But regardless of their changing economic value, children were greatly wanted. Barren women were extremely sensitive to their misfortune and to be taunted about it was one of the worse insults. Young men who had postponed marriage for a few years because they desired to continue their education, talked enviously of their brothers or friends in the same or younger age group who already had children. Some men still took a second wife if the first one was barren.

There is no data to compare birth rates of the tribal past and present. But it is known that the population is increasing, even though syphilis is probably reducing the fertility of some women. There is the usual differential time lag between the reactions of fertility and of mortality rates to cultural changes induced by industrialization. Here, as in many parts of the world, deaths decline in number due to improved medical care, the improved standards of living, and many other scientific advances. In this part of Africa, increasing control over the malarial mosquito and the tsetse fly was also important. All these advances are relatively impersonal, with an obviously good function. But anything related to fertility is deeply personal; and in Africa, as well as in many other societies, a part of traditional religious beliefs. A decline in fertility therefore takes place very slowly and does not depend primarily on the spread of knowledge of contraceptive techniques, but rather on the development of a desire to have fewer children. In all societies this occurs first among a small, sophisticated, upper-class, urban group, whose cultural values are in accord with limiting the number of children.[3]

The Copperbelt was no exception. Most people there appeared to want as many children as possible. But a new attitude existed among an avant-garde group of young girls, in their teens, attending the nearby government boarding school. Fourteen per cent of them said they wanted "as many children as God wills"; the same percentage wanted small families of from one to three children. Between these two extremes were 40 per cent who wanted from four to six children and 32 per cent who desired six or more children. The girls who expressed a desire for fewer than the traditional number of children made the point that they wanted to raise their standard of living.[4] As ambitions grow larger and opportunities increase, the fertility rate will most likely slowly decline.

Childhood

The manner in which children were brought up likewise changed more rapidly among the members of the small group of intelligentsia and the middle class. Unfortunately, there is no quantitative data on the nursing and weaning of babies on the mine township, and my data are fragmentary. Some of the modern young couples shortened the period of nursing and resumed their sexual relations earlier than was customary. Women with some European education tended to nurse their babies periodically according to clock time. The same mothers had a knowledge of calories and introduced European food into the diets of their children quite early. It was my impression, however, that the tribal pattern of complete indulgence and of nursing babies from two to three years was followed by many mothers. I often saw women stop on the streets of the township to nurse a baby who whimpered. Many women to whom I talked apparently never considered any other than the traditional way of nursing and weaning of their babies. But a large number, traditional or modern, went for check-ups during pregnancy and to the hospital for the birth of the baby. Later, if the baby were ill, it was usual to try native medicines first and then, if they did not work, to bring the child to the clinic.

Childhood on the Copperbelt, particularly for the boys, was different from the tribal past. No longer could boys be inducted into adult life through their fathers and other men in the community. Men, like their Western counterparts, disappeared in the morning, or whenever their shift began, to go to their jobs. When they returned, they bathed and sought amusement at the beer hall or in some other gregarious way. Their sons went to school, to the movies, listened to the radio, participated in the numerous activities at the Welfare Center, played in small groups, or roamed around in gangs. Leaders of gangs had names such as John and Jack, the cowboy heroes, or Popeye of cartoon fame.

Ten or fifteen years before the time of my study, when the Welfare Department had not yet begun its work with young people, gangs were more numerous and active than they are today. Then older boys formed their own tribal football teams with an elected "king" who did not play but who knew magic to make his team win and to keep its members from being hurt in the game. The losing team often opposed the decision of the referee, and fights at the end of a game were common. The small boys imitated the older ones and had their tribal football teams and kings. Then gangs became intertribal, and the section (corresponding to neighborhood) of the township became the focus for membership; the new gangs continued to have their football teams and kings. Before playing, the boys annointed themselves with "medicine" (leaves from a special plant, burned and mixed with oil) and buried the teeth of an animal, leaves, or feathers from a bird in the ground near the goal to insure their victory. An egg buried in the center of the playing ground was believed to serve the same purpose. All this was done surreptitiously. Members of the older teams wore something magical sewn into a cloth wrapped around the upper arm and covered by a sleeve. I was told that many of the magical practices persisted in the football games under the auspices of the Welfare Department.

In the past the younger boys used to spend much of their time camping in the bush near the township, killing birds, playing at the Luanshya River, where they made models of automobiles out of mud. Every morning the members of the young gang gathered at the home of the leader, who called the roll; if one stayed away to go to school at the insistence of his parents, he was beaten by the gang. Some boys who were being forced to go to school by their fathers would fool them by scribbling in their copy books and returning home at the time class was dismissed. Those with illiterate fathers were taken in by the trick, but literate ones beat their truant sons.

The boys did not return home during the day to eat but collected food wherever they could, taking some from home and begging the rest from the bachelors, who at that time received rations of cooked food. All the food was taken to the Luanshya River and divided by the king of the gang, who kept a larger share for himself. The grass was tall by the river and good for hiding. They played cowboy games, pretending to shoot each other. If the one who was "shot" did not fall down, there was a real fight. Sometimes, they sat in a circle, and the leader would choose two to fight inside the circle. No one was ever allowed to tell his parents if he were beaten. There were fights between gangs, too, caused mainly when one of them invaded the area of another or when they stole each other's food. A nosebleed was considered the sign of defeat, but to cause bleeding from the mouth was frowned upon.

At the time of my study, gang life, camping in the bush, and playing in the river had diminished. More boys went to school regularly; but there were not enough schools to accommodate all of them, even if they had all desired to attend. Swimming in the Luanshya River had been forbidden, because of the danger of catching the disease bilharziasis. In their free time boys went to the Welfare Center, played games, saw movies, and participated in other activities; playing cowboy and boxing were favorite pastimes. Some boys sold chewing gum, sweets, sheets of writing paper and envelopes, old magazines, and the like to get money. Others went to the Welfare Center to pick the pockets of miners who came there on pay-day. The boys thought the Nyakyusa made particularly good victims because they were supposed to be sleepy. The money, whether earned or stolen, was often used to buy tea, bread, and sweets and for gambling with cards. Money, the new goal, is desired by the boys long before they are old enough to have jobs.

There was much talk by some of the older Africans and among Europeans about juvenile delinquency, but I could get little real information about it. I did learn that the term was used broadly and loosely and often for minor misbehavior such as throwing stones, even though no harm was done. Some young boys did engage in petty thievery, usually from Africans. It was my impression that juvenile delinquency was limited, particularly when compared to that of any American city. Older Africans tended to think of playing cowboy and any departure by the boys from traditional custom as a form of delinquency. In fact, many of the boys were going through the modern process of making a break from traditional African authority figures. Politically oriented youths and men were doing the same in their break from European authorities.

Girls were more with their mothers and, as everywhere, did not tend to form groups like the boys. Older girls looked after younger siblings and easily learned the town household arts by imitation and by helping their mothers. Little girls and boys of five and six played at being married. The beginnings of the menstrual cycle was still marked by a ritual, shortened to a few days. It has already been mentioned that some girls born in town were betrothed in customary manner when quite young and that marriage was planned for them when they came of age.

Attitudes toward Education of Girls

There existed a considerable difference in attitudes about whether girls should be educated and how much education they should have. Education for girls was still new and at the time of my study there were no girls beyond Standard IV in the township school. In the survey of adults, I found that 76 per cent of the women had no European education as compared to 44 per cent of the men without it. Twenty-one per cent of the women as compared to 40 per cent of the men had stopped school somewhere between the end of Standard I and Standard IV. Three per cent of the women as compared to 16 per cent of the men had completed Standard V or gone beyond it. But the government-controlled radio had a series of effective programs advocating education for girls, and there was much propaganda from missions and other sources. Attitudes toward the education of daughters appeared to be correlated with parents' education and occupation. The fathers of 61 per cent of the girls in a nearby government boarding school, which went as high as Standard VI, were in the white-collar class, and the remainder were divided among skilled workers, farmers, a few domestic servants, and three chiefs. Only one of the girls had a father who was a miner.[5]

All the women and men with European education wanted their daughters as well as their sons to be educated. But there was diversity in the attitudes of uneducated parents. An increasing number of them approved of girls being educated up to Standard IV. In these standards the girls would learn not only to become literate, but also how to cook nutritious food and keep the home well. Elementary education for girls was linked to the goal of increased longevity and health for the whole family. Typical statements by men:

I feel that girls should be educated so that they know how to keep their houses properly, and know all the rules of cleanliness and health and how to make some of the European foods. Then they can keep their babies healthy.

I think it is a good thing for girls to be educated, to read and write and to knit and sew as well as to cook. These things are important, because if a girl knows how to knit and to sew, she can save money by not having to buy woolen things. And if she can read and write, she can be reading by herself her husband's letters if he goes away to work. Then cooking is important, too, because we all like to eat good things.

A large majority (79 per cent) of the boys in Standards V and VI in the local school wrote in essays that they desired educated wives because they would know how to keep the house and food clean and how to bring up the children well.[6] Some of the men and boys had values beyond the welfare of their immediate family and added sentiments such as:

If women are educated, they know the value of education and they can then encourage their little children to go to school. In that way the country will be helped to go forward quickly.

Many Africans knew that Europeans lived longer and enjoyed better health, and they thought elementary education for the girls would help them attain the same standards.

The women also wanted their daughters to learn how to cook, sew, and knit in order to be better wives and mothers. But they had other reasons. One woman expressed a common sentiment when she said:

It is not right for my daughters to be uneducated as I am. I want them to have good marriages, with understanding and respect in their home. I have a good marriage, but my husband would like me to know more about keeping a modern home. Then, too, I am sometimes suspicious of how my husband spends his money, and I don't even know how much he earns. But an educated wife might see his ticket to know how much he earns and might even see his savings book.

This point was mentioned often by illiterate women, who could not believe that many literate wives did not know how much their husbands earned.

Many fathers and mothers had ambitions for their daughters, and and wanted them to have the high education which would enable them to become nurses and teachers. These parents had diverse motivations: to enable their daughters to find a place in the modern world, to help them marry educated men, to train them so that they could work if divorced, and to "help the country." Some mentioned how important it was for the country to move forward through educated women. Many mothers thought that marriage to educated men had more chance of lasting. Then, too, divorce could bring hardship to a woman if she had no relatives on the township and if she did not want to return to the village, unless she worked or re-married quickly. There was also the prestige of education. Some women spoke with awe of an occasional woman in the Territory who had gone through Standard VIII.

But there was a minority of men and women, without education themselves, who saw no point in educating their daughters. They feared education would make a girl "too proud" toward her husband and they said that "the main duty of a woman was to marry, nothing else," that a woman had "no chance of doing European work," or that an educated woman would be more apt to get a divorce because she knew she could support herself. The arguments of these traditionalists were losing their strength, as the drive for educating girls gained in momentum. But even if all the girls had wanted to be educated, there were not enough elementary or secondary schools to accommodate them.

New Patterns of Family Life

Even though the data on family life is incomplete, certain patterns emerge quite clearly. New forms of familial behavior are clearly apparent, but the traditional also persists, sometimes in conflict and other times fused. On the Copperbelt, as is many other parts of Central Africa,[7] the conjugal family, with the husband as the head of the household, is developing. This follows inevitably on the township from the man's becoming a wage earner, from the absence of many members of the traditional lineage, and with the emphasis on the individual household rather than on the extended family as the basic unit.[8] The growing tendency of young people to select their own mate also inevitably weakens the control of the extended kinship group who had traditionally arranged marriage. Men, likewise, became more interested in the education and futures of their own children than in their matrilineal nephews and nieces. Ties and obligations to kindred and in-laws existed and loyalties were divided between the extended and immediate family as they were in the past, but there is a reversal in emphasis, as the nuclear family becomes stronger. However, marriage payments by the groom remained important, and gifts to in-laws still had to be given. The strains between the extended and immediate family were focused on money and property, which become increasingly important in the expanding economy and in the revolution of rising expectations. The modern African does not need the social scientist to point this out and his awareness and ability to mingle and carry two sets of responsibilities made for less tension than might be expected. There were also a few who manipulated the situation to avoid any responsibility: they told their sister they could not look after her children because they had adopted the European customs of looking after their own children and then they tried to put the responsibility for that on their wife's brother. Emphasis on the individual family has likewise increased in Western civilization during the last couple of hundred years, but in Africa the changes are taking place in a couple of generations in a society which had an extended kinship system as its core.

As emphasis on lineage weakens, intertribal marriages increase. They occurred frequently in marriages based on choice. Even the young boys no longer had football teams based on tribe, but on locality. The teams of young men were also formed on the same principle. Family life and sports were affected by the same factors which weakened the political significance of tribe.

Meaning of Social Change for Women

Social change involves different factors for women than for men. Although women had economic status in tribal life, men were always their masters. Respect and humility were the proper attitudes of a woman before her husband. Extramarital relations were sanctioned for the men, but not for the women. In the new order, European education has been made available to girls later than to boys and still meets with resistance from a few parents. Opportunities for jobs are still limited for women, as compared to those for men. Women on the township were more traditionally oriented than were the men. This was true even for the avant-garde of young girls in the government boarding school, as compared to the boys in the same standards of school. Although the large majority of both boys and girls wanted to live in town, when they wrote about African life in their essays, more girls than boys described rural life and stressed tribal customs.

Females were more hostile to Europeans than were males. In the essays written by the teen-age boys and girls, 40 per cent of the boys had a favorable attitude to Europeans as compared to 9 per cent of the girls.[9] I have no comparable statistics for adults, but interviewing consistently indicated the greater hostility of women to Europeans, as compared to men. Girls tended to get their attitudes from their mothers, whose image of Europeans was determined largely by what they heard from the men, and this could be quite one-sided. African men have European supervisors, some friendly and some unfriendly, and the human tendency, on returning from the day's work, was to talk more about the indignities suffered than the pleasant casual camaraderie. The women's and girls' hostility to Europeans could also be psychologically related to resentment over their low status in African society. Frequently, people with low status in their own group have greater hostility toward an outgroup than do people of higher status.

Although women had less hard work and an easier life, which they liked, yet men were even more their masters than in the past. In the new economic system only a small proportion of the women were employed outside the home, and they had an economic dependence on their husbands unknown in the past. Adult women, as well as girls, had fantasies about being men and independent. An uneducated woman, annoyed because her husband had not given her money to buy soap, said:

Had I been a man working for myself, I should have been buying a lot of soap. Perhaps, when we go to God, I shall be working as a clerk or as a laborer and earning money.

The absence of her lineage group also contributed to a woman's insecurity. The man's lineage group was also not present, but he had a job, a union, and other organizations which provided status and security. In the emergence of the patriarchally-oriented conjugal family and the weakening of the extended lineage unit, the men gained more economic and psychological independence than did the women. The break from the past, the finding of a new identity, were far more difficult for them.

Comparison with American Negro Women

Exactly the opposite family situation existed among American Negroes in the plantation system of the Old South and, to a slightly lesser degree, in the Negro lower classes of the United States as a whole today. Among these American Negroes, it has been the women who have led the way in taking on the values of the white dominant group. On the Southern plantation, the Negro woman, slave and free, occupied a dominant position economically, socially, and sexually. The matriarchal nature of the southern Negro rural family is well known. As in Africa, the family was unstable, because of the frequency of separations, divorces, and common-law marriages. Men came and went, but the core of grandmother, mother, and children provided the stability. The Negro women enjoyed economic advantages over their men, having more domestic jobs in the white households and, at the same time, sharing equally with men the work in the cotton fields. When schools for Negroes became widespread, more Negro women than men became teachers. In community life, as well as in the family, women were often dominant. They did not have to fear lynching, the threat of which always hovered in the background for men. In my study of Mississippi in the midthirties, I found Negro women in many positions of leadership; and all the women had more contacts with white people than their husbands. The women were also more hopeful about the future than the men.[10]

In recent events connected with desegregation in schools and buses, women have taken considerable initiative. It was a woman who first violated the mores of segregation on buses in Atlanta. In the struggle over school integration at Little Rock, Arkansas, a woman president of the local chapter of the National Association for the Advancement of Colored People has been a leader. Many of the legal cases over entrance to white colleges and universities have been focused on the attempts of young Negro women to be students.

It was not only their high economic status which underlay the dominance of American Negro women, but also the fact that sexual relations between them and white men were frequent before and after the Civil War, while such relations between white women and Negro men were taboo and rare. In the long-time concubinage relationships, love and affection were often a part. Ties of affection were not restricted to these relationships. While there was probably ambivalence between Negro women nurses and cooks with the white children of the household, there was also mutual affection and love. Young children of the Negro nurse and cook were often playmates of the white children. Although fewer Negro men were employed in the household than women, many of both sexes had a strong identification with their "white folks." This does not negate the fact that Negroes resented their inferior position and that there was much hostility to the "white folks." But the identification and closeness of these relationships were responsible, to a large degree, for the subtle and often unconscious taking on of the white men's values by the Negroes, particularly by the women. The internalization of white Protestant values is found frequently in biographies of outstanding Negroes, many of whom praise the character training given them by their mothers.

The different situations in the American Deep South and on the Copperbelt in Northern Rhodesia are part of history and are due to many complex factors. The dominant American Negro mothers helped their Negro children become an integral part of American culture, in spite of barriers erected by white people. But Negro men have had to struggle harder to find their identity and to escape from the domination of women. This has been easier in the middle and upper classes, where the man is the main or only wage earner in patriarchally-oriented households. In Northern Rhodesia, African men are almost exclusively the carriers of European culture. At the same time, their role in childhood training becomes less important because of the hours spent on a job. The African women, more traditional and more anti-European than their husbands, spend their time at home, and their role in training young children has increased. Some of the women's values may therefore become dominant, particularly for the daughters. Of course, the schools, with their male teachers, and the welfare activities for boys that are led by men, somewhat offset the influence of the mothers. But mothers are the first to give values and attitudes to children.

The position of African women in this area and the lag between them and the men in their induction into the modern world may have far-reaching consequences, other than the effect on the structure of the family. The emergence of Africans into modern society may be retarded, and the hostility of women may encourage violence towards Europeans. As opportunities for women increase, their attitudes will probably change. Whatever happens, they are significant in shaping the attitudes of future generations.

12. Women Fighting

Introduction

The conversations that follow illustrate the concern and shame women feel about being barren. Mary Mwenda (Cewa tribe) and Edna Kabeyo (Ngoni tribe), next-door neighbors and friends, were both barren. Mrs. Mwenda had taken her sister's three-year-old son to live with her, and she and her husband were contemplating taking one of her young nieces into the household. There was no child in Mrs. Kabeyo's home.

Mrs. Mwenda and Mrs. Kabeyo were taunted about their barrenness by Mrs. Chisenga (Bisa tribe), who lived in the same section of the township. From her conversation she appeared to be pathological, one of those people who think, without any evidence, that everyone envies them. But the women in the neighborhood regarded her only as a nuisance.

Mrs. Mwenda and Mrs. Kabeyo and six other women were at the public washing stand in their section, washing clothes and talking to each other. Mrs. Chisenga arrived to draw water.

DOROTHY CHISENGA *(to Mrs. Mwenda and Mrs. Kabeyo)*:
> Wash properly. You are letting soap suds fall into my water. I do not want to drink water which is soapy.

[207

MARY MWENDA: How can our soap reach the place where you are washing? *(She turns her back on Mrs. Chisenga, as she and Mrs. Kabeyo continued washing their clothes.)*

DOROTHY CHISENGA: I do not like drinking dirty water, like those who have no children do.

EDNA KABEYO: You are very foolish. Do you think we are fools because we do not have children?

DOROTHY CHISENGA: You are senseless. You only want the husbands of your friends. That is why you do not have children.

(The implication here was probably that Mrs. Mwenda and Mrs. Kabeyo were promiscuous and did not have children because they had syphilis.)

EDNA KABEYO: Do you think we run after men as you do? We do not have children because God did not give us any. You should not be proud of having children just to annoy others.

DOROTHY CHISENGA: You want my husband because you do not have children. Most of you women want my husband.

MARY MWENDA: How wonderful is your husband that we all want him! You fool, go away before we beat you.

DOROTHY CHISENGA: Beat me! You are not even ashamed of yourselves. I know that you have been backbiting me, saying that these are not really a child's diapers I wash at the washing stand. Why can you not produce?

MARY MWENDA: I will beat you! *(Mrs. Mwenda gives Mrs. Chisenga three slaps on the cheek, and Mrs. Kabeyo splashes her with water.)*

EDNA KABEYO: Now, go away, you child of a dog.

DOROTHY CHISENGA: I am going to report that I have been beaten to the Compound Office. Don't you know that my mother is ill. I do not want more troubles now.

EDNA KABEYO: If your mother is ill, why do you provoke other people for nothing? I do not care whether or not your mother is ill. When my mother was alive and became ill, I did not provoke other people for no reason at all.

Mrs. Chisenga walked away. The other women, who have been interested spectators, talked about the episode.

FIRST WOMAN: Has she gone to the Compound Office?

SECOND WOMAN: I can still see her.

THIRD WOMAN: But why does she not go quickly?

FOURTH WOMAN: That woman Chisenga is no good. She also cursed at me one day, and I still do not know what wrong I did.

FIFTH WOMAN: She has quarreled with more than three women in this section already.

SIXTH WOMAN: I know that woman. Before, we both lived in Section Three, and my house was near hers. She did not like to see anyone joke with her husband. If her husband tried to say "my wife" to a small girl, she would grow very jealous and start cursing at the little girl. [Addressing a little girl as "my wife" would usually be regarded as a joke, unless they were in a potentially incestuous relationship.]

FOURTH WOMAN: I wish she would be beaten badly by someone, so that she would stop behaving like this.

THIRD WOMAN: All women are not alike. She will meet a different woman one day who will beat her hard.

EDNA KABEYO: She should not play with us. We will teach her a lesson.

About four o'clock that afternoon Mrs. Mwenda, Mrs. Kabeyo, and several other women were talking outside Mrs. Mwenda's house when Mrs. Chisenga and her husband arrived.

HUSBAND: Who beat you here?

DOROTHY CHISENGA: This one and that one (*pointing to Mrs. Mwenda and Mrs. Kabeyo*).

HUSBAND: Why did you two people beat one person? She came to take me from work so that I should know the reason you have beaten her.

EDNA KABEYO: Your wife is no good. She always curses people at the washing stand because she says she has children. Do you think she is the only one in this

compound who has children? Should we be cursed
at because we have no children?

DOROTHY CHISENGA: You senseless women, you are fools! You only
fought with me because you were jealous. You are
barren; you do not produce.

MARY MWENDA: You are hurting us more. Am I a dog?

Mrs. Mwenda then slapped Mrs. Chisenga on the cheek. Several
onlookers separated the two women.

DOROTHY CHISENGA: Let her beat me now! Let her beat me now. I did
not do anything wrong. She has now given me
four slaps.

WOMAN ON-LOOKER [who had been at washing stand in the morning]:
Yes, she was beaten.

MAN ON-LOOKER: Has she been beaten before?

WOMAN ON-LOOKER: This is now the fourth slap. Let her be taught
a lesson. She always thinks her friends are run-
ners after men. She once called me one.

HUSBAND: You will give the reason you have beaten my wife
at the compound office.

EDNA KABEYO: You can go and report anywhere. We shall state
exactly how your wife approached us. She is a
foolish dog.

Mrs. Chisenga and her husband left just as Mr. Mhango (husband
of Mrs. Mwenda), Mr. Kabeyo (husband of Mrs. Kabeyo), and Mr.
Mwenda (Mrs. Mwenda's brother) came home from work.

JAMES MHANGO: What is wrong here?

MARY MWENDA: That woman always curses at people, and today
she found me washing clothes with Mrs. Kabeyo.
She came to draw water the time I was just putting
soap on the clothes, and she said, "Do not put
soap in my water. Wash properly!" I said, "How
can soap reach the place you are as I am beating
the clothes now." Then I faced the other way, but
she continued talking and said, "I do not want to
drink water which is soapy. You people with no
children are very jealous; you only want your

friends' husbands." I asked her whether she once heard of us committing adultery or saw us standing in the streets with lovers. Then we were angry and I beat her. Yes, I was angry. I beat her!

PETER MWENDA: But do not include your husbands when you quarrel.

MARY MWENDA: She started it. She went to call her husband at work.

JAMES MHANGO: It is useless to join in women's quarrels or fights.

GEORGE KABEYO: It is useless.

JAMES MHANGO: They say they are going to report at the Compound Office. How will they state their case at the Compound Office?

EDNA KABEYO: We do not fear. We can even go to the highest court. It does not matter. If she means to fight we should teach her how we handle people in the Ngoni method. She cannot be fooling with us.

MARY MWENDA: She came to start a fight here at our house, and she will be guilty for doing that. It would have been wrong for us to go to her house.

In the late afternoon of the next day, Mr. Mwenda came home and, finding no one there, went to the home of a neighbor, Mr. Chanda.

PETER MWENDA: Where have all the people gone?

SAM CHANDA: They have gone to the Boma. Mr. Mhango and the others went to report at the branch office.

PETER MWENDA: For what reason?

SAM CHANDA: There was another fight. That woman Chisenga who fought at the washing place came here with her mother and father. Her father is a mine policeman. When he came, he asked why Mrs. Mwenda and Mrs. Kabeyo beat his daughter. He said that he wanted them to fight again so that his daughter could win. So there was another fight, and Mrs. Mwenda beat the policeman's daughter and Mrs. Kabeyo beat her mother. After that Mrs. Mwenda beat the mother and Mrs. Kabeyo beat Chisenga.

PETER MWENDA: What about Chisenga's husband?

SAM CHANDA: He did not come, but remained at home. Mr. Mhango
                    went to the office to report that a policeman had
                    started a fight and then ran away. So they have all
                    been sent to the Boma to register their case.

PETER MWENDA: There are many people who have registered their cases
                    before them, and so it will not be tried until tomorrow.

The next day, about seven P.M., Mr. Mwenda returned home and
found Mrs. Mwenda and Mrs. Kabeyo discussing their case, which
had been tried that day at the court, with neighbors.

PETER MWENDA: Welcome home.

MARY MWENDA: Thank you.

PETER MWENDA: Has your case been settled?

MARY MWENDA: Yes. Mrs. Kabeyo and I had to pay a pound each. Our
                    opponent has not been fined, but the money we paid
                    has not been given to her. It has been given to the
                    government.

PETER MWENDA: Why was she not fined? When people fight, both the
                    victor and the victims are always fined.

MARY MWENDA: They said that I was wrong to beat her at the washing
                    stand and that Mrs. Kabeyo was wrong to splash
                    water on her. They said that had we been patient
                    enough to let the woman curse us, she would have
                    been fined or put in jail. I think her father paid
                    some money to the court elders so that he and his
                    daughter could be favored. Many people think so.

PETER MWENDA: If that is so, then she has not gained anything.

Mr. Mhango came from the beer hall, walking very proudly, and
Mr. Kabeyo also arrived home.

GEORGE KABEYO: How was it?

JAMES MHANGO: I have just come in a taxi-car from the Boma [about
                    five miles away]. Mrs. Mwenda and Mrs. Kabeyo were
                    each fined one pound. I wanted to show my opponents
                    that though I paid these fines, I still had more money.
                    The car came to get us just in front of the court, and
                    the elders there must have been saying, "This man is
                    very proud." I wanted to show them that I have plenty

of money. We were four in the taxi-car: I, my wife, Mrs. Kabeyo, and my sister-in-law, Mrs. Mhango II. We came all the way from the Boma to the road near here. I wanted to be dropped just here in front of my house, but that heap of sand blocked the way.

The elders did not consider the second fight in the evening, when the victim's mother was beaten. Her father, the mine policeman, was despised very much in the court. They said: "You are a very foolish policeman, and you do not know your duty. Why did you run away, after you had persuaded the woman to fight? Our policemen in town do not run away when they see people fighting. If they have no whistles to call for help, they shout with their mouths. You are a foolish policeman." Then this man answered: "Ah, I have been here a long time. This ticket I have is the hundred and twentieth, and I will soon be getting my pension." Then an elder, representing Paramount Chief Mpezeni, said that though the policeman had been here a long time he did not know anything. Moreover, the elders told him that he was not a proper policeman. I was the one who went to report at the branch office that a mine policeman came with his daughter and wife to start a fight.

GEORGE KABEYO: So the Bisa woman has not been charged.

JAMES MHANGO: You see, they said that Mrs. Mwenda and Mrs. Kabeyo were two, and that she was alone, and that they had the intention of beating her. But she was warned not to curse at people again. We were told that if she makes any more trouble she should be taken to court, and she will be put in jail straight away without any trial. If she curses you, just beat her and then take her to court. She will remain in jail.

(The report of what happened in court and of the taxi ride back was repeated many times by Mr. Mhango to neighbors and friends who had come to inquire about the results of the case.)

JAMES MHANGO
(turning to Mr. Mwenda): Where were you today, brother-in-law? You were not in court.

PETER MWENDA: I was doing my work.

JAMES MHANGO: My brother-in-law, you are growing. You are not in
                the stage of a little child who does not reason much.
                Had it been some brothers, they would have gone to
                court to see how their sisters were being tried. You
                see, I got leave for two days, because I did not want
                to miss the case, and had it not been that I was there
                and talking properly, these two women would have
                gone to jail. I stated clearly how the father of the girl
                came to arouse a fight. I was really praised the way I
                talked. My brother-in-law, whenever your sister has a
                case you should be present, no matter what. You can
                never tell what kind of trouble there will be.

Mr. Mwenda, educated and one of the modern intelligentsia, was
the traditional responsible brother looking after his sister's interests
when her husband was philandering during her absence. But he felt
no need to be present in court when she was charged with fighting
the Bisa woman. Traditionally, he should have accepted responsibility
in this situation, too. In contrast to him, Mr. Mhango used the situation, to demonstrate not only his concern for his wife, but his
ability to argue in court, and to vaunt his extravagant spending of
money by taking a taxi home.

13. The Man Who Knocked at the Wrong Woman's Door

Introduction

Unlike the fight between the women, some cases were not considered important enough to take to court. These were settled immediately by the parties concerned, following the same principles and similar procedures of the more formal courts. Friends and neighbors acted as witnesses and judges. Such a case was that of Mr. Harry Chomba (Bemba tribe), a miner without any European education, who when drunk had come knocking on Mrs. Mwenda's door while her husband was working on a night shift. The immediate suspicion was that Mr. Chomba had adulterous intentions; the face-to-face personal relations of the people concerned and of their neighbors demanded that his and Mrs. Mwenda's guilt or innocence be established immediately.

Africans have long had a well-defined system of customary law, and in this area native courts were continued under British administration. The functional principle underlying the law was, and still is, the establishment of a peaceful equilibrium through compensation for wrongs. Litigants acted as their own lawyers, and tribal authorities attempted to reconcile the conflicting interests and assess the amount of compensation.[1] Fundamental to African law was the concept of "the reasonable man,"[2] nicely illustrated in this case and, also, in much of the African's everyday thinking.

Mr. Chomba's case was heard in front of Mrs. Mwenda's house on the day following his midnight knock at her door. Mr. Mwenda, who was a brother of Mrs. Mwenda and who slept in her house, was a witness, as were also the neighbors, Mr. and Mrs. Kabeyo, Mr. Mwape, and Mr. Chomba's wife. Mr. Mhango and Mr. Chomba were the main parties in the case. Three men served as judges: one was a friend of Mr. Mhango; another, a friend of Mr. Chomba; and the third was not a friend of either.

HARRY CHOMBA: Yesterday, I drank a lot of beer at Section One and came home late. I started quarreling with my wife. But I did not want to quarrel, and so I told my wife that I was going to sleep in the kitchen because I was drunk and wanted to keep from quarreling. I left my clothes in the house and went out to the kitchen in my underwear. But I did not stay there. I came out in my underwear and tried to go to Section One for more beer, but I found myself at Section Two. Then I tried to go home, and I thought I had arrived at my house, but instead I was here. I started knocking hard at the door. This boy who sleeps here is the one who answered and told his sister that someone was knocking at the door. But even when he was saying that, I did not know I was lost; I thought it was my wife who was asking who I was. Then Mrs. Mwenda opened the door, and I realized I was lost. She asked my name, and I only answered, "I am." She went to get the light and looked at my face and she said, "Are you the father of Samuel?" I agreed. She asked me where I came from, and I explained how I came here and that I was lost. Then she went to tell Mr. Mwape and Mr. and Mrs. Kabeyo, so that they could be witnesses in the morning, in case either her husband or my wife or other people would be suspicious. Then Mr. Kabeyo and Mr. Mwape and Mrs. Mwenda took me to my wife, and she also explained to them how I left the house to go and sleep in the kitchen and that she thought I was there.

FIRST JUDGE *(friend of Mr.* *Mhango):*	We have heard what Mr. Chomba has told us. He says he got lost because he was drunk.
SECOND JUDGE *(friend of Mr.* *Chomba):*	Is it usual for you, Mr. Chomba, to leave your house after a quarrel and go to sleep in the kitchen?
HARRY CHOMBA:	No, it only happened yesterday.
THIRD JUDGE:	We do not act in the same way always. You cannot say, "I do not do this always, so I cannot do it now!" When people are drunk they do not reason much. Please, Mrs. Chomba, tell us how your husband left the house.
ALICE CHOMBA:	My husband came very late after he had been drinking beer. I was annoyed at him because he was so late and was drunk, and he said, "I am going to sleep in the kitchen because you are talking too much." He left all his clothes in the house and went out in his underwear. I slept, thinking he was in the kitchen. The next time I saw him was when he was brought home by Mr. Mwape and Mr. Kabeyo and the owner of this house, Mrs. Mwenda. She explained how he came to her house and how she called Mr. Mwape and Mr. Kabeyo to be witnesses.
THIRD JUDGE:	We have heard from his wife. We can now hear from the owner of this house, who knows how the man came.
MARY MWENDA:	It was very late at night when he came to knock at the door. I did not hear the knocking, but my brother who sleeps in this front room did. Then my brother shouted, "Someone is knocking at the door." That was after he had asked him who he was, and the reply had been, "I am." I went to open the door and found a man only in his underwear. I asked who he was, and the answer was, "I am." I then went to collect the lamp and looked at his face and found that he was Mr. Chomba. I said, "Are you Mr. Chomba?" and he answered, "Yes." Then I asked why he was naked. He told me he had lost his house. He said, "After I left my house, I went to sleep in the kitchen; then after

that I decided to go for beer to Section One, and when I was coming back, I knocked at this door, thinking I had arrived home." So I decided to call Mr. Mwape and Mr. and Mrs. Kabeyo to come and witness. I explained the matter to them, and then we took him to his house. This morning he came and found me at the washing stand and told me that he was very sorry and would come after work to apologize to my husband with the witnesses present.

FIRST JUDGE: We have now heard the case from the owner of the house.

SECOND JUDGE: The matter is quite all right. It was only a mistake, as we have heard from the main evidence of the owner of the house.

THIRD JUDGE: It is also important to get evidence from witnesses who were there. What do you say, Mr. Mwape?

RICHARD MWAPE: I cannot say more than what you have already heard from the three people. Moreover, the main thing you should all know is how Mr. Chomba came to the house and what he said. If you also find those two things to be important, then let us ask the biggest witness, her brother, to tell us, since he was the first person to hear him.

PETER MWENDA: When I first heard him knocking I was half dreaming. I woke up and then heard him knocking very hard.

FIRST JUDGE: He was sure he had come to his own house.

SECOND JUDGE: Yes, otherwise he should have been knocking very softly, or not at all.

PETER MWENDA: Then I asked who it was. He answered, "I am," with a very strong voice.

SECOND JUDGE: He did not doubt that it was his house where he was knocking.

PETER MWENDA: Then I called my sister, and she came to see who it was and recognized him. My sister asked him why he had come to her house at that time. He explained in the same way my sister has done. All his words he spoke showed me that he was really lost. There was no word out of his mouth that would make me suspicious of his coming to this house at that time.

SECOND JUDGE: We have heard now the evidence from all of them, and the matter is straightforward. He was only drunk.

FIRST JUDGE: It usually happens that when one is drunk he becomes totally useless. This beer we drink is no good.

SECOND JUDGE: It is what I have already seen. One man at home [in the village] drank a lot of beer. He went to his house and found another woman sleeping on his bed and thought she was his wife. His wife, who was drunk, too, slept outside on the veranda, and he thought she was another woman. When his friends came, he told them that there was a woman on the veranda and they could get her. One of his friends went to the veranda, and since the woman too had drunk too much she thought he was her husband. So they slept. Later on, the husband realized that he was sleeping with another woman and that the woman on the veranda was his wife. So he realized he had given his own wife to his friends. That is the trouble with drinking too much beer.

HARRY CHOMBA: I was very sorry when I realized I was lost.

SECOND JUDGE: Oh yes, one can be worried because other people will be talking about it in many different ways, such as saying they found you committing adultery, or you wanted someone's wife, and many other bad things.

JAMES MHANGO: I heard about this thing at my friend's house Mr. Nyawale when I was coming from work. I was told Mr. Chomba went to my house at night for my wife. I was very sorry because I have been with this man for very many years now and we have never quarreled. When I came here I was told about it and that is why I came to call you all. Now we have all heard the evidence you have given and there is, as I have found out, nothing that can make me suspicious. I know that it is the work of beer to confuse people. I was also lost last week. I could not find my house at all. I came from Section Nine through here to the Welfare Center. Fortunately, I met a kind of person who led me home. So I ask you, Mr. Chomba, not to feel unhappy about this. Nearly everyone makes such mistakes.

PART IV

LEISURE

14. The Significance of Leisure in Social Change

ALTHOUGH ALL SOCIETIES have periods for work and for play, anthropologists, with few exceptions, have paid little attention to play.[1] There are descriptions of dances and songs and references to their diffusion; functionalists, such as Radcliffe-Brown, have been interested in the dance as a ritual enhancing the feeling of solidarity in the group;[2] but a theoretical consideration of play and leisure with their social and psychological roots in culture has been largely absent from the works of anthropologists. It may be that they have been culture-bound by the belief that play is frivolous and therefore not worthy of serious theoretical study.

However, two famous anthropologists have included play in their theory of culture. Kroeber, with his usual breadth of interests, noted the links between organic play impulses and the dynamics of human culture. He wrote, "Play impulses in the wide sense are exceedingly significant in man, because in rechanneled form they motivate great areas of human behavior and important achievements of culture. This refers not only to games and sports, but to the influence of curiosity, of desire for variety, of mental restlessness, in the arts and sciences and fashions. If our ancestors had been wholly lacking in playfulness, we should probably have had many fewer aesthetic and intellectual developments in human culture. Not that songs or poems or philoso-

[223

phies are mere play or made in play but they are super-utilitarian: pleasurable outlet for excess energy rather than responses to actual needs, and they are thus based on impulses akin to those of play, sublimated as well as mature."[3]

Malinowski, stressing the functional approach, wrote, "In primitive civilizations the vanguard of progress is often found in works of leisure and supererogation. . . . Advances in skill, scientific discoveries, new artistic motifs [may] filter in through the playful activities of recreation, and thus they receive the minimum of traditional resistence which is associated with activities not yet taken very seriously."[4] New social attitudes and forms of behavior may likewise be introduced, reinforced, or strengthened through play activities.

The social and psychological significance of leisure in the United States has interested a number of sociologists and other social scientists, and among the pioneers have been David Riesman, Reuel Denney, Robert J. Havinghurst, George A. Lundberg, and Mirra Kamaraovsky. Today it is more or less accepted that leisure in modern society is at least as important as work as a subject for research.[5]

In my study on the Copperbelt of Northern Rhodesia, I used leisure activities as an index of social change as well as a means of understanding it. Reuel Denney has pointed out that it is in their leisure activities that we can study the tensions, the frustrations, and the values of man.[6] Max Kaplan has added that it is "in leisure we are freest to be ourselves."[7] Leisure activities on the Copperbelt were all voluntary and included not only play, usually regarded as pleasurable and done for its own sake, but also goal-oriented activities, such as studying English in a night class. My assumption is that given the same opportunities, the choice of leisure activity is based on needs and values, and that the choice then strengthens and reinforces existing attitudes. The process is circular.

The satisfactions and the frustrations in work and in daily life create needs which affect the kinds of activities desired by men in their leisure time. The pick-and-shovel work of underground miners and their round of life in the mining community generate needs different from the needs of those who follow traditional occupations in tribal villages. The miners' needs vary, in turn, from those of the intelligentsia and the skilled and white-collar workers in the same community. Choice is influenced not only by individual needs and values, but also by the norms of the group to which a man belongs. For example, schoolteachers on the Copperbelt, as elsewhere, have different norms for their leisure than do manual workers.

In tribal life men and women enjoyed leisure not according to clock time, but whenever they were free from the routine duties of daily life. They drank beer in small and in large groups, flirted, had sexual affairs, performed tribal dances, played a game of *isolo* (a kind of checkers), told folk tales and riddles, visited neighbors and talked and gossiped about the doings of kindred and friends and about local events. Tribal rituals on the occasion of birth, initiation, marriage, and death were a significant part of religion, but the feasts, the dancing, and the beer-drinking likewise provided a welcome break in the monotony of daily life. Beer-drinking occurred also at the completion of communal tasks, such as clearing bush land, tree-cutting, or hoeing new grass land, and was an important aspect of hospitality. Economic, ritual, religious, and leisure activities were not as sharply differentiated temporarily or spatially as they are in modern society. In the traditional leisure activities men and women, young and old, had their roles; and in all they related in customary ways to their immediate group of kindred and neighbors and to the larger one of tribe.

On the Copperbelt, with a wage economy offering the possibility of a surplus, there was a greater diversity of leisure pursuits and the timing of them was more regular. Traditional leisure activities were pursued with varying degrees of intensity. Tribal rituals still occurred in a rather attenuated form and seemed much less significant than in the past. Tribal dancing, unconnected with any ritual, took place on Sunday afternoons for amusement; the Bemba and most other people in this area have always danced for entertainment as well as for rituals. There was still an intimate circle of kindred, friends, neighbors, and workmates for talk and gossip. Sociability was and is an important value for these Africans. Flirting, sexual affairs, and beer-drinking seemed to occur more today than in the past. The beer hall operated by the mine Welfare Department, and selling commercial bottled beer, was a social center. The stronger native beer continued to be brewed by women in their homes according to custom, but it was now done illegally. The beer was sold and drunk in the homes of the brewers, and the illicit business flourished.

There was a growing richness of choice in new leisure opportunities. Significant among these were listening to the radio, going to movies, and reading newspapers. The activities provided by the Welfare Department—sports, social clubs, ballroom dancing, classes in crafts, and many others—have already been described. Evening English classes were conducted by both the mine Personnel Department and by the government Education Department. Taking correspondence courses and going to church on Sundays or to missionary classes on weekdays were also among the modern activities.

It is assumed that all leisure activities afford pleasure or satisfaction of some kind to the participants. The pleasures and satisfactions are as varied as are the types of activities. These may be private or social, serious or frivolous, physically relaxing or psychologically cathartic (sometimes both) and a means of intellectual or of sensual gratification. For most Africans on the Copperbelt, as for most other men, leisure activities fell into more than one class; but there was often a considerable difference in emphasis. For some, the private activities bringing sensual indulgence were all important; for others, social activities which conferred status or provided an entree into the modern world were significant.

The functions of leisure activities are indirect and direct. They may be a preparation for social mobility, not just through knowledge gained in formal courses or classes, but also through a sense of participation and identification with the larger, modern world. Imagery of self, of human relations, and of the world may be altered by some of the new activities, such as the use of the mass media. Other activities may strengthen and even exaggerate traditional roles. In some activities, there may be a blending of new and old imagery and roles, and this could contribute to an integrated sense of ego identity. Still others may enlarge the group identity.

Leisure may also be the time when a man transcends his limited functions—in the past, as a farmer or herdsman; today, as a miner or clerk—and feels part of life as a whole. It may provide an opportunity for affirmation, to be at one with one's self and with the world. Rituals have this function, and in tribal society they stressed the intimate relationship of man with his land, with his ancestors, with his kindred and his tribesmen, and with king or chief. Among all peoples, religious rituals lead man to accept the reality of creation as he understands it and to celebrate it; and the celebration becomes a reaffirmation.[8] This kind of accord was easier to attain in the relatively homogeneous tribal world than in a modern heterogeneous society. The sense of oneness with the world is of course not limited to religious experience and ritual. Deeply felt love and sexual gratification, esthetic experience, creative work, knowledge and understanding, identification with peoples through literature, drama, or other experience, all may help man transcend the narrowness of his life. "Frivolity, as well as ecstasy, may also provide this mood."[9] A man may abandon himself to gaiety, to jazz, to a movie, to a game of football, to sexual promiscuity, to getting drunk. Some of these activities offer a real catharsis and sense of accord with the world; others, an illusion of it.

This section on leisure is concerned primarily with the mass media, and the chapters following describe and analyze the impact of listening to radio, going to movies, and reading newspapers. Fifty per cent of the adults on the township listened to radio. Thirty-nine per cent were going to the movies and 58 per cent had gone to movies at some time, past or present. Thirty-five per cent were sufficiently literate in English and/or a vernacular language to read a newspaper.

For Africans, as for all of us, the mass media introduced a new form of secondary reality, quite different from the primary reality of oral communication. African people have a rich tradition of the latter in their myths, folk tales, songs, proverbs, and conversation, which persists with vitality. They tell a story dramatically and argue a case in court vigorously. The punch line of a personal discussion is often a proverb, a pointed, brief generalization based on experience.[10]

All communication in tribal society was in the context of African life, in which the personal, the concrete, the detailed, and the sensory were emphasized. These characteristics are not confined to tribal and preliterate peoples. Hoggart uses some of the same terms in describing the essence of English working class life. He writes of it as " 'the dense and concrete life,' a life whose main stress is on the intimate, the sensory, the detailed and the personal."[11] In the United States, our tabloid newspapers, serials on radio and in print, much of literature, and many of our conversations indicate that the same characteristics have considerable strength today. Oral communication obviously involves personal contact and is on a direct and primary level. If it is successful, there is either some similarity of background and experience or an understanding of the different backgrounds of the individual participants.[12] Communication among the preliterate Africans was always on the level of known reality. As Riesman writes, ". . . they [preliterate peoples] are led by folk tales and songs to identify with the tribe as it has been and will be, or possibly with a legendary golden age but they are not incited to imagine themselves outside its comforts and coherence.[13]

The mass media introduced to Africans another form of reality—a world and peoples beyond their experience. The African audience is, in a sense, outside of much of the content of the communication from the mass media; and, therefore, the type of participation is different from that in oral communication. In Western and other historical societies, writing was the first to provide this new and secondary level of reality. Literacy is not just learning how to read but is concerned with comprehending a form of reality beyond immediate experience. Riesman has noted that print helps liberate the individual from his group and from his environment. The rise and increasing influence of the middle class in Western society from the fifteenth century to the end of the nineteenth was marked by the "sway of black print on white paper." In the nineteenth century, the same author stresses the particular significance of the novel in enabling people to project themselves into new situations and into new roles.[14] Although the reader endows the reading experience with an emotional reality, at the same time he is aware of its secondary nature.

In most of the modern historical societies, there were centuries during which the elite and, later, larger groups of people experienced this secondary form of reality through print and established customary forms of response, before the movies and radio were introduced. In Africa, the three media have been introduced in less than half a century and, for most people, within one generation; radio and movies were reaching many people who could not read. Then, too, the reading of the literate minority has been mostly restricted to newspapers, small paper pamphlets or booklets designed to give practical help or tell tales, text books, and the Bible. There has been little reading purely for pleasure.

The sheer mechanics of how radio and movie programs were made and produced were unknown to the African audience. The voice that came out of a box was mentioned over and over again as one of the miracles brought by the Europeans and was often put into the same category with the miracle of an airplane. The technique and art underlying the motion picture camera were likewise a completely new phenomenon. The Africans' ignorance of the techniques underlying these media of communication is particularly significant for the movie-goers and is discussed in the chapter on movies. On the other hand, while reading and writing were also new techniques rather than substitutes for established modes, as Herskovits has pointed out, the literate person mastered them.[15] Africans have emerged directly from a preliterate society with its emphasis on direct oral communication into the latest twentieth century technological developments in secondary communication. The leap into the modern world of communication is dramatic and rewarding but, naturally, brings its problems, too.

The functions of the mass media were personal and social. Among the personal functions, not necessarily to the same degree for each media, are: (1) a source of pleasure; (2) a catharsis; (3) a source of understanding and control over the environment; and (4) a means of extending the range of identifications and a way of relating to other people. On the social level it functioned as: (1) an integrating and stabilizing agent between the past and the present; (2) a disseminator of information and values from other African tribes and from the Western world; (3) Negatively, a break from the parochial past. The personal and social functions overlapped and were often combined in the same media.

The study of the reactions of the Africans to the mass media was particularly rewarding because it extended and deepened my knowledge of their joys and their sorrows, their problems and their attitudes to the world about them. All these were reflected in the discussions of the meanings of the programs for them and of their preferences. I was also interested in those who rejected the mass media and other modern leisure activities. The study of leisure time activities proved to be a useful index of social change, since the traditionalists and modernists tended to emphasize a different use of leisure. We can think of a continuum which has, at one end, the face-to-face private roles of tribal society and, at the other, the more impersonal and cosmopolitan roles associated with modern society. Sex, age, and

European education were among the variables which influenced choice
of leisure activities; and these variables were interrelated, since young
people and males usually had a higher level of education than women
and old people. None of the variables was all-inclusive; personality
needs, as noted earlier, were also important. Choice of leisure activities appeared to be an expression of a life-style, that is, a characteristic way in which many roles are combined.[16] On the Copperbelt
a number of life-styles were available, and my hypotheses are concerned with the voluntary choice of leisure activities and their relationship to changing life-styles. Everywhere, as men become less
fettered to the processes of work, leisure becomes increasingly significant as a means of orientation to society.

We begin the study of leisure in this mining community with the
mass media and the people who participated in them, starting with
the radio, which reached the largest number. The section concludes
with the study of the intransigents, those who refused to enter into
the new world of communication.

15. Listening to the Radio

Broadcasting to africans started in 1941, when a small government station was set up in Lusaka to keep the Africans informed, through community receivers, of the progress of the war, to stimulate their war effort, and to convey orders in case of serious emergency. Harry Franklin, the Director of Information, ran the station in his spare time. After the war he proposed that a central African station be set up in Lusaka to broadcast exclusively to Africans in Northern Rhodesia, Southern Rhodesia, and Nyasaland and that it be used as a medium for mass education, entertainment, and to "play a great part in the sensible enlightenment of the masses."[1] Financial help for buying transmitters and a studio was obtained from the British government in London; and, after three years of searching, Franklin found a company willing to manufacture a dry-battery receiving set cheap enough for Africans to buy. The first sets, known as "The Saucepan Special" because the metal case which protected the set resembled a saucepan, were introduced in October 1949. It was estimated that twelve hundred sets were sold to Africans in Northern Rhodesia during the first four months.[2] Since then the battery sets have been improved, and a number of models were available at the time of the survey, ranging in price from about the equivalent of $16 to $25. Africans living in houses wired for electricity usually had electric radios.

Radio-listening was available to everyone at the township through radios at the welfare centers. Twenty per cent owned their own radios; each home-owned radio reached at least one listener other than the members of the household.[3] Fifty per cent of the adults on the mine township listened to radio, 57 per cent of them at welfare centers. The remainder listened at home or at a friend's home, with naturally more women in this group. Sixty-four per cent of the listeners were men and 35 per cent were women. The majority, 60 per cent were under thirty and 70 per cent had some European education. But a significant minority, 41 per cent of those between thirty and forty years of age and 36 per cent of those over forty—many with no school education—were also among the radio audience.

For the listeners, radio meant a change in sensory perceptions. In the past Africans heard voices and music only directly from human beings. Now they can also hear them from a "box." This new experience seemed to be both a miracle and a new form of reality. For some who did not listen, it seemed "childish to listen to something which is in a box, without seeing the person talking." Some of the same non-listeners also did not want to see "the shadows and unreal things which move as human beings in the cinema." Radio and movies, as forms of indirect and secondary communication, involve an extension of sensory perceptions and the capacity to accept and enjoy new forms of indirect participation. Modern man has been trained to recognize and accept the differences between primary and secondary communication, although many of us still prefer the "live" music of the concert hall to the "canned" music of the record or radio.

The impact of the radio is obviously related to the content of the programs and how they are presented. These depend to a large degree on the type of personnel in charge of broadcasting. At the time of my study, Michael Kittermaster was broadcasting officer. He and his able European and African staff, Dick Sapseid, Peter Fraenkel, Alec Nkhata, Edwin Nlongoti, Sylvester Massiye, and others carried on a tradition set by Harry Franklin of enthusiastic and intelligent hard work and of belief in the usefulness of radio to Africans. It would be difficult to understand the impact of radio at this time without knowing something of the personality, intelligence, and enthusiasm of Kittermaster and his staff. When I first walked into Broadcasting House, I sensed something different from that of any other office (government, research, etc.) in Lusaka. The staff acted as if they were unaware of the color bar. As Peter Fraenkel aptly writes, "Kittermaster . . . seemed somehow unaware of the social pressures outside and did all the things that were simply not done in Rhodesia as if haughtily absent-minded."[4] The European and African members of his staff liked and respected each other and worked enthusiastically and intelligently toward a common goal. Kittermaster's home was the only European one in Lusaka where I met an African (one of his staff) socially, and the occasion was marked by an absence of self-consciousness. Broadcasting House was the one example I found of an actual partnership between Europeans and Africans, the official goal of Federation. Kittermaster and many of his staff are no longer there. Since 1957 there has been the Federal Broadcasting Corporation run by a board of governors, appointed by the Minister of Home Affairs in the federal government.

The staff were not always in their offices. Some toured the country, recording old and new music and events of special interest. Some sat in their offices and compiled bulletins of local news from items sent by African correspondents in villages, or they wrote news of the Territory—political events, strikes, new agricultural schemes, education, sports, etc.—and of the world beyond the Rhodesias and Nyasaland. News was given "straight," without slanting. In interviews with Africans who listened to news on the radio, we found not a single person who doubted the validity and truthfulness of the news reports. The listeners said, "They have not lied to us yet."

In educational talks, infinite care was taken to make them as intelligible as possible to an African audience. Fraenkel tells how he tried to get across an idea of budget expenditure on schools. He spent some time at a bank weighing wads of pound notes, and then went on the air with, "Well, now, if we were to find a big pile of pound notes, as heavy as two bags of maize, then we would have about the same amount of money as our government will be spending on schools this year."[5]

Alec Nkhata, a "dreamer of songs," had a special gift for composing songs, often humorous, about town life. He sang of town "wives" who painted their lips, of the awkwardness of wives from the rural areas, of the loneliness of men away from home, of the fear of dying away from relatives, of the joys of town life, of drinking, of "jiving," and of sex. Often he used traditional music, but his themes were new and so was his guitar. Alone or with his quartet he was exceedingly popular.

Edwin Mlongoti told stories and put on impromptu plays. Africans, with their traditions of singing, of dancing, of arguing cases in their courts, and of being given to much conversation, appear before a microphone without any apparent fear or embarrassment. Four or five of them produce a ten- or fifteen-minute play with almost no rehearsal. The "director" sketches a plot, and then casually assigns the roles. One is a husband; another a wife; a third, a stranger; a fourth, a policeman. Although no visual audience is present, the acting is done with a real sense of drama.

Sylvester Massiye had a novel approach in his "Out of the Whirl-wind" (*Kabvulumvulu*) program on marriage, witchcraft, and other perennially interesting subjects.

The programs to Africans were in a different African language for each of six days, and in English on the seventh. The vernaculars were the main ones in the areas: Bemba, Nyanja, Tonga, Lozi, Ndebele, and Shone. Most of the broadcasts were by Africans.[6] As could be expected, the majority of all listeners (68 per cent) listened on the day of the week when their own language was spoken. But 15 per cent listened three times a week or more; another 18 per cent, whenever they had time.

At the time of my study, broadcasts were from two to nine P.M.[7] From two to four there was continuous music; and after four, a highly diversified program of short items, separated from each other by songs and dance music. In the program were news, plays, stories, educational talks, and "Request" (*Zimene Mwatifunsa*). The last was a request program in which Africans sent messages to relatives and friends in different parts of the Territory, accompanied by the playing of their favorite record.

Practically all of the listeners heard the music and songs. Listeners gave their preferences readily and, in descending order of popularity, they were: music and songs; "Request"; news from districts, Northern Rhodesia, and Central Africa; world news; plays; educational talks; stories and sports.

Like listeners and readers all over the world, some Africans preferred to hear about themselves; and others, about the world; but preferring one program did not exclude listening to and enjoying other programs. Many times, a preference was expressed for a combination of programs, such as "music and news." Whatever the preferred program, the listeners in interviews and in conversations stressed the meanings not only of the most preferred program, but of all they heard—songs, news, plays and stories, educational talks, etc. Radio provided meanings and guidance in a new society as well as entertainment for these African listeners. This was in keeping with tribal oral traditions, in which folk tales, myths, proverbs, and songs had meanings, often direct lessons or morals such as are common in our *Aesop's Fables*. Then, too, as tribal mores and the influence of the elders weakened, the radio offered new group norms, which strengthened the modern attitudes of some listeners and gave direction to the attitudes of others. And, remarkably, the radio was not only concerned with the modern and with town life, but also with villages and the traditional. In the space of an hour or two, it took the listener from one to the other, without giving him any sense of disparity.

Music and Songs

It is not surprising in view of the traditional enjoyment of music that all the radio audience listened to and enjoyed the musical programs and that approximately half of the listeners preferred them. These programs were somewhat more popular among women and the uneducated, but the difference was not significant. Songs were diverse: modern, traditional, cowboy, "jive" songs, Christian hymns. Modern songs were concerned with love, sex, town and rural wives, "goodtime" girls, the loneliness of men away from home, joys and dangers of town life and other choices open to townsmen. Although only a few of the songs expressed the feelings of women, they too enjoyed them. Listeners said the songs helped them; in most songs the listeners were hearing about themselves.

The majority of radio listeners on the mine township said they preferred modern songs and music. But this did not mean European music. The music was often traditional or an altered traditional form, although the singer was accompanied by a modern guitar. The words were in a vernacular language. One who liked the new music said:

I like music best. I enjoy African songs, for I understand the language. I like the songs of Nkhata for two reasons: First, because they are composed of words which are full of meanings; and secondly, I like the guitar-playing. I also enjoy the American music made by coyboys. European music is abominable to me, because it has no life in it. It is slow and dull. Europeans sing as if they are crying.

A minority resented the innovations. One man said:

I like the typical Bemba songs best, because they remind me of Bembaland. I like all kinds of typical Bemba music. I do not like very much the songs by Nkhata, because they are too modern, although Bemba words are used. He even uses a guitar when our forefathers had no guitar. It is merely spoiling the Bemba music, because now many people like his songs, which are half English and half Bemba. And these people do not like the typical old songs. I do not say Nkhata's songs are bad; they are good but they are too English in style. I would suggest that he use English words in them instead of Bemba.

Still others liked both modern and traditional songs. A woman said:

I like best the African tribal music and more especially the Kunda music [she was a Kunda]. When this is on the program, I forget I am in Luanshya and think I am in the rural. Apart from the old songs, I like Alec Nkhata's songs which I think are the leading songs in Northern Rhodesia, as far as modern music is concerned. The variety pleases me.

Others cared only for jive music. One of these said: "Give me only jive music"; and his favorite jiving song was:

> Wa Wa baby
> Oh, baby
> I wanna sing
> Oh, baby
> I wanna jive
> I wanna jive
> Day and night
> With you
> Wa Wa baby
> Oh, baby
> I wanna jive
> Day and night!

Over and over again, we heard: "I forget all about sad things when music is on." "What are these sad things?" we asked; and a typical answer was, "I forget all about death and my relatives who died. When there is no music, one thinks of his relatives who died and in so doing, he, too, will get very thin and may die also which is not a good thing. Let us all be refreshed with music, so that we don't think of death."

Yet some of the songs remembered by these listeners were sad and about death. The refrain in one was:

> I shall die where I wander
> O Mother, O Mother
> I shall die where I wander

Comment of a man: "I like this song because I come from far away to work for money. Now I do not think about returning home, and I have found my home in this place. While seeking a fortune here, I may die. I feel that I shall die far from my home since I am growing old now." For him the function of this song was clearly catharsis.

Other songs concerned with death showed the influence of Christianity. One was:

> Friends, we are visitors on earth!
> Let us always remember that death is at hand.
> Let's not forget our Creator, maker of Heaven and earth,
> Who gave us the world.
> Let's magnify the Lord!

> The world is like a bone
> From which you gnaw a little bit.
> You will die and leave the world.
> Therefore, men and you women, let's not forget!
> Let's remember we will be there on Judgment Day!

> Everyone will receive punishment
> According to his wrongdoing
> There will be the reward for wrongdoers on earth
> The poultry farmer looks after the life of his chickens.
> So are our lives. We are looked after by God!

Christian hymns were likewise heard and their meanings considered. A man repeated the text of "Abide with Me" and said:

I sing this hymn in the evening when I am going to bed. Always I feel God should be near me in everything I do, everything I think about, and in everything I say, so that when I die, I may go to Paradise and not to Hell where I would be in everlasting fires.

There may be a number of reasons for the concern with death in songs. Anxiety about death, particularly death from witchcraft, existed in tribal society and still persists. On the Copperbelt, there was also the fear of dying away from one's home and kindred, which is hard for most people to accept and particularly hard for Africans, who have been so closely tied to their land and to living and dead kindred. It is also possible that Christianity, which adds the fear of Hell and does not take away the fear of witchcraft, may increase anxiety about death. Then, too, death is a much more frequent occurrence on a township of thirty thousand Africans than in a small village; frequent funeral processions winding their way through the township could increase anxiety. I have also another hypothesis: that the generalized anxiety concerning the possible loss of land to Europeans was not unrelated to the anxiety about death, for land was and is symbolic of fertility and life.

Another sad theme was the loneliness of men away from home. A popular song was:

> I try to find you, mother
> But I cannot see you.
> I came outside the house.
> I couldn't see you.
> Sorrow, sorrow. Because I have not seen you.
>
> I have got your picture but it doesn't speak.
> I have got your picture but it doesn't speak.
> If it would have been speaking
> Today I would have been too happy!

Many other popular songs were concerned with town and rural wives, love and sex.

> 1. Goodbye my love, I am going away
>   From where I came.
>   I am tired of waiting for you to change your habits.
>   You will die alone.

Do not forget your responsibility over children.
Although I am going away, I will give you help
In all your difficulties.
You have wronged me by asking for a lot of money
Which I, the unfortunate, cannot afford.

A typical comment:

I like this song because it teaches us that if you marry a town girl, even if you stay with her for two years, you will still divorce each other, because most of them are only after money and not real marriage. If a man is not careful, he is left bankrupt.

2. Some young men are not wise.
   When they see a Kapenta
   They put all their attention to her.
   They forget their houses.
   That is very saddening.
   They start speaking in English,
   "Hulla, Mama, the Beautiful One,
   Come live with me in town.
   You will be very fat, you girl
   If you live with me.
   You're gonna get bread and butter.
   I have everything.
   There are plenty new looks.
   You'll have so many dresses,
   You'll be changing clothes all day.
   In the morning you will eat
   Coffee, toshta, and butter.
   When we two appear in public
   Young men will be shaking
   Because of your beautiful clothes."

Kapenta is the name given to a woman who paints her lips red like a European. She is one of the town good-time girls. This song was regarded as a warning to men not to spend all their money on good-time girls.

3. If you want to choose a girl for a wife
   You better wait for the month of June*

* June is in the Northern Rhodesian winter.

This is the time you will choose a clean girl
Because some bathe in hot season only,
But when it is cold in June, they stop!

4. What a world!
I was surprised when a young townsman married me.
And after only six days,
He said he did not want me any more
Because I had shamed him
In the presence of his people.
Then I begged, "No, no, my love
I'm new to married life
Give me a chance to remain with you
Only another six months."
"No," said the man,
"I asked you to make tea,
But—surprise!
You cooked the leaves like vegetables
And poured on ground-nuts like gravy.
I did not know village women were so ignorant.
You must go back to your house.
Here, take this ticket. It is ready.
The bus is waiting for you there!"

This song, by Nkhata, indicates that all is not necessarily well if a man goes home to the village for a rural bride. The village girl may be awkward in her new surroundings and shame her husband.

5. Let me tell you about the town wives.
Even though I give mine plenty of fish,
Even though there is a bag full of salt—enough to sit in,
Yet she'll complain, "There is not meat."
All day long she is never satisfied.
She threatens, "I'll not stay with you."
Yet . . . she remains, for I satisfy her at night.
At night I fondle her.
Her body becomes our playground.

6. We are the smart men about town. We eat from tables.
We are the smart men about town. We've got the girls.
We are the smart men about town. We put on shoes.
We are the smart men about town. We look like teachers.

> We are the smart men about town. Wonderful wires stretch
>   into our houses.
> We are the smart men about town. We have electric lights
>   and tin roofs.
> Now come and see what-hell-of-a-fellows we are!

Songs 5 and 6 were among the lusty, boasting ones about town life.

Songs with traditional themes were much less popular on this township than those with modern themes and were remembered only infrequently. One of the few was:

> When Maiwaso catches the locusts
> She does not give some to her friends.
> Hm . . . hm . . . hm . . .
> The locusts will mourn for you!

Comment:

It is true that if a person is very stingy he cannot be popular to his friends, and the time will come when he will fall ill, and not many will feel sad with him. That also happens if he dies; there will not be many people at his funeral, and that is not good at all. Even if you have little, you should share some with your friends.

Traditional hospitality was still a much prized value among these Copperbelt Africans.

The songs express well the ambivalences felt by the men in their new situation. Men want the new town wives who ape the looks and clothes of the European women, and who are supposedly "champions" in a strong sex life. Men boast that they have these women. Yet they complain that the same women leave them bankrupt. They also yearn for the supposedly unspoiled rural women, now somewhat romanticized. Yet they are shamed by her awkwardness in the ways of town life. The romantic yearning for one woman exists side by side with the desire for good-time girls, the champions.

A major problem for tribal peoples becoming modern is that for the first time they are faced with many choices. Traditional-minded elders who disapproved of new town customs could not give guidance. The songs offered advice to urban young men faced with alternatives and gave them the comfort of knowing that their temptations and problems were not unique.

"Request" (Zimene Mwatifunsa)

The second most popular program according to our survey was "Request." Twenty-seven per cent of the listeners preferred it, and almost all the listeners heard it with enjoyment. This personal program consisted of messages sent to and from individuals in various towns and villages. It gave news of births and deaths, engagements and marriages, the new address of a man changing his place of work, and other greetings of significance. Each message was accompanied by the sender's favorite song record. Listeners said they liked this program because it was "quicker than a letter" and brought news and "good greetings from people who are far away from me." They also spoke of enjoying the songs which "I hear with the messages."

News

News was impersonal, but gave the listeners some sense of reassurance, of predictability, and even control. "I like the news so that we may know what is going on within our country and in the world." This comment runs like a refrain through the interviews with radio listeners. To know the news from far and near and to know it with the miraculous speed of radio gave the listeners a sense of participation in the near and far worlds. To be ignorant of what is going on arouses anxiety. Knowing the news reduces the imagined fears of the unknown. Then, too, radio news not only lessened the ignorance of illiterate listeners but also reduced the social distance between them and those who could read. One man who had never been to school said:

Since I cannot read and collect information from newspapers to know what is happening in our country, I use my ears and listen to the radio. So I do not remain ignorant of the things my friends who can read may be talking about.

The most frequently remembered news[8] was about equally divided between rural and urban items from Northern Rhodesia and Nyasaland, from which most of the listeners came. Although the adults on the Copperbelt were now part of a larger society, many still had close ties to their rural districts. They were eager to hear of progress

there and of local events, trivial and important. These included reports about activities of chiefs, agricultural developments, schools
being built, passes for mothers to visit sons on the mine, death of an
important person in the rural district, a lion getting in the way of a
bus. Over and over again, listeners expressed their pleasure in hearing news from their home districts:

I bought a radio so that I could listen and hear all that is being said
in Bemba from the different parts of the world, and especially from my
home. I like to hear of things which have been improved or new things
in my country such as dams, schools, and hospitals. Without any time
wasted, the whole world becomes aware of such news.

Urban news was about politics, African trade unions, sports, movement of European government officials, regulations and laws effecting
Africans, and other town events. News of new regulations or laws
often gave a feeling of security to listeners. An uneducated man said:

I like the Northern Rhodesian news best. I heard from the radio an
announcement concerning a new law for Northern Rhodesia. It said that
there was to be a light on a bicycle when moving at night. Any offender
will be dealt with accordingly. I was one of those people who had no light
on their bicycle. So that when I heard that, the following morning I went
to buy my light. I was very pleased, because had I not been attentive,
I should have been the victim of that law.

Reactions to much of the news, particularly any considered political, were clearly influenced by the pre-existing attitudes of the
listeners. Those who had gone as far as Standard IV or further were
interested in political news, and they were primarily concerned with
political progress for Africans and with gaining political equality with
Europeans. One of them said:

I do not like news such as a lion killed a cow at Mkushi or that there
was a fight at Mufilira and so forth, because they do not tell me how my
country is improving. I was pleased to hear three weeks ago that Mr.
Yamba was elected a member of the federal government. You see, long
ago Africans were not allowed to speak for themselves, but now we can be
found even in Parliament. We ought to speak for ourselves. God gave us
minds to think for ourselves.

News of the movements of European officials in the Federation
was remembered quite frequently, but always with hostility or indiffer-

ence, no matter what the news about them was. "They are not our relatives," "They have done us no good," or "They have brought the Federation, which is bad for us." A longer comment was:

I heard that the Governor was going to England to become whom I have forgotten, and that a new Governor was coming to take his place. It did not make any difference to me, since they are only Europeans who favor their fellow Europeans. Had they said that Harry Nkumbula, president of African Congress was going somewhere, I would be sorry, since he is trying to fight for my sake and my children. He does not want Europeans to take our land which God gave us.

Another listener to the same news item, a clerk, said,

. . . The Governor was unfair in some cases by speaking against Africans, especially the time they were talking about Federation. Sometimes he would say that we were not civilized, and that is not good.

Reactions to news about visiting officials from Britain were more mixed: favorable, neutral, or unfavorable. If the officials were linked to Federation, reactions were always negative. But news about the royal family was warmly received. In the imagery of the Africans, the Queen and her family appeared quite different from other Europeans. Some of the uneducated Africans thought that the Queen would not have imposed Federation on them and that their troubles would be over if they could communicate with her.

In making the original survey, I was surprised that even uneducated Africans were listening to world news. Further interviewing revealed that for many the motivation was to find out if a war was going on. For the Africans, a major advantage of the European conquest had been the cessation of intertribal warfare and slavery. But they have experienced the last world war and the older people remember the First World War; they had heard about the Korean War from the radio and they now have news about atomic bombs and other alarming events. The Africans were frightened about the possibility of another world war. Any news they connected with war was heard in the context of suspicions that Europeans had malevolent intentions of sending Africans to war. Typical comments from two uneducated men were:

I like news because I want to know what is happening in other places, whether there is war, and where it is taking place. I heard that Americans wanted to test the atomic bomb in a certain land and the British have agreed. I do not like such things because they are a source of war. Everyone is not happy during a war, and so it is not good. A lot of people are killed and things in the shops are expensive, because they are fewer and difficult to transport, since they are likely to be damaged on the way. If a war comes, I will go to the rural and start hoeing, and then drink beer in the village with my friends. If war comes, I would not remain here in town.

I feel that we have already been subjected by these Europeans, and we shall never be free. We have nothing to do with wars at the present time, since we do not rule any land. It is useless for us to go to war when we know that we shall not gain anything after the war is over. They promise a lot of things while the war is on and when the war is over we do not see these things. In the last war they said that if Africans fight hard and we helped them to win, after war we would be equal to Europeans and would be marrying European ladies. But we do not marry them now. If an African tries to sleep with a European woman, he is imprisoned for years. Yet European men are not even punished for sleeping with African women, and that is why there are so many colored people here. [Colored is used for a mulatto.]

A contemplative African who was a good Christian regarded war as inevitable. He said:

War started when the world was very young, and it is now a thing the world cannot do without. People should fight when they do not agree. Even in the Bible we read of the woman Deborah fighting against the Philistines, and there are more fights or wars in the Bible. Everyone should be prepared to fight, because we read even in Heaven there were wars. There was a war between the angels of God and the angels who followed Satan, the devil. And so how can we avoid wars here on earth?

The only favorable image of Europeans in connection with war was given by a man in his late forties, a clerk with Standard V education, who had traveled around different parts of Africa. He said:

I used to like listening to the wireless during the last war, so that I could know how the war was getting on. I was much interested because that war concerned me, as I am in the hands of the British Empire and the war was between the British and the Germans. I thought that if the British

won, it would be much better for us, but if the Germans won, it would
have been very bad. You see, the British Government is very good indeed,
because it educates its Africans. When the Germans were ruling Tanganyika, Africans were kept as slaves, and they were not educated at all.
That is why Nyakyusa from Tanganyika look very backward, as far as
the use of European things are concerned. If you ask anyone who was
there during the rule of the Germans, he will tell you that they were kept
like animals, and no education given to them. I say that the British government is the best because some of us can now do some good jobs like office
work and can sleep in good houses. I was in Portuguese East Africa from
1927 to 1937, but the Africans there were not so good as I found them
here. Nearly every African there wore torn clothes, and there was no education provided. People were worked like slaves and no African had a
good job. So, from all this one can tell that the British government is the
best.

Many reactions to news were unstructured, but suggested a pleasant
sense of being *au courant*. For instance, an uneducated man reported
his pleasure at hearing news of a football match, a blind man with
deformed hands, a lion hunt, the Pope's illness, and a cold wave in
Canada.

Some news was incorrectly remembered, or confused, or even
imagined. Incorrect recall and the play of imagination are not unique
to Africans; they are universal and not confined to radio listeners.
Whether the recall of news was correct or incorrect, structured or unstructured, the radio listeners, at the time of listening, felt more in
control of their movements, through knowing what was going on in
villages and towns, hearing about new regulations and getting other
information which they considered important. Through the news, the
listeners maintained ties to the rural areas and at the same time felt
more a part of urban life; some extended their range of interest to
places and people in other parts of Africa and in the world.

Plays, Stories, and Educational Talks

In our survey, plays, stories, and educational talks were preferred
by a minority of 10 per cent, but many others listened to them and
liked them. In the more detailed interviewing the recall of plays,
stories, and talks tended to be more accurate than of news. The
listeners did not always distinguish among plays, stories, and talks, all

of which were regarded as a part of life or directly impinging on it. Some of the meanings, or lessons, were in the realm of human relations and morality, while others were about the new material things which have become so important. The themes and the reactions of the listeners to them reflect particularly well the problems, anxieties, and desires of Africans on the township.

Jealousy was a motif running through many of the plays. The highest recall on a play (more than half of those listening to plays) was concerned with a man's jealousy about his wife's possible adultery. The setting of this play was a village and, as told by the listeners, was concerned with a man and his wife going to the bush to collect charcoal. While they were doing this, two young men came there. When the husband saw them, he was suspicious that they were after his wife. So he started asking questions of his wife and quarreled with her. The young men asked what the quarrel was about, and the wife explained. The young men then beat the husband because of his suspicions.

The large majority of listeners to this play thought the jealousy was justified, but they blamed the husband and wife for quarreling in public. Some thought that the wife should have waited and blamed her husband for his suspicions in the privacy of their home; others said that he should have waited to have expressed his suspicions until they were home. A small number thought that the jealousy itself was wrong and unjustified. The earlier discussion of family life indicated that jealousy was a major motif in the relationship of spouses, and the attitude of the majority of listeners is therefore not surprising. But these Africans have a strong sense of decorum, which includes the idea that spouses should not express their jealousy in public. It was likewise significant that a few thought the jealousy was not justified, for this was a new attitude.

Another play on jealousy had a town setting. One of the listeners told the plot:

There was a man who was very jealous of his wife. Every morning before he went to work he swept the yard, making sure that no foot or bicycle marks were there. After work he looked down to see whether any men had come to his house. If he found any marks, he asked his wife who had come there; so a quarrel started. Sometimes when he was at work he would cheat his boss and say that he was very ill and then be given a note to take to the hospital; but instead, he went to his house to see if any man had come there. He did this nearly every week, but no reports came from the hospital to his boss. His wife used to warn him that one day he would be discharged from work, but he did not seem to care. Then one day he said to his boss, "Please, *bwana,* I want to stop work." His *bwana* said, "Are you ill?" Then he answered, "No, *bwana,* I am not ill. I want to stay at home near my wife because some men come in my absence to coax her." His *bwana* and his workmates laughed at him and advised him not to leave his work for that reason. But he gave up his job.

The man in this play seems pathologically jealous, but it dramatizes with great clarity the pervasive jealousy between spouses, accentuating its point by involving the man's job. Here, most of the listeners thought the jealousy was unjustified. One expressed the opinion of many:

It is quite useless for a man to be very jealous of his wife. It does not mean that every man who talks to your wife coaxes her. If you see her talking to a man, do not worry at all. If she does something bad and you discover it, then why not get another wife?

Some listeners said that plays contain the wisdom of their fathers. When asked for an example, one man said,

A few months ago I heard a play about washing woolen things. The husband told his wife to wash the woolen sweater, and the wife agreed that she would wash it, and the husband went away to work. Then his wife, having no knowledge of how to wash woolen things, used hot water, and the sweater shrunk. The husband returned home and asked his wife whether she had washed his sweater, and she answered that she had done so. The husband tried the sweater on, but found that it was too small for him. Then he asked his wife what kind of water she had used, and she told him "hot water." Her husband laughed at her and told her that she should be using lukewarm water for woolen things. The play made people laugh, I know, but it taught them something—that they should use warm water and not hot water for washing woolen things.

What they called the "wisdom of our fathers" was now the knowledge and advice of the young intelligentsia at Broadcasting House on how to wash sweaters and on human relations in the new economic structure. Several plays had themes concerning the relationship of African workers to each other and made the point that men should not bewitch or take other advantage of each other to gain an employer's favor. One man said:

I like plays best because they teach what people ought to do and what they should not do. There was one play I enjoyed very much. It was about bewitching one's co-workers to gain favor with the employer. This teaches people to be good co-workers and to stop the habit of bewitching others.

In another play, a foreman kept reporting to his employer that the Africans under him were not working hard, thus causing them to be fired. Finally the employer sacked the foreman and put one of the former employees in his place. A typical comment was: "This play teaches us not to be cruel to our friends if we are made supervisors."

Africans were always traveling—to the villages for visits and to the towns in search of work or for visits. Some plays were about the hazards of journeys:

One day, Ushifwayo was on a journey to Lusaka, where his brother was very ill. He caught a train, and in the coach there were so many people that there was no fresh air, and he was nearly crushed to death. So he thought of a way in which he could manage to get some fresh air. He started looking this way and that way as if in search of something lost. The people looked at him and asked him what he was looking for. Ushifwayo said that he was looking for a snake which he had caught and was taking to his *bwana* at Lusaka. When the people heard this, they ran away into other coaches in fear that they would be bitten by the snake. In that way Ushifwayo had plenty of room and plenty of fresh air.

Comment: "Had Ushifwao not used a method of getting more air, he would have died."

Trains are relatively new and the concept of the need for fresh air is still newer. But the trick resembles the traditional trickster theme in tribal folk tales.

Hygiene and prevention of illness were common themes:

Three weeks ago I heard a play on hygiene. There was a man who was married and had a child. That child went to school, where he learned about hygiene. The boy used to tell his father about what he learned at school in hygiene lessons. The father did not agree and said diseases had nothing to do with hygiene. Then one day some people were suffering from diarrhea, and the father refused to do as the son wanted. Flies came on the father's food. He drove them away but ate the same food. After a short time he suffered very much from diarrhea and had to be taken to the hospital. When he came out of the hospital, he did not want to be careless again, and started agreeing with his son that what he learned at school was true.

In this play not only was there a lesson about hygiene but also a reversal of the traditional role of a father and his son, with the former refusing at first to accept the new role of learning from his son, but then through experience doing so. The idea that the old should learn from the young seemed to be accepted by the listeners and represented a revolutionary change in attitude.

The traditional stories were usually animal fables with a moral. The role of the radio in taking over some of the functions of the elders is seen in the comment by a man who enjoyed these fables:

I like the stories over the wireless. When I was a small boy, my father and mother used to tell me many. Now I hear them over the wireless, and so I will be able to remember them, and I can tell them to my children when I am seated around the fire with them, as my parents did to me.

The traditional tales which he and others remembered hearing over the wireless were on familiar themes: The small hare gets the better of the big lion, elephant, and leopard; a beautiful girl refuses all suitors and finally marries one who turns out to be a hyena; the son of a chief disobeys his father by going into the jungle where he meets a slave girl whom he marries, and thereby loses his kingdom; a jealous wife turns a co-wife into a hare through witchcraft, but the husband discovers the fact and kills her. The morals or lessons were obvious.

The educational talks people remembered best were those dealing with agriculture, hygiene, and education for girls. A radio talk on how to improve agricultural practices brought favorable comments from those who viewed Europeans as wanting to help Africans:

I like talks on such things as agriculture because they help the well-being of the people, so that they will not be hungry and will have more clothing and more wealth; and trade, too, is increased.

I remember one lecture on how to fight soil erosion. I heard that we should not burn the bush late in the dry season because the grass and the plants are destroyed by this fire. Much of the good soil is washed away by the rain when it comes because the ground is then bare. The other thing is that we should try by all means to preserve the fertility of the soil by not planting the same crop in the same garden for many years. I like agricultural lectures because I intend to become a farmer when I have collected enough money.

Similar talks brought negative reactions from those who viewed Europeans as basically unfair to Africans.

These Europeans have come here and introduced the new methods of farming, but they have pushed the Africans to rocky places. Now they force Africans to use the European methods of farming in these rocky places. How can they expect us to grow food on rocks? If they know better, then why didn't they occupy these rocky places and improve them? The Europeans are unfair.

I remember hearing a talk about agriculture. I heard that ridges would be introduced so as to keep the fertility of the soil unharmed by running water or wind. I also heard that people were refusing to make these contour lines or ridges because it was such hard work. I feel that people were right to refuse, because we have no special machines to work with. Europeans have tractors, ploughs, and other special farm equipment to make the contour lines. But we Africans don't have them. How can we make contour lines with hoes only? This is very hard work.

The main themes of talks on education for girls were these: If educated, girls would have more knowledge of hygiene and would know how to cook the new foods necessary for good health; as a result, their husbands and children would enjoy better health and live longer. The reactions to these talks were predominantly favorable.

Very few liked or remembered academic talks, but a clerk with a Standard VI education said:

When I heard the talks on history of ancient famous men like Socrates, that is when I started liking wireless, since I knew I would learn some history from it, and this would help me in my private studies. I cannot go to school now, since I am married and I have to send a child to school.

I heard in February [interview in May] that in Greece there lived a man called Socrates. Socrates was a great thinker and used to ask questions to find out things. People did not like him for such questions, and he was given poison to drink, and he died after drinking poison in

339 B.C. One of his followers was Plato, who started a school or academy
for philosophers. One of his students was Aristotle, who was a naturalist
and teacher of Alexander the Great. That is what I learned from the
wireless.

I thought it very good that the wireless should be teaching us. I
think it was very bad for people to kill Socrates. He had introduced a
good way of thinking by asking questions. It is no good doing something
if you do not know how to do it or what you are doing. I like these talks,
but I do not like the stories from the wireless since they are untrue. Have
you ever seen any animal speak like a person or have a big garden?

This man had moved away from his tribal folklore. He was more
interested in the wisdom to be learned from history. Socrates was
teaching him.

Listening to the radio had many functions. It was, first, a source
of much pleasure. It seemed also to provide a catharsis: Africans
listening to songs, stories, and plays about their personal problems
such as adultery, lonesomeness, jealousy, felt "refreshed." Radio also
gave meanings and clues to many problems in the new world and
some sense of control over it. Through radio, knowledge and the
possible range of identifications was extended beyond village and town
to the larger community of Northern Rhodesia, Nyasaland, and
Southern Rhodesia and, to a lesser degree, to the African continent
and the world beyond. Finally, radio served as a bridge between
the tribal and the modern world, for listeners could send messages
to kindred and friends at home, receive news of villages and hear
traditional tales as well as new ones.

The African listening to the radio—for the joy of music, for the
meanings in songs and plays, for news, for the knowledge of the European know-how in hygiene, agriculture and bringing up babies—
became more a whole person. He was not just a miner, a carpenter,
a clerk, or a housewife. He affirmed his relationships with the tribal
village, with the new environment on the Copperbelt, and with the
world, still rather dimly realized, beyond that. Because so many of
the radio programs were concerned with the concrete and the intimate, because the songs and music gave sensory pleasure, and, of
course, because it was aural, radio also provided a not too difficult
transition from the primary reality of tribal auditory communication
to a new secondary level of communication.

Radio was particularly important for those Africans who were predisposed to change. In Africa, as elsewhere, radio is rarely the sole agent of change, but rather a reinforcing and contributing agent functioning with other social and economic agencies of change.[9] Underlying radio's strength as an agent of social change in Northern Rhodesia was the fact that it was non-commercial and controlled.[10] Its programs to Africans were the result of careful planning and intelligent work by a small staff of devoted and enthusiastic people, European and African, at Broadcasting House in Lusaka.

There is a basic difference between the controlled radio programs to Africans in Northern Rhodesia and the commercial programs in the United States. Here, the commercial radio tends to express only such attitudes as are already virtually universal. There, the programs stressed some attitudes which were not universal. For instance, in the beginning, the programs advocating education for girls appealed only to a minority. The programs reinforced and strengthened the attitudes of this group and at the same time introduced a new idea to many other listeners, giving them persuasive reasons for adopting the new customs of sending girls to school. Of course, the fact that an African listened to radio indicated a certain modernity in outlook and a probability that he was open to persuasion. Yet interviews indicated that the radio programs were probably among the influential factors which increased the proportion of girls going to school.

There was nothing comparable on the radio programs for Europeans, who were also living in a world of rapid change, to help them understand it. Some of the Europeans had come to Africa thinking to escape the changes in their own country, but had jumped from the frying pan into the fire. A radio program which would have helped Europeans comprehend the Africans' growing nationalism and the social and political changes occurring all over Africa might have been useful.[12] However, such a program would not have been possible in the Federation, since the Prime Minister and other political leaders appeared unable to accept the reality of African nationalism.

16. Going to the Movies

Iₙ ᴛʜᴇ ᴘᴀꜱᴛ the visual experience of Africans was limited to the direct perception of their immediate environment. Movies introduced a secondary form of visual reality, ranging widely over the known and the unknown. Their surface realism and sensory appeal tend to disguise fantasy and give it the appearance of reality. In the news films Africans see people, places, and events which they know to be real though not always within their experience. They see Queen Elizabeth, European statesmen, African leaders, sportsmen, and many others in the news. They see real places: villages, towns, mines, schools, Victoria Falls, European cities, and so on. On the same programs they see cowboy films. The cowboys come from a real place, America. The cowboys' boxing is not too different from the boxing matches in the *British News*. But nothing in their background prepares the African audience to distinguish between fictional and documentary films.

Unlike Broadcasting House, the Motion Picture Section of the Information Department had no people dedicated to using the medium to help Africans make a transition to the modern world. Instead, there were technicians making movies of African scenes and going on movie-truck tours in rural areas, and there was a censorship board. Its "guiding principles" were modeled on the Production

254]

Code of the Motion Picture Association of America and were concerned with taboos on showing nudity, crime, and other scenes considered unsuitable.[1] The Motion Picture Section of the Information
Department lacked all awareness of the sociological significance of
movies and of problems inherent in their introduction to Africans.
A basic problem for the audience was one of reality: What is real?
What is "cheating"? Another was how to interpret what was seen.
Africans, like all peoples, tend to interpret what they see in terms
of their own limited experiences.

Movies (called cinema or bioscope by most Africans) are older
than radio and were first shown in this community in 1928. Unlike
the radio, they were a commercial "package" purchased by the mine
Welfare Department from a film company in South Africa. The
package was much the same at each showing: a cowboy film (old and
grade B), *British News, The Northern Spotlight* (Northern Rhodesia
News), an animal cartoon (*Kadoli*), *The African Mirror* (incidents of African life), an adventure serial such as *Superman,* and,
occasionally, a very old American slapstick comedy. The movie-goer
saw the entire package without enjoying the selectivity of the radio
listener, who usually listened only to the program which interested
him.

My initial survey indicated that 58 per cent of the adults on the
township have attended the movies at some time, and of these, 39
per cent were going now. Among the latter, 53 per cent went once a
week; 3 per cent, once in two weeks; 6 per cent, once a month;
and the remainder, less frequently. There was usually one showing
a week on the mine township; and the audience averaged twelve to
fifteen hundred people, about half of whom were children under sixteen. The audience was diverse: old and young, men and women, educated and uneducated. Although there were more men than women
in the audience and more people under thirty with some school education, yet 47 per cent of all the women and of all the uneducated,
48 per cent of all people in the thirty-to-forty year age group,
and 36 per cent of those over forty were also going to movies.

At seven o'clock on a clear evening, adults and children lined up
for their tickets—"thruppence" (three pennies) for adults and a penny
for children—at the large, unroofed white stone amphitheatre connected with the mine Welfare Hall. (Today there is a roofed theater.)

As the theater began to fill up, friends greeted each other, some young men attempted to make assignations with young women, children jostled and pushed each other and were told to be quiet and to make way for their elders. There was a continuous hubbub. The large audience spilled over into the center aisle, sitting on the steps of the inclined floor. Late-comers stood by the walls. Talk, laughter, and a sense of expectation pervaded the theater.

Going to the movies was a social experience, whereas listening to radio was relatively private, whether done at home or in a small group at a welfare center. There was an excitement in being part of a movie audience of more than a thousand people, constantly commenting to each other, shouting their pleasure and booing their displeasure. The comments often revealed the audience's basic problem of distinguishing between reality and acting as well as its reactions and attitudes to the content of the films. The following comments, typical on any movie evening, were recorded verbatim by African assistants sitting in various parts of the amphitheater. I was also present, observing and recording.

The show began with *The African Mirror,* showing incidents of African life:

Pictures of a mining town
This is Luanshya! Luanshya! (*several men shouting*).
Wake up, you old people from the villages, who don't know towns (*a boy, shouting*). "This is not Luanshya. It is Mufilira. Didn't you see it? It was written before you saw the picture. Couldn't you read?
Ah, are you sure it is Mufilira?
Sure, sure, it is Mufilira. I know that shaft.

A group of African first-aiders on the mine
These are the people who do very little work underground. They just go to sleep. The machine boys are the ones who work very hard.
Look, those people are very lazy—four people carry one sick person. Why can't he be carried by two? Boo! Boo! (*a few others join his boos*).

Lozi people dancing
Ah, the Ngoni dance.
No, it is a Lozi dance. This is most interesting. See the women dancing like mad women. Women are dancing by themselves. It would be better if they were dancing together with men, like we do today. Europeans

are wonderful people, because here are the Lozi beating drums, singing and dancing in the bioscope as they did long ago. All those whom you see are dead and buried, but we still see them move.

Large, healthy looking cattle
Oh, hiii, Halo hii!
These cows are Southern Rhodesian *(a man speaking)*. When they are brought here for slaughtering, meat is sold to the Europeans only. We are sold thin meat [without fat].

THE NORTHERN SPOTLIGHT [news from Northern Rhodesia]
Dedication of home for the aged
These are very good houses. They look very beautiful.
Are they for Africans?
Hm, Do you think they can build houses for Africans like that? Can you see any Africans in the crowd listening to that speech? No, these houses are for Europeans.

Europeans in a club house
Oh, see those people are playing drafts as we play here.
See, others are reading newspapers.
Very many Europeans like reading newspapers.
It is because they are written in their own language, and the other reason is that most of them know how to read.
But there are a lot of Africans who do not read newspapers, and yet they can read.
Europeans always like keeping themselves busy. We like sleeping.

THE BRITISH NEWS
The Queen's visit to America
Ah, what nice cars these are!
This Queen will go around the world. She has already visited many places.

A snow-covered mountain
Oh, that is a very beautiful mountain. Do we have them here with ice on top?
Oh yes, in Kenya there is one which goes above the clouds. The top is white.
When did you see it?
I saw it when I was in the army in the last war.

ANIMAL CARTOON
(Much laughter and appreciative shouts by children.)

COWBOY FILM

[During this film men, women, and children rose to their feet in excitement, bending forward and flexing their muscles with each blow the cowboys gave. The shouting could be heard several miles away.]

Wheoo! He is intoxicated with a blow!

I know this cowboy. He does not play with anyone except his brother.

They all fear him because they cannot fight him.

Oh, that man will soon receive a blow.

He has let him go because the man is a weakling.

Ahass! One! One! Waan!

Look at that other man!

Oh, yes, that is the only man who can fight Jack!

Look at his ears, they indicate that is a furious man!

That man in feathers is a Negro!

No. You do not know Negroes! He is a red Indian.

Look at that man. He is smoking opium.

What is it for?

Oh, so you do not know that it removes the sense of fear.

Hmm, Jack is very clever, he can fight them all.

Oh! Oh! OOO! The cowards have retreated!

That is what I said.

Oh! Oh! Ooo! There they are. They are found by Jack.

One! Waan! (*in unison with the blows*).

Now next time he is going to that man who was smoking opium, who seems to be the leader of those cowards.

Oho! He is down already.

He is going to revenge on what they did to his son.

Whip. Oh-oo, he is caught by the neck by that whip.

One! Waaani!

Now the fight is hot.

Waan! Waan! There he goes through the window!

Wheooo! Wheooo! Waaan!

Ohoo, now those two heroes are the winners.

Yes, this is the kind of Jack we want.

It is nine-thirty, and the movie is over. The audience comes out into the night and goes home. Some are on bicycles; most walk. The township is dark, but flames from the smelter are silhouetted against the bright star-filled sky. Soon all are in their darkened houses.

Among the types of movies, cowboy films were the most popular. 35 per cent of the audience preferred them, 10 per cent more of those with education than without, and 7 per cent more males than females. The remainder of the preferences were scattered in quite small percentages. Twenty per cent said they enjoyed the whole show without any preferences. This was in contrast to the radio listeners, all of whom enjoyed parts of the program more than others. For the 20 per cent of movie fans without preferences and for many others, too, the total experience of movie-viewing was important. One woman said:

> I like the movements of the picture. Now, about what I like best, I cannot say; I like anything that is shown; the cowboys beating each other, football, and all the others. They all please me.

The novelty of movement on the screen was the major attraction in the days of the nickelodeon when movies were first shown in the United States. Movement is still the essence of films.

There were "talkies" and silent films. Practically none of the talk, however, could be understood because the conversations and shouting in the audience drowned out the voices from the screen. But when the audience was relatively quiet, even those who knew English could understand little of the American cowboy's English. As the movie finished one evening, several fourteen- or fifteen-year-old schoolboys commented to each other that they could not understand the words.

> "American English" is all mbam, mbam; you can't understand it.
> Oh, yes, it is very quick, and you write as you speak it. Professor Powdermaker is the only one who understands it. [I was a familiar figure at the movies.]

In a tour of the rural areas with a movie truck, which showed a British talking film, I learned that the English-speaking members of the audience understood very little of the talk. The British-movie English was different from the school-learned English of the Africans; the talk in the films was also too rapid for the audience to catch; and there was, again, the competition from the noisy conversations of the audience.

The cowboy and other American films were usually fairly old and in black and white. Some of the films made in Africa were in color. The original survey had no question on preference for black and

white or color films, but later interviews showed 100 per cent preference for black and white films. The main objections to the color
films were that the colors were not "natural-looking" and that Africans looked too black in them. The attempt to make the films seem
more real with colors evidently made them seem more unreal.

Movies were a significant individual and social experience for the
mass audience: men and women, young and old, educated and
uneducated. The experience was individual through identification
with the cowboy hero and in the expression of strong emotions, particularly during the fighting when men (and women, too) flexed
their muscles and shouted. This identification with the cowboy was expressed particularly well by a relatively well-educated (secondary
school), law-abiding young man in his early twenties, who held a
responsible job:

> When the people are fighting, I feel as if I am also going to fight some-
> one. My muscles feel it (*tensing his arm muscles to show me*), and I feel
> as if I am fighting. I always want to see how strong Jack is and whether
> he can be knocked out early. But I expect the hero, Jack, to beat everyone
> and to win every time. When the hero doesn't rise up after a fight, it is
> useless, and I feel discouraged. We don't want Jack to be beaten, and we
> will not come again if he is beaten. He *must* always rise up after he is
> hit and the enemy *must* always run away.
>
> I like the way they ride and fight with their hands. I do not like to
> fight, but I enjoy seeing other people fighting, but not killing each other.
> I used to fight when I was a boy, up to about when I was twelve years
> old. But I cannot fight now, because I would not want to lose the respect
> of people.

A member of the intelligentsia, to which this young man belonged,
was not supposed to fight. He was supposed not only to dress like
a European, but also to act with dignity. Behavior is an important
class distinction on the mine township.

Uneducated men, whose status did not depend on refraining from
fighting, had the same kind of identification. One said:

> I like to see cowboys run after one another on horses, and the fighting.
> Jack beats his friends skillfully, and it pleases me to see him plant blows
> on other men's faces. I also like their music. They sing very lovely songs.
> If I went to America, I would very much want to be a cowboy.

Others not only identified with the cowboys but felt they could improve their fighting and boxing from watching them. A typical comment was:

I like best the cowboy films, because they teach us how to fight others and how to win lovers. I learned how to box people better than I did in the past, and in this way I have become popular on the township, and people fear me. This I like.

Women enjoyed the cowboy films for very similar reasons and additional ones. Two typical comments:

I like the cowboy films best because I like to see how to throw good blows, so that I can kick anybody who interferes with my business; for example, if my husband interferes.

I enjoy very much the cowboy fighting. I like their boxing, and it is really exciting. In addition I see the way in which the girls in the film are dressed. I am particularly interested in seeing women ride horses and in trying to shoot men. I also like the music very much.

The repetitive quality of the plot in cowboy films is not unlike the same quality in many African folk tales, and in popular stories and movies over the world. The African audience often anticipated what was going to happen in their comments to each other. The struggle is between good and bad people. The brave hero, always on the side of the good people, fights hard, sometimes infatuates a girl, and always triumphs through his manly strength. The symbols are clear, the emotions direct. The drama is acted over and over again, somewhat like a ritual, and offers release and hope. The catharsis was different from that of the radio songs of individual loneliness, love, joys, and troubles in town. Through the cowboy films, pent-up aggressions were played out in a group; and the African became free and triumphant. The individual's enjoyment was heightened by the sharing of his feeling with a thousand or more others, who were shouting their reactions. There was much greater excitement and overt emotional participation at the movies than at the Sunday afternoon tribal dances.

It is not difficult to understand why the Africans strongly identified with the cowboy hero, Jack, or Jake as he was also called. In the past, intertribal wars were part of African life, and success in fighting was one way of gaining prestige. But we do not have to look only to the past. Probably even more important is the manner in which identification with the cowboy hero fits into the present power relations between European and Africans. It was obvious that Africans resented their low political, economic, and social status in relationship to Europeans and that there was relatively little outlet for the consequent aggressive feelings. The hard-fighting cowboy, moving freely on his horse in wide-open spaces, surmounting all obstacles and always winning, is indeed an attractive hero for a people intensely fearful of losing some of their wide-open spaces to Europeans, who until recently held all the power. The cowboy is white, but not European. Through identification with him, the African can fantasy, unconsciously or consciously, being as white as the dominant group and always winning over them. The film likewise gave him an opportunity to learn the popular skill of boxing, which he could then use immediately in intra-African fighting.

Yet boos were frequent when the coyboys used pistols. Several men in the audience expressed the general feelings when shooting was taking place in a cowboy film:

Oh, those people are not kind. I hate to see a gun being used for killing human beings. I tremble. Boxing is fine but not shooting like that.

Why should they use pistols for shooting human beings instead of wild animals? Could any Africans dare to do that? I think America is a lawless country, if they can shoot people like that.

Guns are fearful things. In the past, African chiefs and kings got them in exchange for ivory and slaves and thus were able to enslave more efficiently. Today, Europeans have guns and Africans do not have them. But in boxing, it is physical strength and skill which count. Africans often boasted about their strength—how they do the hard work on the mines, while Europeans only sit at desks. Thus, the cowboys' boxing pleased them, while their use of guns aroused anxiety.[2]

The universal popularity of the cowboy films is well known, but has not been studied in detail. My hypothesis is that they would particularly please those in a weak position in the power structure. Male adolescents in the United States, feeling their growing male strength and powerless to use it against the control of their parents and other adults in authority enjoy cowboy films. For the Africans, a better folk hero could not have been invented.

The cowboy has become part of the African world and has even taken on African characteristics. He is supposed to have witchcraft, to be the son of a "big" man, and to show traditional respect toward his elders.

> Eh, the cowboy has medicines [witchcraft] to make him invisible. His enemies have failed to see him hiding in the bush.

> Jack knows he is younger than Chibale [older cowboy who plays the part of a clown]. So Jack has to respect him. Cowboys show respect. And Jack is also the son of a big man.

It was difficult for many of those who loved the cowboy films to believe that they were not portraying actual reality. In this context it should be remembered that the motion picture camera and the production of movies, so familiar to contemporary movie-goers in the modern world, were unknown to the African movie audience. When I talked to a group of teen-age boys in Standards V and VI (about seventh and eighth grades), one of them asked me if the cowboys were real. I tried to explain the nature of acting in the films. They were loth to accept it. "Then how do they show red blood when they are hurt?" Even older and better-educated young men in their early twenties also found it emotionally difficult to accept cowboy films as fictional. To them the blows were actually heavy ones, men were really hurt, houses really burned, and horses galloped at incredible speed. Many in the audience were worried or angry if something in the film disturbed their sense of its reality. The remarks of a young man in his early twenties when he saw a cowboy being given shooting lessons were revealing. "They are cheating us. He is an expert in shooting. I saw him before, and he could shoot; now he is just pretending." There was the same sense of being "cheated" if a cowboy who "died" in one film appeared alive two weeks later in another.

The complex problem of reality in the films is seen also in the reactions of a group of fourteen- and fifteen-year-old school-boys to a religious picture, *The First Easter*. The following comments were exchanged among three boys during the show.

The Disciples of Jesus Appear
  Ah, these are only Europeans.
  This is Palestine.
  Do they speak English there?
  These are only ordinary Europeans. They just choose a nice place
where they could act.
  Europeans are liars. Were there any records from Jesus?

Scene of soldiers before king
  Just like Superman. [Refers to cape which king is wearing and which is
similar in style to Superman's.]
  That is Mary.
  Yes, that is whom she resembles.
  These are modern Europeans. When Jesus was dying, there were no
films taken.

At the end of film
  It is just a play. Did you not see how we acted it at school?

Yet, the concept of acting was slowly making its way. A woman,
commenting on a cowboy film she had just seen, said,

  I like cowboy films because of the fighting. I enjoy seeing people
beaten by the cowboy. Fighting is no good if I am in it myself. With
cowboys it is interesting, because it is all acting.

  There were others who knew and sensed that films were "pretend."
One man watching a cowboy movie said, "Those people [the cow-
boys] are very clever. They make one pretend that he has died."
But for many in the movie audience the film was either real or
"cheating"; in the latter case the Europeans who made the film
were "liars."
  Like Jack the cowboy, Superman was powerful and invincible,
with the additional characteristic of being able to fly through space.
Two men, among those who preferred the Superman film, said:

  I like Superman best because I have not seen any human being fly
before, and it was very interesting to see our friend, Superman, do it
without any difficulties.

  Superman could change his features any time he wished. He could
see hidden things when he opened his eyes, and he could stop moving
cars by holding them with his hands. He could stop a big burning flame

A literate man relaxes with a newspaper outside his home.

Mother and children: babies are nursed wherever and whenever they wish.

The new bungalow type homes provided for Africans in the upper pay group.

A public washstand with its running water is a busy place for women. Houses in background represent the norm.

with his little breath. He could hold elderly people in the air with his hands. Many men tried, but failed to kill him. At the end, I saw him wave his hands, as though he said, "This land and world is mine!"

Typical comments by women were:

I like Superman best. He was a very brave man and saved the life of a girl whom he loved, when she was captive under a certain king in the country where Superman lived. I liked his flying, because before I saw this film I thought it was impossible for a human being to fly, except the *Kadoli* [cartoon characters], and they are champions of the impossible.

I liked Superman best because he used to fly and destroy some people's homes with blows and iron bars. He wore a black suit with a gray hat and spectacles, and black shoes and a necktie. I liked his complexion and his dressing. Had he been an African, girls would have been fighting for him.

Children in the audience, as children in other parts of the world, loved Superman and identified with him. A sad tale was told of how a ten-year-old boy, wrapped in a piece of cloth resembling Superman's cape, climbed to the top of a high ant hill, raised his arms to fly, lifted his feet, and fell to the bottom of the ant hill, dead.

Old Charlie Chaplin comedies were sometimes shown at childrens' afternoon shows and were popular among them. The only adult reactions I have are from a rural tour with a movie truck which included an old slapstick comedy called *The Rink,* in which Chaplin is on roller skates. The audience thought the skates were a special kind of shoes and viewed the skating as a dance. They responded most enthusiastically when Chaplin glided into a graceful rhythm, even more than at the slapstick episodes. Chaplin was often referred to as *kaumuntu,* a Bemba term of good-humored derision, meaning a small man, not quite normal, and sometimes sexless. The following were among the comments:

Is he [Chaplin] a real person? Or is it someone from imagination?
Is there a school to give training to people to act in that way?
He is a funny man. He is like a lunatic and makes me laugh.
What kind of shoes are these that run like everything?
It is a wonderful dance.
Europeans are clever. They make wonderful things.
Charlie is making nonsense. If he were an African, he would have

been put in prison. I did not like it. It is good for school boys. [This comment was from a middle-aged man.]

Adults on the township also thought Chaplin films were only for children. The little man, not physically strong, who saves himself in difficult situations by his naïveté was not like the trickster of African folk tales, who used his wits.

The animal cartoons (*Kadoli*) were greatly enjoyed by the children, who shouted enthusiastically, "Dolly, dolly, hallow dolly!" whenever the cartoons appeared. Some of the adults accepted them as "just pretend for fun." Others resented the make-believe, and still others were confused by the problem of make-believe *versus* reality. Comments were:

> The *Kadolis* are very good in dancing without music.
> But it is a surprising thing that the *Kadolis* are keeping the same steps and movements.
> This is only cheating us. You think a *Kadoli* dog can dance so nicely?
> White men are clever; these are only drawings.
> The *Kadolis* should be brought only for children.
> Ah, look at that, it is wonderful. The monkey is dressing.
> See the monkey putting on trousers and pretending to walk like a human being.
> But is it true that the monkey could push a bar like that? I do not think so.

(*Two boys, about twelve or thirteen years old, discuss a cartoon film they have just seen*)

> Hm . . . These *Kadoli* are wonderful.
> Is it true that there is a *Kadoli* world?
> Yes, if you went where the world ends, you can find them. They depend on the sky for food, because there it is very low, and so they can cut pieces from it, and they eat that just as we eat bread.
> They must be very fortunate.
> Yes, they are.

For the first time Africans—the man-on-the-street type and not just an elite—were receiving communications from and about the larger world. Yet, many in the audience were *outside the content* of the communication, and they could interpret it only in terms of their own limited experiences. They tended to see film characters in terms of familiar kinship relationships. Men and women in the same age group must be either siblings, spouses, or lovers, depending on whatever clues were seen (often mistakenly) in the film. During a brief film showing of a European quartet of mixed voices, people said:

These two on the left, the lady and the gentleman, are not active. But look, the other two are smiling at each other.

Likely the first ones are sister and brother and the other pair are darlings.

Many European customs were misunderstood. It has already been noted that kissing, about which many Africans appear to have learned from films, is regarded as a direct prelude to sex relations. African parents do not kiss their children. In a film, when a man kissed a child, some of the audience assumed that the man was the child's father and that the kiss was a prelude to incest, regarded with horror. There was an appreciation of physical beauty, African and European, but again with frequent misunderstandings. Some scenes of European life produced these comments:

Men and women in a European café

Are these proper ladies or are they clowns?

I think they are clowns.

It is the behavior of white ladies. They are not ashamed.

They play hopelessly; yet they are beautiful.

But are these ladies mad?

Oh yes, of course! Can't you see them smoking those big cigarettes? [Cigarette in holder.]

The dancing is interesting. Look, that one wrings her waist like a developed caterpillar.

Bathing beach, with men and women lying on the sand
Comments of men.

See? Our friends [Europeans] can swim together with women.

I do not like it. It encourages immorality.

Many Africans regarded the Europeans as immoral in much the same way that Europeans viewed Africans as immoral. Most of the Europeans and Africans were basically ignorant of the mores of the other and both were parochial in their point of view.

Reactions to current events in news films were diverse, and depended, as might be expected, on the educational background and pre-existing attitudes of the audience. In our original survey, 13 per cent preferred the news programs, 18 per cent of the men as compared to 7 per cent of the women. Thirty-one per cent of those with Standard V or better education preferred the news as compared to 11 per cent of those with no education or less than Standard V. In the Standard V and above group, 26 per cent preferred *The British News,* and 7 per cent preferred *The African Mirror* and *The Northern Spotlight.* It appeared that the intelligentsia were primarily interested in the larger world. For them it had the same functions as radio news: extending their spatial imagery, increasing their knowledge of the world, and widening the range of possible identifications. They were pleased to see foreign places, to look at people in other parts of the world, and to learn about their ways of life. The news films took people visually into a modern world and gave them some feeling of being part of it. The following comment was typical:

I was interested in the football match, "England versus the rest." It was a very good match, and I saw that their standard of playing is much better than ours. I am interested in athletic activities in the films because I am a sportsman. I also like to see films on farming in England because farming is done with ease there. It is not so tough as is farming in Northern Rhodesia, where you use hoes, axes, and picks. In England machinery does everything.

I also enjoyed the program in the news which showed how Mr. Scott discovered the South Pole. I like his courage very much. And it interested me to see how cold it is at the poles. Only snow is there. I also enjoyed seeing the Queen visit different places and open important buildings.

The uneducated members of the audience usually enjoyed the sports—football and boxing in particular—and pictures of the British royalty. Much of the other news was selectively perceived and interpreted in terms of anxieties and pre-existing imagery. Comments made during a news film of floods in Europe which showed people being evacuated from their homes, revealed not only misunderstanding, but also the ever-present anxiety that Europeans may take the African's land.

Those people do not have an easy time at home. Perhaps that is the main reason why they have made this Federation of theirs, so that those who have no homes in England or anywhere in Britain, may come and live here, where we do not have floods.

Yes, my friend, you have said it.

See how these people are suffering. Airplanes come to get their clothes and their food, and their houses are very damaged. Do they think we will be sympathetic and allow them to come here? No, they can come here only by force.

See those people throwing clothes on a lorry! I think they are the clothes they bring to us second-hand.

So, we put on clothes of dead people. I will stop buying second-hand clothes. Otherwise, ghosts of dead people will come to me.

Look, the village is in the river. Houses built in waters. How did they manage that? How can they lay bricks in water?

You forget it is the rainy season now. In England it rains heavily now.

Ah, there is trouble. I pity them.

Ah, why worry? Look, those Europeans are working hard. [Europeans are heaping filled bags of earth to stop the flood waters.] But when they come here they don't do any hard work at all. They are all supervisors.

So you think Europeans don't do any hard work in England! They must work there. I have seen pictures of them doing shoveling work. It is only here where they have servants to chop wood for them, wash for them, and cook for them, that they do nothing.

Yes, I have heard the same thing. My *bwana* used to tell me about it.

Any picture of Europeans doing manual work evoked surprise.

Scene in a European Hospital

A very nice hospital.

That nurse is very beautiful.

Does it mean those two ladies are sick?

Why should they trouble patients in that way?

Are those the treatments for sick people?

But from what are they suffering?

Their disease is unknown.

We only see two patients in that big hospital. It is all a lie.

Of course, they are only making funnies.

A scene in Formosa

Soldiers! Are they from war?

Yes, war is on. They will kill us all.

Look at those girls typing [in office of one of the officers]. I wish my sister went to that school.

H'mm, You think African girls here could do that? They just want to eat.

All news about Federation officials was viewed in the context of the African's hatred of it. Comments on a visit of the Federal Prime Minister to Ndola:

> Look, two motorcycles in front of the car.
> They usually do that when a governor visits anywhere.
> Look, that short white man speaking to many white men.
> If you see Europeans talking like that, they are talking about Federation.
> But they talk to themselves. No Africans are there.
> We do not want Federation.
> Yes, you people there (*shouting to those in the film*) stop talking about it!
> This is our country!

Whatever was seen was commented on, interpreted, criticized. Questions were asked. Sometimes a friend answered them—or no one answered. The interpretations were often distorted or incorrect. We remember the Broadcasting House officer weighing pound notes so that the audience could get some idea of the amount of money being spent on schools. Nothing similar was done to make news items in the movies intelligible. Nor were any Africans used to interpret films in their own language, as in radio. In addition, the action in news films was in very rapid succession: Queen dedicating a public building, a horse race, a flood, statesmen talking. At the end of a news program, two men talked:

FIRST MAN: Ah, that is why I do not like *The British News*.
HIS FRIEND: Why?
FIRST MAN: Well, it is because it is always such a mixture of subjects. Now it is about horses; before, airplanes, and the Queen; and all those other things. . . . Why?

There was no answer to this "why."

The problem of reality in the mass media is complex, not only in Africa, but everywhere. In the modern theatre the illusion skillfully created on the stage has a reality apart from life. But often in radio and television programs the audience finds it difficult to keep the fiction apart from reality. American viewers of the soap operas, so popular on radio not long ago, sent gifts and messages to fictional characters when they were in trouble. The 1938 radio production of Orson Wells' "War of the Worlds" though announced as a play, produced genuine confusion and even panic among thousands.[4]

The opposite happened in the United States in 1960 when rehearsed and "rigged" television programs were presented as spontaneous and true. The resentment of some of the audience was similar to the reactions of some of the Africans when they learned that the fictional movies were not true. Americans, too, felt "cheated." In 1961, James T. Aubrey, Jr., president of the Columbia Broadcasting System's television network wrote, "The viewer, faced with so great a variety of programs and techniques of presentation, needs a guide to help him cross the bridge between fact and fiction, between truth and artifice, between reality and illusion."[5] If such is true in the United States of 1961, how much more does it apply to an audience in transition from tribal to modern life!

Of all the mass media, the movie is the most subjective and "potentially the least rationalistic."[6] The director with his camera is a powerful person, as he "subtly invites us to embrace one character and exclude another—to look up and feel awe of a noble man or fear of a villain; to look down and feel contempt or pity."[7] For many of us movies are a pleasant and easy form of escape. For the Africans and other inexperienced audiences they were much more. Drama, adventure, documentary, and news films—all of them—gave the African access to a new and wide variety of places, people, events, and styles of life. The audience watched a new world unfold before them. With the exception of the almost uniform response to cowboy films, the reactions of the individual members differed, depending largely on their education or lack of it. But the questions "What was real?" "What was cheating?" were a problem for many, educated and uneducated. The confusion was due in large part to ignorance of how movies were produced. Also, since much that was portrayed in the films was completely outside the knowledge and experience of the audience, it was inevitable that interpretation of the screen imagery would be in terms of the Africans' world, with the resulting misunderstandings. Nevertheless, understood or misunderstood, the movies gave pleasure, extended the boundaries of the world, and the imagery of the African audience. The cowboy films offered an effective release of aggressive impulses. For the African audience was never passive; it was as always actively participating and with emotion.

Many of the functions of movies and radio were similar. But the reality problem of movies did not exist in radio. Moreover, the staff in the Motion Picture Department appeared not to know about the problem and certainly made no attempt to cope with it. There are no easy answers to the problems inherent in introducing movies to a largely illiterate audience. But, assuredly, the answers do not lie in censorship or in casually presenting commercial packages. Perhaps they lie in communicating the nature of the medium and indicating what is real and what is "just pretend." The larger answer is, of course, in more education and in more direct contact with modern culture. The mass media were a main source for the communication of Western culture to many Africans. As long as there is an almost complete absence of personal relations between Africans and Europeans, other than that of employer and employee, the resulting ignorance is bound to distort communication from movies.

17. Education and the Printed Word

Anyone can listen to a radio or look at a movie, but reading and writing require the use of abstract symbols, learned through formal education. Even when achieved, literacy requires greater intellectual effort than do the other two media. It is, therefore, not surprising that the shift from a preliterate to a literate culture is more gradual and seemingly less dramatic than the response to radio and to movies. This was true in the Western world as well as in contemporary Africa. After the invention of printing only a small minority could read and write, and it took several centuries for literacy to become almost universal in the Western world. In many parts of the world it is still limited.

In Africa the problem is complicated by the fact that the usefulness of literacy in an indigenous language is limited. Only a European language provides the entree into the modern world; in Northern Rhodesia the language is, of course, English.

Although change from a preliterate to a literate society is slow, its significance is far reaching, especially in Africa. As Fallers has noted, in tribal Africa there were no "high" and "low" cultures such as characterized Europe, Asia, and Latin America, where folk cultures were a kind of "counter culture" to "high" cultures. The same author writes, "Africans very commonly perceive themselves as being differentiated in terms of wealth and power but they do not often, except in the few real conquest states, view their societies as consisting of 'layers' of persons with differential possession of a high culture."[1] Social stratification was based on age, sex, wealth, and rank, but everyone belonged to the same culture and shared its common values. But under colonialism, European culture has been the high one, with access to it for the African through literacy and education. The literate Africans were culturally and, often, socially separated from the illiterate.

Africans on the Copperbelt were quick to recognize this new stratification. Although there was no reason why they could not communicate with each other in their vernacular language, a man who did not speak English felt inferior when he was talking to an English-speaking African. This sentiment was vividly expressed in essays written by adult Africans attending English night classes. They said:

I desire the English which my friends speak. Anytime I hear a man speaking English, I become sick and wish to be the one so speaking.

I do not feel well when my fellows speak English in my presence.

One of these men asked me to take his picture reading a newspaper, although actually his reading ability was not that good.

The Africans who were literate in English were well aware of their social superiority. A white-collar worker said:

You will not see many educated people listening to news on the wireless; you will find more of them reading newspapers. The news announced on the wireless is only for those who are lowly educated.

This new stratification based on education and literacy weakened traditional divisions based on sex and age.[2] Anticipating this change when education for girls was first proposed, Africans argued that educated girls would be "too proud" and not show the proper respect for their husbands. However, the campaign succeeded because it stressed that educating girls would make them better wives and mothers: they would know more about hygiene, cooking, and other homecraft; and their husbands and children would be healthier and live longer. But like any other social change, education for women has consequences unforeseen by its advocates. Some women have become teachers, nurses' aides, welfare workers; others will go eventually into more advanced positions. This gives them the opportunity of regaining an economic status which they enjoyed as members of the tribal economic system, and, sooner or later, going beyond that as they advance into the modern world.

The relative status positions of young people and elders have also been profoundly affected. In the past the elders had wisdom and knowledge. A riddle told in the course of an intra-African conversation illustrates how the argument for educating the young has been set in traditional mores, as was education for girls.

THE RIDDLE

There was a man who had three sons, and he sent them all to school. The first son was trained as a telescopist; the second son, as a hunter; and the third, as a boatman. When they finished all their courses, they came home.

One day a beautiful girl fell in a big lake and was caught by a very big snake. When the news came to their ears, the first son, who was a telescopist, got his telescope and saw the girl still alive under the water, but caught by the big snake. He said, "Oh, I have to get my brother who is a boatman, and then we can rescue her." So he called the boatman. When they were together, they said, "Yes, we can go there, and we can see her, but how shall we rescue her from the big snake?" They then called their brother, the hunter, and they all went in the boat on the lake.

When they reached the middle of the lake, the telescopist saw the girl under the water. He and the hunter went under the water, and the boatman remained in the boat. The telescopist told the hunter where the snake was, and the hunter shot it. The girl was then rescued and put in the boat and off they went to the shore.

Now the question is, who did the most useful work, so that he could marry the girl?

The riddle was given by an uneducated man to two men, one with European schooling and the other without. Both failed to guess the answer; finally they gave up and one said, "Ah, this is a very difficult riddle. Tell us the answer, because we have failed."

THE ANSWER

The key is that none of the three brothers could marry the girl because their duties were equally important. These boys took the girl to their father who married her. For he had done the most important work of sending them all to school to learn their knowledge.

The reactions were: "Yes, yes, that is true!" and "Yes, we are convinced."

The themes are traditional: the rescue of a young girl, the riddle of who contributed the most to the rescue, and the father winning over his sons. But the reason for his winning, namely, that he sent his sons to school, is new. A nice blending of old and modern patterns.[3]

Education

Contemporary problems concerned with education and literacy are understandable only in the historical context of educational opportunities for Africans in this area. Although much progress has been made during the last decade, the development of educational facilities in Northern Rhodesia has been slow. As indicated earlier, European education began at mission schools. The year 1885, when the Paris Evangelical Society established a mission station in Barotseland, is (apart from the journeys of David Livingstone) usually considered the beginning of missionary enterprise in Northern Rhodesia. During the next forty years this society and others established mission schools primarily to train African evangelist teachers. Training in literacy in order to read the Bible, and other religious teaching, were accompanied by medical help and by practical instruction in hygiene, crafts, and skills in the household, in the garden and in the cattle kraal. Shortly after 1925, when Northern Rhodesia became a protectorate, a subdepartment of native education was established under the Department of Native Affairs and five years later became an independent department. It gave financial help to missions for their primary and teacher-training schools and shared secondary and vocational training with them. This cooperation continues, but the government assumes an ever-increasing share of responsibility. The copper companies in the beginning gave elementary training in the use of tools to unskilled Africans; now there is also intensive training for skilled work. The mining companies have likewise assumed increasing responsibility for general school education.

This policy began with adult evening classes in English, but has extended to African education in the whole Territory. In 1960 the two major groups (Rhodesian Selection Trust and the Anglo-American) contributed £323,000 for African education in Northern Rhodesia.[4]

The normal age for beginning school is seven years for boys and eight for girls. Elementary school education is divided into:

Lower primary—Sub-Standards A and B and Standards I and II
Middle primary—Standards III and IV
Upper primary—Standards V and VI

Finishing Standard VI, which is comparable to our eighth grade, is analogous to graduating from what we used to call grammar school, and carried considerable prestige in this part of Africa.

Although the number of schools was growing, opportunities were still limited. As late as 1958, it was estimated that there were school facilities in Northern Rhodesia for only 59 per cent of the children in the primary age group, i.e., from Sub-Standard A through Standard VI and that 90 per cent of the lower primary-school age group, 30 per cent of the middle primary-school age group, and 14 per cent of the upper primary-school age group were attending classes.[5]

An urgent problem was the large proportion of students who never went beyond Standard II of the lower primary school. In 1958-1959, it was possible for only one African child out of every three in Northern Rhodesia to go from the lower primary to the middle primary course and for two out of every five to advance from the middle primary to the completion of the upper primary course (Standard VI).[6] The masses of children who did not go beyond the lower primary classes could acquire and retain little of value to them.

The number of young people who gained the humanistic education associated with completing secondary school was much smaller. Secondary school consists of six forms and requires six and a half years. It is divided into:

Junior secondary—Forms I and II, taking two years
Senior secondary—Forms III and IV, taking two and one-half years
Higher School Certificate and university entrance qualification—Form
   VI, taking two years

From 1948 to 1958 the number of secondary schools in Northern Rhodesia had increased from two to seventeen; and their number of pupils, from 198 to 1,890. But of these seventeen schools, only one prepared students to meet college entrance requirements, five went as far as Form IV, and eleven offered only junior secondary courses. The enrollment in all the secondary schools had increased from 570 in 1953-1954 to 1,890 in 1958-1959, but the bulk of it was in the junior forms. On the senior level up to June 1959, eleven girls and 490 boys in Northern Rhodesia had gained the Cambridge School Certificate; eighteen boys had gained the full Higher School Certificate, and no girls had reached this level.[7]

In 1958 there were ten teacher-training colleges, one technical college and twenty-one trade schools. Admission to all of them was after the completion of Standard VI. The combined enrollment (as of September 1958) in the teacher-training colleges was 1,249, of whom 220 were women.[8] In 1959 the enrollment in the technical college and trade schools was 1,437.[9]

The biracial University College of Rhodesia and Nyasaland, established in Salisbury in 1955, offered the first college training in the Federation for either Africans or Europeans. Previously, Africans desiring a college education went, usually with the help of government scholarships, to Fort Hare College in South Africa, Makerere College in Uganda, or to institutions in the United Kingdom and the United States. The total number of Africans in Northern Rhodesia who had completed courses in higher education by June 1959 were thirty-four men and one woman. Twenty of these had taken an arts degree; eleven, a science degree; and one each, a degree in engineering, fine arts, domestic science, and law.[10] But in the same year twenty-six Northern Rhodesian African men were taking courses of higher education, fourteen of them in arts degree courses, five in science, three in medicine, two in law, and two in postgraduate education courses.[11] Two years later, in 1961, sixty-one Africans were attending the biracial Salisbury University College.[12] If all the students now in college complete their work, there will be approximately 122 Africans in Northern Rhodesia with a college degree, almost all men, the majority of whom will have an arts degree.[13]

Given this situation, adult education is obviously important. It began about 1944, and comprehensive plans have existed since 1953. In 1959, approximately thirty-seven hundred students were enrolled in adult education classes registered with the African Education Ministry. These do not include the classes run by the copper-mining companies and other private organizations.[14]

On the Copperbelt, the educational level of Africans is probably higher than in the Territory as a whole, because of the contributions from the mining companies. The first schools for Africans in the mining communities were opened in 1937 by the United Missions. In 1943, compulsory education was introduced by the government at certain Copperbelt centers. But this regulation was suspended eight years later because of inadequate accommodations and the rapid increase of children of school age.[15] In 1953-1954 it was estimated that there were about 11,000 children under sixteen years of age (including those too young for schooling) on the Roan Antelope Mine township. Of these, 1,300 were attending primary school, with the majority in the lower primary standards.[16] In 1960-1961 out of 14,100 (again including those too young for school), 3,310 were attending primary classes.[17] Thus, the percentage attending has nearly doubled, rising from 12.7 per cent in 1953-1954 to 23.4 per cent in 1960-1961. An even more dramatic increase is shown in the proportion of girls to boys attending primary schools in the same period. In 1954 of those attending primary schools on the mine township and the municipal location, 72 per cent were boys and 28 per cent were girls. (The two communities were grouped together under the heading "Luanshya" by education officials.) In 1960-1961 on the Roan Antelope township, the proportion was 58 per cent boys and 42 per cent girls.[18] Plans for 1961 on the Roan Antelope township included education for every child on it and the commencement of one secondary school.[19]

The economic, social, and political situation has changed so rapidly, particularly during the last decade, that it has been impossible for education to keep its pace. The building of schools and the training of teachers take time, as well as large amounts of money. Long-range successful campaigns urging education for girls had to be waged. Nor were the goals of education changed overnight. The mission originally wanted to educate Africans to be good Christians, to be healthier, and to become better farmers and herdsmen. The colonial government had a long-range goal covering a century or more of helping Africans to become black Europeans. The mining companies at first thought it necessary to give only the necessary instructions in the use of tools, safety precautions, and other elementary essentials for unskilled miners. Today the missions, the protectorate government, and the mines are speeding up the educational process to help Africans take their economic and political place in the modern world, not in another century, but in the immediate present.

The Printed Word

The impact of literacy cannot be underestimated. As Riesman notes, once literacy enters the environment, neither the social organization nor the individual can ever be the same again. He writes, "Books bring with them the detachment and a critical attitude that is not possible in a society dependent on the spoken word. We can occasionally have second thoughts about a speech, but we cannot hear it, as we can read a book. . . . that is, the writer can be checked up on in a way that the speaker or, as we shall soon discover, the movie-maker cannot be."[20] A twenty-year-old white-collar worker, educated through Standard VI, who read newspapers regularly and who, of course, had never heard of David Riesman or read any sociology, used almost the same words when he explained why he preferred getting news from the newspapers rather than from radio or movies.

In a newspaper you can read and re-read the news, and so you can understand it properly. Also, a newspaper keeps a record of what has happened or been said, but the wireless only says something once and leaves no record for the future which one can refer to, and so it is simple to cheat there. And the bioscope sometimes does not tell the truth. For example, the *Kadoli* [animal cartoons] are not true. There is no world where *Kadoli* do such extraordinary things like breaking themselves to pieces and then living again.

Although this young African might be naïve about movies and in a long interview indicated a belief in witchcraft, he and others like him had real sociological insight into one of the functions of the printed word in a preliterate society. They were likewise aware of their satisfaction in extending their horizons and knowledge, of breaking their bonds with the relatively closed world of the past, and, of course, of the practical advantages in relationship to jobs.

It was not easy to find out the exact proportion of literates in this African community. In our original survey, some of the respondents tended to say that they were literate in English if they knew the alphabet and had learned to read in an elementary fashion in their early years at school, but had lost, through disuse or lack of interest, whatever ability to read and write that they once possessed. I therefore counted as literate only those who were able to say what they had last read and give at least a few details of it. Thirty-three per cent were literate in English and/or a vernacular. Fifty-one per cent of the males and 14 per cent of the females were in this group, as were 100 per cent of those who had gone through Standard V and 23 per cent of those in the Standards I-IV group.[21] Literacy in English is supposed to be attained after completion of Standard IV and in a vernacular after Standard II. But all schools did not reach the expected norms, and some who had only gone through Standard II forgot what they had learned.

What the literate read has naturally changed since literacy was first introduced through mission schools. At that time, reading was usually restricted to the Bible and other religious books which had been translated. As late as 1950, in villages between two mission stations on the Mushiri Reserve, "of those who could read, by far the most used their ability to read only in connection with religious worship."[22] But on the mine township at the time of my study the major reading was of newspapers. The literate were reading in order to enter a larger secular world rather than the kingdom of Heaven. For the religious, the Bible was, of course, still important.

No newspapers or magazines were published in Northern Rhodesia by Africans, and there are still none at this writing. But there were several published for Africans by Europeans, with Africans on their staff. The three most widely read papers, in the order of their popularity on the mine township, were: the *Roan Antelope,* the *African Eagle,* and the *Northern News.* These papers differed markedly and appealed to different groups of readers.

The *Roan Antelope,* an eight-page monthly (now, ten pages fortnightly) was published by the Roan Antelope Copper Mines for its African employees and sold for one pence. The paper was focused on orienting the readers to life on the township. Its tone was personal, friendly, non-political, designed to spread a feeling of good will between management and workers and to encourage employees to take advantage of the many welfare activities. News stories and articles were about sports, clubs, classes, health, hygiene, adult aducation, pensions, housing, bonuses, women's clothes and house-keeping, people going on leave and returning from it, major agricultural developments in rural areas, visits of chiefs and of important Europeans, and success stories of individual Africans. There were many pictures. As a house organ, the paper was not concerned with the larger African scene. Instead, it captured some of the intimacy and unity characteristic of the village, which also pervaded the township. At this writing the feeling-tone of the paper is much the same, although the topics covered are broader. Profiles of local trade union leaders are included with those of teachers and other prominent men in the community. In 1961 there was a series of articles on life in British universities and another on suggestions for buyers of second-hand cars, indicating a rise in economic and educational interests. The same issues also carried traditional folk tales, such as the story of how a hare tricked a hyena. The paper, written in English and Bemba, was read, at the time of my study, by 53 per cent of the readers on the mine township and preferred by 40 per cent of them.

The *African Eagle,* the second most popular paper on the mine township, was a twelve-page weekly, selling for two pence, published in Lusaka as a commercial enterprise by Europeans for Africans. Five pages, including the first one, were in English; and the remainder, in Bemba, Tonga, Lozi, and Nyanja. The paper combined both a personal and an impersonal approach. It was generally apolitical in tone, but carried some political news. The range of interest was broad: African affairs in towns and rural areas, with particular emphasis on Northern Rhodesia; a small section on world news; "Home Notes and Social News"; "What to do when baby cries"; recipes; and editorials, usually nonpolitical. Much of the writing was in an African tradition. For instance, in reporting a theft or a case of adultery, a moral was always drawn. There were articles and letters from readers, admonishing readers to give up "bad" customs such as feeding children with left-overs, laughing at barren women, believing in the spirits of the dead; and there were others which encouraged readers to build brick houses when they returned to their villages, to take hats off when entering a house, and to follow similar points of European etiquette. Advertisements picturing Africans as users of fountain pens, bicycles, radios, sewing machines, soap, shoe polish, dried milk, cocoa, margarine, aspirin, etc., were frequent. This paper was read by 43 per cent of the mine township readers and was preferred by 21 per cent.

The *Northern News,* third in popularity, selling for three pence, was a ten-page daily, published in Ndola (capital of the Western Province) for Europeans and, of course, only in English. It was politically oriented, generally impersonal, and covered news of the Copperbelt, Northern Rhodesia, the Federation, and to a much smaller degree, the world beyond. Social notes and news of sports were naturally exclusively European. It was read by 34 per cent of the township readers and was preferred by 17 per cent of the readers.[23]

The order of preference for the three papers varied according to the education and tastes of the readers. Some people liked to read (as well as to listen on the radio) primarily about themselves; and others, about the world. Many enjoyed both. The *Roan Antelope,* with its local orientation and personal tone, appealed most to the least educated men and to the women. At the other end was the *Northern News,* published for Europeans, impersonal, politically oriented, and most popular among the educated males. Although both were contemporary urban papers, they seemed to symbolize some of the differences between tribal and modern life in the contrast between the parochial and personal orientation of the one and the broader impersonal orientation of the other. The *African Eagle,* midway between the other two papers, had both functions and was similar to those radio programs which served as a bridge between village and urban life. But in spite of differences in spatial and cultural range, all the papers provided an entree into some aspect of the modern world. Among both Europeans and Africans, broader reading correlated with greater education. The Europeans reading the *Northern News* were reading about themselves. Only the more highly educated Europeans were interested in the *London Times* with its broader coverage of news.

About a third of the African newspaper readers said they had no preference for any particular section of the paper, and among these were many readers of the *Roan Antelope.* They liked the whole paper as some of the movie audience enjoyed the whole show. But some of the *Roan Antelope* readers had preferences: articles on sports, health, cooking, and sewing.

Comments of men.

I like best the part about sports because I am interested in them and would like to be a sportsman. Last week I read about the team which had won the cup in football.

I like best the part about hygiene. Two weeks ago I read about how to keep food clean, and this is essential. If we are to keep healthy, food must be clean. If you live according to what you are told, then you can have good health and live longer. I would very much like that I live very long.

Comments of Women.

I read how to keep the house clean, and I learned a lot. I thought, perhaps, it might be the reason why my husband divorced me, that I did not keep the house clean. The paper clearly stated that some husbands do not like dirt in the house.

I like best the part which talks about the activities of women. I read about the women's classes at the subwelfare centers. The African women are taught there to use the right materials and to sew well.

Of the 124 readers who expressed a preference, the largest category (35 per cent) was for news and politics. As might be expected, these were readers of the *Northern News* and the *African Eagle*. Most of them, but not all, had a Standard V or better education. Interest in news and politics represents an engagement of the self with the world. However, it was quite apparent that none of the mass media were being used as instruments for political propaganda or, consciously, for political education.

The prevailing political awareness of Africans—literate and illiterate, adults and adolescents—had come primarily through the power of events, rather than through propaganda or formal education, and, obviously, the main event was Federation. Before this the British protectorate government had been more or less taken for granted and generally regarded as benevolent. A small group of better educated and politically aware men had assumed that independence would come eventually when they were ready for it. But Federation made everyone politically aware. As one man with a Standard IV education who read the *Northern News* and preferred the political news, said:

I like best the page on which political matters are written. A long time ago Africans seemed to be very thoughtless about these things. But as soon as the question of Federation was asked, it made Africans think. They must make sure they understand the questions that come up. As Federation is still being talked about, I want to be sure that I know about it.

A teacher with Standard VI education, who preferred the *Northern News,* said:

I like the political part of the paper, so I can understand how the government of Northern Rhodesia is going on with its people. The Africans are not satisfied with present conditions, because Europeans have more representatives in the government and Africans have only a few.

Some men in the lower educational group were also interested in reading about politics. One with a Standard II education and literate only in the vernacular, who read those pages of the *African Eagle* written in his language, said:

I like to read about politics. Last week I read about the Native Authority objecting to the meeting of any Congress organization in the Mumbwa district. They suspect a meeting will bring much hatred between Africans and Europeans because of Federation, which is enforced against the wish of Africans. The Native Authority said that if one desires to hold a Congress meeting in Mumbwa district, he must be given permission by the Native Authority, and no one must address an audience of more than three people. This is a blow for the African Congress, for most of the funds come after a huge public meeting. The Native Authority is justified, but now the African Congress will not be able to talk to the African people in this district and hear their views about Federation.

Not all the interest in news was concerned directly with Federation; some was more general. A shopkeeper with Standard V education who preferred the *African Eagle,* said:

I like to read the page which contains the news of the world, because I can come to know how other people of the world are being ruled. I would like to compare them with how we are being ruled here, so that I may know whether we are, or are not, ruled properly. If I find we are not ruled properly, then I start to raise complaints, so that our living is improved.

Pictures was the preferred section for 16 per cent of the readers, and sports, for 10 per cent. A miscellaneous category, in which the sections on etiquette, advice to readers, and letters to the editor were the most numerous was preferred by 23 per cent of the readers.

Lack of time prevented me from doing much systematic work on book-reading, but it was clear from my observations and from the statistics of the Publications Bureau that book-reading was not habitual for most of the literate Africans. "Books" were usually small booklets of less than a hundred pages, designed to be of practical help in family life, morals and manners, housekeeping, the writing of letters, and similar problems. Other practical books were grammars, phrase books, dictionaries, and text books. A third group was concerned with traditional and modern stories, folklore and proverbs, and African history. These booklets were published by the Publications Bureau of Northern Rhodesia and Nyasaland or by British publishers in cooperation with the Bureau, and were distributed in Northern Rhodesia by the United Society for Christian Literature.[24] The price of booklets ranged from seven pence to six shillings.

The Publications Bureau was established in 1940, with headquarters in Lusaka. In addition to the publication and distribution of books (the term used by the Bureau for its booklets) to Africans, it encouraged local African authorship and the growth of country libraries and also cooperated with education departments. Besides the director, the late Mr. H. G. Wilson, there were two other Europeans, an editorial assistant and a supervisor of production, and there were eight Africans, functioning as readers, translators, and writers. The books were written in the major vernaculars and in English. Sales in the two territories of Northern Rhodesia and Nyasaland at the time of my study ranged from less than a thousand to between seven and eight thousand, and the Bureau considered anything over a thousand as a "best seller."[25]

Of the twelve best sellers in Northern Rhodesia, six were concerned with practical help in the modern world, five with traditional customs and stories, and one with both old and new customs in the family.

Banja Lathu (Our Family Group), in Nyanja, by E. W. Chafulumira, selling for ten pence, headed the best-selling list for a number of years and far outsold any other book. (Its closest rival was a Standard I vernacular reader.) The author of *Banja Lathu,* when interviewed, said that the book was designed to teach young people, marrying in the towns, the traditional family customs and those new ones which he considered good. The major points are:

A woman should not call her husband by his first name, but should address him as the father of her child.

A woman should cook food and bring it to her husband.

A husband should work hard, earn money, and buy clothes and food for his wife and children; the wife should know how to cook food well and to look after the children.

A husband and wife should love each other and stay together a long time.

A pregnant woman should be looked after by her husband, because of his love for her. If she is tired and speaks "rudely" the husband should understand and not be "mad."

Cleanliness is necessary for all members of the family.

When going on a journey, older and stronger men and women should carry things.[26]

The book takes a middle path, stressing traditional respect of a wife for her husband and of young people for their parents and, at the same time, urging the European patterns of cleanliness, of special care and tenderness for a pregnant woman, and of adults rather than young people carrying things.

On the mine township market there was a bookstall with forty-two books on it. The bookseller could not give even approximate sales of the ten which he said were the best sellers; of these, six were concerned with the European world, whether through the Bible or through learning English and arithmetic, three were fiction, and one was traditional stories.

Thirty-seven fictional booklets, called novels, have been published by or in association with the Bureau.[27] Of these, twenty-five have a modern theme and setting, but most of them use the traditional form of a parable to convey a lesson. The following are examples:

Caro Ncinonono (The World is Not a Happy Place), in Tumbuka, by M. W. K. Chiume (1956), is the life story of a man who overcame all handicaps and became a respected leader of his people.

Umupashi Wa Mwaico (It's Never Too Late to Mend), in Bemba, by Duncan T. Tembo (1957), is about a man who falls in with bad companions, but later reforms and rises to prosperity.

Uwakwensko Bushiku (A Friend in Need is a Friend Indeed), in Bemba, by S. A. Mpashi (1951), is a detective story set on the Copperbelt.

Mkoko (The Story of a Man Who Went Astray), in Nyanja, by A. U. Mwale (1954), is the story of a man and the various jobs he tried.

A few novels do not emphasize the moral lesson, although it is usually not completely missing. Examples:

Cekesoni Aingila Ubusoja (Jackson Becomes a Soldier), in Bemba, by S. A. Mpashi (1950), portrays the lighter side of army life.

Pio Akobekela Vera (Pio Becomes Engaged to Vera), in Bemba, by S. A. Mpashi (1957), set on the Copperbelt, is a sequel to *Uwakwensho Bushiku,* which told how Pio saved Vera's brother from a false charge of murder.

Contemporary social problems were the themes of a few novels, among which were:

Mubekwabekwa, in Tonga, by J. B. Mwema (1958), is about a boy who upset the customary Tonga matrilineal law of inheritance.

Cimuka, in Tonga, by Milimo (1958), illustrates some of the attitudes of Tonga people toward getting rich and toward charms, and also the conflict between traditional and European beliefs.

Twelve of the fictional books had a historical or tribal setting, and among these were:

Pano Calo (Here on Earth), in Bemba, by S. A. Mpashi (1958), is an allegorical story of a chief.

Makandauko A Imute Wa Kalilo (Adventure of Imute of Kalilo), in Lozi, by T. M. M. Muwindwa (1958), is a story of a brave hunter who lived in olden times.

Ku Harare (Journey to Southern Rhodesia), in Tumbuka, by A. Mbeea (1958), is a novel about a journey south early in the century.

The contemporary African literature produced in this area is not of the same high order or as creative as the books which have been written in other parts of Africa, particularly in the Union of South Africa, Western Nigeria, the French Cameroons, Senegal-Mali, Guinea, and Sierra Leone. It might be worthwhile to translate and make available novels from other African countries and from other cultures, European, American, and Asian. Unfortunately, I do not know how much, if any, emphasis is placed on reading English and American novels in the secondary schools of Northern Rhodesia. But my impression is that adults who were literate in English, with or without a secondary school education, were primarily interested in reading non-fiction books, which they thought would be technically helpful to them. The significant role of the novel in nineteenth century England and the United States was missing in this part of Africa. In Western society, Riesman writes, "The novel of the nineteenth century, as its critics contended, doubtless disoriented many chambermaids and a few duchesses, but on many occasions it helped prepare individuals for their careers in a disorienting world of rapid industrialization and urbanization, where, indeed, fictional moves and actual ones were not so unlike, and life and art could almost imitate each other."[28] As the same author notes, "In a society depending on oral tradition, individuals have life-cycles—they live through childhood; they are initiated; they become adult; they grow old; they die—but they do not have careers in our abstract sense of the term."[29] Today, Africans, living in a period of rapid change, with increasing opportunities for new careers involving urbanization, could imaginatively prepare themselves for playing new roles through novel-reading, called "anticipatory socialization" by psychologists. The humanities may be as important in helping Africans become modern men as technical education, although the effect of the latter is more obvious.

Change from a preliterate to a literate society is of far-reaching significance, but progress is slow. Funds and trained personnel are inadequate. Many of the newly independent countries debate whether it is better to use their limited funds in training an elite or in providing a broad mass education. Often, educational policies are argued in terms of economics. The values of substituting a theory of natural causation for witchcraft in the minds of the masses or of having women keep pace with men educationally are often not considered.

When the illiteracy rate is high and there are not enough schools to accommodate the young, obviously radio and movies become more significant in helping induct Africans into a modern world. But there were some Africans who did not want to listen to the radio, go to movies, or become literate. They did not take advantage of any of the available mass media and new leisure activities. In the next chapter, it is these Africans whom we try to understand.

18. The Intransigents

THE INTRANSIGENTS wanted the jobs, the money, and the material goods which the new economic order offered, but they had no emotional commitment to the new moral order and they resisted its values. Complex problems related to the behavior of the intransigents involve unconscious as well as conscious factors, and my understanding is limited largely to hypotheses based on clues and inferences from overt behavior.[1]

The new leisure activities—listening to the radio; going to movies; attending evening classes; belonging to a social club; learning European dances, ways of cooking and making clothes; playing football—were part of the modern world. Participation in any of them symbolized, to some degree, an acceptance of it and a desire to enter it. The new activities were available to everyone on the township. But half of the people did not listen to the radio, and more than half did not go to movies.[2] Many in the same group did not participate in any of the Welfare Department activities, and only a minority of the illiterate were attempting to become literate. These non-participants were from the same tribal backgrounds as were the participants; and some of them were in the same age and sex groups, although they included more old people and more women. This group seemed to be on the township only to earn money and to get the things that money would buy. Everyone wanted money and the new material possessions, but in this period of rapid change some adults had also accepted the new moral order and internalized some of its values, while others found this process too difficult.[3]

There are a number of hypotheses to account for the difference between the two groups: Individuals committed to the new moral order have faith in eventual rewards from it and an ego sufficiently strong to accept the risks and anxieties which always accompany change; they have a desire for the more personal autonomy inherent in the new order and do not always think in terms of opposing polarities. Conversely, the intransigents do not have these characteristics or possess them to a much smaller degree. Doob also has a hypothesis that "at the outset only the stronger members of the tribe were attracted to learn certain new forms of behavior."[4] But he does not define strength or the conditions underlying its initial possession and, presumably, he is referring to overt learning. My hypotheses are concerned with unconscious internalization of values, as well as overt learning, and with some of the theories underlying the concept of ego strength.

In giving up traditional values and goals and in taking on those from another culture, the rewards can rarely be completely certain. An African living in the rural area of Northern Rhodesia can be reasonably certain of monetary rewards if he becomes a miner in town, and to get them he does not have to change basic attitudes or traditional values. However, to want to become literate, to save money for future goals, to be interested in a world beyond tribe and township, to practice new forms of social relationships—these indicate a commitment to a new moral order in which the rewards are still uncertain and the path not always clear.

The sources of ego strength could be several. Innate genetic differences between individuals could be influential, although there are almost no data to prove it. On another level, psychoanalytical theory gives clues from individual life histories. Returning to Erickson's theory of ego strength, the assumption is that an infant's feeling of basic trust in his mother is a primary condition for trust in one's self and that this is followed by the ability to trust and relate to many peoples. The long period of indulgent nursing which could engender basic trust was noted in the modal tribal life history, as was also the abrupt weaning which could lead to distrust. There have probably been many significant changes and considerable diversity in the bringing up of children over the last thirty-five or fifty years on the township and in the villages. As indicated earlier, women with some education were tending to shorten the nursing period, and the nuclear patriarchal family was gaining in strength while the lineage ties were weakening. Nor are experiences on which basic trust is built limited to infancy or to early childhood. Later childhood and youth are significant, as is also adult experience. Some adults had been sent to mission boarding schools when they were children and had close contact with European missionaries, while others never went to any school and had no contacts beyond family, lineage, and village. Most of the African political and trade union leaders and the intelligentsia of this area (and in other parts of Africa) had contacts in childhood with benevolent European mission teachers, who provided new models for identification. The missionaries did not think or teach in terms of polarities—African *versus* European— but preached instead that all men were brothers and the children of God. Because of this convergence, the Africans influenced by missionaries did not have to endure the anxiety of trying to choose between being African or European. Implicit also in the missionaries' teaching was the concept of autonomy, that no one necessarily had to follow a traditional role. These young Africans were able to imagine playing a role in modern society and becoming a part of it. "I am what I can imagine I will be," as Erickson has written.[5] Once having played a new role, the ego becomes stronger and development of other new roles is apt to be continuous. As Feldman and Moore point out in their theory of labor commitment, change is cumulative; multiple involvements in several contexts reinforce one another and increase the general level of commitment.[6] The same authors emphasize the significance of adult socialization during a transitional stage in the development of a society.[7] Data from this mining township seems to confirm their theories. However, my hypothesis is that those who are successful in the process of adult socialization may have had a different form of socialization in infancy, childhood, or youth which gave them the desire and the ego strength to change attitudes and commitments when they become adults.

Parents of twenty or thirty years ago who sent their children away to a mission school were probably different in character from those who did not believe in educating their children. The latter offspring would, therefore, have been handicapped not only by their lack of education, but also by their parents' attitude toward education and by the absence of other models for identification. Uneducated Africans rarely had any contacts with Europeans until they were adult, and then the relationships were superficial and of the "command and serve" type, such as between the European "gangers" and their African "boys." These Africans apparently did not change their internalized values and could not imagine themselves being different from their parents and ancestors. They tended to accept the traditional power-status theme in which inequality between young and old, men and women, chief and commoner was taken for granted. This attitude was often expressed by those who did not desire to become literate and who expressed no regret over their lack of education; for some, this conservative attitude was now sanctioned by a Christian God:

I did not go to school to learn how to read because God did not say we should all go to school. That is the reason why some are well educated, some a little educated, and others are without education. The world would not have been interesting, if we were all equal. There should be some to be above others, and these should serve those who are above.

I did not go to school and the reason is that we cannot all be the same. For example, two people come to town to work. Then after two years they both stop work. One of the two will definitely be much better than the other. This is only because God did not make us equal in all things. I am better than some educated men in some ways. I am able to produce [children], but sometimes an educated man may not be able to produce.

I do not know how to read or write because my father told me it was useless for me to go to school. He told me that I should work and earn money, because that is the most important thing today. And he told me that even if you are educated, you will not be a white man. I do not want to learn, because I know it is a waste of time. It is more important for me to drink beer.

These people thought in terms of polarities: those who command and those who serve, Africans and Europeans, education versus procreation. They thought they had to choose between them. Certainly, the European "gangers" on the mine, as contrasted to the missionaries, encouraged thinking in opposing polarities. This could only increase anxieties and make change more difficult.

Underlying other negative attitudes toward education was an idea that it had little connection with the primary goal of earning money, and on the mine township at the time of my study there was some reality behind this notion. The boss boy, who was in one of the higher paid groups, could be illiterate and without education, while youths with a Standard V or VI education might earn less or be unemployed. A man in his twenties said:

I did not go to school because I did not see any value in education, and I do not go to a night school for adults because I am not a fool. There are lots of people with high education, Standards V and VI, but they wander about without employment. Even when some of them get employed they are paid the same rate with someone who did not go to school. I am a driver, and I earn more money than an educated person can get. The other reason for not going to night school is that it is wasting time, when I want to be looking for girls.

Recently the situation has changed. Boss boys must now have a Standard III education, and many new jobs requiring education have been opened to Africans.

Under the new mine policy of advancement for Africans into more skilled and responsible jobs, higher levels of education become increasingly necessary. The changing economic structure is an important agent of adult socialization. Not only do education and high wages become closely connected, but commitments are made to other values introduced in the schools.

It has been noted that radio and movies also introduce new values as well as give pleasure and that they were accessible to all, which was not the situation with schools. Why were 50 per cent of the adults not listening to the radio and 61 per cent not going to the movies? (There was much overlapping between the two groups.) For approximately half, among the major reasons were: movies were only for children, dislike of Westerns, too busy with their work, taking a correspondence course, going to night school, or learning to be carpenters in spare time; some women were afraid of the advances of men at the movies or did not think it womanly to go to the Welfare

Center. But the remainder of the non-participants for radio as well as movies had different reasons, the most numerous being "not interested" or "too lazy," which were similar in meaning. In this context, women said they were "too lazy" and men "not interested." A man in his thirties, on the Copperbelt for ten years, said:

I have no time for the radio or bioscope or such things. Nothing interests me in them at all. They are only fit for Europeans who bought them. Why should we pretend to be Europeans? I do not go to any of them because they do not interest me.

Women often said they were "too lazy." Laziness for them had no immoral connotations and was mentioned without self-consciousness or apology:

I am not interested in either radio or movies and that is because I am lazy. I do have time to go to the Welfare Center; it is just laziness.

Men also said that they could not take time from their beer drinking. Their interest was not just in drinking, but rather in getting drunk. There was the same casualness and lack of self-consciousness in talking about being drunk as in saying one was lazy. One man told another that he could not make an appointment for the next day, because it was pay-day and he expected to be drunk then.

These people regarded the mass media as primarily for Europeans and not for Africans, and for them the two races were opposing polarities. Therefore, they could not psychologically make the effort to enter or commit themselves to a modern world which they regarded as purely European. They were not interested in hearing over the radio about "the progress my country is making," in news of the larger world, in Nkhata's songs of town life, or even in traditional songs and stories; nor did they desire the exciting catharsis afforded by the cowboys' fighting in the movies. Instead they gave the impression of passivity toward anything remotely modern. At the same time, they were not yearning to return to their villages except for visits. The men liked being on the mine township for the money that could be earned, and women liked the easier life there. They were apparently enjoying life, but appeared unable to imagine becoming modern and accepting European values. Instead, some of them seemed to regress to exaggerated traditional values, one of which was beer drinking.

Beer was an integral part of tribal life: essential to hospitality, a payment for labor and a necessary part of rituals. In the past it was impossible for anyone except a chief to get enough beer to become a regular drunkard, and chiefs who drank regularly apparently "carried" their liquor. But more than a quarter of a century ago, when Richards was doing her work among the Bemba, she noted that those Africans who lived in villages near the town of Kasama (the capital of the Northern Province) did not follow the traditional etiquette of beer-drinking and that they drank more than did the people in remote rural villages. These Africans near Kasama felt no obligation to share beer purchased with money; the owner who had brewed her own supply shared it with fewer people; occasionally beer was even drunk alone. Instead of drinking in the evenings as was traditional, some began drinking in the morning and kept at it all day. Richards writes that "in the circle of villages round a town like Kasama it would be fair to say that a large proportion of the younger men are regularly drunk every Saturday and Sunday in a way that is quite unlike the slight intoxication of an ordinary village beer-drink."[8]

In the tribal villages, beer-drinks were a major form of entertainment. On the mine township, it was one of many. Among the different kinds of beer, the most popular was the traditional native beer brewed illegally by women in their homes and sold and drunk there. Occasionally, the illegal brewers were caught, fines were paid, and the brewing continued. Legal bottled beer was sold at the beer halls. The European authorities did not permit whiskey or wine to be sold to Africans.

I met very few Africans who did not like drinking beer and who did not drink it. Members of the Watch Tower Sect were the only group who never drank. But there was a great difference between individuals in the amount drunk and in the emphasis placed on drinking. For some, getting drunk was the major way of spending their leisure time and a goal of life. As these men came off their day or night shift, the question they asked each other was, "Where shall we drink beer today; at whose house is native beer for sale?" As one man put it, "When you are in the morning shift and knock off in the afternoon, you fear your friends have finished all the beer. Then when you are in the afternoon shift, you fear your friends will drink all the beer you have left in the compound." The beer hall, with its legal beer, was the last resource if no native beer could be found, and it was also a place for sociability for both heavy and mild drinkers. Men, and women, too, talked about their great need for beer quite freely:

Comments of men.

I don't feel well if I pass a day without drinking beer. It is my food.

I have no time to go to the bioscope, as I must go looking for beer. I like the beer brewed in the compound better than that sold at the canteen.

I have no time to go and listen to the radio, because most of my time, when I am not working, is spent in drinking beer. This is my game. I can't do well in life without beer.

Comments of women.

Cinema shows and radio are there to entertain youth. We people of old age [she was in her thirties] cannot attend such things where small boys go. Our form of entertainment is beer. This is the only thing we like.

I do not attend radio. My wireless is the beer, because when I am drunk, I can sing and dance and can be proud.

A woman, in her thirties and without any schooling, was quite sociological in her explanation of why she did not go to the movies or listen to the radio. She said:

Cinema is a strange thing to me. At home we did not have it, and how can I develop the habit of going to cinema now? The people who enjoy it are those who have been born here, and this is their home. They start early going to cinema, and they have developed great interest in it. It is the same with wireless. I drink beer on the Copperbelt, because beer is not a new thing to me. I started drinking beer while at home, and here it is just a matter of continuing what I have always done. At home the only "cinema" I had seen was to watch people dancing, and I have not stopped watching people dance here, because I had this sort of thing at home. But I do not want to follow strange European entertainments. I must stick to my own.

Although she was aware of what we call her social conditioning, she was not correct in her generalization from it. The majority of people on the township were born in rural areas as she was. Yet in our survey, 45 per cent of the rural-born were listening to radio. For them security did not lie in "continuing what I have always done";

and "strange European entertainments" did not threaten the stability of their world as they seemed to threaten hers.

The goal of the habitual drinkers was to get drunk. A general complaint against bottled beer was that it had little effect on the drinkers. Many times such sentiments were heard as, "it [bottled beer] makes no change in me. I drank much on Sunday, but it did not make me much drunk."

As among all peoples, reactions of Africans when they were drunk varied. They included the expression of hostility, boasting about being important, or going to sleep to avoid quarreling, and fighting. A few joked and danced. A man in his twenties said, "You know, after drinking much beer I do not feel shy, and so I say anything I want to say without fear. That is why I like drinking beer very much." When drunk this man quarreled with another drinker and said, "Ay, you, I shall kill you as I killed a man in Makoma Dam." Another man boasted incorrectly that he was a chief, although he was not even related to the royal family.

The general pattern was either to express aggression or to avoid it by falling asleep. Habitual drunkards often expressed their fear of getting into quarrels and were apparently anxious about their hostile feelings. A man who had been drinking a great deal said to his friend, who was sober: "My friend, I am drunk and I must go to sleep. It is not for one who is drunk to move among so many people, in case he pushes one of them and gets into a fight." Another said, "You see, I have no time for going to Welfare Center to listen to wireless or going to bioscope because I spend most of my time, when I do not have to work, in drinking beer. I like beer because when you have drunk much you must go to sleep and you do not quarrel with others. Those who make much noise only pretend to be drunk. One who is really drunk is usually very quiet or sleeps."

It should be remembered that tribal tradition emphasized the keeping of peace in the village. Today, European laws strengthen this tradition. Hostilities were formerly expressed mainly through witchcraft, gossip, and warfare. The first two still function. Getting drunk appears to be increasing as another outlet for hostility or anxiety. As in the past, there was a limit on the Copperbelt to what was considered proper for the extent of drunkenness. It was bad to drink so much that one became completely senseless. A man might leave his bicycle and go home without it, and then it would be stolen. Or he might do things which brought abuse and ridicule on himself. At one beer-drink at which everyone had been drinking heavily, one man, for no apparent reason, tried to lift a large, heavy bucket of beer, dropped it, and the beer ran over the ground and the clothes of the men. They were very much annoyed at the waste of beer and the spoiling of their clothes and wanted to beat the offender. But he ran home quickly. One member of the beer party later told his workmates about it, and they all started laughing very much and began exaggerating and adding to the story, saying that the man had excreted in someone's beer.

One man, listening to a similar tale, boasted, "I know how to drink. If I went to a school where they teach how to drink beer, I should have passed P.S.D., Public Service Drinker."

Some of these men who boasted that they knew how to drink liked to drink in what they considered European style, sitting on chairs in special-group houses.

No matter whether these habitual drinkers drank sitting on the floor in a small hut, or on a chair in a special-group house, whether they fought or boasted about fighting, or went peacefully home and fell asleep to avoid fighting, drinking beer to get drunk was an urgent need for them. When one of them received his pay, he could not be found at home. Many times he bought beer for his friends or workmates. It was both an act of friendship and a way of showing off that he had money. When there was no money, friends loaned it to each other. "Where is the beer today?" was a never-ending question. If a man knew where native beer was brewed, it was considered discourteous not to tell his friend who asked the question.

There were many other Africans who drank beer, but whose drinking did not consume so much of their money or of their leisure time. They might occasionally get drunk, particularly at a funeral or wedding or some other special occasion. But drinking and getting drunk was not their major form of recreation. These men were content with the commercial bottled beer at the beer hall and enjoyed meeting their friends there. When they returned from work, like the others they bathed and ate, and then they might go to the beer hall. But they also had other leisure-time interests, such as visiting friends, practicing football, listening to the radio, going to a club, reading a newspaper, and for a few, going to night classes. The men who were trying to advance to better jobs said they were too busy to spend much time drinking.

I did no quantitative survey of those who habitually became drunk as compared to those who drank in moderation.[9] But it was my strong impression, based on those Africans I knew, those interviewed, and from innumerable recorded conversations, that the habitual drunkards did not have modern goals, except for the one of making money. Nor did they regret their illiteracy or tend to participate in the new leisure-time activities. They were primarily interested in making as much money as possible and displaying their wealth through the clothes they bought, the amount of beer they drank, the gifts they gave to relatives, the occasional taking of a taxi, and other such luxuries. Those who were interested in furthering their education, in educating their children, in becoming skilled workers, or in eventually owning a shop also drank beer, but rarely became drunk. These men usually participated in some of the new leisure-time activities. The clerks, teachers, and highly skilled workers had an image of themselves which excluded drunkenness. They also did not want to spend too much money on beer because they were saving to further their own careers, for the education of their children, or for some other long-range ambitions. Europeans on the Copperbelt also had a reputation for drinking heavily and getting drunk, but I made no study of this.

It is obvious that drinking to excess is not peculiarly African. In the United States and many other modern societies, alcoholism is a major social problem. Nor is intoxication a modern phenomenon. The first use of intoxicating beverages is bound up with the development of agriculture. Made from barley, and then from rice, they are believed to have spread from India originally. Barley beer is thought to have been introduced into Africa from Egypt.[10]

The physiological effects of alcohol are several: It is an anesthetic, a sedative, a relief of fatigue, and a food. It is generally recognized that the reduction of anxiety is the primary psychological function of drinking alcoholic beverages and that the other factors such as food and the reduction of fatigue are secondary.[11] As Horton points out, anxiety as the primary drive is usually unconscious and "the most common motive expressed verbally is simply the wish to become intoxicated. Not drinking but drunkenness is valued."[12]

Tribal Africans recognized the food value of their beer. But on the Copperbelt, where food was both more plentiful and diverse, the habitual heavy drinkers drank to get drunk whenever they had the money and could find native beer. Nevertheless, they did not appear to be alcoholics as the term is used in Western society. Their drinking did not seem to affect their emotional relations with their wife and children and, with a few exceptions, they were able to work satisfactorily. At the same time, the drinking was more than a Saturday night spree, customary among workers in many parts of the world. Heavy drinking among the Africans seemed to be a more or less culturally approved form of alcoholic delinquency, through which was expressed a passive resistance to European status values, which they had been unable to achieve.[13]

The habitual hard drinkers in this community were miners, who ranged from pick-and-shovel workers to boss boys. Mining is a dirty job and entails hard physical work; and for those who work underground it is hazardous. Nor did the miner's job have high status. None of the adolescent boys in Standards V and VI in the township school wanted to be miners; half of them were the sons of miners.[14]

Adults going to night school hoped to get jobs other than mining when they became literate or had more education. Europeans who worked in the mine had supervisory positions and did not do the dirty, hard physical jobs. As Mitchell and Epstein have pointed out, new status categories among the Africans have been determined primarily by the European way of life.[15] The miners, low in the social hierarchy, appeared to think they were raising their status by drinking often and heavily. In the past chiefs drank more than commoners, elders more than young people, and men more than women. They were also "showing off" (a traditional and contemporary value) in their display of wealth, necessary for heavy drinking. Important, too, was the fun and conviviality which accompanied the drinking. This was true likewise for those who drank more moderately in the beer hall.

But there are also unconscious functions in getting drunk, and the major one was probably the usual relieving of anxieties, caused in this situation by living in a world of change and being unable to change with it.

An interesting comparative situation exists among the Soga people in Buganda, also living through a period of rapid change. There, some village headmen achieve high status through becoming part of the Europeanized civil service bureaucracy. However, other headmen refuse these position and emphasize, instead, the traditional aspects of their role. Still others do neither and usually drink to excess. This passive reaction can be described as a state of anomie.[16] The intransigents on the mine township were unable to take the road to autonomy, a goal of modern Africans; the new economic organization and resulting structure prevented a return to tribal life. Like the passive Soga headmen, they drank to excess. The heavy drinkers on the mine township may have suffered from what psychiatrists call separation anxiety, and, as a result, had regressed to excessive gratification on an oral level.

The excessive promiscuity on the mine township is likewise an exaggeration of a tribal pattern and may also be caused by undue anxieties. Although extramarital relations were more or less the norm on the township, they seemed to be more common and more frequent among the intransigents than among the intelligentsia and others who were trying to enter the modern world. Some men said they could not attend night classes or listen to the radio because it would take time from looking for girls. The ever-present suspicion of unfaithfulness in many marriages had a considerable basis in reality. According to Freud, the development of civilization presupposes the ability of individuals to restrain, postpone, and sometimes renounce powerful instinctual urgencies, particularly those of sex and aggression.[17] This concept is widely accepted by many. The anthropologist Shalin's theory of the origin of civilization is that human nature is superimposed on animal nature, that is, restraints are laid on the sexual and aggressive impulses; and he notes Freud's famous allegory of the conflict between the sexually inclined id and the socially conscious superego.[18] The social psychologist Doob ends his *Becoming More Civilized* with the statement, as if it were a new concept, "Civilization, let it be whispered and shouted, requires people to exercise self-control, and such control is achieved by forfeiting some other tendency such as spontaneity."[19]

Restraints on both these instincts existed in tribal societies. Sexual relations were forbidden with a wide number of people at all times and to all at certain times; the expression of aggression between kindred and toward those in authority was carefully controlled. Tradition sanctioned these taboos, and it was believed that supernatural and social punishment would follow their violation. Then, as now, men differed in their ability to endure these restraints: taboos were sometimes broken; some men engaged in more extramarital relations or had more divorces than the society considered proper. In the tribal past men had to postpone another powerful desire—the achievement of adult status and becoming head of a household. In some tribes full adult status was not attained until people became grandparents. On the Copperbelt, in contrast, young men can enjoy high status through becoming educated and having a successful modern career. This achievement means hard and purposeful work for new goals introduced by Europeans, which could only function within the new future-oriented image of time. The Christian religion, as well as the modern economic system, emphasize the renunciation of present satisfactions for the sake of future rewards. Going to school, saving money, and other career-directed activities are the results of internalized values oriented toward the future, and they seemed to be frequently accompanied by more instinctual restraints than that practiced by the intransigents. A causal correlation is inferred. Some men apparently had a lower threshold for toleration of instinctual restraint and were less able than others to internalize new values. As already noted, individual differences in ability to endure restraints on instinctual impulses apparently existed in tribal society, as they do also among contemporary Europeans. Recent varations in the Africans' childhood conditioning at home and the factor of school education for some and not for others probably increased individual diversity in respect to control over instinctual life. The rewards for such restraints come from society and expand with economic and political advancement. But the controls have to come from within the individual, who must be strong enough to integrate sex needs with economic goals. There are no supernatural or tribal punishments for lack of control. The habitual heavy drinkers and excessively promiscuous people evidently did not have the desire or the necessary strength to impose inner controls. It was mostly from this group (a minority) that the intransigents seemed to come.

Another hypothesis is that those who resisted change (on any but material values) had more conscious and unconscious resentment toward Europeans than did the modern African, which could be channeled in heavy drinking. Overt resentments were primarily over wages and attitudes of supervisors. Unskilled and uneducated workers, among whom were many of the intransigents, tended to have more uneducated and intolerant supervisors than did educated Africans. Nor were unconscious hostilities channeled in the formal etiquette of the past, customary in relations with the first Europeans. Neither did the intransigents enjoy a catharsis through identification with the victorious cowboy hero of the movies. There may likewise have been unconscious hostility toward the Africans who were becoming part of the modern world. The intransigents knew their world was moving, but they did not have the ego strength to risk the ambiguities of change. Not in the past or today did they have the kind of experiences with Europeans which would make identification possible. They saw the two races as polarities, which must remain forever differentiated. "Why go to night school, or to the movies, or listen to the radio—this will not make us Europeans." But they could not return to a tribal past which no longer existed. In the opera *Fledermaus,* there is a song, "Happy Is He Who Forgets What Cannot Be Changed." Perhaps the Africans who drank to get drunk were trying to forget their inability to change in a changing world, and this could also apply to heavy-drinking Europeans.

In the next and concluding chapter, we turn to those Africans and Europeans who are in the vanguard of their changing world.

PART V

CONCLUSION

19. Freedom

"WE MAY STATE tentatively that the elite which emerges from historical change are groups which out of the deepest common identity crises manage to create a new style of coping with the outstanding danger situation of their society."[1]

Such an elite is always small in number, but they have a significance far out of proportion to their numbers, particularly in crises situations such as those caused by the rapid social change in Northern Rhodesia. These crises are inherent in the progressive development of new identities in modern society. In tribal societies men tended to get their identity from their status of sex and rank, due to the accident of birth. The tribe formed the limits of the group identity. Many of the Europeans in Northern Rhodesia got their identity in a similar manner; their status also depended on an accident of birth— belonging to the white race—and their group identity was often confined to people with the same skin color in this particular African setting. However, as noted earlier, several centuries ago in other parts of the world, the Industrial Revolution, the Protestant Reformation, and the development of capitalism freed man to make his own place, regardless of the accident of birth. But this dramatic change was limited in its application; in the period in which colonial empires were formed masses of men were used as means for other peoples' purposes. Of course, men have been objects to others at all times. But increasingly, people began to see themselves as objects for their own ends and to take account of the meaning of their lives for themselves. The gradual relinquishment of empires and the revolt of former colonial peoples are part of the increasing demand of people to serve their own ends.

This historical development, taking centuries in some countries, has been happening in Northern Rhodesia in less than half a century. Even in the countries where social change has been relatively gradual, its influence on ego and group identity have, of course, not been uniform. Always in critical situations there is a psychological elite; men of individual strength and of broadening group identity, able to forge a synthesis of old and new life-styles, capable of self-direction and aware of the realities of the situation. These can be called the autonomous. Others in time of danger or in critical situations cling fanatically to old patterns, because they lack the strength to go forward or because they oscillate between the old and the new, depending on the situation of the moment; still others are at an impasse because of strong ambivalences. In the contemporary crises in this part of Africa, all these types are found among both Africans and Europeans. My analysis is in sharp contrast to the popular and oversimplified interpretation that, for example, "the natives thus exist in the void between a traditional tribalism which is beyond recovery and a total Europeanization which would, to be realized require far more opportunities for exposure to environmental conditioning."[2] A social crisis exists for Africans in the change from a tribal to a modern way of life, but not necessarily to total Europeanization. No people has ever totally taken on any culture, and it is evident that the Africans during this period of change do not live in a void.

A distinction must be made between tribalism and tribal structure, since they are not necessarily synonymous.[3] It is possible for tribal values and a system of social relationships to have considerable strength, after the tribe no longer functions as a political structure. On the Copperbelt the tribe, still a significant point of reference for the individual, had relatively little political significance; the tendency was toward the expansion of a group identity beyond the tribe. Even in the early days of the mining community, Africans had begun to group tribes, other than those from their home area, into three or four major categories, such as the Bemba, Ngoni, and Lozi, who were dominant when the Europeans arrived. Or, all tribes from one geographical area were grouped together, e.g., all from Nyasaland were called "Nyasa."[4] The Federation has also been an impetus in weakening tribal pluralism. An uneducated man, in his thirties, said:

It is true that we should copy some of the things Europeans have brought, but good ones only. It is right for me to learn to speak Bemba, Nyanja, or any other tribe's language, because we are of the same country, like water in the same jar. Water in the same container cannot have two tastes. Therefore, we people in Northern Rhodesia should be one, and not say, "I am a Bemba, or Ngoni, or such and such." We should ourselves be federated, like the Europeans have done with the three countries.

The opposing tendency also existed. Another man, in discussing the elections of Africans to the Legislature, said:

As a Tumbuka I would not represent the Bemba well, because I would not understand well what they really meant or wanted. So the best way is for a Tumbuka man to represent the Tumbuka people, and a Bemba man for the Bemba. Then things would be going well, if we, and the Europeans, and the Asiatics had equal representation.

My impression was that this man represented a minority. Inter-tribal marriages, association in political organizations and trade unions which cut across tribal lines, working with men of different tribes as well as having them as friends and neighbors,[5] and the unity resulting from common opposition to Federation: all these blurred tribal boundaries. There was also the knowledge that beyond these, beyond the Copperbelt, beyond the Federation, there were other Africans struggling for autonomy and freedom. Radio, movies, newspapers, and people brought news of the world still farther away, beyond Africa. Some members of the intelligentsia, through scholarships from their own government or fellowships from foreign countries, and a few trade union and political leaders on missions abroad were having direct experience of this expanding world.

Within this expanding universe, some of the basic tribal themes—common to all the tribes in this area—persisted. Power, status, land, and kinship were and still are the focus for strong sentiments. The

strength of the new African nationalism in part lies in the fact that it
represents a convergence of old and new values; it offers a broader
group identity, which, however, retains some traditional elements;
it alleviates present anxieties and offers promises of rewards to many
Africans—educated and illiterate, modern and traditional-oriented.
There are many other aspects of nationalism; here my interest is
limited to its relationship to the emerging new group identity.

On the mine township with its modern wage economy, land was
still of paramount importance, and fear of losing it because of the
Federation was all-pervasive. We recall that land and its fertility were
mystically interrelated with the ancestors buried on it, with the chief's
power, and with his sex life. He held the land for the tribe, and its
use by members was taken for granted. Survival depended upon it.
This dependence has been weakened in the new economy. But residence on the mine township was contingent on a job. Returning to
the village, whether desired or not, might be necessary when a man
stopped working. Confidence was strengthened in the strike, described
earlier, because, as some of the strikers said, even if they were fired
they could return to the village and farm. The fear of losing land
was also expressed by many whose economic survival and plans for
the future had no connection with farming. Schoolteachers and careerists in the civil service expressed the same anxiety about losing land
as did illiterate miners. A man who had been to England for his
training and who held an important position in the civil service said,
apropos of nothing, at the end of a conversation about the impact
of radio and movies, "Soon, because of this Federation, we will be
wandering around the bush like pigs." Spontaneously, and without
any questioning, this fear was universally expressed. When it was
pointed out that the federal government had no control over native
lands in Northern Rhodesia and that no land had been alienated by
it, the answer was, "Ah, wait and see. Look at Southern Rhodesia."
Sometimes there was also a reference to South Africa.

It is difficult to assess the exact degree of reality underlying the
all-pervasive fear of losing the land. Certainly the Federation was
planned by the settlers to bring a greater degree of independence
from the Colonial Office, and it was no secret that many Europeans
wanted the greater freedom of dominion status. It was also true that
in Southern Rhodesia, a self-governing colony and a part of the

Federation, the Africans had lost land to the settlers. The Africans
therefore concluded that the Federation, which enhanced the power
of the European settlers and reduced that of the Colonial Office,
would follow the policies of Southern Rhodesia. The fact that the
capital of the Federation, Salisbury, was located in Southern Rhodesia,
strengthened the fear. It was logical that the Africans should predict
the future on the basis of their knowledge of the past and of a
comparative situation.[6]

The rational fear of losing their land was probably deepened by
the unconscious symbolism of land and mother, particularly mother's
breast. This symbolism is not unique to Africans. "Mother earth"
is a common concept. In tribal Africa, a generous nursing mother,
a generous chief, fertility of land, fertility of men and women were
all, consciously and unconsciously, linked with survival. The possible
trauma due to the sudden weaning after long indulgence has likewise
been noted. This kind of symbolism endures a long time, even in a
changing situation. The early benevolent Europeans—missionaries and
civil servants—had been likened by Africans to protective fathers
leading their children into a modern world.[7] They had, to some
degree, taken the place of African chiefs, who had led the way in
the tribal world. The Protectorate had lived up to its name; African
rights were paramount and protected. With the Federation, the Europeans, as represented by the politically powerful settlers, were believed to threaten the source of life—the land. Even the civil servants,
the protective "fathers," had passively acquiesced in the formation of
the Federation. At the time it came into existence, the Africans
thought they were being pushed into a position where they must
fight for political independence from Europeans before they were
quite ready for it. They would then have preferred the Colonial Office
to have retained its power until they were more highly educated and
better trained for political independence. They had been deserted by
the protective fathers, and danger loomed.

Potential and present dangers often stir the hidden anxieties rising
from unresolved early crises. But the present crisis was being faced
not by infants, but by adults, some of whom were an elite who had
started on the path to autonomy and who would not be turned back.
They had the strength to try and resolve the crises, and their solution
appealed to others. The nationalist movement, directed against the

Federation and the political power of European settlers, alleviates fears about the loss of land and, apparently, deep anxieties—conscious and unconscious—about annihilation. Since these fears are universal, it unites all Africans, regardless of tribe, education, or membership in newly formed social classes. The movement safeguards a traditional and elemental security, land, as it leads them into a modern world.

The nationalist movement fights for political control by the Africans, who are an overwhelming majority of the population. When the Europeans first arrived in this part of Africa, they had certain capabilities which the Africans did not have. Now, increasingly, Africans are aware that they have similar capabilities and the mystique of race has been questioned. The new African leaders have been relatively successful in the modern world and are committed to helping other Africans to success and to freedom from the dominance of Europeans. There is reason to believe that the African leaders would welcome some loose form of federation of the Rhodesias and Nyasaland, particularly on the economic level, if it was not controlled by Europeans.

The African nationalist movement, however, represents much more than freedom from Europeans. It also reflects and strengthens the shifting locus of intra-African power and the changing nature of African leadership. While the power of tribal chiefs was in some ways strengthened, as well as curtailed, by British indirect rule, it obviously depended, to a large degree, on the good will of the district and provincial commissioners rather than on supernatural sanctions. In the reality politics of today these and the power of the chiefs have much weakened. Even the chief's custodianship of the land rests ultimately on decisions made by the Colonial Office. Africans pay taxes to the government rather than tribute to a chief, who can, therefore, no longer practice the tribal virtue of generosity. The new leaders have no control over natural resources, and their fame does not depend on generosity or on supernatural sanctions, but on their ability to deal with Europeans and to wrest political power from them. The young leaders have achieved power rather than inherited it. They are educated and have many of the capabilities formerly thought to be exclusively European. Their success depends on planning ahead, knowing when to use violence, when to exercise restraint, when to use other forms of strategy, and on continuous work and struggle. The young African leaders dress like Europeans, speak the same language, often with the same British accent, and have much of the European know-how. Yet they do not seem to be black Europeans. The polarities of African versus European appear to have been merged in them. They have apparently integrated a series of identifications and become autonomous men, internally anchored and capable of self-direction.[8] They formed their own nationalist movement and party, and in Northern Rhodesia and Nyasaland have been successful in gaining the support of most of the chiefs as well as the masses of people. One successful African, who had in the past demonstrated an ability for leadership, lost his opportunity for it when he joined the European party in power and accepted office in its government. Many Africans regarded him as a traitor. My impression was that he was really a black European and was happy to receive recognition as such. Previously he had been bitter over the lack of this recognition.

The relative youthfulness of African political leaders symbolizes well the shift in the status positions of age *versus* youth. Young people are not only breaking from the domination of Europeans, but also from their own fathers, grandfathers, uncles, and other tribal authority figures. The young leaders, with more power now than the elders or chiefs, are more like older brothers, and thus escape being symbols for the familiar ambivalences of the parent-child relationship inherent in many leader-followers situations.

Kinship ties are more persistent than the sentiments underlying the status positions of age and youth. The nationalist movement does not seem to affect lineage bonds directly, although indirectly the broader group identity, as well as the modern economic system, weakens them. Like land, but perhaps to a lesser degree, lineage ties still represent security. Even educated men have too precarious a foothold in the modern world to give up either. An African can still count on his kindred for help in times of trouble: unemployment, illness, or some other crises. He also needs their assistance when he marries, when he starts a new enterprise such as opening a tea shop, or engages in some other modern undertaking. So the intelligentsia continue to give cash and gifts to their kindred, even though they do it grumblingly. The uneducated seem to do it more as a matter of course.

The traditional conflict between conjugal family and lineage is stronger and more open for the modern African than for his ancestors. They knew the pull between family and lineage: two sets of men having rights in the same women and one spouse having to change his residence upon marriage and to live more or less as an outsider in a new community. The lineage was always the stronger and the family always the weaker. Spouses were divorced, remarried, and started new families, while the close ties of lineage members remained throughout life and, supposedly, after death. The lineage was a part of the daily economic and social round of life, one spouse being a functioning member and the other adapting to it as an outsider. Today on the Copperbelt the conjugal family has become much stronger. It is an economic unit, with a closeness unknown in the tribal past. The husband is usually the sole wage earner in the family, and his wife and children are far more dependent on him than they had been. The decreasing emphasis on polygamy adds to the closeness. Then, too, marriages, particularly of the intelligentsia, are increasingly based on choice instead of being arranged by kindred, and this presumably leads to emotional closeness.

It was not possible to determine definitively whether extramarital relations and divorces were more, or less, frequent on the Copperbelt than in the tribal villages. In the early days of the township, when men usually came without their wives, relations with any available women were the necessary norm. In the recent period the large majority of men have wives with them. Still, there was the pull of the traditional pattern of extramarital relations, coupled with greater opportunities and a relative anonymity as compared to the village. There appeared to be, nevertheless, a growing stability in the families of the intelligentsia, from whom the elite came.

Children growing up in a monogamous family, with the lineage absent, are conditioned to a closer relationship with one mother and one father, rather than to the closer emotional ties with a number of adults functioning as surrogate parents. These children, when grown, might have deeper and more stable relationships in their marriages than were customary in tribal society. Then, there seemed to have been no pattern in the family for exclusive, deep emotional relationships during childhood and youth.

Although ties in the modern conjugal family are closer than in its tribal counterpart, at the same time autonomy for its members is even permitted and encouraged. Through education, sons and even daughters can prepare for a different kind of life than that of their fathers and mothers. This was unknown in tribal society. The Wilsons, in their early classic on social change in Central Africa, wrote, "Greater autonomy in the narrow relations as well as greater subordination in the wider, is thus an aspect in the increase in scale."[9] Expanding this point and put more psychologically, my hypothesis is that a relatively stable conjugal family and a relatively unstable and partially absent lineage convey a sense of basic trust—the necessary basis for both a strong ego and an expanding group identity— more than an unstable family and a stable functioning lineage. Ego identity can be more deeply rooted in the nuclear family because its biological ties *are* closer than in the lineage. The modern Africans were more concerned about the future of their own children than about plans for their sister's children, and this was supported by the new social structure in which children grew up apart from their lineage and in which the father was the head of the household.

Many other aspects of the new economic order weakened the lineage structure. Pensions and systems of voluntary savings, new opportunities in skilled jobs and for advancement in other fields, the possibility of owning a town house rather than having its occupancy dependent upon a particular job—all these meant less dependence on the lineage for security and a greater sense of being able to take care of one's self and family. This is part of a process af adult socialization in a transitional period, strengthened in the next generation by childhood socialization. Parents everywhere pass on to their children what they have learned about the world.

But conflicts still exist between the family and the lineage. Field, in her study of mental illness in a Ghana village, wrote that kinship disputes were more potent causes of disputes than marital disharmony.[10] The lineage still makes its demands, and in a crisis the conflict between individual and family interests may be acute. Such a predicament arose at the time of my study in the life of a modern young man, in his midtwenties, with a secondary school education, who held an interesting and challenging job. Although married and the father of two children, he was saving money to go to England for university study. He had strong intellectual interests, was politically aware, moderately active in politics, and ambitious. One day his older brother was in a severe accident and was rushed to a hospital. The doctors said his death was imminent. Lineage members assembled and decided that the young careerist must follow the tribal custom and marry his brother's widow. This meant not only taking on an additional wife, but also becoming father to his brother's three children. To take responsibility for two wives and five children would mean the end of his plans for study in England. Besides, he and his wife were content with their monogamous marriage, which was in keeping with their status among the urban intelligentsia. But if he did not follow the wishes of his kindred on this important matter, he faced excommunication from his lineage. He would have to stand alone in a new society, in which he was only partly established. He had, for instance, counted on some help from kindred for his family during his contemplated absence in England. The decision was not an easy one but finally he made it: He decided to marry his brother's widow. His foothold in the modern world was too precarious to let him give up completely the security represented by his lineage and to break the ties he had been conditioned to in childhood. Difficult as the decision was, the young careerist did not present the familiar picture of the neurotic torn in unconscious conflict between two cultures. His fears were open and manifest and he made the decision on what, to the best of his knowledge, was a reality situation. He could not at this moment afford to lose the support of his lineage.

The incident has an anticlimax. The brother, close to death, recovered. The careerist's son would probably make a different decision in a similar situation. A group identity beyond that of lineage (and tribe) grows stronger with the developing economic order and the increasing success of the nationalist movement. Nor will the careerist's son have the same early commitments to his lineage as his father. Childhood and adult socialization will have more continuity. In each there will be more freedom from the ties and demands of the lineage group.

Freedom is also related to an increasing acceptance of empirical concepts of reality and the decline of witchcraft thinking, "an *a priori* assumption about reality" not subject to proof.[11] The extent of contemporary witchcraft-thinking is difficult to measure. On the

Copperbelt, it functioned in new situations such as jobs and sports. A man who was fired sometimes placed the blame on the witchcraft of an envious fellow worker. A team which lost a football game might think it due to the superior magic of the winning team.[12] But even in the thirties, when the Wilsons made their study, they thought that the *relative* importance of magic was declining.[13] Richards, working in the same period in a rural area of Northern Rhodesia, thought it was increasing.[14] At the time of my study, Africans on the mine township said there was less witchcraft on the Copperbelt than in the rural areas. My strong impression was that education continuously increased the number of those who replaced witchcraft-thinking with the empirical thinking of science. The intelligentsia, particularly those with secondary education, schoolteachers, and men learning the new skills of advanced jobs were gaining a view of the universe in which witchcraft was not a principle of causation. A student in secondary school, home on vacation, argued with his uneducated family that witchcraft did not exist. He then put his lack of belief to an empirical test. His family told him that under certain conditions a witch was bound to appear. He fulfilled all the conditions; no witch came. He thought his lack of belief was scientifically proved. His uneducated family thought he must be a witch, because only a witch could afford to argue in that way. A belief in witches has a universality far beyond Africa and in many historical periods, including our own not too distant past. It tends to weaken or disappear on conscious levels when the social order no longer sanctions it, when anxieties are reduced or channeled in other ways, and when empirical thinking becomes a norm. It may continue to lurk in the unconscious and become conscious in times of anxiety or in cases of mental illness.

In the early fifties, there was witchcraft-thinking in the anti-federation propaganda that Europeans had poisoned the sugar to make African men impotent and African women sterile. Today in the propaganda of the nationalist movement and in the speeches of their leaders, witchcraft-thinking is absent. They are based instead on political realities: reports of a recent meeting with a government minister in London, comments and criticisms of the Federation's Prime Minister, discussion of a new franchise proposal, economic problems, and other such hard facts.

The intransigents, on the other hand, who have not been able to accept the realities of social change other than those concerned with money and material goods, believed in witchcraft, and some presumably practiced it. Yet, even among them, it has probably decreased. Africans said there was less envy of material possessions, which leads to witchcraft, because most everyone had the opportunity to acquire them for himself. There were also other outlets for aggressive impulses, such as getting drunk, fighting (personal rather than warfare), and stealing, all of which appear to have increased in intra-African life; and there were, also, demonstrations of hostility to the European-led Federation.

In any transitional or revolutionary period, the reactions of individuals to change show a wide latitude, and even in times of relative stability there is a difference of pace in the acceptance of new ideas and values. In the preceding chapter and in this one, the focus has been on the two extremities: the intransigents, who resist change; and the elite, who have been able to forge a new identity out of the crises. Obviously, there are many gradations between these contrasting types, some of which have been indicated throughout the book. The human species is remarkably ingenious in the multitude of ways it combines old and new patterns, and no two individuals do it in exactly the same way.

The new freedom has many sides. Men no longer have to fear the ever-recurring famines of the past. On the Copperbelt men did not often go hungry, although they were not always satisfied with their food. The fear of being empty (and its probable unconscious association with a weaning trauma) and the great dependence on the traditional giving and receiving aspects of many relationships were weakening. Instead, there is a growing reliance on one's own ability not only to get enough to eat, but to advance in new ways of life. The individual's ego is strengthened by every experience of its own power. In the process of adult socialization, there seems to be a relationship between changes in economic and political structure and in personality, since the structural changes provide the new opportunities for further growth. The shift from a subsistence to a surplus economy does not present the frequent situations which could call forth the early weaning trauma. On the other hand, as already suggested, the alleged desire of the European settlers for the

African's land probably does awaken early anxieties.

The growing differentiation and freedom from ancestral ties and lineage bonds increase the desire of Africans to be responsible for their own fate and to make their own traditions. At the same time, the elite, who have incorporated new models presented to them by a changing society, have begun to close the gap between Africans and Europeans by merging the former polarities, rather than by becoming black Europeans, which was the initial tendency. This elite participates in an expanding group identity, represented by the nationalist movement, and is nourished by it. Again, there is a circular process with roots in the changing social structure; the elite are the new models with whom other Africans can identify.[15]

The desire for freedom and the expanding group identity are expressed through the African nationalist movement. In Northern Rhodesia it is represented at this writing by the United National Independence party, led by Mr. Kenneth Kaunda. Its program is not strikingly racial. In an address to the people of Northern Rhodesia, in April 1961, Mr. Kaunda said, "The basic thoughts that guide me I must admit are nationalistic, but they accept the various elements that make up the country of Northern Rhodesia and of the interdependence of these various elements on each other. . . . I am asking our white people to show they are Northern Rhodesians and I am asking them for a manifestation of white Northern Rhodesian nationalism, when I ask them to line up with us in the common cause for freedom. If I read the temper of my people correctly, they are ready to accept their common lot and are prepared to go forward accepting a common discipline and a common desire for all our people. Surely this is the strongest assurance that one can have that we will endure as a nation. The acceptance of this unity, which we are ready to assure by a policy of respect for present valuations, obligations and agreements, is a step forward by my people to nationhood."[16] Mr. Kaunda made similar speeches to small and large groups of Europeans, trying to reduce their fears.

During 1961 there was a three-sided struggle among Mr. Kaunda, Sir Roy Welensky, and the British government over a constitution for Northern Rhodesia, with the British government vacillating in its position. When Sir Roy protested against a plan which was acceptable to Mr. Kaunda and his party, even though they did not get all they had asked for, concessions were made to Sir Roy. The result was a proposed constitution with a mechanism for the franchise that literally no one could understand. But it was clear that the new constitution would not give the Africans a majority. Mr. Kaunda had staked his standing on gaining political advancement through negotiations or, at the most, non-violent resistance. He is a follower of Gandhi's philosophy. But when he had presumably failed, there was violence, sabotage, and arson in the Northern Province, which has had a long history of belligerence. According to the *Central African Examiner,* the violence was not directed against people, but against schools, clinics, roads, and other symbols of government services to Africans. The same source editorially writes that "it is, in a deep sense, imposed authority and rule without consent which is being challenged."[17] Negotiations over the Northern Rhodesian constitution were reopened, and at this writing there are rumors that concessions will be made to Mr. Kaunda and the nationalists he leads. It is fairly certain that if Mr. Kaunda fails, he will be replaced by another African leader, who will not have his principles against violence.

The nationalist movement, with its goal of freedom from European political control, is part of the larger democratic social movements of our time. It is linked to Britain's gradual swing, even under the Conservative party, to the Left and to the welfare state, and to the movements of peoples in many parts of the world to establish their own identity and determine their own fate. Even if Federation had not come into being, Africans in this area would probably have had their nationalist movement, although its course might have been different. The fears aroused by the increased power of the European settlers through Federation gave it an impetus. So, also, did the remembrance of being habitually treated by many Europeans as less than human.

A pressing problem is whether the Europeans will recognize the African's new personality, the new identity which is revealed in the nationalist movement. In the thirties, the Wilsons noted that "the increasing assumption by Africans of European dress and manners, though it symbolizes an increasing civilization, is accompanied by more rather than less discourtesy from Europeans, who sense it as a bid for conventional equality."[18] At the time of my study on the mine township, many Europeans systematically and openly insulted or degraded Africans. The lines before the hatches of the European stores, the segregation even at post office windows and other public buildings, the likening by European supervisors of Africans to "monkeys just down from the trees," all threatened the new identity, as did the lack of opportunities for political power and the relatively slow economic and social advancement to some kind of parity with Europeans. Even strong men need recognition in order to maintain their self-esteem.

There has been much improvement during the last few years. The segregation in stores, public buildings, movies, and cafés in Northern Rhodesia is now legally forbidden. Schools are rapidly multiplying under the sponsorship of mine and government, and there is a strong drive for literacy and mass education. The mines have opened up many new opportunities for advancement and are providing the necessary training. Some political concessions have been made. But at this writing, the important and controversial issue is that of political power; and the Europeans, led by the Federation's Prime Minister, appear to be making a last-ditch stand to retain their political dominance.

This brings us to the problem of changes in the ego and group identity of the Europeans. They, like the Africans, have their intransigents and an elite, with all the gradations between the two extremes. Europeans have their form of tribalism, a parochial, closed ideological world built on mystical beliefs about the alleged superiority and inferiority of white and black people. The Europeans enjoyed not only political power, a monopoly of skilled jobs and of opportunities for advancement, but also what Thackeray called "the pleasure of associating with inferiors." Not, of course, that there was any true association. The limited relations of Europeans with a few Africans could bring little knowledge and less understanding, particularly since there was no desire for either. There are innumerable examples of the Europeans' ignorance of Africans, but the most glaring was the Prime Minister's (and many others') repeated statements that the majority of Africans were not opposed to Federation and that the opposition came only from a few agitators. During the first few months of my study, when the Federation had just come into being, it was readily obvious that everyone, from school boys to illiterate

adults, were against Federation. The 1960 "Monckton Report" found
the same attitude after the Federation had been in existence six
years. It reports, "The dislike of Federation among Africans is widespread, sincere and of long standing."[19] The Europeans' ignorance
maintained the barriers surrounding his small world in much the
same way as the refusal of the intransigent African to listen to the
radio protected the small circle of his existence.[20] Then, too, as
Clegg has pointed out, contact with technically backward Africans
has given Europeans a mistaken confidence in their own abilities
and powers, which leads to an unrealistic political attitude.[21]

There are a number of reasons, obvious and subtle, why many
Europeans want to hold on to their traditional identity and keep
the cozy exclusiveness of their small world. Like the African intransigents, their only commitment to change is in raising their
material standards of living, and they fear Africans' competition.
Some of the European managerial group commented that the color
bar kept the incompetent European on the job. The 1959 annual
report of the Department of Labour, as reported in the *Federation
Newsletter,* noted that:

> The advance of the African worker is having a pronounced impact on
> the availability of work for Europeans in Northern Rhodesia. Increasing
> numbers of European school leavers are finding it more difficult each
> year to find employment owing to the inadequacies of their education.
> A youth employment service involving co-operation between the edu-
> cational authorities, the Department of Labour, employers and the parents
> of school leavers was established during the year.
> It was clear, however, that some European youths would be competing
> against African school leavers with comparable and sometimes higher
> academic qualifications.[22]

Europeans were not accustomed to competing economically with
Africans on equal terms. Nevertheless, I do not think the problem
of economic competition is the major one. It is inevitable that the
European incompetents will be weeded out. Although they may
become more bitter and hostile, they are too insignificant politically
to become an issue, and European employers will probably not regret
their exit. Then, too, new opportunities for training and advancement
in skilled jobs were created for Europeans on the mines, at the time
that Africans were advanced into more responsible and skilled jobs.

The most significant problems are political and psychological, and they are closely interwoven. The European settlers have been battling with the Colonial Office for an extension of their political power, at the same time that Britain has been relinquishing its colonies and giving power to Africans. The feeling of the Europeans, therefore, is that they are being "sold down the river" by Britain. This is the culmination of a long-standing feeling against the early British decree of the paramountcy of African interests, and the alleged partiality of district officers and other civil servants toward Africans. The increasing demands of the Africans, the development of their nationalist movement and its victories in other parts of the continent deepened the fears of the European settlers. They, therefore, thought it necessary to gain independence from the Colonial Office quickly, while they were still politically dominant.[23] When the first Federal conference was held in 1948, one of the leading members said quite openly, "The main reason why we need a Federal State in Central Africa is because this will enable us to loosen the grip of the Colonial Office on the Territory."[24] As Clegg writes, the Europeans "struggle to oust the Colonial Office, for the modern concept of Trusteeship, of helping technically backward peoples to bridge the gap between the past and present and fashion a new national synthesis, is equally incompatible with the *sine qua non* of the European community."[25]

It is this new African national synthesis, similar to what I have called the new group identity, which most Europeans resist. They cling to the symbols and the actualities of an old and weakening order because it has given them power. Like the intransigent Africans, they have not the ego strength to move forward into a new order or "take" the anxieties which such change involves for them. They fear they would have no place in a society in which their privileged position and authority over Africans was not maintained by statute. They have no confidence in their ability to learn how to maintain a position through ability and the earned respect of Africans. Like the black intransigents, the personality (the conscious aspects) of the white ones is closely identified with traditional status roles. The European intransigent, like his African opposite number, tends to think in terms of polarities. If the European loses his sense of total identity with his allegedly superior racial group, he is in danger of losing himself.[26] Any such threat may produce for the white man, as well as for the black, heavy drinking, aggressive behavior, violent antipathies, phobias, and other irrationalities.

The concept of partnership between the two races, the alleged basis for the Federation, was never taken seriously by the politically dominant Europeans. The Africans were not to become partners until they had achieved European standards, economically and educationally. It would thus be an extremely long time before the majority of Africans could have the political privilege of a vote. Clegg writes, "In a strictly European context it was as though the two per cent of the population having the highest income in the land should stipulate that no one could enjoy their privileges unless and until they [the Africans] had achieved their 'standards,' and that in the meantime, political power and control over society should be vested exclusively in their persons."[27]

However, the Europeans pledged themselves to raise African standards and made what seemed to them many concessions. Among these were: The federal civil service was opened to all races; segregation was abolished in state-owned railway dining cars; in Northern Rhodesia, discrimination in post offices and in shops ceased; multi-racial clubs were established; in Southern Rhodesia, African professional men could have offices in urban areas previously open only to Europeans.[28] The Europeans were hurt when Africans were still not satisfied and kept demanding more—including the vote for all.

The most frequent reason given by the Europeans for resisting this demand is that the Africans are not sufficiently "responsible" to exercise political power. However, chiefs and kings exercised political responsibilities in the past, and Africa is outstanding among preliterate peoples for its high level of political development. Under the British rule, an increasing number of Africans have been in responsible positions. The Africans' responsibility in running the Native Courts has not been questioned, and both the logic and flexibility of African law has been pointed out by many students of it.[29] Mine management is advancing Africans into responsible jobs. Eventually, the majority of Africans will be literate. In the meantime, there is no certainty that an illiterate person lacks political wisdom, particularly in a society where literacy is a recent innovation. India has universal suffrage in spite of mass illiteracy. On the

Copperbelt I heard illiterate Africans talk with clarity and logic about the issues of the day and the affairs of their own lives. Their illogic was no greater than that of Europeans. Certainly, Africans, from school boys to adults, literate and illiterate, were politically aware.

The Europeans appear to think that anything they do is "responsible" behavior, even when, as in 1961, the Prime Minister boycotted a conference at which he and African representatives were supposed to confer with high British government officials in London. The Prime Minister's sense of responsibility was questionable when, in February of the same year, he called out federal troops in Northern Rhodesia; the action was regarded by many as unnecessary and provocative. He aroused the fears of Europeans by playing up the chaos in the former Belgian Congo after it was given independence, and talked as if the situation would be the same if Africans were given universal suffrage in Northern Rhodesia. He never mentioned the well-known differences between British and Belgium colonial policies or the peaceful transition of former British colonies to independence. He took the initiative, in the latter part of 1961, in the disturbed Congo situation, although constitutionally the Federation's foreign policy is supposed to be determined by Great Britain. The *Rhodesia Herald*'s comment was: "Officially the Federation's foreign policy lies in the hands of the British Government, but . . . the Federation's Prime Minister will act in the manner which he considers to be in the best interest of the Federation—whether Britain likes it or not. . . . Rhodesians to a man must give their loyalty and support to Sir Roy."[30] Constitutionality is usually an essential of political responsibility; the *Rhodesia Herald*'s comment would have probably been quite different if African political leaders had acted outside of a constitution. An African riot because of frustration and because political means of redress are unavailable is regarded as a sign of irresponsibility of all Africans. When some Europeans riot over the desegregation of cafés and movies, no one says this is a sign of the irresponsibility of the white race.

Sir Roy's attitudes are described in detail because he is the Prime Minister of the Federation, head of the party in power, and because for Africans he is *the* symbol for the European dominated Federation. No one questions his political ability or skills, and he is by no means the most conservative of the Europeans. He thinks of himself as a moderate, and there are die-hards to the political right. But he has been singularly inept with Africans, constantly disparaging them. He refers to them at home and abroad as "primitive," a term regarded as insulting by contemporary Africans. In a signed article in the *New York Times* about Nyasaland, he writes that the majority of Africans there are "extremely primitive," citing as proof that the wheel was practically unknown until seventy years ago.[31] The great progress made by Nyasalanders, initially through the educational work of the missions, is not cited, nor is the career of Dr. Hastings Banda, the leader of African Nyasalanders, mentioned. Probably the article was designed as public relations for Americans, but there are many African students, including some from the Federation, in New York; and the African intelligentsia at home as well as abroad know that this is the Prime Minister's opinion of them.

A basic problem for the Prime Minister and many settlers is the same. They are honestly attached to their country. They talk of how they or their parents came as immigrants and worked hard to build the economy and to make a place for themselves and their descendants. Their attitudes are similar to those of the pioneers who settled in North America, and Sir Roy often mentions the analogy, particularly when he complains about the lack of understanding Americans show of the Rhodesian settlers' problems. Granted that the feelings of attachment to the country to which they have migrated are as deep for the Rhodesian settlers as for the American colonists (although there are differences in the two situations), yet even Sir Roy with all his strength cannot move the timetable back several hundred years. The Prime Minister and his followers lack a sense of history and do not know that the present situation demands new, bold thinking. Instead they cling to a past form of racial nationalism. They cannot imagine being part of a community in which they, a small minority, are not politically dominant. They are not able to merge the polarities of European and African in a common identity.

Mr. Kaunda talks of Northern Rhodesian nationalism. But for Europeans the term Northern Rhodesian is reserved for white men. A black man, according to them, is an African and not a Northern Rhodesian. For example, the European Mine Workers' Union is called The Northern Rhodesia Mine Workers' Union, while the Africans belong to the African Mine Workers' Union. To many settlers, *the* people of Central Africa are the one-thirtieth of the population which is European. The European political leaders in power at this writing, represented by Sir Roy, are not an elite in the sense that they can realistically appraise the contemporary crises as a historical event and forge a new style of living, which would include contemporary Africans rather than their ancestors to whom a wheel was unknown.

But a European elite in this psychological sense does exist and the characteristics which they share are a sense of history and an understanding of both the direction and the speed of changes in African society. Among these leaders are Sir John Moffat and Sir Stewart Gore-Browne. Sir John, born in Northern Rhodesia of a distinguished missionary family, is a leader of the Liberal party, which frequently battles for the Africans and endeavors to plan for a transition to African political power in the immediate future, rather than in some far-distant time when presumably every African would be economically and educationally on a par with Europeans. Sir Stewart, a resident of Northern Rhodesia for over forty years, a former member of the colony's Legislative and Executive Councils, has joined the African nationalist movement led by Mr. Kaunda. Behind these and other outstanding men are a minority of Europeans, who may, however, play a significant role because they are not alarmed by the possibility of living in a country where the majority of the population —the Africans—would be politically dominant. Their identity is not cued to a traditional status role based on an accident of birth. They are autonomous men, able to learn from experience, with an awareness of historical and social forces, who have created new styles of coping with the crises of the period in which they live.

Among this European elite are also men who hold high positions in the ownership and management of the copper mines. They are best represented by Sir Ronald Prain, chairman of the Rhodesian Selection Trust. The contrast between his statements and those of Sir Roy are illuminating. Sir Ronald writes: "The determination of indigenous peoples to assume an increasing share in the political affairs of their countries is one of the strongest human and political forces of the 20th century, perhaps the outstanding historical feature of our times. It is a factor which must be faced squarely, and dealt with realistically if changes are to occur on an orderly basis."[32] In

approving the Monckton Report, which was attacked by the United
Federal party, he wrote: "In accepting the general principles, it
does not follow that one is in agreement with every one of the
recommendations, but in my opinion the report is one of the few
realistic documents to appear in relation to these territories, based
as it is on the recognition that in countries where non-whites are in a
majority, the day must come when a majority of the electorate will
be non-white, and that any attempt to preserve a permanent barrier
against this is short-sighted and doomed to failure. No one is sug-
gesting that major changes can be achieved overnight, but the only
realistic course is that major steps towards this should be taken with
a minimum of delay. In the context of Africa today a sense of
urgency leading to bold decisions may well be the course which
contains the least risks."[33]

Sir Roy's philosophy is best expressed in his frank statement: "I
am determined to stop the tide of African nationalism if it lies in
my power."[34] The Europeans in power play for time, some to maintain their power as long as possible or indefinitely, and others to
extend the education and training of Africans. But whatever the
reason, when time is unduly emphasized without a realization of the
Africans' sense of urgency and of the rapid growth of nationalism,
the hostility of the Africans grows stronger and the chances of a
peaceful transition weaken.

Of course, Sir Roy knows that an electorate representing an
African majority would not elect him Prime Minister. On the other
hand there is no reason to think that copper-mining could not function well under a government which represented the majority of
Africans in Northern Rhodesia. The major problem for any industry
is stability of government rather than its complexion. Ownership and
management efforts seem to be directed to strengthening the possi-
bilities for stability in a transition period. In addition to the already
noted policies for speeding up economic advancement for Africans,
increasing their responsibilities in running the mine townships, and
making large financial contributions to African education, they have
also supported and sponsored the seven-year Kafue River project,
designed to open up a million acres of land to agricultural cultiva-
tion. Even more, they recognize African nationalism as a powerful
social movement which cannot be stopped or long held back.

This European elite, whether in politics or in mine ownership, differ from the political leadership represented by the Prime Minister not only in their sense of history and of urgency but apparently in a greater degree of psychological security, permitting them to participate in a more universal group identity, which, as Erikson notes, Western man is developing almost against his will.[35] Similarly, the group identity of the modern African and of their elite, such as Mr. Kaunda, becomes steadily broader. If this new group identity of Africans and of Europeans is sustained economically, politically, and emotionally, then energy may not only be released but also be created for the continued development of civilization in this part of Africa.

TABLES

TABLE 1

Description of Sample Used in Survey

Location			Sex			Place of Birth		
Mine Township	363	66%	Males	286	52%	Rural	468	85%
Municipal Location	188	34	Females	265	48	Urban	83	15
Total	551	100		551	100		551	100

Age Groups			*Education*		
Late Teens	61	11%	None or substandards		
20-30 years	262	48	A and B	326	59%
30-40 years	178	32	Standards I-IV	170	31
40 and over	50	9	Standards V-VI and over	55	10
Total	551	100		551	100

Education According to Sex

	Males (286)		Females (265)	
None or Sub-Standards A and B	125	44%	201	76%
Standards I-IV	114	40	56	21
Standards V-VI and over	47	16	8	3
Total	286	100	265	100

Tribal Groups

Northern Province (Bemba, Bisa, Lala, Lungu, Luunda, Ushi)	199	36%
Eastern Province (Chewa, Chikunda, Kambo-Nsenga, Kunda, Ngoni, Nsenga, Nyanga)	115	21
Western Province (Lamba, Lima, Kaonde)	51	9
Central and Southern Provinces (Ila, Lenje, Soli, Swaka, Toka, Tonga)	31	6
Barotse and Northwestern Province (Lozi, Luchazi, Luvale, Kachokwe, Mbundu)	10	2
Nyasaland (Henga, Tonga, Tumbuka, Yao)	93	17
Foreign (largely from Tanganyika)	52	9
Total	551	100

Church Affiliation*

Free Church and C.M.M.L.	206	37%
Anglican Church	12	2
Watch Tower	59	11
Dutch Reformed Church	49	9
Roman Catholic Church	111	20
African Church	10	2
Seventh Day Adventists	8	1
Mohammedan	7	1
Pagan	89	16
Total	551	99

* The free Church is a rather loose combination of the Methodists, Congregationalists, and Presbyterians who have united in their missionary work in Northern Rhodesia. Grouped with it are also the Christian Missions in Many Lands (C.M.M.L.). Church affiliation does not necessarily mean that the individual is an active member. It may mean that at some time in the past he had a connection with a mission station or school. Also, many Africans claim a membership in a church, whether or not this is technically correct; in this area they would be apt to claim the Free Church.

TABLE 2
Radio Listeners

Place of Listening	Mine	Township		Municipal Location			Total		
Home	36	20%	(178)	14	15%	(96)	50	18%	(274)
Welfare center	102	57	(178)	62	65	(96)	164	69	(274)
Friend's home	40	23	(178)	20	21	(96)	60	22	(274)
Total	178	50	(363)	96	51	(188)	274	50	(551)

	Males			Females			Total		
Home	32	18%	(177)	18	19%	(97)	50	18%	(274)
Welfare center	118	67	(177)	46	47	(97)	164	60	(274)
Friend's home	27	15	(177)	33	34	(97)	60	22	(274)
Total	177	61	(286)	97	37	(265)	274	50	(551)

Age Groups				Place of Birth			
Late teens	40	65%	(61)	Rural	208	45%	(468)
20-30 years	143	54	(262)	Urban	66	79	(83)
30-40 years	73	41	(178)	Total	274	50	(551)
40 and over	18	36	(50)				
Total	274	50	(551)				

Education

None or Sub-standards A and B	119	33%	(326)
Standards I-IV	105	62	(170)
Standards V-VI and over	50	91	(55)
Total	274	50	(551)

Frequency of Listening	Total listeners (274)		Owners of Radio (50)	
Once a week when listener's language is spoken	185	68%	28	56%
3 times a week or more	40	15	15	30
Any time listener has time	49	18	7	14
Total	274	101	50	100

NOTE: Number in parentheses after percentage indicates base number, when it is not quickly obvious.

TABLE 3

Preferred Radio Programs

	Sex		Location		Total	
	Males (177)	Females (97)	Mine (178)	Municipal (96)		
Music and songs	70 40%	62 64%	86 48%	46 48%	132	49%
News*	67 38	18 18	48 27	37 38	85	31
*Zimene Mwatifunsa***	52 29	22 23	53 30	21 22	74	27
Plays	8 5	4 4	7 4	5 5	12	4
Education talks	8 5	3 4	3 2	8 8	11	4
Stories	1 .6	4 4	3 2	2 2	1	.4
Sports	1 .6	0 0	1 .6	0 0	5	2

NOTE: Some of the 274 listeners gave more than one preference, and the most frequent combination was news and music.
* Northern Rhodesian, Central African, District, World.
** Request Program.

TABLE 4

Attendance at the Movies

Sex				Age Group			
Male	187	66%	(286)	Late teens	50	82%	(61)
Female	130	47	(265)	20-30 years	164	63	(262)
				30-40 years	85	48	(178)
				40 and over	18	36	(50)
Total	317	58	(551)	Total	317	58	(551)

Education				Location			
None or Sub-Standards A and B	154	47%	(326)	Mine township	196	54%	(363)
Standards I-IV	121	71	(170)	Municipal location	121	64	(188)
Standards V-VI and over	42	76	(55)				
Total	317	58	(551)	Total	317	58	(551)

Frequency of Attendance		(213)
Once a week	112	53%
Once in two weeks	7	3
Monthly	13	6
Not reporting on frequency	81	38
Total	213	100

NOTE: Number in parentheses after percentage is base number. Of the sample of 551, 317 (58 per cent) have attended the movies at some time, and 213 of the 551 (39 per cent) were attending the movies at the time the survey was made.

TABLE 5

Preferred Films

	(a) *Total*		Males (187)	(b) *According to Sex*	Females (130)	
Cowboy	112	35%	71	38%	40	31%
Superman	47	15	22	12	25	19
British News	29	9	23	12	6	5
African Mirror and Northern Spotlight	14	4	12	6	2	2
Cartoons	19	6	8	4	11	8
Son of Guardsman	15	5				
Chaplin	5	2				
Other farces	5	2				
Religious	4	1				
Education	2	1				
Romance	1	*				
No preference	64	20				
Total	317	100	187	100	130	100

(c) *According to Education*

	None and Sub-Standards A and B (154)		Standards I-IV (121)		Standards V-VI and Over (42)	
Cowboy	40	26%	43	36%	16	39%
Superman	11	7	32	26	4	10
British News	8	5	1	1	11	26
African Mirror and Northern Spotlight	6	4	1	1	3	7
Cartoons	12	8	1	1	0	

NOTE: The data are based on the 317 who were going to the movies at the time of the survey or who had gone at some other time. Only the first five preferences are given in (b) and (c). When the tables were first worked on in Africa, the percentages of the remaining preferences were obviously insignificant and not tabulated on the original tables. The "No preference" was significant; but, unfortunately, the original data on the division of this number according to sex and education have been lost.

* Less than 1 per cent.

TABLE 6

Reasons for Non-Participation in Movie-going or Radio-listening

Not Going to the Movies

Not interested or too lazy*	75	32%
Only for children	52	23
Teaches bad ways of living	39	17
Fear of being beaten on way home	29	12
Would rather drink beer	27	12
Must stay at home**	29	12
Women fear sexual advances	11	5
Women not allowed by husband to go	15	6
No money	17	7
Religion against it	5	2
No reason given	16	7

Not Listening to Radio (277)***

Not interested or too lazy*	163	58%
Too old	25	10
No time	47	19
Prefer to drink beer	17	6
No reason given	25	10
Total	277	50

NOTE: Of the total sample, 234 were not going to the movies. A considerable number gave more than one reason. Percentages are based on 234.

* The two expressions are grouped together because their meaning seemed to be the same for the respondents.

** To take care of children or to keep things from being stolen.

*** This group, half of the total sample of 551, gave only one answer.

TABLE 7

The Readers

Location				Sex			
Mine township	121	33%	(363)	Male	147	51%	(286)
Municipal location	62	33	(188)	Female	36	14	(265)
Total	183	33	(551)	Total	183	33	551)

Education

None or Sub-Standards A and B	0	0	(326)
Standards I-IV	128	23	(170)
Standards V-VI and Over	55	100	(55)
Total	183	33	(551)

NOTE: As already indicated in text (p. 281) the survey of literacy was not usable. Our strong impression was that among the people claiming to be literate were: those who could write only their name; those whose literacy in a vernacular, gained many years ago in the first few years of schooling, had been lost through disuse; those who knew only the alphabet. The survey therefore concentrated on those who were reading now, whether in English or in a vernacular, and could describe something they had read relatively recently.

Number in parentheses after percentage is base number.

TABLE 8

Newspapers and Magazines Read

	Total (183)		Mine Township* (121)		Municipal Location* (62)	
African Eagle	75	41%	52	43	23	37%
Roan Antelope	72	39	64	53	8	13
Northern News	71	38	41	34	30	48
African Weekly	51	28	36	30	15	24
Zonk and Drum	45	24	34	29	11	18
Central African Post	38	21				
Church papers	27	15				
African Miner**	7	4				
Bantu Mirror and Bantu World**	8	5				

NOTE: One hundred eighty-three, or 35 per cent, of the sample read a newspaper or a magazine; and a considerable number read more than one.

* The differences between mine township and municipal location are noted for only the five mostly widely read periodicals. The numbers in the others were too small to be significant.

** The three most popular periodicals are described in Chapter 17; and most of the others, in note 23 of the same chapter. The remaining three which need description are: the *African Miner,* a monthly ten-page mimeographed organ of the African Mine Workers' Union, selling for three pence, which was new at the time of the survey, not attractive in format, and was then reaching very few of the miners; the *Bantu Mirror* and the *Bantu World,* which were published in Southern Rhodesia, and had an extremely small circulation on the Copperbelt.

TABLE 9
Preferred Papers

	Total (183)		Mine Township (121)		Municipal Location (62)	
African Eagle	47	25%	25	21%	22	34%
Roan Antelope	51	28	49	40	2	3
Northern News	48	26	20	17	28	42
African Weekly	24	13	18	15	6	9
Zonk and *Drum*	39	21	30	25	9	14
Central African Post	18	10	16	13	2	3
Church papers	22	12	8	7	14	22

	Sex				*Education**			
	Male (147)		Female (36)		Standards I-IV (128)		Standards V-VI and Over (55)	
African Eagle	42	28%	5	14%	32	25%	14	25%
Roan Antelope	37	25	14	39	43	16	8	14
Northern News	44	30	4	11	18	14	28	50
African Weekly	22	15	2	5	15	12	8	14
Zonk and *Drum*	34	23	5	14	19	16	20	36
Central African Post	18	12	4	11	8	6	10	18
Church papers	14	9	8	22	18	14	2	3

NOTE: *African Miner, Bantu Mirror,* and *Bantu World* are omitted from this list because the division of preferences was not significant for these papers: two persons expressed preference for *Bantu Mirror* and *Bantu World,* and *African Miner* was not selected at all.

Some readers gave more than one preference.

* The group with no education or only Sub-Standards A and B was omitted because the number of readers in it was insignificant.

TABLE 10
Preferred Sections of Paper

News and politics	45	35%
Pictures	20	16
Sports	12	10
Fiction	7	6
Food, health, cooking, and sewing	7	6
Social activities	5	4
Miscellaneous*	28	23
Total	124	100

NOTE: Preferences were expressed by 124 of the 183 readers, and percentages are on the 124 base.

* Miscellaneous included etiquette, advice, and letters to editor.

TABLE 11

Summary of Participation in the Mass Media

		Per Cent of Sample (551)
Reading a paper or magazine (English and/or vernacular)	183	35
Listening to radio	274	50
Going to movies (at time of survey)	213	39
Listening to radio and going to movies	193	35
Reading, listening to radio, and going to movies	122	22

TABLE 12

Territorial Distribution of the Population, 1951-1959
(population in thousands)

Year (at 30th June)	Southern Rhodesia	Northern Rhodesia	Nyasaland	Total for Feder- ation
Europeans				
1951	138	38	4	180
1952	152	42	5	199
1953	157	49	5	211
1954	158	53	5	216
1955	165	58	6	229
1956	178	66	7	251
1957	193	72	7	272
1958	207	72	8	287
1959	215	73	9	297
Average Compound Annual Rate of Increase	5.7%	8.5%	10.7%	6.5%

TABLE 12 *(Continued)*

Territorial Distribution of the Population, 1951-1959

(population in thousands)

Year (at 30th June)	Southern Rhodesia	Northern Rhodesia	Nyasaland	Total for Federation
Africans				
1951	2,080	1,860	2,330	6,270
1952	2,140	1,910	2,370	6,420
1953	2,210	1,960	2,420	6,590
1954	2,270	2,010	2,470	6,750
1955	2,340	2,060	2,530	6,930
1956	2,420	2,110	2,580	7,110
1957	2,480	2,160	2,630	7,270
1958	2,550	2,220	2,690	7,460
1959	2,630	2,280	2,750	7,660
Average Compound Annual Rate of Increase	3.0%	2.6%	2.1%	2.5%
Other Races				
1951	10	4	6	20
1952	11	4	7	22
1953	11	5	8	24
1954	12	6	8	26
1955	13	6	9	28
1956	13	7	10	30
1957	14	8	11	33
1958	15	9	11	35
1959	15	10	12	37
Average Compound Annual Rate of Increase	5.2%	12.1%	9.0%	8.0%

SOURCE: Advisory Commission on the Review of the Constitution of the Federation of Rhodesia and Nyasaland. *Report: Appendix VI, Survey of Developments since 1953,* (Report by Committee of Officials), Her Majesty's Stationery Office, London, 1960, Table 25, p. 327.

TABLE 13

Average African Monthly Wage Rates, Northern Rhodesia

	1953		1954		1955		1956		1957		1958	
	s.	d.	s.	d.	s.	d.	s.	d.	s.	d.	s.	d.
Agriculture												
Farm labourers	55	10	60	10	65	1	71	8	73	11	78	0
Bakeries												
Workers	82	6	89	10	109	5	104	7	107	11	119	2
Building												
Bricklayers	177	7	192	5	210	2	216	11	209	2	201	8
Carpenters	161	0	183	8	197	2	222	6	206	2	205	5
Hotel and Catering												
Waiters	84	6	92	4	116	4	117	1	129	11	141	4
Labourers												
Unskilled	70	9	78	0	93	8	97	2	97	11	101	5
Transport												
Drivers, M. T.	158	9	182	11	212	0	215	3	214	3	251	11
Wholesale and retail												
Shop Assistants	95	0	98	10	102	8	106	7	135	1	187	11
Deliverymen	70	0	78	0	93	0	93	11	104	5	113	9
Tailors	100	0	102	11	110	2	114	6	115	9	142	6
Copper Mines												
Surface	147	11	162	4	211	9	218	5	238	4	294	7
Underground	156	9	173	10	217	7	253	10	262	10	353	9

SOURCE: Advisory Commission on the Review of the Constitution of the Federation of Rhodesia and Nyasaland. *Report: Appendix VI, Survey of Developments since 1953*, (Report by Committee of Officials), Her Majesty's Stationery Office, London, 1960, Table 44, p. 346. The figures shown are based on a twenty-six day month and including rations but excluding the value of housing.

TABLE 14

Importance of Mining in the Federal Economy

Heading	Period	Total for the Federation as a whole	Mining Industry	Percentage of Total Represented by Mining
Gross Investment	1954-58	629,000,000	100,000,000	16
Rhodesia Railways: Tonnage Hauled	1958	10,725,000	6,173,000	58
Electricity Consumption (KWh)	1958	2,956,000,000	1,746,000,000	59
Domestic Exports,* including Gold	1958	138,000,000	94,100,000	68
Africans in Employment**	1956	1,037,343	98,770	10
Europeans Economically Active**	1956	111,778	9,790	9

* The figures cover copper, asbestos, chrome ore, zinc, cobalt, lithium ore, lithium and uranium salts, manganese ore, coal, and gold.

** The figures exclude those employed in refineries.

SOURCE: Advisory Commission on the Review of the Constitution of the Federation of Rhodesia and Nyasaland. *Report: Appendix VI, Survey of Developments since 1953*. (Report by Committee of Officials), Her Majesty's Stationery Office, London, 1960, Table 81, p. 427

TABLE 15

Primary School Enrolment, Northern Rhodesia, 1953-1954 and 1958-59:

(number)

	1953-54	Planned for 1958-59	Actual 1958-59
Sub-Standard A to Standard II	147,822	201,200	200,383
Standards III and IV	20,467	27,800	30,143
Standards V and VI	6,011	13,100	13,400
Total	174,300	242,100	243,926

SOURCE: Advisory Commission on the Review of the Constitution of the Federation of Rhodesia and Nyasaland. *Report: Appendix VI, Survey of Developments since 1953,* (Report by Committee of Officials), Her Majesty's Stationery Office, London, 1960, Table 35, p. 190.

TABLE 16

Secondary School Enrolment: Northern Rhodesia

	Enrolment 1953-54	Enrolment 1958-59
Junior Secondary	433	1,401
Senior Secondary	137	489
Total	570	1,890

SOURCE: Advisory Commission on the Review of the Constitution of the Federation of Rhodesia and Nyasaland. *Report: Appendix VI, Survey of Developments since 1953,* (Report by Committee of Officials), Her Majesty's Stationery Office, London, 1960, Table 38, p. 192.

NOTES

Notes

INTRODUCTION

1. For example, see Herskovits, Melville J., "The African Cultural Background in the Modern Scene" in *Africa Today*, ed. C. Grover Haines, Johns Hopkins Press, Baltimore, 1955, p. 36; and *Continuity and Change in African Cultures*, ed. William R. Bascom and Melville J. Herskovits, University of Chicago Press, Chicago, 1959, *passim*.

2. Richards, Audrey I., "The Village Census in the Study of Culture Contacts," *Methods of Study of Culture Contact in Africa*, International Institute of African Languages and Cultures, Memorandum XV, Oxford University Press, Oxford, 1958, p. 46.

3. Mannheim, Karl, *Ideology and Utopia, An Introduction to the Sociology of Knowledge*, trans. Louis Wirth and Edward Shils, Harcourt, Brace, New York, 1936, pp. 52-53.

4. This is in contrast to field work in the Southwest Pacific and some other parts of the world where educated assistants have been unavailable.

5. Powdermaker, Hortense, "Social Change through Imagery and Values of Teen-age Africans in Northern Rhodesia," *American Anthropologist*, LVIII, 5, 1956, *passim*.

6. The same point has been made recently by Epstein, A. L., "The Network and Urban Social Organization," *The Rhodes-Livingstone Journal*, 1961, pp. 29-62. See also Philip Mayer's *Xhosa in Town, Townsmen or Tribesmen*, Oxford University Press, Capetown, 1961, *passim*.

7. Pool, Ithiel de Sola's review of Erik H. Erikson's *Young Man Luther*, in *Public Opinion Quarterly*, XXIII, 1, 1959, p. 138.

CHAPTER 1

1. Taylor, Ostrander F., "Problems of African Economic Development," *Orbis, A Quarterly Journal of World Affairs,* 1960, IV, 2, 1960, p. 195.

2. Prain, Sir Ronald, Talk to the American Institute of Mining, Metallurgical and Petroleum Engineers, New York City, February 7, 1957.

3. *Hearings on Activities of Private United States Organizations in Africa,* Subcommittee of House Committee on Foreign Affairs, 87th Cong., 1st sess., May 8, 11, 12, 16, 25, and June 1, 1961, p. 33.

In 1959, the population of Northern Rhodesia was approximately 2,280,000 Africans, 73,000 Europeans, and 10,000 of other races (Advisory Commission on the Review of the Constitution of the Federation of Rhodesia and Nyasaland, *Report: Appendix VI, Survey of Developments since 1953,* Her Majesty's Stationery Office, London, 1960, Table 25).

4. Other mines owned by them on the Copperbelt are Mufulira and Chibuluma. Mines owned by the Anglo-American Corporation are Rhokana, Nchanga, and Bancroft.

5. Communication from the African Personnel Department of the Roan Antelope Copper Mines, Ltd.

6. *Ibid.*

7. Rhodesian Selection Trust Froup of Companies, *The African Mine Worker on the Copperbelt of Northern Rhodesia,* Salisbury, 1960, p. 31.

8. Mitchell, Clyde J., *African Urbanization in Ndola and Luanshya,* Rhodes-Livingstone Communication No. 6, 1954, p. 4.

CHAPTER 2

1. Hartmann, Heinz, *Ego Psychology and the Problem of Adaptation,* trans. David Rapaport, International Universities Press, New York, 1958, p. 23.

2. Inkeles, Alex, "Personality and Social Structure," *Sociology Today,* ed. Robert K. Merton, Leonard Broom, and Leonard S. Cottrell, Jr., Basic Books, Inc., New York, 1959, p. 251.

3. *Ibid.,* p. 261.

4. Teilhard de Chardin, Pierre, *The Phenomenon of Man,* trans. Bernard Wall, Harper & Brothers, New York, 1959, *passim.*

5. *Ibid,* Introduction by Julian Huxley, p. 14.

6. Hartmann, p. 43.

7. Herskovits, Melville J., "The African Cultural Background in the Modern Scene," *Africa Today,* ed. C. Grove Haines, Johns Hopkins Press, Baltimore, 1955, p. 36.

8. Smelser, Neil J., *Social Change in the Industrial Revolution,* Chicago University Press, 1959, p. 2, and *passim* for the study of industrial differentiation. See also Weber, Max, "Bureaucracy" *From Max Weber: Essays in Sociology,* trans. ed., and with an introduction by H. H. Gerth

and C. Wright Mills, Kegan Paul, Trench, Trubner & Co., London, 1947, pp. 198-199.

9. Redfield, Robert, *The Primitive World and Its Transformations,* Ithaca, 1953, pp. 20-22.

10. Frank, Lawrence K., "Cultural Implications of Man in Space," *Annals of the New York Academy of Sciences,* LXXII, 4, 1958, p. 199.

11. "Scale" is the term used by Godfrey and Monica Wilson in their *Analysis of Social Change;* their criteria for it include the number of people in relationship to each other and the intensity of the relationship, (first published 1945) Cambridge University Press, Cambridge, England, 1954, pp. 24-30.

12. See Boulding, Kenneth, *The Image,* University of Michigan Press, 1956, pp. 47-63, for changes in imagery of time and space.

13. Wilson, p. 9.

14. Cf. Fallers, L. A., "Despotism, Status Culture and Social Mobility in an African Kingdom," *Comparative Studies in Society and History,* II, 1, 1958, pp. 11-32.

15. See Robinson, Ronald, Gallagher, John, and Denney, Alice, *Africa and the Victorians,* MacMillan, London, 1960.

16. Herskovits, p. 36.

17. Chardin, pp. 165-168; see also Boulding, pp. 47-63.

18. For a technical discussion of progressive and regressive adaptation, see Hartmann, p. 402.

19. Cf. Smelser, p. 402.

20. Axelrad, Sidney, and Maury, M., "Identification as a Mechanism of Adaptation," *Psychoanalysis and Culture,* ed. George B. Wilbur and Warner Muensterberger, International Universities Press, New York, 1951. pp. 168-174.

21. Erikson, Erik H., "The Problem of Ego Identity," *Identity and the Life Cycle, Selected Papers by Erik H. Erikson, Psychological Issues,* Vol. I, No. 1, 1959, p. 89.

22. *Ibid.,* pp. 111-113.

23. See Moore, Wilbert E., and Feldman, Arnold S., *Labor Commitment and Social Change in Developing Areas,* Social Science Research Council, New York, 1960, p. 1-12, 67, and *passim.*

24. Erikson, "Ego Development and Historical Change," *Identity and the Life Cycle,* p. 44.

25. Axelrad, and Maury, p. 172.

26. Erikson, "The Problem of Ego Identity," p. 125.

CHAPTER 3

1. The historical data in this chapter represents a synthesis from reading most of the published pertinent data on the tribal past in Northern Rhodesia and on some of the Nyasaland tribes. The references below are the major ones on which the synthesis is based.

The sources most heavily relied on for historical data are:

BARNES, J. A., "Some Aspects of Political Development Among the Fort Jameson Ngoni," *African Studies*, VII, 2-3, June-September, 1948.

————, (a), "History in a Changing Society," *Rhodes-Livingstone Journal*, XI, 1951.

————, (b), "The Fort Jameson Ngoni," *Seven Tribes of British Central Africa*, ed. ELIZABETH COLSON and MAX GLUCKMAN, Oxford University Press, London, 1951.

————, (c), *Marriage in a Changing Society*, Rhodes-Livingstone Paper, No. 20, 1951.

————, *Politics in a Changing Society*, Oxford University Press, London, 1954.

BRELSFORD, W. V., *Fishermen of the Bangweulu Swamps*, Rhodes-Livingstone Institute Papers No. 12, 1946.

————, *The Succession of Bemba Chiefs*, 2nd ed. The Government Printer, Lusaka, 1949.

————, *The Tribes of Northern Rhodesia*, The Government Printer, Lusaka, 1957.

CIBAMBO, Y. M., *My Ngoni of Nyasaland*, United Society for Christian Literature, London, 1942.

COILLARD, F., *On the Threshold of Central Africa*, Hodder and Stoughton, London, 1897.

COLSON, ELIZABETH, "The Plateau Tonga of Northern Rhodesia," *Seven Tribes of British Central Africa*, ed. ELIZABETH COLSON and MAX GLUCKMAN, Oxford University Press, London, 1951.

————, "Every Day Life Among the Cattle-keeping Plateau Tonga," *Rhodes-Livingstone Museum Papers*, N. S. No. 9, 1953.

————, *Marriage and the Family Among the Plateau Tonga of Northern Rhodesia*, Manchester University Press, Manchester, Eng., 1958.

COXHEAD, J. C., *The Native Tribes of Northern Rhodesia*, Royal Anthropological Institute, Occasional Papers, No. 5, London, 1914.

CUNNISON, I., *History on the Luapula*, Rhodes-Livingstone Papers No. 21, 1951.

————, "Headmanship and the Ritual of Luapula Villages," *Africa*, XXVI, 1956.

————, "Perpetual Kinship: A Political Institution of the Luapula peoples," *Rhodes-Livingstone Journal*, XX, 1956.

FORTES, N., and EVANS-PRITCHARD, E. E., "Introduction," *African Political Systems*, ed. M. FORTES and E. E. EVANS-PRITCHARD, 3rd ed., Oxford University Press, London, 1948.

GANN, L. H., "The End of the Slave Trade in British Central Africa," *Rhodes-Livingstone Journal*, XVI, 1954.

————, *The Birth of a Plural Society*, University of Manchester Press, Manchester, Eng., 1958.

GLUCKMAN, MAX, *Economy of the Central Barotse Plain*, Rhodes-Livingstone Institute Papers No. 7, 1941.

————, "Kinship and Marriage among the Lozi of Northern Rhodesia and the Zulu in Natal," *African Systems of Kinship and Marriage*, ed. A. R. RADCLIFFE-BROWN and C. D. FORDE, Oxford University Press, London, 1950.

————, "The Lozi of Barotseland in North-Western Rhodesia," *Seven Tribes of British Central Africa*, ed. ELIZABETH COLSON and MAX GLUCKMAN, Oxford University Press, London, 1951.

————, (a), *The Judicial Process Among the Barotse of Northern Rhodesia*, Free Press, Glencoe, 1955.

————, (b), *Custom and Conflict in Africa*, Free Press, Glencoe, 1955.

GOULDSBURY, C., and SHEANE, H., *The Great Plateau of Northern Rhodesia*, Edwin Arnold, London, 1911.

HANNA, A. J., *The Story of the Rhodesias and Nyasaland*, Faber and Faber, London, 1960.

MAIR, L. P., "Survey of African Marriage and Family Life," *African Marriage and Social Change*, ed. ARTHUR PHILLIPS, Oxford University Press, London, 1953.

MITCHELL, J. C., with M. GLUCKMAN and J. A. BARNES, "The British Headman in British Central Africa," *Africa*, XIX, 2, April 1949.

————, "The Yao of Southern Nyasaland," *Seven Tribes of British Central Africa*, ed. ELIZABETH COLSON and MAX GLUCKMAN, Oxford University Press, London, 1951.

————, *African Urbanization in Ndola and Luanshya*, Rhodes-Livingstone Communication No. 6, 1954.

————, *The Yao Village*, Manchester University Press, Manchester, Eng., 1956.

READ, MARGARET, "The Moral Code of the Ngoni and their Former Military State," *Africa*, XI, 1938, pp. 1-24.

————, *Native Standards of Living and African Cultural Change*, Memorandum XVI, International African Institute, London, 1938.

————, *The Ngoni of Nyasaland*, Oxford University Press, London, 1956.

————, *Children of their Fathers*, Yale University Press, New Haven, 1960.

RICHARDS, A. I.: "Mother-right among the Central Bantu," *Essays Presented to C. G. Seligman*, ed. E. E. EVANS-PRITCHARD, R. FIRTH, B. MALINOWSKI, and I. SCHAPERA, Kegan, Paul, London, 1933.

————, "The Life of Bwembya, A Native of Northern Rhodesia," *Ten Africans*, ed. M. PERHAM, Faber and Faber, London, 1936.

————, *Hunger and Work in a Savage Tribe*, Free Press, Glencoe, 1948.

————, "Variations in Family Structure among the Central Bantu," *African Systems of Kinship and Marriage*, ed., A. R. RADCLIFFE-BROWN and C. D. FORDE, Oxford University Press, London, 1950.

————, *Land, Labour and Diet in Northern Rhodesia*, (first published 1939), 2nd ed., Oxford University Press, London, 1951.

————, "The Political System of the Bemba of North-Eastern Rhodesia," *African Political Systems*, M. Fortes and E. E. Evans-Pritchard, eds., (first published 1940), Oxford University Press, London, 1955.

————, *Chisungu, A Girl's Initiation Ceremony Among the Bemba of Northern Rhodesia,* Grove Press, New York, 1956.

SMITH, E. W., and DALE, A. M., *The Ila Speaking People of Northern Rhodesia,* 2 vols., Macmillan, New York, 1920.

TUDEN, ARTHUR, "Ila Slavery," *Rhodes-Livingstone Journal,* XXIV, December 1958.

WILSON, GODFREY, "An African Morality," *Africa,* IX, 1936.

WILSON, MONICA, *Good Company: A Study of Nyakusa Age-Villages,* Oxford University Press, London, 1951.

In the theoretical discussion of the instability of African marriage, indebtedness is primarily to:

BARNES, J. A. "Measures of Divorce Frequency in Simple Societies," *Journal of the Royal Anthropological Institute,* LXXIX, 1949.

FALLERS, L. A., "Some Determinants of Marriage Stability in Busoga: A Reformulation of Gluckman's Hypothesis," *Africa,* XXVII, 2, April 1957.

GLUCKMAN, MAX: "Kinship and Marriage among the Lozi of Northern Rhodesia and the Zulu of Natal," *African Systems of Kinship and Marriage,* ed. A. R. RADCLIFFE-BROWN and C. D. FORDE, Oxford University Press, London, 1950.

————, *Custom and Conflict in Africa,* Free Press, Glencoe, 1955, Chap. 3.

HOMANS, GEORGE C., and SCHNEIDER, DAVID M., *Marriage, Authority and Final Causes,* Free Press, Glencoe, 1956.

SCHNEIDER, DAVID M., "A Note on the Bridewealth and the Stability of Marriage," *Man,* LIII, April 1953.

For the theoretical concepts concerned with the relation of ritualized etiquette to rank and power, indebtedness is primarily to:

COHEN, YEHUDI, "Some Aspects of Ritualized Behavior in Interpersonal Relationships," *Human Relations,* XI, 3, 1958.

LINTON, RALPH, *The Study of Man,* Appleton-Century, New York, 1936.

MERTON, ROBERT, *Social Theory and Social Structure,* rev. and enlarged ed., Free Press, Glencoe, 1957, Chap. VI.

For data on judicial procedure, the reliance is primarily on:

EPSTEIN, A. L., "Some Aspects of the Conflict of Law and Urban Courts in Northern Rhodesia," *Rhodes-Livingstone Journal,* XII, 1951.

————, "The Role of the African Courts in Urban Communities of the Copperbelt in Northern Rhodesia," *Rhodes-Livingstone Journal,* XIII, 1953.

————, *Juridical Techniques and the Judicial Process,* Rhodes-Livingstone Papers, No. 23, 1954.

——, "Divorce Law and the Stability of Marriage among the Lunda of Kazembe," *Rhodes-Livingstone Journal*, XIV, 1954.

Specific footnotes are for quotes, references to authorities other than those cited above, and comparative material:

2. Mitchell, 1951, p. 308.
3. Quoted in Gann, 1958, p. 14.
4. Powdermaker, Hortense, "Social Change through Imagery and Values of Teen-Age Africans in Northern Rhodesia," *American Anthropologist*, LVIII, 5, October 1956, pp. 800-806.
5. Powdermaker, Hortense, *Life in Lesu: The Study of a Melanesian Society in New Ireland*, W. W. Norton, New York, 1933, *passim*.
6. A lineage consists of an original male or female ancestor, depending on whether descent is patrilineal or matrilineal, and all the descendants through males or females. The lineage group is all the members alive at a given time. A clan is formed on the same principle but is larger than a lineage; in the latter, a member can usually trace his relationship with other members from the common ancestor, but in the clan this has to be assumed (Radcliffe-Brown, A. R., "Introduction," *African Systems of Kinship and Marriage*, ed. A. R. Radcliffe-Brown and Daryll Forde, 3rd ed., Oxford University Press, London, 1956, pp. 14, 39-40).
7. Barnes, 1951 (b), pp. 220-221.
8. Colson, 1958, p. 102.
9. Among the exceptions to this practice were the Cewa, who had large villages and who practiced cross-cousin marriage; among the Plateau and Valley Tonga intravillage marriage was also common.
10. Mair, 1953, pp. 99-100.
11. Barnes, 1951 (c) p. 116.
12. Fallers, 1957, p. 113.
13. Powdermaker, *Life in Lesu*, pp. 150-151.
14. Gluckman, 1955 (a), p. 138.
15. Gluckman, 1955 (b), pp. 30-31.
16. Richards, 1951, p. 214.
17. Cohen, Yehudi A., "Food and Its Vicissitudes: A Cross-Cultural Study of Sharing and Nonsharing," *Social Structure and Personality*, ed. Yehudi A. Cohen, Holt, Rinehart and Winston, New York, 1961, pp. 312-341.
18. Richards, 1951, p. 29.
19. This same point is made for the Spanish-speaking people in northern New Mexico in an unpublished paper by Rudolph Kieve, "The Meaning and Use of Illness and Disability among Spanish-speaking People in Northern New Mexico," Fourth Western Divisional Meeting of the American Psychiatric Association, Salt Lake City, Utah, September 21, 1961.
20. Cohen, Yehudi A., "Some Aspects of Ritualized Behavior in Interpersonal Relationships," *Human Relations*, XI, 3, 1958, *passim*.

21. Field, M. J., *Search for Security: An Ethno-Psychiatric Study of Rural Ghana*, Northwestern University Press, Evanston, 1960, p. 38.

22. *Ibid.*, p. 87.

23. *Ibid.*, p. 116.

24. Nadel, S. F., "Witchcraft in Four African Societies: An Essay in Comparison," in *American Anthropologist*, LIV, 1, January-March 1952, p. 29.

25. Turner, W. W., *Schism and Continuity in an African Society: A Study of Ndembu Village Life*, Manchester University Press, Manchester, Eng., 1957, p. 294.

26. Bohannan, Paul (ed.), *African Homicide and Suicide*, Princeton University Press, Princeton, 1960, pp. 266, 252-262.

27. Erikson, Erik H., "Growth and Crises of the Healthy Personality," *Identity and the Life Cycle, Selected Papers by Erik H. Erikson, with a Historical Introduction by David Rapaport, Psychological Issues*, I, 1, 1959, p. 52.

28. Richards, 1948, pp. 40-41.

29. Colson, 1958, pp. 238-239.

30. Read, 1960, p. 59.

31. Kieve, in his unpublished paper on the Spanish-speaking peoples in northern New Mexico (see note 19) writes, "The conscious aspect of each personality was so nearly identified with his role that individuality as we know it could not come into being through mental activities such as the gaining and utilizing of experiences but only through the manifestation of temperament, of idiosyncracies of behavior, of powerful empathies, of phobias and other individualizing irrationalities" (p. 7). The situation was not too dissimilar among the tribal Africans described in this chapter.

32. For this point of view about African personality, see Ritchie, J. F., *The African as Suckling and as Adult*, Rhodes-Livingstone Paper, No. 9, 1943, *passim*.

33. Field, p. 28.

CHAPTER 4

1. The major indebtedness for the historical data in this chapter, unless otherwise indicated, is to Gann, L. H., *The Birth of a Plural Society: The Development of Northern Rhodesia under the British South Africa Company, 1894-1914*, Manchester University Press, Manchester, Eng., 1958.

2. Gann, p. 37.

3. Cf. Carpenter, George W., "The Role of Christianity and Islam in Contemporary Africa," *Africa Today*, ed. C. Grove Haines, Johns Hopkins Press, Baltimore, 1955, pp. 101-107.

4. Shepperson, George, and Price, Thomas, *Independent African: John Chilembwe and the Origins, Setting and Significance of the Nyasaland*

Native Rising of 1915, Edinburgh University Press, Edinburgh, 1959, p. 421.

5. *Ibid.,* pp. 421-422.

6. Cohen, Andrew, *British Policy in Changing Africa,* Routledge and Kegan Paul, London, 1959, p. 9.

7. Gann, p. 76.

8. *Ibid.,* p. 145.

9. *Ibid.,* p. 151.

10. Mair, L., "African Chiefs Today," *Africa,* XXVIII, 3, July 1958, p. 195. Unless otherwise indicated, the description of the Native Authority System is based on this article.

11. *Ibid.,* p. 196.

12. *Ibid.,* p. 197.

13. Great Britain, *Parliament Sessional Papers,* 1923. 17. (Cad. 1922).

14. Cohen, p. 22.

15. *Northern Rhodesian African Representative Council, 1947,* The Government Printer, Lusaka, No. 2, p. 81.

16. *Ibid.,* p. 35.

17. Barnes, J. A., "History in a Changing Society," *Rhodes-Livingstone Institute Journal,* XI, 1951, p. 3.

18. Mitchell, J. C., *The Yao Village,* Manchester University Press, Manchester, Eng., 1956, p. 38.

19. Cunnison, Ian, *History of the Luapula,* Rhodes-Livingstone Papers, 21, 1951, pp. 27-28.

20. Shepperson and Price, p. 9.

21. *Northern Rhodesian African Representative Council, 1948,* The Government Printer, Lusaka, No. 3, pp. 37-38.

22. *Ibid.,* p. 10.

23. Powdermaker, Hortense, "Communication and Social Change Based on a Field Study in Northern Rhodesia," *Transactions of the New York Academy of Sciences,* Ser. II, Vol. 17, No. 5, March 1955, pp. 437-439.

24. *New York Times,* February 6, 1960.

CHAPTER 5

1. The data on the Europeans in this and in the following chapter are more or less restricted to those factors which influence their relations with Africans.

2. *Census of Population, 1956, Federation of Rhodesia and Nyasaland,* Central Statistical Office, Salisbury, 1960, p. 7.

3. *Ibid.,* p. 62, Table 20.

4. This stereotype does not seem to be held by Africans outside of the Copperbelt. Dr. Elizabeth Colson in a personal communication writes that although there were Afrikaaners farming in the Masabuka district in Northern Rhodesia where she worked, they were almost invariably

grouped with other Europeans by Africans. Dr. L. A. Fallers makes the same point, also in a personal communication, for Uganda.

5. Franck, Thomas M., *Race and Nationalism: The Struggle for Power in Rhodesia-Nyasaland,* Fordham University Press, New York, 1960, pp. 3, 243-245.

6. *Ibid.,* p. 3, 134.

7. *Ibid.,* p. 134.

8. *Ibid.,* pp. 239-243.

9. Press release of the National Institute for Personnel Research in Johannesburg, December 30, 1960.

10. Cole, D. T., "Fanagalo and the Bantu Languages in South Africa," *African Studies,* XII, 1, 1953, pp. 1-9. See also Epstein, A. L., "Linguistic Innovation and Culture on the Copperbelt, Northern Rhodesia," *Southwestern Journal of Anthropology,* XV, 3, 1959, pp. 236-237.

11. This concept of projection is quite familiar, and much work has been done in the United States which demonstrates its role in prejudice. See, for example, Adorno, T. W. *et al., The Authoritarian Personality,* Harper & Brothers, New York 1950, *passim.*

12. *Hearings on Activities of Private United States Organizations in Africa,* Subcommittee of House Committee on Foreign Affairs, 87th Cong., 1st sess., May 8, 11, 12, 16, and June 1, 1961, pp. 45-46.

CHAPTER 6

1. In this chapter only economic aspects of African life are stressed. Marriage, family life, leisure time, political freedom, and other aspects of Copperbelt life are discussed in subsequent chapters.

2. Mitchell, J. Clyde, *African Urbanization in Ndola and Luanshya,* Rhodes-Livingstone Communication No. 6, roneoed, Lusaka, 1954, Table V, p. 7.

3. *Hearings on Activities of Private United States Organizations in Africa,* Subcommittee of House Committee on Foreign Affairs, 87th Cong., 1st sess., May 8, 11, 12, 16, and June 1, 1961, p. 36.

4. *Northern Rhodesia Chamber of Mines Year Book, 1960,* Salisbury, 1961, Table XXI, p. 36.

5. Rhodesian Selection Trust Group of Companies, *The African Mine Worker on the Copperbelt of Northern Rhodesia,* Salisbury, 1960, p. 15.

6. *Hearings,* p. 45.

7. *Ibid.,* p. 37.

8. *Federation of Rhodesia and Nyasaland Newsletter,* Washington, D.C., November 11, 1960.

9. *Ibid.*

10. Rhodesian Selection Trust Group of Companies, pp. 21-22.

11. *Roan Antelope,* August 5, 1961, p. 1.

12. *Northern Rhodesia Chamber of Mines Year Book, 1960,* p. 35.

13. *Ibid.,* p. 31.

14. Northern Rhodesian Selection Trust Group of Companies, pp. 16-17.

15. Gouldsbury, Cullen, and Sheane, Hubert, *The Great Plateau of Northern Rhodesia,* Edwin Arnold, London, 1911, p. 251.

16. Richards, A. I., *Land, Labour and Diet in Northern Rhodesia,* Oxford University Press, London, 1939, p. 217.

17. *Hearings,* p. 36.

18. Mitchell, p. 19.

19. *Ibid.,* p. 20.

20. Rhodesian Selection Trust Group of Companies, pp. 17-18.

21. Powdermaker, Hortense, "Social Change through Imagery and Values of Teen-age Africans in Northern Rhodesia," *American Anthropologist,* LVIII, 5, October 1956, pp. 799-801.

CHAPTER 7

1. Epstein, A. L., *Politics in an Urban African Community,* Manchester University Press, Manchester, 1958, pp. 123-127.

2. *Ibid.,* pp. 126-127.

3. Epstein's book, as the title indicates, is mainly concerned with politics in the mine community, and his excellent discussion of the African Mine Workers' Union is in this context. He gives no attention to the welfare activities of management.

4. Personal communication from Welfare Section, African Personnel Department, Roan Antelope Copper Mines, Ltd., 1958.

5. Roan Antelope Copper Mines, Ltd., "Notes on African Education," March 3, 1955, p. 5.

6. Rhodesian Selection Trust Group of Companies, *The African Mine Workers in the Copperbelt of Northern Rhodesia,* Salisbury, 1960, p. 37.

7. *Ibid.,* pp. 34-36.

8. Roan Antelope Copper Mines, Ltd., *African Personnel Department, Welfare Section Report,* 1958, pp. 3, 10, 11.

9. Powdermaker, Hortense, "Social Change through Imagery and Values of Teen-age Africans in Northern Rhodesia," *American Anthropologist,* LVIII, 5, October 1956, pp. 799-801.

10. Data on the history of the African Mine Workers' Union and on the system which preceded it is from Epstein, unless otherwise indicated.

11. *Roan Antelope,* No. 60, March 1958, p. 1.

12. *Ibid.,* No. 115, July 9, 1960, p. 7.

13. Epstein, p. 112.

14. *Hearings on Activities of Private United States Organizations in Africa,* Subcommittee of House Committee on Foreign Affairs, 87th Cong. 1st Sess., May 8, 11, 12, 16, 2nd June 1, 1961, p. 44.

15. Personal communication from African Personnel Department,

Roan Antelope Copper Mines, Ltd.

16. Epstein, p. 129.

17. Personal communication from African Personnel Department, Roan Antelope Copper Mines, Ltd.

18. *Ibid.*

19. *Northern Rhodesia Chamber of Mines Year Book, 1960,* Kitwe, 1961, p. 38, Table 23.

20. *Roan Antelope,* June 11, 1960, p. 1.

21. Cf. *Hearings,* p. 38.

CHAPTER 8

1. The description of this strike, the only one which occurred during my study, is from conversations recorded while it was in progress (see Introduction for method of recording conversations). The names of those participating in the conversations are all fictitious, but are representative of the tribes to which the participants belong. Members of some tribes use clan surnames. First names are usually English ones. Since married women keep their own surnames and do not take their husbands', it is less confusing to designate them in the conversations by their first name. Parents are frequently referred to as "Father of —— " and "Mother of —— ". The prefixes for male and female vary according to the vernacular language, and it has therefore seemed better to use the uniform English prefixes of *Mr.* and *Mrs.*

2. The Lozi have a saying that a chief was supposed to have only one subject who demanded immediate attention. The union may have transferred this attitude to the general manager of the mine.

3. The president's remark might be interpreted as an indirect boast that the uneducated miners are more virile sexually than the educated Africans. He belonged to the intelligentsia, and possibly he was trying to win over the uneducated men, who had recently elected an illiterate man as their chairman. The word *marry* in his remarks probably refers to extramarital relations as well as to marriage.

4. Mr. Katilungu, the president of the African Mine Workers' Union at the time of this strike, was considered a moderate leader who usually lived up to the contractual agreements between union and management. As he stated in an earlier speech, he had not been consulted in advance about the strike and heard of it only through a government labor office. According to the intelligentsia, he had to support the belligerent chairman out of fear of losing the support of the local. But since he knew the local's complaint did not come within the contract with management and that the strike was illegal, he had obviously worked to change the alleged issue. His threat to call out the other mines may have been window-dressing to demonstrate to the members of the local that he, too, could be warlike. He was apparently trying to control the situation, and it seems to have been his influence which ended the outlaw strike.

CHAPTER 9

1. There is relatively little published information on family life on the Copperbelt.

Clyde Mitchell's excellent survey in 1951 of marriage on the Copperbelt gives significant statistics of marriage and divorce but was limited on the problems considered (Mitchell, J. Clyde, "Aspects of African Marriage on the Copperbelt of Northern Rhodesia," *Rhodes-Livingstone Journal*, XXII, September 1957).

Godfrey Wilson's study in 1939-1940 of the economics of detribalization in the town of Broken Hill (a short distance from Luanshya) has a valuable but relatively brief section on marriage (Wilson, Godfrey, *An Essay on the Economics of Detribalization in Northern Rhodesia,"* Parts I and II, Rhodes-Livingstone Papers Nos. 5 and 6, 1941, 1942).

An early study by Audrey Richards on Bemba marriage included only some comments about marriage on the Copperbelt (Richards, Audrey, *Bemba Marriage and Present Economic Conditions,"* Rhodes-Livingstone Papers No. 4, 1940).

Elizabeth Colson's excellent structural study of marriage and the family among the agricultural Plateau Tonga offers interesting points for comparison with the family on the Copperbelt but obviously no data on the latter (Colson, Elizabeth, *Marriage and the Family among the Plateau Tonga of Northern Rhodesia,* University of Manchester Press, Manchester, Eng. 1958).

J. A. Barnes' early study of Ngoni marriage also offers comparative material: (Barnes, J. A., *Marriage in a Changing Society,* Rhodes-Livingstone Papers, No. 20, 1951).

Max Gluckman, Audrey Richards, Margaret Read, and many other authors cited in Chapter 3 give detailed information about family life in the tribes they studied some time ago, but there is no comparable data for the Copperbelt.

Mair gives an excellent summary of African marriage and social change, as of the late forties, but with little data for the Copperbelt (Mair, L. P.: "African Marriage and Social Change" in *Survey of African Marriage and Family Life,* ed. Arthur Phillips, Oxford University Press, London, 1953).

2. Cf. Wilson, 1942, p. 40.

3. Mitchell, p. 21.

4. Phillips, Arthur, "Marriage Laws in Africa," *Survey of African Marriage and Family Life,* ed. by Arthur Phillips, p. 242.

5. Mitchell, p. 2.

6. Wilson, 1941, p. 21.

7. However, data on this point for the traditionalists is quite incomplete, and this is one of the many problems on which further research should be done.

8. Colson, pp. 118-119.

9. Wilson, 1942, p. 64.

10. Mitchell, p. 13.

11. *Ibid.*, p. 16.

12. Wilson, 1942, p. 41.

13. Mitchell, p. 8.

14. *Ibid.*, pp. 10-11.

15. Wilson, 1942, p. 41.

16. Mitchell, p. 5.

17. The same type of jealousy and marital insecurity was found in the township of Kisenyi, part of Kampala, in Uganda (See Southall, A. W., and Gutkind, P. C. W., *Townsmen in the Making,* East African Studies, No. 9, mimeographed, East African Institute of Social Research, Kampala, 1956, p. 79).

18. Cf. *Ibid.*, p. 106.

19. A study should be done to ascertain the degree of correlation between stability of marriage and education, income, type of job, intratribal and intertribal marriage.

20. Epstein, A. L., "The Role of the African Courts in Urban Communities of the Northern Rhodesian Copperbelt," *Rhodes-Livingstone Journal,* XIII, 1953, pp. 1-17.

21. Epstein, A. L., *Judicial Techniques and the Judicial Processes,* Rhodes-Livingstone Papers No. 32, 1953, p. 37.

CHAPTER 11

1. Powdermaker, Hortense, "Social Change through Imagery and Values of Teen-Age Africans in Northern Rhodesia," *American Anthropologist,* LVIII, 5, October 1956, pp. 804-806.

2. *Ibid.*, pp. 799-801.

3. See Reed, Stephen W., "World Population Trends," *Most of the World,* ed. Ralph Linton, Columbia University Press, New York, 1949, p. 11.

4. Powdermaker, pp. 800-801.

5. *Ibid.*, p. 784.

6. *Ibid.*, pp. 799-801.

7. Cf. Colson, Elizabeth, *Marriage and the Family Among the Plateau Tonga of Northern Rhodesia,* Manchester University, Manchester, Eng., 1958, *passim.*

8. However, there are other situations in rural areas where the husband is absent, in which the woman becomes more or less the head of the household and the ties with lineage are strengthened. This point was made by Elizabeth Colson in an unpublished paper, "Family Change in Contemporary Africa," read at a conference, "Anthropology and Africa" held at the New York Academy of Sciences, May 1-3, 1961.

9. Powdermaker, p. 794.

10. Powdermaker, Hortense, *After Freedom, A Cultural Study in the Deep South,* Viking Press, New York, 1939, p. 367.

CHAPTER 13

1. Epstein, A., "Some Aspects of the Conflict of Law and Urban Courts in Northern Rhodesia," *Rhodes-Livingstone Journal,* XII, 1951.
2. Gluckman, Max, *The Judicial Process Among the Barotse of Northern Rhodesia,* Free Press, Glencoe, 1955.

CHAPTER 14

1. This deficiency has been noted by Keesing (see Keesing, Felix M., "Recreative Behavior and Culture Change," *Selected Papers of the Fifth International Congress of Anthropological and Ethnological Sciences, September 1-9,* 1956, University of Pennsylvania Press, Philadelphia, pp. 130-133).
2. Radcliffe-Brown, A. R., *The Andaman Islanders,* Cambridge University Press, 1933, *passim.*
3. Kroeber, Alfred L., *Anthropology,* rev. ed., Harcourt, Brace, New York, 1948, p. 29.
4. Malinowski, Bronislaw, "Culture," *Encyclopedia of the Social Sciences,* IV, Macmillan, 1931, 642-643.
5. Kaplan, Max, *Leisure in America: A Social Inquiry,* John Wiley and Sons, New York, 1960.
6. Denney, Reuel, *The Astonished Muse,* University of Chicago Press, Chicago, 1957, *passim.*
7. Kaplan, p. 4.
8. Pieper, Josef, *Leisure the Basis of Culture,* Faber and Faber, London, 1952, pp. 54-55.
9. Huizinga, Johan, *Homo Ludens, A Study of the Play Element in Culture,* Beacon Press, London, 1955, pp. 20-21.
10. Doob, Leonard, *Communication,* Yale University Press, New Haven, 1961, describes other forms of tribal communication through drums, dances, physical movements, personal adornments, etc.
11. Hoggart, Richard, *The Uses of Literacy. Aspects of Working Class Life with Special Reference to Publications and Entertainments,* Penguin, London, 1958, p. 81.
12. Cf. Innis, Harold A., *The Bias of Communication,* University of Toronto Press, Toronto, Can., 1951, pp. 191-192.
13. Riesman, David, *The Oral Tradition, the Written Word, and the Screen Image,* Antioch College Founders Day Lecture, No. 1, Antioch Press, Yellow Springs, 1956, p. 34.
14. *Ibid.,* pp. 27-28.
15. Herskovits, Melville J., "The African Cultural Background in the

Modern Scene," *Africa Today,* ed. C. Grove Haines, Johns Hopkins Press, Baltimore, 1955, pp. 43-44.

16. The term "life-style" is used in this way in a study of leisure in contemporary Western society by Havinghurst, Robert J., and Feinenbaum, K., "Leisure and Life-Style," *American Journal of Sociology,* LXIV, 4, January 1959, pp. 396-404.

CHAPTER 15

1. Franklin, H., *Report on the Development of Broadcasting to Africans in Central Africa,* Government Printer, Lusaka, 1949, p. 7.

2. *Ibid.,* pp. 1-6.

3. Statistical data, unless otherwise indicated, is from my initial survey with its random sample of 551. Tables are given in the Appendix.

4. Fraenkel, Peter, *Wayleshi,* Weidenfeld and Nicolson, London, 1959, p. 23.

5. *Ibid.,* p. 34.

6. In an unpublished study by Peter Fraenkel and C. Clyde Mitchell, "Some Factors in the Comprehensibility of English Broadcasts to African Listeners," the results suggest that the English spoken by an African announcer is more easily understood by Africans, but that the majority preferred English announcers because they thought they could better learn the correct English pronounciation from them.

7. In 1960, the Federal Broadcasting Corporation increased the number of broadcasting hours to Africans to two hundred; the programs were in nine African languages and in English (*Federation of Rhodesia and Nyasaland Newsletter,* Washington, D. C., November 14, 1960, p. 14).

8. The data on the remembering of news comes from the longer and more detailed interviews with about seventy people (not randomly selected) rather than from the initial survey. The results are not as significant quantitatively as those of the random sample of 551, but give data of considerable importance.

9. See Klapper, Joseph T., *The Effects of Mass Communication,* Free Press, Glencoe, 1960, p. 92.

10. In March 1960, it was announced that commercial advertising on the African Service of the Federal Broadcasting Corporation would begin between July and September of that year (*Federation of Rhodesia and Nyasaland Newsletter,* March 3, 1960).

11. Klapper, p. 51.

12. In 1960, a series of articles on this subject were published in *Horizon,* a monthly magazine published by Roan Antelope Mines for its European employees.

CHAPTER 16

1. According to the Native Film Censorship Board, scenes must be deleted which show women of easy virtue; prolonged embraces; scantily

dressed women; wearing of masks; manhandling of women; fights between women; capture and tying of Europeans by natives, including North American Indians; deliberate murder at close quarters; war atrocities; out-of-date war scenes; all scenes of obnoxious crime, readily understood by Africans; all scenes of knife attacks; all scenes of arson, rioting, or insurrection; political demonstrations with rioting, clubbing; any other scenes which the Board considers unsuitable. (From *Guiding Principles in Use by the Native Film Censorship Board in Northern Rhodesia* Motion Picture Section, Information Department, Lusaka).

In 1960, racial bars were removed for admission to all commercial movie houses in Northern Rhodesia. I do not know whether this has affected the censorship code.

2. A study of the effect of violence in television movies on children, by Himmelweit, Hilde, T., Oppenheim, A. N., and Vince, Pamela, (*Television and the Child*, 1958), summarized by Klapper, showed that "violence which follows a conventional pattern, the outcome of which is predictable, apparently disturbs very few children . . . Because the children know the ending will be happy, with no harm done to the hero, the violence does not matter" (Klapper, Joseph T., *The Effects of Mass Communication*, Free Press, Glencoe, 1960, p. 146).

The same study of reactions to "Westerns" indicated the "intense involvement during the showing of the programme with complete release of tension at the end . . ." (*Ibid.,* p. 147). I assume that similar mechanisms were underlying the Africans' reactions to the fighting in cowboy films.

3. Superman was preferred by 19 per cent in our original survey, insignificant statistically because the film ended halfway through the survey.

4. The play was concerned with strange beings from another planet who were supposed to have landed in New Jersey, as the vanguard of an invasion from Mars. Thousands of the radio listeners believed the play was a news report of facts, although it had been plainly described as fiction.

5. Aubrey, James T., Jr., "Point of View, Program Practices," CBS Television Network, New York, 1961, p. 2.

6. Riesman, David: *The Oral Tradition, the Written Word, and the Screen Image,* Antioch College Founders Day Lecture, No. 1, Antioch Press, Yellow Springs, 1956, p. 31.

7. *Ibid.,* p. 31.

CHAPTER 17

1. Fallers, L. A., "Are African Cultivators to be called 'Peasants' " *Current Anthropology,* II, 1961, p. 110.

2. Epstein makes the same point of the prestige attached to the speaking of English by Africans (Epstein, A. L., "Linguistic Innovation and

Culture on the Copperbelt, Northern Rhodesia," *Southwestern Journal of Anthropology*, XV, 3, 1959, pp. 237-240.

3. A study of folklore, riddles, and proverbs as they function in a contemporary African situation might give interesting clues to both continuity and change.

4. *Federation of Rhodesia and Nyasaland Newsletter*, Washington, D. C., October 28, 1960.

5. Advisory Commission on the Review of the Constitution of the Federation of Rhodesia and Nyasaland, *Report: Appendix VI, Survey of Developments since 1953*, Her Majesty's Stationery Office, London, 1960, p. 190.

6. *Ibid.*, p. 191.

7. *Ibid.*, p. 192.

8. *Ibid.*, p. 175.

9. *Ibid.*, p. 193.

10. *Ibid.*, p. 197.

11. *Ibid.*, p. 197.

12. *Federation of Rhodesia and Nyasaland Newsletter*, February 24, 1961.

13. Advisory Commission, p. 197.

14. *Northern Rhodesia African Education, Annual Report*, 1952, pp. 5-11.

15. *Ibid.*, pp. 5-11.

16. Data from local education officials.

17. Communication from African Personnel Department, Roan Antelope Copper Mine, 1961.

18. *Ibid.*, The exact figures are:

1954—Luanshya (including mine and municipal townships): 1,568 boys; 618 girls.

1960-1961—mine township only (Roan Antelope, Ltd.): 1,917 boys; 1,393 girls.

19. *Ibid.*

20. Riesman, David, *The Oral Tradition, the Written Word, and the Screen Image*, Antioch College Founders Day Lecture, No. 1, Antioch Press, Yellow Springs, 1956, pp. 7-8.

21. Tables giving the data from the survey are in the Appendix. Only the pertinent percentages are given in the text.

22. In a study, done in 1950 by a Rhodes-Livingstone Institute Research team, of the reading habits in ten villages in the Mushiri Reserve, 25.5 per cent of a sample of 165 were literate; but this group included those who were not reading regularly or at the particular time of the survey. The proportion of literates is smaller than in our survey not only because of a lapse of four years in time, but probably also because the study was done in villages rather than in a town (a Rhodes-Livingstone Institute Research Team, "Reading Habits in a Part of the Mushiri Reserve," *Rhodes-Livingstone Journal*, XI, 1951, pp. 61-62).

23. Other papers, with a smaller circulation on the township, were the *African Weekly,* similar to the *African Eagle,* except that the former was published in Salisbury and was concerned mostly with news from Southern Rhodesia; the *Central Africa Post,* a European daily published in Lusaka and not as much concerned with the Copperbelt as was the *Northern News. Zonk* and *Drum,* monthly magazines published in South Africa, contained fiction, articles, sports news, and many pictures. Twenty-nine per cent of the literate read one or the other; and they were preferred by 16 per cent, most of whom had Standard V or more education.

24. In 1960, it became possible for any bookseller in Northern Rhodesia and Nyasaland, who had been granted trade terms by publishers to order his supplies directly from them (Publications Bureau of Northern Rhodesia and Nyasaland, *Annual Report for the Year 1960,* Government Printer, Lusaka, 1961, p. 4).

25. Publications Bureau, *Annual Report for the Year 1954,* p. 7.

26. Even at the time of my study I often saw young men in their twenties ask boys of ten or eleven years to carry small things for them. Similarly, most Europeans did not carry anything if there was an African around to do it for them.

27. The description of them is from a communication from the Northern Rhodesian and Nyasaland Publications Bureau, May 6, 1961.

28. Riesman, p. 28.

29. *Ibid.,* p. 28.

CHAPTER 18

1. An intensive and more psychoanalytical study of individuals would obviously be rewarding in this context.

2. All detailed statistics are in the Appendix.

3. Doob distinguishes between central and segmental change (see Doob, Leonard W., *Becoming More Civilized, A Psychological Exploration,* Yale University Press, New Haven, 1960, p. 88). Mead makes a similar point in her study of the changing Manus people (see Mead, Margaret, *New Lives for Old: Cultural Transformation, Manus, 1928-1953,* Morrow, New York, 1956, p. 172).

4. Doob, p. 19.

5. Erikson, Erik H., "Growth and Crises of the Healthy Personality" in *Identity and the Life Cycle, Selected Papers, Psychological Issues,* I, 1, 1959, p. 82.

6. Feldman, Arnold S., and Moore, Wilbert E., *Labor Commitment and Social Change in Developing Areas,* Social Science Research Council, New York, 1960, p. 64-65.

7. *Ibid.,* p. 367 and *passim.*

8. Richards, Audrey, I., *Land, Labour and Diet in Northern Rhodesia, An Economic Study of the Bemba Tribe,* (first published 1939), 2nd.

ed., Oxford University Press, London, 1951, p. 81.

9. Given the time and the necessary assistants, such a comparative survey could be done and, if correlated with sociological factors, would be decidedly rewarding.

10. Loeb, Edwin M., "Primitive Intoxicants," *Quarterly Journal of Studies on Alcohol,* IV, 1943, pp. 287-298.

11. Horton, Donald, "The Functions of Alcohol in Primitive Societies: A Cross-Culture Study," *Quarterly Journal of Studies on Alcohol,* IV, 1943, pp. 216-223.

12. *Ibid.,* p. 249.

13. Erikson, Erik: *Childhood and Society,* W. W. Norton, New York, 1950, p. 115.

14. Powdermaker, Hortense: "Social Change through Imagery and Values of Teen-age Africans in Northern Rhodesia," *American Anthropologist,* LVIII, 5, October 1956, p. 799.

15. Mitchell, J. Clyde, and Epstein, A. L., "Occupational Prestige and Social Status among Urban Africans in Northern Rhodesia," *Africa,* XXIX, 1, January 1959, pp. 24-35.

16. Fallers, Lloyd A., *Bantu Bureaucracy,* W. Heffer & Sons, Cambridge, England, 1956, pp. 178-179.

17. Freud, Sigmund, *Civilization and Its Discontents,* Joan Riviere, trans., first published in 1930, reprinted Doubleday Anchor Book, 1958, pp. 42-43, *passim.*

18. Shalin, Marshall D., "The Origin of Society," *Scientific American,* CCIII, 3, 1960, pp. 78-80.

19. Doob, p. 267.

CHAPTER 19

1. Erikson, Erik H., "The Problem of Ego Identity," *Psychological Issues,* I, 1, 1959, p. 160.

2. Franck, Thomas M., *Race and Nationalism: The Struggle for Power in Rhodesia-Nyasaland,* Fordham University Press, New York, 1960, p. 205.

3. See Mitchell, J. Clyde, *The Kalela Dance,* Rhodes-Livingstone Papers, No. 27, 1956, p. 30 and *passim.*

4. *Ibid.,* pp. 28-30.

5. Cf. Epstein, A. L., *Politics in an Urban African Community,* Manchester University Press, Manchester, England, 1958, pp. 224-240, and *passim;* and Gluckman, Max, "From Tribe to Town," *Nation* (Sydney, Australia) No. 53, September 24, 1960, pp. 7-12.

6. Powdermaker, Hortense, "Communication and Social Change Based on a Field Study in Northern Rhodesia," *Transactions New York Academy of Sciences,* Ser. II, Vol. 17, No. 5, March 1955, pp. 436-437.

7. *Northern Rhodesian African Representative Council, 1947,* Government Printer, Lusaka, No. 2, p. 81.

8. See Riesman, David, Glazer, Nathan, and Denney, Reuel, *The Lonely Crowd*, Doubleday Anchor Book, New York, 1953, pp. 275-297; Axelrad, Sidney, and Maury, M., "Identification As a Mechanism of Adaptation, *Psychoanalysis and Culture*, George B. Wilbur and Warner Muensterberger, eds., International Universities Press, New York, 1951, p. 183.

9. Wilson, Godfrey and Monica, *The Analysis of Social Change, Based on Observations in Central Africa*, first published, 1945, University Press, 1954, p. 41.

10. Field, M. J., *Search for Security*, Northwestern University Press, Evanston, 1960, p. 115.

11. Wilson, p. 73.

12. Cf. Scotch, N. A., "Magic, Sorcery and Football Among the Urban Zulu: A Case of Reinterpretation under Acculturation," *Journal of Conflict Resolution*, V, 1, March 1961, pp. 70-74.

13. Wilson, pp. 120-121.

14. Richards, Audrey I., "A Modern Movement of Witchfinders," *Africa*, VIII, 3, October 1935, pp. 448-461

15. These Africans provide a decisive contrast with many North American Indian tribes. For instance, the Sioux Indians have passively resisted integration of their past identity—closely associated with a seeming inexhaustible buffalo supply, unlimited space, and centrifugal activities—with the American middle-class values and centripetal localized goals of savings and bank accounts, presented by white teachers in Indian schools. The teachers never became models with whom Indians identified. Instead, the Sioux fantasied restoration of their past, while they accepted government help, often in the form of relief. (See Erikson, Erik H., *Childhood and Society*, W. W. Norton, New York, 1950, pp. 137-140.)

16. *Northern Rhodesia News Survey*, II, 1, June 1961.

17. *The Central African Examiner*, September 1961, p. 3.

18. Wilson, p. 15.

19. Advisory Commission on the Review of the Constitution of Rhodesia and Nyasaland, *Report*, Her Majesty's Stationery Office, London, 1960, p. 16.

20. Moore and Tumin have pointed out the social function of ignorance in excluding other cultural alternatives. Moore, Wilbert E., and Tumin, Melvin, "Some Social Functions of Ignorance," *American Sociological Review*, XIV, 1944, pp. 787-795.

21. Clegg, Edward, *Race and Politics, Partnership in the Federation of Rhodesia and Nyasaland*, Oxford University Press, London, 1960, p. 256.

22. *Federation of Rhodesia and Nyasaland Newsletter*, Washington, D.C., September 2, 1960.

23. Clegg, p. 256.

24. Quoted in Clegg, p. 161.

25. *Ibid.*, p. 210.

26. The same point is made by Rudolph Kieve, M.D., in his discussion

of traditional Spanish culture in his unpublished paper, "The Meaning and Use of Illness and Disability among Spanish-speaking People in Northern New Mexico," given at the Fourth Western Divisional Meeting of the American Psychiatric Association, Salt Lake City, September 21, 1961.

27. Clegg, p. 227.

28. *Ibid.*, p. 229.

29. See Epstein, A. L., *Juridical Techniques and the Judicial Process, A Study in African Customary Law,* Rhodes-Livingstone Papers No. 23, 1954; and Gluckman, Max, *The Judicial Process Among the Barotse of Northern Rhodesia,* Free Press, Glencoe, 1955.

30. Quoted in *The Central African Examiner,* V, 2, January 1962, p. 8.

31. *The New York Times,* March 21, 1959, p. 14.

32. Sir Ronald L. Prain, "Statement by the Chairman, Rhodesian Selection Trust Group of Companies," New York, October 22, 1961, p. 8.

33. *Ibid.,* October 22, 1960, p. 9.

34. Dispatch from Salisbury by Drew Middleton, *New York Times,* February 23, 1961, p. 1.

35. Erikson, Erik H., "Ego Development and Historical Change," *Identity and the Life Cycle, Psychological Issues,* I, 1, 1959, p. 46.

REFERENCES

References

ADORNO, T. W., et al., *The Authoritarian Personality*, Harper & Brothers, New York, 1950.

Advisory Commission on the Review of the Constitution of the Federation of Rhodesia and Nyasaland, *Report: Appendix VI, Survey of Developments since 1953*, Her Majesty's Stationery Office, London, 1960.

AUBREY, JAMES T., JR., "Point of View, Program Practices," CBS Television Network, New York, 1961.

AXELRAD, SIDNEY and MAURY, M., "Identification as a Mechanism of Adaptation," *Psychoanalysis and Culture*, ed. by George B. Wilbur and Warner Muensterberger, International Universities Press, New York, 1951.

BARNES, J. A., "Some Aspects of Political Development Among the Fort Jameson Ngoni," *African Studies*, VII, 2-3, June-September, 1948.

———, "Measures of Divorce Frequency in Simple Societies," *Journal of the Royal Anthropological Institute*, LXXIX, 1949.

———, "History in a Changing Society," *Rhodes-Livingstone Institute Journal*, XI, 1951.

———, *Marriage in a Changing Society*, Rhodes-Livingstone Papers, Rhodes-Livingstone Institute, No. 20, 1951.

———, "The Fort Jameson Ngoni," *Seven Tribes of British Central Africa*, Elizabeth Colson and Max Gluckman, eds., Oxford University Press, London, 1951.

———, *Politics in a Changing Society*, Oxford University Press, London, 1954.

BARNETT, H. G., *Innovation*, McGraw-Hill, New York, 1953.

BASCOM, WILLIAM R. and HERSKOVITS, MELVILLE, J., eds., *Continuity and Change in African Cultures*, University of Chicago Press, Chicago, 1959.

BOHANNAN, PAUL, ed., *African Homicide and Suicide*, Princeton University Press, Princeton, N.J., 1960.

BOULDING, KENNETH, *The Image*, University of Michigan Press, 1956.

BRELSFORD, W. V., *Fishermen of the Bangweolu Swamps*, Rhodes-Livingstone Institute Papers, No. 12, 1946.

———, *The Succession of Bemba Chiefs*, 2nd ed., The Government Printer, Lusaka, 1949.

———, *The Tribes of Northern Rhodesia*, The Government Printer, Lusaka, 1957.

CARPENTER, GEORGE W., "The Role of Christianity and Islam in Contemporary Africa," *Africa Today*, C. Grove Haines, ed., Johns Hopkins Press, Baltimore, 1955.

Census of Population, 1956, Federation of Rhodesia and Nyasaland, Central Statistical Office, Salisbury, 1960.

Central African Examiner, September 1961, January 1962.

CIBAMBO, Y. M., *My Ngoni of Nyasaland*, United Society for Christian Literature, London, 1942.

CLEGG, EDWARD, *Race and Politics, Partnership in the Federation of Rhodesia and Nyasaland*, Oxford University Press, London, 1960.

COHEN, ANDREW, *British Policy in Changing Africa*, Routledge and Kegan Paul, London, 1959.

COHEN, YEHUDI A., "Some Aspects of Ritualized Behavior in Interpersonal Relationships," *Human Relations*, XI, 3, 1958.

———, "Food and Its Vicissitudes: A Cross-Culture Study of Sharing and Nonsharing," *Social Structure and Personality*, by Yehudi A. Cohen, ed., Holt, Rinehart and Winston, New York, 1961.

COILLARD, F., *On the Threshold of Central Africa*, Hodder and Stoughton, London, 1897.

COLE, D. T., "Fanagalo and the Bantu Languages in South Africa," *African Studies*, XII, 1, 1953.

COLSON, ELIZABETH, "The Plateau Tonga of Northern Rhodesia," *Seven Tribes of British Central Africa*, Elizabeth Colson and Max Gluckman, eds., Oxford University Press, London, 1951.

———, "Every Day Life Among the Cattle-Keeping Plateau Tonga," *Rhodes-Livingstone Museum Papers*, N.S. No. 9, 1953.

———, *Marriage and the Family Among the Plateau Tonga of Northern Rhodesia, Manchester University Press*, Manchester, Eng., 1958.

———, "Family Change in Contemporary Africa," unpublished paper read at a conference, "Anthropology and Africa," held at the New York Academy of Sciences, May 1-3, 1961.

COLSON, ELIZABETH, and GLUCKMAN, MAX, (eds.), *Seven Tribes of British Central Africa*, Oxford University Press, London, 1951.

Coxhead, J. C., *The Native Tribes of Northern Rhodesia,* Royal Anthropological Institute, Occasional Papers, No. 5, London, 1914.

Cunnison, I., *History of the Luapula,* Rhodes-Livingstone Papers No. 21, 1951.

———, "Headmanship and the Ritual of Luapula Villages," *Africa,* XXVI, 1956.

———, "Perpetual Kinship: A Political Institution of the Luapula People," *Rhodes-Livingstone Journal,* XX, 1956.

Denney, Reuel, *The Astonished Muse,* University of Chicago Press, Chicago, 1957.

Doob, Leonard W., *Becoming More Civilized, A Psychological Exploration,* Yale University Press, New Haven, 1960.

———, *Communication,* Yale University Press, New Haven, 1961.

Dunn, Cyril, *Central African Witness,* Victor Gollancz, Ltd., London, 1959.

Eisenstadt, S. N., "Sociological Aspects of Economic Adaption of Oriental Immigrants in Israel: A Case Study in the Problems of Modernization," *Economic Development and Cultural Change,* IV, 3, University of Chicago Press, April 1956.

Epstein, A. L., "Some Aspects of the Conflict of Law and Urban Courts in Northern Rhodesia," *Rhodes-Livingstone Journal,* XII, 1951.

———, "The Role of the African Courts in Urban Communities of the Copperbelt in Northern Rhodesia," *Rhodes-Livingstone Journal,* XIII, 1953.

———, "Divorce Law and the Stability of Marriage among the Lunda of Kazembe," *Rhodes-Livingstone Journal,* XIV, 1954.

———, *Juridical Techniques and the Judicial Process,* Rhodes-Livingstone Papers No. 23, 1954.

———, *Politics in an Urban African Community.* Manchester University Press, Manchester, Eng., 1958.

———, "Linguistic Innovation and Culture on the Copperbelt, Northern Rhodesia," *Southwestern Journal of Anthropology,* XV, 3, 1959.

———, "The Network and Urban Social Organization," *Rhodes-Livingstone Journal,* XXIX, 1961.

Erikson, Erik H., *Childhood and Society,* W. W. Norton, New York, 1950.

———, "Growth and Crises of the Healthy Personality," "The Problem of Ego Identity," "Ego Development and Historical Change," *Identity and the Life Cycle, Selected Papers by Erik H. Erikson, with a Historical Introduction by David Rapaport, Psychological Issues,* I, 1, Monograph I, International Universities Press, Inc., New York, 1959.

Fallers, Lloyd A., *Bantu Bureacracy,* W. Heffer & Sons, Cambridge, England, 1956.

————, "Some Determinants of Marriage Stability in Busoga: A Reformulation of Gluckman's Hypothesis," *Africa*, XXVII, 2, April 1957.

————, "Despotism, Status Culture and Social Mobility in an African Kingdom," *Comparative Studies in Society and History*, II, 1, 1958.

————, "Are African Cultivators to Be Called 'Peasants'?" *Current Anthropology*, II, 1961.

Federation of Rhodesia and Nyasaland Newsletter, Washington, D. C., March 3, 1960; September 2, 1960; October 28, 1960; November 11, 1960; November 14, 1960; February 24, 1961.

FIELD, M. J., *Search for Security: An Ethno-Psychiatric Study of Rural Ghana*, Northwestern University Press, Evanston, 1960.

FORTES, M., and EVANS-PRITCHARD, E. E., (ed.), "Introduction," *African Political Systems*, 3rd ed., Oxford University Press, London, 1948.

FRAENKEL, PETER, *Wayleshi*, Weidenfeld and Nicolson, London, 1959.

FRAENKEL, PETER, and MITCHELL, J. CLYDE, "Some Factors in the Comprehensibility of English Broadcasts to African Listeners," an unpublished study, Rhodes-Livingstone Institute.

FRANCK, THOMAS M., *Race and Nationalism: The Struggle for Power in Rhodesia-Nyasaland*, Fordham University Press, New York, 1960.

FRANK, LAWRENCE K., "Cultural Implications of Man in Space," *Annals of the New York Academy of Science*, LXXII, 4, 1958.

FRANKLIN, H., *Report on the Development of Broadcasting to Africans in Central Africa*, Government Printer, Lusaka, 1949.

FREUD, SIGMUND, *Civilization and Its Discontents*, trans. Joan Riviere, (first published 1930), Doubleday Anchor Book, New York, 1958.

GANN, L. H., "The End of the Slave Trade in British Central Africa," *Rhodes-Livingstone Journal*, XVI, 1954.

————, *The Birth of a Plural Society, The Development of Northern Rhodesia under the British South Africa Company, 1894-1914*, Manchester University Press, Manchester, Eng., 1958.

GLUCKMAN, MAX, *Economy of the Central Barotse Plain*, Rhodes-Livingstone Institute Papers No. 7, 1941.

————, "Kinship and Marriage among the Lozi of Northern Rhodesia and the Zulu in Natal," *African Systems of Kinship and Marriage*, ed. A. R. RADCLIFFE-BROWN and C. D. FORDE, Oxford University Press, London, 1950.

————, "The Lozi of Barotseland in Northwestern Rhodesia," *Seven Tribes of British Central Africa*, eds. ELIZABETH COLSON and MAX GLUCKMAN, Oxford University Press, London, 1951.

————, *Custom and Conflict in Africa*, Free Press, Glencoe, 1955 (a).

————, *The Judicial Process Among the Barotse of Northern Rhodesia*, Free Press, Glencoe, 1955 (b).

————, From Tribe to Town," *Nation* (Sydney, Australia) September 24, 1960.

GOULDSBURY, C., and SHEANE H., *The Great Plateau of Northern Rhodesia,* Edwin Arnold, London, 1911.

Great Britain, *Parliament Sessional Papers,* 1923, 17. (Cad. 1922)

HANNA, A. J., *The Story of the Rhodesias and Nyasaland,* Faber and Faber, London, 1960.

HARTMANN, HEINZ, *Ego Psychology and the Problem of Adaptation,* trans. DAVID RAPAPORT, International Universities Press, New York, 1958.

HAVIGHURST, ROBERT J., and FEINENBAUM, K., "Leisure and Life-Style," *American Journal of Sociology,* LXIV, January 1959.

HERSKOVITS, MELVILLE J., "The African Cultural Background in the Modern Scene," *Africa Today,* ed. C. GROVE HAINES, Johns Hopkins Press, Baltimore, 1955.

———, "African Economic Development and Cross-Culture Perspective," *Journal of the American Economic Association,* XLVI, 2, May 1956.

———, *Anthropology and Cultural Change in Africa,* Communications of the University of South Africa, Pretoria, 1957.

HODGKIN, THOMAS, *Nationalism in Colonial Africa,* New York University Press, New York, 1957.

HOGGART, RICHARD, *The Uses of Literacy. Aspects of Working Class Life with Special References to Publications and Entertainments,* Penguin, London, 1958.

HOMANS, GEORGE C., and SCHNEIDER, DAVID M., *Marriage, Authority and Final Causes,* Free Press, Glencoe, 1956.

Horizon, Roan Antelope Copper Mines, Ltd., 1960.

HORTON, DONALD, "The Functions of Alcohol in Primitive Societies: A Cross-Culture Study," *Quarterly Journal of Studies on Alcohol,* IV, 1943.

Hearings on Activities of Private United States Organizations in Africa, Subcommittee of House Committee on Foreign Affairs, 87th Cong., 1st sess., May 8, 11, 12, 16, 25, and June 1, 1961.

HUIZINGA, JOHAN, *Homo Ludens, A Study of the Play Element in Culture,* Beacon Press, London, 1955.

INKELES, ALEX, "Personality and Social Structure," *Sociology Today,* ed. ROBERT K. MERTON, LEONARD BROOM, LEONARD S. COTTRELL, JR., Basic Books, Inc., New York, 1959.

INNIS, HAROLD A., *The Bias of Communication,* University of Toronto Press, Toronto, Can., 1951.

KAHL, JOSEPH A., "Some Social Concomitants of Industrialization and Urbanization," *Human Organization,* XVIII, 2, 1957.

KAPLAN, MAX, *Leisure in America: A Social Inquiry,* John Wiley and Sons, New York, 1960.

KEESING, FELIX M., "Recreative Behavior and Culture Change" in *Selected Papers of the Fifth International Congress of Anthropological and Ethnological Sciences,* University of Pennsylvania Press, Philadelphia, 1956.

KIEVE, RUDOLPH, "The Meaning and Use of Illness and Disability among Spanish-speaking People in Northern New Mexico," unpublished paper given at the Fourth Western Divisional Meeting of the American Psychiatric Association, Salt Lake City, Utah, September 21, 1961.

KLAPPER, JOSEPH T., *The Effects of Mass Communication,* Free Press, Glencoe, 1960.

KROEBER, ALFRED L., *Anthropology,* rev. ed., Harcourt, Brace, New York, 1948.

LERNER, DANIEL, *The passing of traditional society: Modernizing the Middle East,* Free Press, Glencoe, 1958.

LEYS, COLIN and PRATT (eds.), *A New Deal in Central Africa,* Crawford, Heinemann, London, 1960.

LINTON, RALPH, *The Study of Man,* Appleton-Century, New York, 1936.

LOEB, EDWIN M., "Primitive Intoxicants," *Quarterly Journal of Studies on Alcohol,* IV, 1943.

MAIR, L. P., "Survey of African Marriage and Family Life," *African Marriage and Social Change,* Arthur Phillips, ed., Oxford University Press, London, 1953.

————, "African Chiefs Today," *Africa,* XXVIII, 3, July 1958.

MALINOWSKI, BRONISLAW, "Culture," *Encyclopedia of the Social Sciences,* Macmillan, 1931.

MANNHEIM, KARL, *Idealogy and Utopia, An Introduction to the Sociology of Knowledge,* trans. LOUIS WIRTH and EDWARD SHILS, Harcourt, Brace, New York, 1936.

MAYER, PHILIP, *Xhosa in Town, Townsmen or Tribesmen,* Oxford University Press, Capetown, 1961.

MEAD, MARGARET, *New Lives for Old: Cultural Transformation, Manus, 1928-1953,* Morrow, New York, 1956.

MEERLOO, JOOST A. M., *Conversation and Communication,* International Universities Press, New York, 1952.

MERTON, ROBERT, *Social Theory and Social Structure,* rev. and enlarged ed., Free Press, Glencoe, 1957, Chap. 6.

MITCHELL, J. CLYDE, "The Yao of Southern Nyasaland," *Seven Tribes of British Central Africa,* ed. ELIZABETH COLSON and MAX GLUCKMAN, Oxford University Press, London, 1951.

————, *African Urbanization in Ndola and Luanshya,* Rhodes-Livingstone Communication No. 6, Lusaka, 1954.

————, *The Yao Village,* Manchester University Press, Manchester, Eng., 1956.

————, *The Kalela Dance*, Rhodes-Livingstone Papers, No. 27, 1956.

————, "Aspects of African Marriage on the Copperbelt of Northern Rhodesia," the *Rhodes-Livingstone Journal*, XXII, September 1957.

————, (with M. Gluckman and J. A. Barnes), "The British Headman in British Central Africa," *Africa*, XIX, 2, April 1949.

MITCHELL, J. C., and EPSTEIN, A. L., "Power and Prestige among Africans in Northern Rhodesia: An Experiment," *Proceedings and Transactions of the Rhodesian Scientific Association*, XLV, 1957.

————, "Occupational Prestige and Social Status among Urban Africans in Northern Rhodesia," *Africa*, XXIX, 1, January 1959.

MOORE, WILBERT E., and FELDMAN, ARNOLD S., *Labor Commitment and Social Change in Developing Areas*, Social Science Research Council, New York, 1960.

MOORE, WILBERT E. and TUMIN, MELVIN, "Some Social Functions of Ignorance," *American Sociological Review*, XIV, 1949.

NADEL, S. F., "Witchcraft in Four African Societies: An Essay in Comparison," *American Anthropologist*, LIV, 1, January-March, 1952.

New York Times, February 6, 1960, and March 21, 1959.

Northern Rhodesia African Education Annual Report, 1952.

Northern Rhodesia Chamber of Mines Year Book, 1960, 1961, Kitwe.

Northern Rhodesian African Representative Council, 1947; 1948, The Government Printer, Lusaka.

Northern Rhodesian News Survey, II, 1, June 1961.

PHILLIPS, ARTHUR, "Marriage Laws in Africa," *Survey of African Marriage and Social Change*, ed. Arthur Phillips, Oxford University Press, 1953.

PIEPER, JOSEF, *Leisure the Basis of Culture*, Faber and Faber, London, 1952.

POOL, ITHIEL DE SOLA, review of ERIK H. ERIKSON's *Young Man Luther*, in *Public Opinion Quarterly*, XXIII, 1, 1959.

POWDERMAKER, HORTENSE, *Life in Lesu: The Study of a Melanesian Society in New Ireland*, W. W. Norton, New York, 1933.

————, *After Freedom, A Cultural Study in the Deep South*, Viking Press, New York, 1939.

————, "Communication and Social Change Based on a Field Study in Northern Rhodesia," *Transactions of the New York Academy of Sciences*, Ser. II, Vol. 17, No. 5, March 1955.

————, "Social Change through Imagery and Values of Teen-Age Africans in Northern Rhodesia," *American Anthropologist*, LVIII, 5, 1956.

PRAIN, SIR RONALD, Talk to the American Institute of Mining, Metallurgical and Petroleum Engineers, New York City, February 7, 1957.

————, *Statement by the Chairman, Rhodesian Selection Trust Group of Companies, to accompany the Directors' Reports and Accounts, for the*

year ended June 30, 1960 and *for the year ended June 30, 1961*,
Browne and Company, Inc., New York, 1960 and 1961.

Publications Bureau of Northern Rhodesia and Nyasaland, *Annual Report for the Year 1954; 1960*, Government Printer, Lusaka, 1955, 1961.

RADCLIFFE-BROWN, A. R., *The Andaman Islanders*, Cambridge University Press, 1933.

——, "Introduction," *African Systems of Kinship and Marriage*, ed. A. R. Radcliffe-Brown and Daryll Forde, 3rd ed., Oxford University Press, London, 1956.

READ, MARGARET, "The Moral Code of the Ngoni and Their Former Military State," *Africa*, XI, 1938.

——, *Native Standard of Living and African Cultural Change*, Memorandum XVI, International African Institute, London, 1938.

——, *The Ngoni of Nyasaland*, Oxford University Press, London, 1956.

——, *Children of Their Fathers*, Yale University Press, New Haven, 1960.

REDFIELD, ROBERT, *The Primitive World and Its Transformations*, Cornell University Press, Ithaca, 1953.

REED, STEPHEN W., "World Population Trends," *Most of the World*, RALPH LINTON, ed., Columbia University Press, New York, 1949.

Rhodes-Livingstone Institute Research Team, "Reading Habits in a Part of the Mushiri Reserve," *Rhodes-Livingstone Journal*, XI, June, 1951.

Rhodesian Selection Trust Group of Companies, *The African Mine Worker on the Copperbelt of Northern Rhodesia*, Salisbury, 1960.

RICHARDS, AUDREY, I., "Mother-right among the Central Bantu," *Essays Presented to C. G. Seligman*, ed. E. E. EVANS-PRITCHARD, R. FIRTH, B. MALINOWSKI, and I. SCHAPERA, Keegan Paul, London, 1933.

——, "A Modern Movement of Witchfinders," *Africa*, VIII, 3, October 1935.

——, "The Life of Bwembya, A Native of Northern Rhodesia," *Ten Africans*, ed. M. PERHAM, Faber and Faber, London, 1936.

——, *Bemba Marriage and Present Economic Conditions*, Rhodes-Livingstone Papers No. 4, 1940.

——, *Hunger and Work in a Savage Tribe*, Free Press, Glencoe, 1948.

——, "Variations in Family Structure among the Central Bantu," *African Systems of Kinship and Marriage*, ed. A. R. Radcliffe-Brown and C. D. Forde, Oxford University Press, London, 1950.

——, *Land, Labour and Diet in Northern Rhodesia*, (first published 1939), 2nd ed., Oxford University Press, London, 1951.

——, "The Political System of the Bemba of North-eastern Rhodesia," *African Political Systems*, (first published 1940) 5th ed., Oxford University Press, London, 1955.

——, *Chisungu, A Girl's Initiation Ceremony among the Bemba of Northern Rhodesia*, Grove Press, New York, 1956.

————, "The Village Census in the Study of Culture Contacts," *Methods of Study of Culture Contacts in Africa,* International Institute of African Languages and Cultures, Memorandum XV, Oxford University Press, New York, 1958.

RIESMAN, DAVID, *The Oral Tradition, the Written Word, and the Screen Image,* Antioch College Founders Day Lecture, No. 1, Antioch Press, Yellow Springs, 1956.

RIESMAN, DAVID, GLAZER, NATHAN, and DENNEY, REUEL, *The Lonely Crowd,* Doubleday Anchor Book, New York, 1953.

RITCHIE, J. F., *The African as Suckling and as Adult,* Rhodes-Livingstone Papers, No. 9, 1943.

Roan Antelope, March 1958, June 11, 1960, August 5, 1961 (formerly, *The African Roan Antelope*).

Roan Antelope Copper Mines, Ltd., *Notes on African Education,* March 3, 1959.

ROBINSON, RONALD, GALLAGHER, JOHN, and DENNEY, ALICE: *Africa and the Victorians,* MacMillan, London, 1960.

SCHNEIDER, DAVID M. "A Note on the Bridewealth and the Stability of Marriage," *Man,* LIII, April 1953.

SCOTCH, N. A., "Magic, Sorcery and Football Among the Urban Zulu: A Case of Reinterpretation under Acculturation," *Journal of Conflict Resolution,* V, 1, March 1961.

SHALIN, MARSHALL D., "The Origin of Society," *Scientific American,* CCIII 3, 1960.

SHEPPERSON, GEORGE, and PRICE, THOMAS, *Independent African: John Chilembwe and the Origins, Setting and Significance of the Nyasaland Native Rising of 1915,* Edinburgh University Press, Edinburgh, 1959.

SMELSER, NEIL J., *Social Change in the Industrial Revolution,* Chicago University Press, Chicago, 1959.

SMITH, E. W., and DALE, A. M., *The Ila-speaking People of Northern Rhodesia,* 2 vols, Macmillan, New York, 1920, Vol. I.

SOUTHALL, A. W., and GUTKIND, P. C. W., *Townsmen in the Making,* East African Studies, No. 9, mimeographed, East African Institute of Social Research, Kampala, 1956.

SPEARPOINT, F., "The African Native and the Rhodesian Copper Mines," Supplement, *Journal of the Royal African Society,* XXXVI, July, 1937.

TAYLOR, OSTRANDER F., "Problems of African Economic Development," *Orbis, A Quarterly Journal of World Affairs,* IV, 2, 1960.

TEILHARD DE CHARDIN, PIERRE, *The Phenomenon of Man,* Bernard Wall trans., and Introduction by Julian Huxley, Harper & Brothers, New York, 1959.

TUDEN, ARTHUR, "Ila Slavery," *Rhodes-Livingstone Journal,* XXIV, December 1958.

TURNER, W. W., *Schism and Continuity in an African Society: A Study of Ndembu Village Life,* Manchester University Press, Manchester, Eng., 1957.

WEBER, MAX, *From Max Weber: Essays in Sociology,* trans., ed., and with an introduction by H. H. Gerth and C. Wright Mills, Kegan Paul, Trench, Trubner & Co., London, 1947.

WILSON, GODFREY, "An African Morality," *Africa,* IX, 1936.

————, *An Essay on the Economics of Detribalization in Northern Rhodesia,"* Parts I and II, Rhodes-Livingstone Papers Nos. 5 and 6, 1941, 1942.

WILSON, GODFREY and MONICA, *Analysis of Social Change, Based on Observations in Central Africa* (first published 1945), Cambridge UniversityPress, Cambridge, Eng., 1954.

WILSON, MONICA, *Good Company: A Study of Nyakusa Age-Villages,* Oxford University Press, London, 1951.

Index

ABOUT THE AUTHOR

A noted anthropologist, HORTENSE POWDER-
MAKER's principal studies have included a stone-age
culture in the southwest Pacific, a rural community
in the Deep South, problems of race and prejudice,
the influence of mass media. The fruits of that experience have been summoned to this new book which
promises to stand as a major work in the field of
African studies.

The author of *Life in Lesu: The Story of a Melanesian Society in New Ireland, After Freedom: A
Cultural Study in the Deep South, Probing Our Preju-
dices,* and *Hollywood the Dream Factory,* Dr. Powdermaker studied under the distinguished anthropologist,
Bronislaw Malinowski, at the University of London
where she received her Ph.D.

She has held a number of fellowships for field re-
search as well as visiting lectureships, and is currently
Professor of Anthropology at Queens College, City
University of New York.

5 mins home ownership
left residue 97   muddle   Jackson
                                   not war   no real
                                     716   810
d Court — guardian public morals 109   distinct
influ by social Ds

         neighbors social control   radio
                         203   res home 102
                         269   people
                                                      342

                                               Welfare
ders 112   women   ong 109
utan adviser councils 113

13 V elders
tubs skilly place under

Coffeey/Stuart 120 / educ'ing 140
             141 / suffrage deal

                                               unitary mun
                                                        105

                                               sponsor other 105
un deff mining 9
trade under rules 5

family life (9) 187 used guls le 87 integral (188-9)
                     Reg < D

201
         educ 199   leave kids 195-6
         alone wishlist 202-4 & 7

on leisure as index 224

diff norms 225

leis functions 226

funct mass media 229

%/o 227

tool + med
diff response

(310) revid astul function
tubar
new leaders achieved N 314

life style 230

mores no
diu
254
ordr reality
256 end

radio stuff 232 + (253) planned ▷✱
noise 233   reinforce
request bd fo ill 242

net ill
mores
(270)

riddle + redr 275

stan diff
304 achevement
+ head house
(308)

newspapers 281

inhabitants 289
diff specializ 292
families 292
mass media for tv (096)
305

mores new status categories for ∅
det by Eur (302)